WDA&A2E

The Wordsworth Dictionary of

Abbreviations &

Acronyms

SECOND EDITION

Rodney Dale &
Steve Puttick

Wordsworth Reference

The edition published 1999 by Wordsworth Editions Limited
8B East Street, Ware, Hertfordshire SG12 9HJ

ISBN 1 85326 766 X

Typeset by Antony Gray
Printed and bound in Great Britain by
Mackays of Chatham plc, Chatham, Kent

2 4 6 8 10 9 7 5 3 1

INTRODUCTION TO THE SECOND EDITION

Our First Edition was well received and sold out, which has given us the opportunity to rearrange our classifications, correct some errors, and incorporate our continuing collection of A&As. We are particularly grateful to all those correspondents who sent comments and further entries. They confirm our view that there is a strong 'information stratum' of people who like to read books such as this just for the fun of it.

In what way, and why, have we altered our classifications? Our previous arrangement made the book a good read, but less convenient for finding a given entry from scratch. We have therefore amalgamated some of our more general sections, but have left those which relate to well-defined categories. The contents list should make this clear; in our first 'General' section we have incorporated a code against certain entries to indicate how they were arranged in the First Edition.

One of our correspondents pointed out that some entries were not, strictly speaking, As or As, but where better than in this book to find them? Please keep the comments coming.

RODNEY DALE   STEVE PUTTICK
Haddenham, Cambs   *St Ives, Hunts*

INTRODUCTION TO THE FIRST EDITION

No reference book can ever be complete. During our period of compilation, we have carried our notebooks everywhere with us, and not a day passes without another gem or two to add to our lists. But as well as the very latest additions, we have sought out lists from days gone by; in that way, too, our work provides material which may not be found in other contemporary publications.

We live in a world of A&As; some are well established and here to stay – others of course will pass – but we want our compilation to have an historical value in years to come. We suspect that, although some will use this book to look up A&As, they will also browse in it to learn, and to find inspiration. This is particularly true of people in the 'information stratum', for whom quizzes and Trivial Pursuit ™ are the stuff of life, and we have added a little explanation – and some tongue-in-cheek editorial bias – here and there to enhance entries.

New A&As are arising all the time; we propose to continue our collection, and would welcome (via our publishers) individual submissions, or specialist lists, for consideration.

Capital letters in expansions can be overdone, so we have confined them to titles, proper nouns and the like. Generally, we have used roman type for A&A expansion, and italic for explanation. As for the A&As themselves, we have adopted what we think is the common, or perhaps the sensible, choice of upper or lower case (or occasionally shown both *eg* AC, ac). In accordance with modern trends, we have avoided peppering our pages with full points.

RODNEY DALE
Haddenham, Cambs

STEVE PUTTICK
St Ives, Hunts

ACKNOWLEDGEMENTS

We thank the many people and organisations who have contributed to our lists, particularly The Bank of England, The College of Arms, Stephen Adamson, Angela Devlin and her publishers Waterside Press for allowing us to reproduce A&As from her fascinating glossary of insiders' terms *Prison Patter* – a manual essential for all those interested in words and the living language (ISBN 1 872 87041 4); Wayne (almost an angel) Debeugny of Ordnance Survey; Tony Burnley of Cambridgeshire Constabulary; Cambridgeshire County Fire & Rescue Service; Tim & Andrea Dale; The Jockey Club; Court of the Lord Lyon; The Institution of Mechanical Engineers; Valerie & Michael Grosvenor Myer of Haddenham, Cambs; Francis Pullen of Cambridge Consultants Ltd; The Royal Institute of British Architects; Two Counties Ambulance NH Trust; Tina Starling lately of GER; and all the helpful and long-suffering Library Assistants – particularly at St Ives District Library, Huntingdonshire – who tracked down obscurities and suggested sources.

Our particularly helpful correspondents include Andrew Buxton of Lewes; Grandborough Inquizitor John Forster; Adrian Room of Stamford; and Michael Vnuk of Queensland. We are most grateful for their help and interest.

On the editorial and production side we thank Zoë Dale, Vicki Morrison & Matthew Pettitt who have spent long hours organising the contents; designer Antony Gray; and Marcus Clapham & Clive Reynard of Wordsworth Editions for their help & support.

We apologise to anyone we have left out.

CONTENTS

1 General

A

AA professional/upper managerial occupational grade (COM)

A amphetamine (PRP)

A Associate of . . .

A approved

A mass number (SCI)

A America or American

A major arterial road (*as in A30 – London to Penzance*)

A & C Black Adam & Charles (*British publishers*)

A A Milne Alan Alexander (*English writer 1882–1956*)

A C Benson Arthur Christopher (*man of letters; author of poem* Land of Hope and Glory *1862–1925*)

A horizon topsoil layer in soil profile

A J Cronin Archibald Joseph (*British novelist & physician 1896–1981*)

A J P Taylor (Alan John Percivale (*British historian, 1906–90*)

A licence *formal permission given under Road Traffic Act 1960 in Britain to a road transport company to operate as general carriers*, ie *carrying goods of other parties*

A list most sociably desirable category

A Mus LCM Associate in Music, London College of Music (MUS)

A Mus TCL Associate in Music, Trinity College of Music, London (MUS)

A P Herbert Alan Patrick (*English writer & politician, 1890–1971*)

A S Byatt Antonia Susan (*novelist, 1936-*)

A to Z from start to finish

A&L Alliance & Leicester Building Society (COM)

A&P Agricultural & Pastoral (*Show, Association, NZ*)

A/c account

A/F as found

A/S level advanced/supplementary level examination

A1 first class (COM)

A1, A–1 physically fit (SPR)

A1, A–1 a ship in first class order (*Lloyd's Register*)

A320 Airbus model A320-200

A340 Airbus model A340-300

A4E Arts for Everyone (*Arts Council initiative*) (FPA)

AA Alcoholics Anonymous

AA Automobile Association

AA Agent's Association

AA&QMG Assistant Adjutant and Quartermaster General

AAA Amateur Athletic Association (SPR)

AAA Automobile Association of America

AAA Association for Autonomous Astronauts

AAAM American Academy of Arts & Music (FPA)

AAAS American Association for the Advancement of Science

AAB assault & battery (PRP)

AABB American Association of Blood Banks

AAC All-American Football Conference (SPR)

AACCA Associate of the Association of Certified and

Corporate Accountants (*see* ALAA)

AACO Arab Air Carriers Organisation

AACR Association for the Advancement of Civil Rights

AAEE Aircraft & Armament Experimental Establishment (*Boscombe Down*) (MIL)

AAF Auxiliary Air Force (*now* R Aux AF)

AAFTCO Army Air Force Training Command Orchestra (*under Capt Glenn Miller*) (MUS)

AAI Associate of the Chartered Auctioneers' and Estate Agents' Institute

AAIB Air Accident Investigation Branch

AAL above aerodrome level

AAM Association of Assistant Masters/Mistresses

AAMC Australian Army Medical Corps

AAO Affirming Apostolic Order (*against female priests*)

AAU Amateur Athletic Union (SPR)

AB aggravated burglary (PRP)

AB Bachelor of Arts (*USA*)

AB Alan Bennet Hargreaves (*1904–96; Wales & Lake District rock-climbing pioneer, known as 'AB' to distinguish him from AT Hargreaves*)

AB able-bodied seaman

AB *Art Bulletin* (*The College Art Association of America*) (FPA)

ABA Amateur Boxing Association (SPR)

ABA American Basketball Association (*from 1967*) (SPR)

ABA Aerotransport (*Swedish airline*)

ABAE Amateur Boxing Association of England (SPR)

Abb, abbrev(s) abbreviation(s)

ABC accurate; brief; clear (*maxim for writers*)

ABC American Broadcasting Corporation (FPA)

ABC Australian Broadcasting Corporation (FPA)

ABC American Bowling Congress (*tenpin*) (SPR)

ABC An Bol Cumann (*Irish road bowling*) (SPR)

ABC Australian Bowling Council (*lawn bowls*) (SPR)

ABC airway, breathing, circulation

ABC process a process of sewage treatment in which alum, blood, clay and charcoal are used as precipitants. ((ARC))

ABCFM American Board of Commissioners for Foreign Missions

ABCM Associate of the Bandsmen's College of Music (MUS)

ABCM Associate of the Bandsmen's College of Music (MUS)

ABH actual bodily harm (PRP)

ABI Association of British Insurers (COM)

Abl ablative

ABL American Basketball League (*to 1967 –see ABA*) (SPR)

ABM anti-ballistic missile defence system (MIL)

Abo non-PC word for Australian Aborigine

ABP Associated British Ports

Abp, abp Archbishop

Abr abridged

ABS Association of Broadcasting Staff (UNI)

ABS acrilonitrile/butadiene/styrene (*a range of copolymers based on cyanoethene/but 1,2:3,4-diene/phenylethene*) (CHM)

ABS anti-lock braking system

ABS automatic booking system

ABSA Association for Business Sponsorship of the Arts (FPA)

ABSAPS Association for British Sponsorship of the Arts Pairing Scheme

ABSM Associate of the Birmingham School of Music (MUS)

ABSM (TTD)

Associate of the Birmingham School of Music (Teacher's Training Diploma) (MUS)

ABSRE Association of British Sound Reinforcement Engineers (SCI)

ABT American Ballet Theater (MUS)

ABTA Association of British Travel Agents

Ac aircraft (MIL)

AC account current; account (COM)

AC Arts Council (COM)

AC Companion of the Order of Australia

AC Athletic Club (SPR)

AC Appellation Contrôlée (*French wine classification*) (F&D)

AC altocumulus (*meteorological*)

AC ante Christum (*Latin: before Christ*)

AC, A/C aircraftman/woman (MIL)

AC/DC a bisexual person

AC/DC, ac/dc capable of running on either AC or DC electricity (SCI)

ACA Associate of the Institute of Chartered Accountants

ACAB Alcohol Concern Advisory Board

ACAB all coppers are bastards (PRP)

ACAC Curriculum Authority for Wales

ACADS Auctioneers' Completion and Deposit Scheme

ACAS Advisory, Conciliation and Arbitration Service

ACAS Assistant Chief of the Air Staff

Acc accusative

ACC Army Catering Corps (MIL)

ACC Australian Croquet Council (SPR)

ACC Auto-Cycle Club (SPR)

ACCA Associate of the Chartered Association of Certified Accountants

ACCI Autoglass Car Confidence Index

ACCLOC access overload control (*cutting off mobile phones at the request of the Cabinet Office or police in emergencies: Categories 1-9: public, depending on tariff level, 12: emergency services, 13: higher government officials, 14 & 15: 'reserved'*)

Accn accommodation (MIL)

ACCS Associate of the Corporation of Certified Secretaries

ACCUS Automobile Competition Committee of the United States (SPR)

ACE Advisory Centre for Education

ACE Association of Cost Engineers (*estd 1961*)

ACE Automatic Computing Engine (SCI)

ACE Allied Command Europe (MIL)

AcEm actinium emanation; actinon (CHM)

ACER Australian Council for Educational Research

ACF Army Cadet Force

ACF diagram a triangular diagram used to represent the chemical composition of metamorphic rocks (SCI)

ACGI Associate of the City & Guilds Institute

ACID Arts Cinema in Danger (Cambridge)

ACIS Associate of the Chartered Institute of Secretaries

ACM Air Chief Marshal

ACN Australian Corporation/ Company

ACNI Arts Council of Northern Ireland (FPA)

ACO Assistant Chief Officer (FRS)

ACOG Atlanta Committee for the Olympic Games (*also suggested: Atlanta can't organise games, and Athens cheated of games*) (SPR)

ACORN a classification of residential neighbourhoods (*by postcode*)

ACP African, Caribbean & Pacific States

ACR Automatic Conditional Release (PRP)

ACR approach control radar

ACRA Aluminium Can Recycling Association

ACRE Action with Communities in Rural England

ACS Airfield Construction Service (military) (MIL)

ACS Additional Curates Society

ACSDID Against Compulsory Sex Differentiation in Dress

ACSP Advisory Council on Scientific Policy

ACT Association of Cycle Traders (COM)

ACT Association of Christian Thinkers

ACT Australian Capital Territory

ACT Association of Corporate Treasurers

Actg acting (FRS)

ACTS Actions for Churches Together in Scotland

ACTT Association of Cinematograph & Television Technicians (*see* BACTA) (UNI)

ACTU Australian Council of Trade Unions (UNI)

ACU Auto-Cycle Union (SPR)

ACV air-cushion vehicle

ACV armoured command vehicle (MIL)

ACW Arts Council of Wales (FPA)

ACWW Associated Country Women of the World

AD Air Defence; Air Despatch; Army Department (MIL)

AD Anno Domini (*Latin: in the year of our Lord; see* CE)

AD Corps Army Dental Corps

AD eund ad eundem gradum (*Latin: admitted to the same degree*)

Ad fin ad finem (*Latin: to the end*)

Ad lib ad libitum (*Latin: freely; at pleasure*)

Ad, A/d after date

Ad, adv advantage (tennis) (SPR)

AD[&]C advise duration and charge (*whereby the operator rings you back after connecting your call and does just that*) (SCI)

ADA air defended area (MIL)

ADA Amateur Diving Association (SPR)

ADAPT Access for Disabled People to Arts Today

ADAs additional days added (PRP)

ADC aide-de-camp

ADC Amateur Dramatic Company (FPA)

ADC analogue-to-digital converter (SCI)

ADC Aviation Development Corporation (*Nigerian airline*)

ADC (P) personal ADC to the Queen

ADCM Archbishop of Canterbury's Diploma in Church Music (MUS)

ADE American Dramatists in Europe

ADF automatic direction finder (SCI)

ADFW Assistant Director of Fortifications and Works

ADGB Air Defence of Great Britain

ADGMS Assistant Director-General of Medical Services

ADI acceptable/available daily intake (F&D)

Adj adjustment (COM)

Adj adjunct; adjourned

Adj(s) adjective(s)

Adj, Adjt Adjutant (MIL)

ADJAG Assistant Deputy Judge Advocate General

Adm Admiral (MIL)

Adm/admin administrative/administration

Admin O administrative order (MIL)

ADMS Assistant Director of Medical Services

ADO Assistant Divisional Officer (FRS)

ADOS Assistant Director of Ordnance Services

ADP automatic data processing (MIL)

ADPCM adaptive differential pulse code modulation (SCI)

ADRs additional days remitted (PRP)

ADS Amateur Dramatic Society (FPA)

ADS air data system (SCI)

ADS&T Assistant Director of Supplies and Transport

ADSL asymmetric digital subscriber loop (SCI)

ADSL asynchronous digital subscriber line

ADT Addictive Diseases Trust (*now RAPT*) (PRP)

Adv advice

Adv adversus (*Latin: against*)

Adv adverb

Adv adverbial

Adv advocate

Adv, advt advertisement

ADVS Assistant Director of Veterinary Services

Ae aetatis (*Latin: at the age of, aged*)

AE & P Ambassador Extraordinary & Plenipotentiary

AE Housman Alfred Edward (*English poet 1859–1936*)

Æ, AE George William Russell (*Irish poet and journalist 1867–1935*)

AE, AEA Air Efficiency Award

AEA Atomic Energy Authority

AEAF Allied Expeditionary Air Force

AEC Army Educational Corps (*now RAEC*)

AEEU Amalgamated Engineering & Electrical Union (*merged AEU & EETPU*) (UNI)

AEF Allied Expeditionary Force (*WWI*) (MIL)

AEG all edges gilt (of a book) (FPA)

AEM Air Efficiency Medal

AENA All-England Netball Association (SPR)

AERE Atomic Energy Research Establishment

AES Audio Engineering Society (*set up in USA 1948*) (MUS)

AESOP Association of Europeans for Safety in Ordnance & Propellants (*Jonathan Coe – What a Carve-up*) (FPA)

AET after extra time (*sport; also the name of a football-inspired concert piece by Michael Nyman, punning* *on his Estonian wife's name Aet (pronounced eye-et)* (SPR)

AETC Arts & Entertainment Training Council (FPA)

AEU Amalgamated Engineering Union

AEWHA All-England Women's Hockey Association (SPR)

AEWU Amalgamated Engineering Workers' Union (UNI)

Af Africa(n)

AFA automatic fire alarm (FRS)

AFA Amateur Fencing Association (SPR)

AFA American Football Association (SPR)

AFC Air Force Cross

AFC automatic frequency control (SCI)

AFC Australian Football Council (SPR)

AFC Association Football Club (SPR)

AFC Air Force Cross

AFC Australian Flying Corps (became RAAF)

AFCENT Allied Forces Central European Theatre (MIL)

AFD automatic fire detection (FRS)

AFD accelerated freeze drying (F&D)

AFG Action for Governors *(information and training)*

Afg, Afgh Afghanistan

AFHQ Allied Force Headquarters

AFI American Film Industry (FPA)

AFIA Associate of Federal Institutes of Accountants (Australian)

AFIAeS Associate Fellow of the Institute of Aeronautical Sciences

AFL American Football League (SPR)

AFL Australian Football League (SPR)

AFM Air Force Medal

AFM American Federation of Musicians (MUS)

AFM atomic force microscope (SCI)

AFmr Assistant Firemaster (Scotland) (FRS)

AFN American Forces Network (FPA)

AFNOR Association Française de Normalisation *(the standards organisation of France)*

AFP Agence France Presse (FPA)

AFPU Allied Forces Photographic Unit

AFR Automatic Fingerprint Recognition

AFRAeS Associate Fellow of the Royal Aeronautical Society

AFRC Agricultural and Food Research Council

AFSLAET Associate Fellow of the Society of Licensed Aircraft Engineers & Technologists

AFT anyone for tennis? *(genre of drama)* (FPA)

AFTAR Awards for Trivial Animal Research *(Animal Aid's annual awards)*

AFV armoured fighting vehicle (MIL)

AG Aktiengesellschaft *(German: joint-stock company)* (COM)

AG Assistant Governor *(when staff were recruited to the Prison Service at Governor level)* (PRP)

AG Adjutant General

AG Attorney General

AGC automatic gain control (SCI)

AGE Age Concern England

AGI Associate of the Institute of Certificated Grocers

AGI Action for Governors Information

AGL above ground level ((ARC))

AGLO Action for Gay & Lesbian Ordinands

AGM Award of Garden Merit (RHS)

AGM air-to-ground missile

AGM Annual General Meeting

AGO American Guild of Organists (MUS)

AGR advanced gas-cooled reactor (SCI)

AGSM Associate of the Guildhall School of Music & Drama (MUS)

Agt agreement (COM)

Agt agent

AH anno Hegirae (*Latin: In the year of the Hegira*)

AHA Australian Hotels Association

Ahm ampère-hour meter (SCI)

AHQ Army Headquarters

AHWC Associate of Heriot-Watt College (*Edinburgh*)

AI Amnesty International

AI artificial intelligence (SCI)

AIA Associate of the Institute of Actuaries

AIAE Associate of the Institute of Automobile Engineers

AIB Allied Irish Banks

AIBA Association Internationale de Boxe Amateur (*French: International Amateur Boxing Association*) (SPR)

AIBD Associate of the Institute of British Decorators

AIBP Associate of the Institute of British Photographers

AICA Associate Member Commonwealth Institute of Accountants

AICE Associate of the Institute of Civil Engineers

AICR Association of International Cancer Research

AIDS Accumulated Income Deposited in Switzerland

AIEE Associate of the Institute of Electrical Engineers

AIF Australian Imperial Forces

AIFV armoured infantry fighting vehicle (MIL)

AIG Adjutant-Inspector-General

AIIA Associate of the Insurance Institute of America

AIJO Association of Independent Joint Operations

AIL Associate of the Institute of Linguists

AILocoE Associate of the Institute of Locomotive Engineers

AIMarE Associate of the Institute of Marine Engineers

AInstPl Associate of the Institute of Patentees

AIPAC American/Israeli Public Affairs Committee

AIR Art Information Registry (COM)

AIR All India Radio (FPA)

Airmob airmobile Mil

AISA Associate of the Incorporated Secretaries' Association

AJ Archaeological Journal (*Royal Archaeological Institute*) (FPA)

AJA Australian Journalists Association (FPA)

AJAG Assistant Judge Advocate General

AJC Australian Jockey Club (SPR)

Aka, AKA also known as

AKC Associate of King's College (*London*)

AKL Auckland (*New Zealand airport*)

ALA all letters answered

ALAA Associate of London Association of Certified Accountants (*name now changed; see AACCA*)

ALADI Asociación Latino-Americana de Integratión (*Spanish: Latin-American Integration Association*) (COM)

ALARM All London Against the Road-building Menace (*1986–98*)

ALARP as low as reasonably practicable

Alas Alaska (*USA*)

Alb Albania(n)

ALBA American Lawn Bowls Association (SPR)

ALCM Associate of the London College of Music

ALCS Authors' Licensing and Collecting Society (FPA)

Ald, Aldm Alderman

Aldaniti Grand National Winner, 1981, named after the owner's children Alistair, Daniel, Nichola and Timothy (SPR)

ALERT Automated Law Enforcement Response Team

A-level Advanced level examination

ALF Animal Liberation Front

Alfa Romeo Anonima Lombardo Fabbrice Automobili Romeo (*Italian: Romeo's Lombardy Automobile Manufacturing Company*)

ALFSEA Allied Land Forces South-East Asia

Alg Algeria(n)

ALGOL alogorithmic language (SCI)

ALI Argyll Light Infantry

ALIS Association du Locked in Syndrome

ALITALIA jocularly: Always Late In Take Off, Always Late In Arriving

ALOE A Lady of England – pseudonym of Charlotte Marie Tucker (*English author, 1821–93*)

ALP aerial ladder platform (FRS)

ALP Australian Labor Party (spelt Labor not Labour) (POL)

ALRA Academy of Live & Recorded Art

ALS advanced life support MED

Alta Alberta (*Canadian Province*)

ALU air lifting unit (FRS)

ALU arithmetic & logic unit (SCI)

AM Artium Magister (*Latin: Master of Arts*)

AM Master of Arts (*USA*)

AM Albert Medal

AM Member of the Order of Australia

AM Associate Member

AM ancient monument

Am- ammonium ion (*or radical* NH_4+; amyl ((*pentyl*) *radical* C_5H_{11}) (CHM)

AM, am amplitude modulation (FPA), (SCI)

Am, Amer America(n)

AMA American Motorcycle Association (SPR)

AMBOV, Ambov Association of Members of Boards of Visitors (PRP)

AMC air material command (MIL)

AMCO Association of Media Companies (COM)

AMF Australian Military Forces

AMF(L) Allied Mobile Force (*Land Element*) (MIL)

AMGOT Allied Military Government of Occupied Territory

AMIAE Associated Member of the Institute of Automobile Engineers

AMICE Associate Member of the Institution of Civil Engineers

AMIChemE Associate Member of the Institution of Chemical Engineers

AMIE (Ind) Associate Member of the Institution of Engineers (*India*)

AMIEE Associated Member of the Institute of Electrical Engineers

AMINA Associate Member of the Institution of Naval Architects

AMMA Assistant Masters' & Mistresses' Association

AMO Association of Magisterial Officers (UNI)

AMOB automatic meteorological oceanographic buoy

AMOC Aston Martin Owners' Club

Amoco American Oil Company (COM)

Amos nickname for teacher who perpetually opened 'At my old school . . .'

AMP Aksialnym Magnittym Polem

AMP Australian Mutual Provident

AMPA advanced mission planting aids

AMS American Musicological Society (MUS)

AMS Amsterdam (*Netherlands airport*)

AMS Assistant Military Secretary

AMS Army Medical Service

AMTA designer drug known as DOB, Golden Eagle or Flatliner

AMTPI Associate of the Town Planning Institute

AMU Associated Metalworkers Union (UNI)

Amu atomic mass unit (SCI)

AMusD Doctor of Musical Arts (MUS)

AMusTCL Associate in Music, Trinity College of Music, London (MUS)

AMVETS American veterans

AN direction finding system in which two signals corresponding

to morse A&N (• — and — •) are received simultaneously. When on course these are of equal intensity and blend into a continuous steady tone (SCI)

ANA Associate National Academician (*America*)

ANAC Australian National Athletic Council (SPR)

Anat anatomy; anatomical

ANC Advanced National Certificate

ANC African National Congress (POL)

ANEC Inst Associate of NE Coast Institution of Engineers and Shipbuilders

ANF Atlantic Nuclear Force (MIL)

ANFO ammonium nitrate & fuel oil (CHM)

ANFS Australian National Film School (FPA)

ANHRA American National Hot-Rod Association (SPR)

ANJ The Antiquaries' Journal (*Society of Antiquaries of London*) (FPA)

Ann annuity (COM)

Ann annuals; annals (*yearly publications*) (FPA)

Anon, anon anonymous (*unnamed; a prolific poet*); anonymously

Anoprop anomalous propagation (*radar clutter*)

ANSI American National Standards Institute

Ant antonym (*word of opposite meaning*)

ANU Australian National University

ANZAAS Australian & New Zealand Association for the Advancement of Science

ANZAC Australian and New Zealand Army Corps

AO Officer of the Order of Australia

AO Air Officer

AoA Articles of Association (COM)

AoA angle of attack (MIL)

AOABH assault occasioning actual bodily harm (PRP)

AOB, aob any other business

AOC any other colour

AOC Air Officer Commanding

AOC Appellation d'Origine Contrôlée (*highest French wine classification*) (F&D)

AOCB any other competent business

AOC-in-C Air Officer Commanding-in-Chief

AOE Association of Organ Enthusiasts (MUS)

AOER Army Officers Emergency Reserve

AOF Ancient Order of Foresters

AOG aircraft on ground

AOH Ancient Order of Hibernians (*Nineteenth-century foundation*)

AOL America online (SCI)

AONB Area of Outstanding Natural Beauty (SCI)

AOR album-oriented rock; album-oriented radio (*USA*) (MUS)

AOV any other variety

Ap additional premium (COM)

AP Associated Press (FPA)

AP amtlicher Prüfungsnummer (*German wine classification*) (F&D)

AP aerial photograph/photography

AP armour piercing

AP ammunition point

AP Air Publication (*Ministry of Defence*) (MIL)

APACS Association for Payment Clearing Services

APC automated processing centre (COM)

APC automatic phase control (SCI)

APC armoured personnel carrier (MIL)

APCIMS Association of Private Client Investment Managers and Stockbrokers

APCS Association of Payment Clearance Services (COM)

APCS advanced passenger clearance system

APD Army Pay Department

APD antisocial personality disorder

APDS armour piercing discarding sabot (MIL)

APEX Association of Professional, Executive, Clerical & Computer Staff (UNI)

APF accidental phosphate fluoride

APLEG All-Party Landmass Education Group

A-PN Author-Publisher Network (FPA)

APO Army Post Office (MIL)

App apparatus

App applied; appointed; approved

App apprentice

App appendix (FPA)

APP trade name for bismuth carbonate (CHM)

App, approx approximate(ly)

Appro approval

Apptd appointed

APPU Australian Primary Producers Union (UNI)

APR annual percentage rate (COM)

APRO Aerial Phenomena Research Organisation

APS accelerated promotion scheme (*introduced 1988 for staff considered to have potential to reach the rank of at least Governor 2*) (PRP)

APS advanced photo system

APS Assisted Places Scheme

APSC Asia Pacific Space Centre

Apt apartment

APTC Army Physical Training Corps (MIL)

APU audience participation unit (FPA)

APU auxiliary power unit (SCI)

APV Assisted Prison Visit (PRP)

APVU Assisted Prison Visits Unit (PRP)

Aq cal aqua calida (*Latin: hot water*)

AQMG Assistant-Quartermaster-General

Ar Aramaic (FPA)

AR actual reality (SCI)

AR analytical reagent (*indicating a standard of purity of a chemical*) (SCI)

Ar argon; general symbol for an aryl, or aromatic, radical (CHM)

AR all round (ARC)

AR autonomous region

Ar- indicating substitution in the aromatic nucleus. (CHM)

Ar, Arab Arabia(n); Arabic (FPA)

Ar, arr arrive(s)(d); arrival

ARA Associate of the Royal Academy (FPA)

ARA Amateur Rowing Association (SPR)

ARAEN Appareil de Référence pour la détermination de l'Affaiblissement Equivalent pour la Netteté (*French: a standard telephone transmission reference system that uses comparative articulation tests to assess in decibels (or nepers) the transmission performance of telephone equipment*) (SCI)

ARAeS Associate of the Royal Aeronautical Society

ARAM Associate of the Royal Academy of Music (MUS)

ARAS *see* RAS

ARBA Associate of the Royal Society of British Artists

ARBC Associate of the Royal British Colonial Society of Artists

ARBN Australian Registered Business Number

ARBS Associate of the Royal Society of British Sculptors

ARBS angle rate bombing set

ARC Aid to Russian Christians (*founded by Jane Ellis (1951–98)*)

ARCA Associate of the Royal Cambrian Academy

ARCA Associate of the Royal Canadian Academy

ARCE Academical Rank of Civil Engineers

Arch archaic; archaism

Arch archipelago

Arch archery (SPR)

Arch, Archbp Archbishop

Archd Archdeacon

Archd Archduke

Archt Architect

ARCM Associate of the Royal College of Music

ARCO Associate of the Royal College of Organists (MUS)

ARCO-CHM Associate of the Royal College of Organists – Choir-master (MUS)

ARCS Associate of the Royal College of Science

ARCS Admiralty Raster Chart Service (MIL)

ARCUK Architects' Registration Council UK (ARC)

ARD automatic release date (PRP)

ARE Associate of Royal Society of Painter Etchers

Arg Argentina

ARHA Associate of the Royal Hibernian Academy (FPA)

ARIBA Associate of the Royal Institute of British Architects

ARIBA Associate of the Royal Institute of British Artists

ARIC Associate of the Royal Institute of Chemistry

ARICS Professional Associate of the Royal Institution of Chartered Surveyors

ARINC Aeronautical Radio INCorporated (*a US organisation whose membership includes airlines, aircraft constructors and component manufacturers. It publishes agreed standards and finances research*)

ARISE Association for Research into the Science of Enjoyment

ARL Army Research Laboratory (*Adelphi MD*) (MIL)

ARLA Association of Registered Letting Agents (COM)

ARM Advanced RISC Machines (SCI)

Arm Armenia(n)

Arm Armoric(an) (*ancient name for Brittany, France*)

ARM Anglican Renewal Ministries

ARMCM Associate of the Royal Manchester College of Music (MUS)

Armr armoured (MIL)

ARMS Associate of the Royal Society of Miniature Painters

ARP air raid precautions (MIL)

ARPA Advanced Research Projects Agency (*US Dept of Defense*) (MIL)

ARPO50 Association for Retired Persons Over 50

ARPS Associate of the Royal Photographic Society

ARRC Associate of the Royal Red Cross (not if RRC)

ARRC Allied Rapid Reaction Corps (MIL)

ARSA Associate of the Royal Scottish Academy (FPA)

ARSM Associate of the Royal School of Mines

Art Article

Art artificial

ART assisted reproduction technology

ARTC Associate of the Royal Technical College, Glasgow

Artic articulated lorry

Arty artillery (MIL)

ARV armed response vehicle

ARV armoured recovery vehicle (MIL)

ARVIA Associate of the Royal Victorian Institute of Architects

Arvo afternoon (*Australian*)

ARWA Associate of the Royal West of England Academy

ARWS Associate of the Royal Society of Painters in Water-Colours

AS Anglo-Saxon

AS air-seasoned (*of timber*) (ARC)

As Asia(n); Asiatic

AS Anglo-Saxon

As- asymmetrically substituted (CHM)

ASA Advertising Standards Authority (COM)

ASA Amateur Swimming Association (SPR)

ASA American Standards Association

ASAA Associate of the Society of Incorporated Accountants and Auditors

ASAD all singing, all dancing (*hot and cold swinging everything*)

ASAGB Amateur Swimming Association of Great Britain (*was MSCA*) (SPR)

ASAM Associate of the Society of Art Masters

ASAP, asap as soon as possible

ASAT anti-satellite weapon (MIL)

ASB American Shipping Bureau (COM)

ASB Accounting Standards Board

ASB alternative service book

ASBA Association of Self-Build Architects (ARC)

ASBSBSW Amalgamated Society of Boilermakers, Shipwrights, Blacksmiths & Structural Workers (UNI)

Asc ascendant (SCI)

ASC Army Service Corps

ASCAP American Society of Composers, Authors & Publishers (MUS)

ASCII American Standard Code For Information Interchange (*pronounced 'Askey' as in Arthur*) (SCI)

Asda Associated Dairies (COM)

ASDIC anti-submarine detector indicator (MIL)

ASE Amalgamated Society of Engineers

ASEAN Association of South East Asian Nations

ASH Action on Smoking and Health (*see* CFT)

ASI Anti Slavery International

ASIC application-specific integrated circuit (SCI)

A-side more important side of record (MUS)

A-side supposedly the more important side of a record (FPA)

ASL Amerslan/g; American Sign Language

ASLEF Associated Society of Locomotive Engineers & Firemen (UNI)

ASLIB Association of Special Libraries & Information Bureaux (UNI)

ASM Assistant Stage Manager (FPA)

ASM Automation Systems Manager (SCI)

ASPAC Asian & Pacific Council

ASR Air Sea Rescue

ASRA Albert Square Residents' Association

ASSAP Association for the Scientific Study of Anomalous Phenomena (SCI)

ASSD Association of Social Services Directors

Assn association

Assoc associate; association

ASSR Autonomous Soviet Socialist Republics

Asst, asst assistant

Assyr Assyria(n)

ASTM American Society for Testing Materials (SCI)

ASTMS Association of Scientific, Technical and Managerial Staffs

Astr Astronomy

Astr, astron astronomy; astronomer; astronomical (SCI)

Astrol astrology; astrologer; astrological

ASU Air Support Unit

ASV advance safety vehicle

ASW Association of Scientific Workers

ASW Approved Social Worker

ASWE Admiralty Surface Weapons Establishment (*see* AUWE) (MIL)

ASX Australian Stock Exchange

Asym asymmetrical

AT attainment target

AT augmented transition network (SCI)

At no atomic number (SCI)

At wt atomic weight (*now relative atomic mass*) (SCI)

AT&T American Telegraphs & Telephones (COM)

ATA Air Transport Association

ATA air transport auxiliary

ATAF Allied Tactical Air Force (MIL)

ATAPS Association of Tarot & Associated Psychic Services

ATB aeration test burner (SCI)

ATB all-terrain bicycle

ATC Automatic Telephone Company (COM)

ATC Air Training Corps (MIL)

ATC air traffic control

ATC Air Tanzania Corporation; any time cancelled

ATCL Associate of Trinity College of Music, London (MUS)

ATF Bureau of Alcohol, Tobacco & Firearms (*US*)

ATGW anti tank guided weapon (MIL)

ATM asynchronous transfer mode (SCI)

ATM automated teller machine

ATMT American Telephone Manufacturing Company (COM)

ATOC Association of Train Operating Companies

ATOL Air Tour Organisers Licence

ATP Association of Tennis Professionals (SPR)

ATP advanced turbo-prop

ATR air turbo-ram jet engine (SCI)

ATR tube anti-transmit-receive tube (SCI)

ATS Auxiliary Territorial Service (MIL)

ATSC Associate of the Tonic Sol-fa College (MUS)

Att at this time

Att attached

Att Attorney

Att Gen, Atty Gen Attorney General

Attn attention

ATV Associated Television (FPA)

ATV all-terrain vehicle

ATWM army transition to war measure (MIL)

AU artist unknown (*Joseph Pennell*)

AU assessment unit (PRP)

AUA another useless acronym

AUC Australian Universities Commission

AUC anno urbis conditæ (*Latin: From the foundation of the city* (*Rome*)

AUR automatic unconditional release (PRP)

AUT Association of University Teachers (UNI)

Auto automatic transmission

Auto- aut- prefix from autos (*Greek: self*)

AUWE Admiralty Underwater Weapons Establishment (*see* ASWE) (MIL)

AV accumulated visits (PRP)

AV Artillery Volunteers (MIL)

AVC automatic volume control (SCI)

AVC additional voluntary contribution (*to pension scheme*)

AVD all very different/difficult

Ave Avenue

AVLB armoured vehicle launched bridge (MIL)

AVM Air Vice-Marshal

Avoird avoirdupois

AVR Army Volunteer Reserve

AVRO AV Roe and Co (*aeronautics*)

AVT argenine vaso-toxin

AW all widths (*of cut timber*) (ARC)

AWACS airborne warning & control system (MIL)

AWBC Australian Women's Bowling Council (*lawn bowls*) (SPR)

AWLA All-England Women's Lacrosse Association (SPR)

AWLA Australian Women's Lacrosse Association (SPR)

AWN Pugin Augustus Welby Northmore (*British architect 1812–52*)

AWOL absent without leave (MIL)

AWU Australian Workers Union (UNI)

Ax axiom

AYM angry young man (*becomes COD*)

Azerty European version of keyboard with az taking place of qw – as in qwerty (COM)

AZT azidothymidine (*also called zidovudine*) (CHM)

B

B middle managerial occupational grade (COM)

B benzedrine (PRP)

B biennial

B Bishop (*chess*) (SPR)

B bowled

B- military aircraft bomber (US) (MIL)

B horizon solid zone of accumulation below A in soil profile

B licence for those carriers who combine carrying their own goods with those of others

B road secondary road

B&B 50/50 brandy & Benedictine mixture (F&D)

B&B; b&b bed & breakfast

B&D Black & Decker (COM)

B&E breaking & entering (PRP)

B&H Benson & Hedges (COM)

B&H Boosey & Hawkes (COM)

B&H Bourne & Hollingsworth (COM)

B&H Benson & Hedges English Cricket cup (SPR)

B&Q Block & Quaile (*Richard Block and David Quayle opened 050369; nearly called Always*) (COM)

B&S brandy & soda (F&D)

B&W Boulton & Watt (COM)

B&W, B/W, b/w black & white (*photography*) (FPA)

B, b born

B, B&EM bed, breakfast & evening meal

B, Bib Bible (FPA)

B/H curve also called magnetisation curve (SCI)

B/H loop also called hysteresis loop (SCI)

B'ham Birmingham

B'head Birkenhead

B3 bullshit baffles brains (*pronounced 'B cubed' – used as a verb 'to B-cube' somebody*) (SCI)

BA Baccalaureus Artium (*Latin: Bachelor of Arts*)

BA British Academy

BA British Association (*for the Advancement of Science*)

BA breathing apparatus (FRS)

BA Bachelor of Arts

BA British Association (*a system of metric screw threads, confined to small sizes, used in instrument work. It is designated by numbers from 0 to 25, ranging from 6mm to 0.25mm in diameter and from 1mm to 0.072mm pitch*) (SCI)

BA British Airways (*see BOAC*)

BAA British Agencies for Adoption

BAA British Airports Authority

BAA British Astronomical Association

BAAF British Agencies for Adoption and Fostering (*not in favour of Kimiko, the Taiwanese virtual pet Dec 97*)

BAAL British Association for Applied Linguistics

BAC British Aircraft Corporation (COM)

BACB British Association of Communicators in Business (*formerly BAIE*)

BAcc Bachelor of Accountancy

BACC Broadcast Advertising Clearing Centre

B-acid 1-amino-8-naphthol-3,5-disulphonic acid; an intermediate in dyestuff manufacture (CHM)

BACM British Association of Colliery Management (UNI)

BACS Bankers' Automated Clearing System

BACTA Broadcasting, Entertainment & Cinematograph Technicians' Union (*merged ACTT & BETA*) (FPA)

BACV breathing apparatus control van (FRS)

BADA British Antique Dealers' Association (COM)

BADC British Academy of Dramatic Combat (*to achieve stage fighting credibility*)

BADN British Association of Dental Nurses

BAe British Aerospace (COM)

BAe146 British Aerospace model 146-300

BAECO breathing apparatus entry control officer (FRS)

BAF British Athletics Federation (SPR)

BAFO British Air Forces of Occupation

BAFSV British Armed Forces Service Vouchers (*pronounced baffs – an internal currency*) (MIL)

BAFTA British Academy of Film & Television Arts (*see BAF and SFTA*) (FPA)

BAGS Butchers' Arms Golf Society (Oxford) (SPR)

BAGUPA Bishops' Advisory Group on Urban Priority Areas

BAI Bachelor of Engineering (*Latin: Baccalaurius in Arte Ingeniaria*)

BAIE British Association of Industrial Editors (*now BACB*)

Bal balance

Bal balneum (*Latin: bath*)

BAL British anti-lewisite (*dimercaptol – antidote to war gas and metal poisoning*) (CHM)

BALI British Association of Landscape Industries (UNI)

BALPA British Air Line Pilots Association (UNI)

Balt Baltic

BAMPAA British Actors, Models & Performing Artists' Association

B-amplifier amplifier following mixers or faders associated with microphone circuits in broadcasting studios, the faders and mixers following the A-amplifiers. Not the same as a class-B amplifier (SCI)

BAO Bachelor of Obstetrics

BAOR British Army of the Rhine (MIL)

BAPS British Association of Plastic Surgeons

Bapt Baptist

Bapt, bp baptism; baptised

BAR Browning Automatic Rifle (MIL)

Bar barrister

Bar barometer; barometric

BARB British Audience Research Board (FPA)

BARC British Automobile Racing Club

BArch Bachelor of Architecture

BARNA Brown & Root North Africa (COM)

Barr Barrister

BART Buildings at Risk Trust

Bart, Bt Baronet

BAS Bachelor of Agricultural Science

BAS British Acoustical Society (*see* IOA) (SCI)

BAS British Antarctic Survey

BASDA Business and Accounting Software Developers Association

BASF Badische Anilin und Soda-Fabrik (*German chemical and electronics factory*) (COM)

BASI British Association of Ski Instructors

BASIC beginners' all-purpose symbolic instruction code (SCI)

BASW British Association of Social Workers

BAT British-American Tobacco (COM)

BAT breathing apparatus tender (FRS)

BAT British Antarctic Territory

Batt Battalion

Batt Battery

Bav Bavaria(n)

BAWLA British Amateur Weight Lifters Association (SPR)

BB Boys' Brigade

BBA British Bankers' Association (COM)

BBA British Beekeepers Association

BBBC British Boxing Board of Control (SPR)

BBC British Broadcasting Company (*until 31 December 1926, when it became the British Broadcasting Corporation*) (FPA)

BBCM Bandmaster of the Bandsmen's College of Music (MUS)

BBE best before end (F&D)

BBFC British Board of Film Censors (FPA)

BBM Best of British Motorsport

B-boy male rap-music fan (MUS)

BC back cover (*publishing*) (FPA)

BC bayonet cap (*fitted to an electric lamp, consisting of a cylindrical outer wall fitted with 2 or 3 pins for engaging in slots in a lampholder*) (SCI)

BC Before Christ (*ie counting backwards from the supposed year of Jesus's birth, as determined by the Council of Nicea in 325; see* BCE)

BC back cross (SCI)

BC British Colombia (*Canadian province*)

BC Battery Commander (MIL)

BC&CS British Cactus & Succulent Society

BCA Bachelor of Commerce & Administration (*NZ*)

BCA Book Club Associate (FPA)

BCA British Chocolate Alliance (F&D)

BCAR British Civil Airworthiness Requirements

BCC British Coal Corporation (*formerly* NCB) (COM)

BCC British Chambers of Commerce

BCCA British Cyclo-Cross Association (SPR)

BCD binary-coded decimal, a decimal code in which each digit is represented by its binary equivalent. Four binary digits are required to represent each decimal digit

BCE before common (or Christian) era

BCE Boundary Commission for England

BCF bromochlorodifluoromethane (*organic liquid used for extinguishing fires*) (CHM)

BCF British Cycle Federation (SPR)

BCGBA British Crown Green Bowling Association (SPR)

BCh Bachelor of Surgery

BCL Bachelor of Civil Law

B-class insulation a class of insulating material to which is assigned a temperature of 130°C. (SCI)

BCMS Bible Churchmen's Missionary Society

BCNET Business Co-operation NETwork (COM)

BCNZ Broadcasting Corporation of New Zealand (FPA)

BCOF British Commonwealth Occupation Force

BCom Bachelor of Commerce

BCP British Car Parks (COM)

BCP Book of Common Prayer

BCS British Computer Society (*estd 1957, Royal Charter 1984*) (SCI)

BCTF British Craft Trade Fair (*Harrogate*)

BD bank draft; brought down (COM)

BD bills discounted (COM)

BD Bachelor of Divinity

BD bipolar disorder

Bd board

Bd bound (FPA)

Bd bond (COM)

Bd ft broad foot

Bd(s) board(s)

BDA British Dental Association

BDB British Digital Broadcasting

BDC Bentley Drivers' Club

BDC, bdc bottom dead centre (SCI)

BDE business development exercise (COM)

Bde, bde Brigade (MIL)

BDPO broken down press officer

BDS Bachelor of Dental Surgery

BDS Bomb-Disposal Service (MIL)

BDSA British Diplomatic Sponsors' Association

BDV breakdown voltage (SCI)

BDV broken down vehicle

BDV Borna disease virus (*carried by animals, thought to cause depression*)

BE bill of exchange (COM)

BE British Energy (= *NE* + *SN*) (COM)

BE Board of Education (US)

BE Bachelor of Education

BE Bachelor of Engineering

BE Baltic Exchange

BE Belgium

BEA British East Africa

BEA British European Airways (*jocularly: Britains Excuse for an Airline*)

BEA British Egg Association

BEAB British Electrical Approvals Board

BECTU Broadcasting Entertainment & Cinematograph Technicians' Union (*amalgamation of BETA and ACTT*) (FPA)

BEd Bachelor of Education

BEF British Expeditionary Force (MIL)

BEJAM Brian Eric John Apthorp & Marion/Millie (*frozen food store, now Iceland*) (COM)

BEM British Empire Medal

BEN best end of neck

BENELUX Belgium, the Netherlands & Luxembourg

BEng Bachelor of Engineering

BENHS British Entomological & Natural History Society

BEPO British Experimental Pile O (*principal source of UK radioisotope production until superseded by DIDO at Harwell in 1969*) (SCI)

BER Board for Engineers' Regulation (SCI)

BES Biological Engineering Society (*see* IPEMB) (SCI)

BES Building Engineering Services (ARC)

BESA British Engineering Standards Association (*now British Standards Institution*)

BET British Electric Traction (COM)

Bet between

BET absorption theory Brunauer, Emmett & Teller postulated the building up of multimolecular absorption layers on the catalyst surface, and extended Langmuir's derivation for single molecular layers to obtain an isothermal equation for multimolecular absorption (SCI)

BET surface area surface area of a powder calculated from gas absorption data, by a method devised by Brunauer, Emmett & Teller (SCI)

BETA Broadcasting & Allied Trades Alliance (*see* BACTA) (FPA)

BEUC Bureau Européen des unions de consommateurs (*French: Bureau of European Consumer Organisations*)

BEV Black English Vocabulary (*sociolinguistics*)

BEV black English vernacular

BF brought forward (COM)

BF British Fascists (*in 1924, the name superseded Fascisti. Party members, and especially opponents, often abbreviated this to BF*) (POL)

BF bedroom farce (FPA)

Bf bold face (FPA)

BFA British Footwear Association (COM)

BFA British Film Academy (*forerunner of SFTA & BAFTA*) (FPA)

BFAWU Bakers, Food & Allied Workers Union (UNI)

BFBS British & Foreign Bible Society

BFBS British Forces Broadcasting Service (FPA)

BFG British Forces in Germany (MIL)

BFG Big Friendly Giant (*book by Roald Dahl*) (FPA)

BFG Black Forest gâteau (F&D)

BFI British Film Institute (FPA)

BFM breast-feeding mother (PRP)

BFO beat frequency oscillator (SCI)

BFPO British Field/Forces' Post Office; British Forces Posted Overseas (MIL)

BFPO bisdimethylaminofluoro-phosphine oxide (*dimefox, an insecticide*) (CHM)

BFSS British Field Sports Society

BG battle group (MIL)

BGA British Gliding Association (SPR)

BGHQ Battlegroup Headquarters (MIL)

BGM Burma Gallantry Medal

BGO blinding glimpses of the obvious

BGP British Grand Prix

BGS Brigadier General Staff

BGSU Barclays Group Staff Union (*ceased 1995 – see* UNiFI) (UNI)

BH Broadcasting House (FPA)

BH Bush House (FPA)

BHA British Hospitality Association (COM)

BHB British Horseracing Board (SPR)

BHC benzene hexachloride (CHM)

BHIPA British Honey Importers' & Packers' Association (COM)

BHP broken-hearted Pommies

BHP Broken Hill Proprietary (*Australia*) (COM)

BHP, bhp brake horsepower (rate at which an engine does work, measured against a brake) (SCI)

BHS British Home Stores (COM)

BHS British Hypertension Society

BHSVA JG's edible plastic – Justin White and Gus Gray of Bluestone High School, VA invented this by accident

Bi bisexual

BIB business improvement bulletin (COM)

Bib bibliothèque (FPA)

Bib, Bibl Biblical (FPA)

BIBC British Isles Bowls Council (lawn bowls) (SPR)

BIBF British & Irish Basketball Federation (SPR)

BIBIC British Institute for Brain-Injured Children

Bibl bibliographical; bibliography (FPA)

Bibliog bibliographer; bibliography (FPA)

BIC Business Information Centre (COM)

BICC British Insulated Callenders Cables (COM)

BIFU Banking, Insurance & Finance Union (UNI)

Big 3 Harvard, Yale & Princeton (*American East Coast Colleges*)

Big A Aids (PRP)

Big H heroin (PRP)

BIHA British Ice-Hockey Association (SPR)

BIM British Institute of Management (COM)

BINDT British Institute of Non-destructive Testing (*estd 1954*) (SCI)

Bio biography (FPA)

Biog biographical; biography (FPA)

Biol biological; biology (SCI)

BIOS basic input/output system

BIOT British Indian Ocean Territory

BIP Benefits Investigation Programme

BIP Brigade Internatonale Patisserie (*also known as Entarteurs – Belgian surrealists who shove cream cakes into people's faces, especially – Have I Got News for You 241098*)

BIRPS British Institutions Reflection Profiling Syndicate (*imaging the earth's sub-structure*)

BIS Bank for International Settlements (Switzerland) (COM)

BIS Bureau of Indian Standards

BISRA British Iron & Steel Research Association (COM)

BIT battle inoculation test (MIL)

Bit binary digit/unit (0 or 1) (SCI)

BITCH Black Intelligence Test of Cultural Homogeneity

BJA British Judo Association (SPR)

BK Battery Captain (MIL)

Bk(s)

Book(s) (FPA)

Bk, bk bank; book; backwardation (COM)

Bkcy bankruptcy (COM)

BKFS British-Kuwaiti Friendship Society

Bkg, bkg banking (COM)

Bkpt, bkpt bankrupt (COM)

Bks barracks (MIL)

BKV best-kept village

BL bill of lading (COM)

BL British Leyland (COM)

BL breakdown lorry (FRS)

BL Bachelor of Law

BL Bachelor of Letters

BL Barrister-at-Law

BL British Library (FPA)

Bl blue

BLA British Liberation Army

BLAC British Light Aviation Centre (SPR)

Blad book layout and design (*a dummy with sample spreads*) (FPA)

BLAM Barrel-Launched Adaptive Munitions (*small bullets*)

B-layer weakly reflecting and scattering layer 10-30km above the earth's surface

BLDSA British Long Distance Swimming Association (SPR)

BLDSC British Library Document Supply Centre (FPA)

BLE Brotherhood of Locomotive Engineers

BLEATERS born losers expending all their energy rubbishing success

BLEU blind landing experimental unit (*operated by the RAE which developed such a system*) (MIL)

BLit, BLitt Bachelor of Letters or Literature

Blk block; bulk

Blk, bl, blk black

BLL Bachelor of Laws

BLRA Brewers & Licensed Retailers Association (COM)

BLRRG British Library Regular Readers' Group (FPA)

BLT bacon, lettuce & tomato (*roll or sandwich*) (F&D)

Blubo Blut und Boden (*German: blood & soil – a film genre*) (FPA)

BM Bachelor of Medicine

BM British Museum (FPA)

BM Burlington Magazine (FPA)

BM bench mark

BMA British Midland Airways

BMD births, marriages & deaths (*see* HMD)

BMEP Brake Mean Effective Pressure (SCI)

BMG one of the big five record companies (*BMG, EMI, Polygram, Sony, Warner*) (MUS)

BMH British Military Hospital (MIL)

BMHA British Music-Hall Association (FPA)

BMHS British Music-Hall Society (FPA)

BMI Broadcast Music Incorporated (MUS)

BMJ British Medical Journal

B-movie a supporting film, supposedly less attractive than the main feature (FPA)

BMPA British Medical Pilot's Association

BMus Bachelor of Music (MUS)

BMW better make way

BMX bicycle motocross

Bn Battalion (MIL)

BNAF British North Africa Force

BNB British National Bibliography (FPA)

BNC British National Committee

BNF Bibliothèque Nationale de France (*French: French National Library*) (FPA)

BNOC British National Oil Corporation (*became BritOil*) (COM)

BNTM British New Town Movement

BO brought over; buyer's option (COM)

BO Banker's Order (COM)

BO branch office (COM)

Bo back order; broker's order (COM)

BO body odour (*identified by Lifebuoy soap*)

BO box office (FPA)

BO blackout (FPA)

Bo's'n boatswain (*pronounced bosun*)

BOA British Olympic Association (*name under which Great Britain entered the Moscow Olympics (1980) because politicians wanted Britain to boycott the games in protest at the Russian invasion of Afghanistan. It caused consternation in some quarters because some thought Boa was a new country*) (SPR)

BOAC British Overseas Airways Corporation (*see* BA)

BOAC better on a camel

BOB breathing observational bubble

BOBMF Battle of Britain Memorial Flight (MIL)

BOC British Opera Company (MUS)

BOCDO Breach of Conditional Discharge Order (PRP)

BOCM British Oil & Cake Mills

BOE sill brick-on-edge sill (ARC)

BOF British Orienteering Federation (SPR)

BOGOF buy one, get one free (*trade jargon for such an offer*)

BOIS basic output/input system

Bol Bolivia(n)

BOLA Betting Office Licensees' Association (SPR)

Bolly Bollinger (*champagne*) (F&D)

BomCS Bombay Civil Service

BomSC Bombay Staff Corps

BOPO Breach Of Probation Order (PRP)

Bor Borough

BOS British Orthoptic Society (UNI)

BOSCO Breach Of Community Service Order (PRP)

BOSS Breach Of Suspended Sentence Of Imprisonment (PRP)

BOSS Bureau of State Security (*South Africa*)

BOT Board of Trade (COM)

Bot botanical; botany (SCI)

BOTB British Overseas Trade Board

BOV Board of Visitors (PRP)

Bovril from bos (*Latin: ox*) and vril, the term applied to the life force in Bulwer-Lytton's novel The Forgotten Race (1871) (F&D)

BP [Lord] Robert Stephenson Smyth Baden-Powell (1857–1941, founder of the Boy Scouts (1908) and (with his sister Agnes) of the Girl Guides (1910)

BP bill(s) payable (COM)

BP British Petroleum (COM)

BP between perpendiculars

Bp birthplace

Bp below proof (F&D)

Bp Bishop

Bp, b pt boiling point (SCI)

BPA British Parachute Association

BPA Bicycle Polo Association (1895–1930) (SPR)

BPAGB Bicycle Polo Association of Great Britain (*from 1930*) (SPR)

BPC British Pharmaceutical Code

BPC British Printing Corporation (COM)

BPharm Bachelor of Pharmacy

BPhil Bachelor of Philosophy

Bpi bits per inch (SCI)

BPI British Photographic Industry

B-picture/side secondary to the A-side of the record, or the feature film, sometimes superior to the main attraction (FPA)

B-position in a manual exchange, any individual switchboard section that is mainly equipped for the reception and completion of calls originated by subscribers foreign to that exchange (SCI)

BPRS Brief Psychiatric Rarity Scale

Bps bits per second (SCI)

BPSG Black Prisoners' Support Group (PRP)

BPTM British Publishers' Traditional Market (FPA)

BQ bill of quantities (ARC)

BR bill(s) receivable (COM)

Br branch (COM)

Br Brother

Br Breton

Br bronze (SCI)

Br, Brit British

Br, Brit Britain (*United Kingdom of England, Scotland, Wales & Northern Ireland*)

Bra brassière

BRA The British Reflexology Association

BRA Brigadier Royal Artillery

BRC British Reinforced Concrete (COM)

BRC Business Research Centre (COM)

BRC British Retail Consortium

BRCS British Red Cross Society

BRDC British Racing Drivers' Club

BRE Building Research Establishment

Bren gun Brno (*in Czechoslovakia*) + Enfield (*the manufacturers*) (MIL)

Brev Brevet

BRFI Brewing Research Foundation International

BRG British Racing Green

Brig Brigadier

Brig Gen Brigadier General (MIL)

BRITE Basic Research in Industrial Technologies for Europe (COM)

BritOil British Oil (*formerly BNOC*) (COM)

BRIXMIS British Military Exchange Mission (*The British Commander-in-Chief's Mission to the Soviet Forces in Germany*) (MIL)

BRM binary rate multiplier (SCI)

BRM British Racing Motors

BRN Berne (*Swiss airport*)

Bro(s), bro(s) brother, brothers

BROSCAOR Bloodless Revolution of Senior Citizens and the Occupationally Rejected (*young age pensions, Age Hostels, no redundancy, etc*) (*marching on Whitehall on 20 April. Booked around 2,000 coaches*) (*Reggie Perrin BBC TV*)

BRS British Road Services (COM)

BRSC British rear support command (MIL)

BRSCC British Racing & Sports Car Club

Brt bought

BS bill of sale (COM)

BS balance sheet (COM)

BS Bachelor of Surgery

BS brilliant acid green (food colouring) (F&D)

BS British Standard

BS2 Biosphere-2 (*experiment*) (SCI)

BSA Building Societies' Association (COM)

BSA Burma Star Association (MIL)

BSA British Surfing Association (SPR)

BSAA British South American Airways

BSAC British Sub Aqua Club (SPR)

BSAD British Sports Association for the Disabled

BSAO British Staff Admin Office

BSAP British South Africa Police

BSAS British Sausage Appreciation Society

BSB British Sky Broadcasting (FPA)

BSB British Satellite Broadcasting (FPA)

BSC British Shoe Corporation (COM)

BSC British Steel Corporation (COM)

BSC British Sugar Corporation (COM)

BSC Broadcasting Standards Council (UK) (COM)

BSc Bachelor of Science

BSC base-station control (SCI)

BSC Building Societies Commission

BSc(Dent) Bachelor of Science in Dentistry

Bsd besonders (German: particularly)

BSE blame someone else

B-service-area region surrounding a broadcasting transmitter where the field strength is between 5 & 10mV/m (SCI)

B-setting photography setting where shutter stays open until it is closed manually (FPA)

BSF British Salonica Force

BSF Brotherhood of St Francis

BSI Baker Street Irregulars (*Holmesian gang*) (FPA)

BSI British Standards Institution

B-side the single-current channels in a quadruplex system (SCI)

B-side less important side of record (*which may turn out to be better received than the A-side*) (MUS)

BSIT Building Societies' Investment Trust (COM)

BSkyB British Sky Broadcasting (*union of BSB and SkyTV*)

BsL Bills of Lading (COM)

BSL Botanical Society of London

BSM Barker, Storey, Matthews (COM)

BSM British School of Motoring (COM)

BSO Bournemouth Symphony Orchestra (MUS)

BSSc, BSocSc Bachelor of Social Science

BST Bible Speaks Today

BST bovine somatotrophin (*growth hormone to promote milk yield*)

BSt E Bury St Edmunds

BT British Telecommunications Plc (*British Telecom*) (COM)

Bt bought (COM)

Bt, Bart Baronet (*the lowest hereditary title of honour – Sir X Y*)

BTA British Troops Austria

BTB Lord Ian Basil Gawaine Temple Blackwood (*illustrator of Belloc's Bad Child's Book of Beasts, 1870–1917*)

BT-cut special cut of quartz crystal to obviate temperature effects, such that the angle with the z-axis is -40° (SCI)

BTCV British Trust for Conservation Volunteers

BTE British Troops in Egypt

BTEC Business & Technical Education Council

BTG British Technology Group (COM)

BTGSS British Telecom Global Satellite Services (SCI)

BTH British Thomson-Houston (COM)

BTh Bachelor of Theology

Btm bottom

BTO British Trust for Ornithology

BTO Brigade Training Officer (FRS)

BTP Buoni del Tesoro Poliennali (Italian bond)

BTR British Telecommunications Research (COM)

Btu British thermal unit

BTW by the way

Bty, btry battery (MIL)

Bu butyl (-C_4H_9 *radical*) (CHM)

BUFORA British UFO Research Association

Bulg(n) Bulgaria(n)

BUM broadcasting under management (*Kenny Everitt joke*)

BUNDY but unfortunately not dead yet

BURP bankrupt, unemployed, rejected person

BV bene vale (*Latin: farewell*)

BV Beata Virgo (*Latin: Blessed Virgin (Mary)*

BVA British Video Association (FPA)

BVCA British Venture Capital Association

BVI British Virgin Islands

BVM Beata Virgo Maria (*Latin: Blessed Virgin Mary*)

BVMS Bachelor of Veterinary Medicine & Surgery

BW biological warfare (MIL)

BWA Journal of Welsh Academy (writers) (FPA)

BWB British Waterways Board

BWI British West Indies

BWIA Trinidad & Tobago Airways

B-wire in a 2-wire telephone line to a manual exchange, that wire which under normal conditions is further from the earth potential (SCI)

BWM British War Medal

BWR boiling-water reactor (SCI)

B-Y signal Component of colour TV chrominance signal.

Combined with luminance (Y) signal, it gives primary blue component (SCI)

BYO Australia & New Zealand – an unlicensed restaurant where diners can bring their own drink (F&D)

BYOB bring your own bottle/booze/beer (F&D)

Byz Byzantine

Bz benzoyl (CHM)

Bz, bz benzene (CHM)

C

C cocaine (PRP)

C commended

C Conservative

C centre stage (FPA)

C Champion

C club(s) (*cards*)

C circa (*Latin: about*)

C cum (*Latin: with*)

C- military aircraft cargo transporter (*US*) (MIL)

C- cis- (*containing the two groups on the same side of the plane of the double bond or ring*) (CHM)

C- cyclo- (*containing an alicyclic ring*) (CHM)

C Chem Chartered Chemist

C horizon partly decomposed bedrock below B in soil profile

C licence for those carrying only their own goods

C of E Church of England

C of I Church of Ireland

C of S, COS Chief of Staff (MIL)

C P E Bach Carl Philipp Emanuel (*German composer, 1714–88*)

C S Lewis Clive Staples ('*Jack*', *English novelist 1898–1963*)

C sups Combat Supplies (MIL)

C&G City & Guilds

C&M care & maintenance (COM)

C&S Colyer & Southey (*artboard*) (COM)

C&S clogs & shawls (*genre of novel*) (FPA)

C&W country & western (MUS)

C/- care of (*Australian*)

C/o carried over; care of (COM)

C/P charter party

C/s cases

C1 supervisory, junior managerial or clerical occupational grade (COM)

C14 dating carbon 14 dating (*for living, or once-living, organisms*) (SCI)

C2 skilled manual worker (COM)

C3 command, control & communication (MIL)

C3I command, control, communication & intelligence (MIL)

C3PO Star Wars robot

C4 Channel 4

C5 Channel 5 (FPA)

C5 Sir Clive Sinclair's electric vehicle launched January 1984

CA Chartered Accountant (COM)

CA Consular Agent

CA Church Army

CA Consumers' Association (UK)

CA Chief Accountant

CA compressed air (ARC)

CA The Croquet Association (SPR)

CA The Camanachd Association (*shinty*) (SPR)

CA controlled atmosphere (*gas storage technique for fresh fruit & vegetables and pre-packed meat*) (F&D)

CA Central America

CA, COA, CoA Certificate of Airworthiness

CAA Civil Aviation Authority

CAAA Child Abuse Accountability Act (US)

CAAC Civil Aviation Administration of China

CAB Citizens' Advice Bureau

CAC Crown Appointments Commission (advises Prime Minister on appointment of Dioscesan Bishops)

CAC cubic air capacity (PRP)

CACLB The Churches Advisory Council for Local Broadcasting

CACM Central American Common Market

CACS centralised automatic control system (PRP)

CAD compact audio disc (FPA)

CAD computer-aided design (SCI)

CAD Central Ammunition Depot (MIL)

CADCAM, CAD/CAM computer-aided design, computer-aided manufacturing (SCI)

CADD Campaign Against Drinking & Driving

CADDIA Co-operation in Automation of Data & Documentation for Exports, Imports & Agriculture

CAE College of Advanced Education (*Australia*)

CAE computer-aided engineering (SCI)

CAF cost & freight (COM)

CAF Charities' Aid Foundation

CAFE Christianity and the Future of Europe

CAI common air interface (SCI)

CAI Camogie Association of Ireland (*women's Irish field sport – a form of hurling*) (SPR)

CAIR Council on American-Islamic Relations

CAL computer-assisted/aided learning

CALA Citizens Against Lawsuits Abroad (*California*)

Cam camouflaged (MIL)

CAM computer-aided manufacture (COM)

CAM crassulacean acid metabolism (SCI)

CAMD Centre for Applied Microbiological Research (*a Department of Health Institute at Porton Down*) (MIL)

CAMEO come and meet each other

CAMP Campaign Against Moral Persecution

CAMPFIRE Communal Area Management Programmes For Indigenous Resources

CAMRA CAMpaign for Real Ale (F&D)

CAMS catapult armed merchant ship (*releasing Hurricanes*) (MIL)

CAMS Confederation of Australian Motor Sports (SPR)

CAMS Chautiers Aéro-Maritimes de la Seine

CAMW Central Association for Mental Welfare

CAN Control Area Network (*Bosch standard*)

Can Canada

CANA Clergy Against Nuclear Arms

Canad Canadian

Can-Am Canadian-American Challenge Cup (*series of annual motor races*) (SPR)

Canc cancelled; cancellation

Cant Canterbury

Cantab Cantabrigiensis (Latin: of Cambridge)

CANTAB Cambridge Neuropsychological Test Automated Battery (*for early detection of Altzheimer's disease*)

Cantuar Cantuariensis (*Latin: of Canterbury*)

CAP Common Agricultural Policy

Cap capacity; capital; capitalise

Cap capital letter (FPA)

Cap capitulum, caput (*Latin: heading, chapter*) (FPA)

CAP combat air patrol (MIL)

Cap, cap capital

Capt Captain

CAPU Campaign Against Peptic Ulcers

Card Cardinal

CARE Co-operative for American Relief Everywhere

CARE Christian Action for Research and Education

CARICOM Caribbean Community & Common Market

CARIFTA Caribbean Free Trade Area

Carliol Bishop of Carlisle

Cart cartridge (*magnetic tape container*) (FPA)

Cas Casualty (MIL)

CAS Chief of Air Staff

CAS calibrated airspeed

CASE Campaign for the Advancement of State Education

CASEVAC CASualty EVACuation (MIL)

CASH Campaign Against Stage Hypnosis

CAST Creative & Supportive Trust (PRP)

CAT charges, access, terms

CAT common assessment task

CAT computer-assisted trading (COM)

CAT College of Advanced Technology

CAT computer-aided teaching

CAT Cosmic Anisotropy Telescope (SCI)

Cat catalogue (FPA)

Cat catechism

Cat catalytic converter

Cat catamaran

Cat catering (MIL)

Cat A, B, C, D categories of security: A for the highly dangerous, B for those who should not be allowed to escape, C for those who are unlikely to attempt a difficult escape, and D for those suitable for open prison. (PRP)

CAT valve cooled-anode transmitting valve (SCI)

CATA Cutlery & Allied Trades Association (COM)

Cata- containing a condensed double aromatic nucleus substituted in the 1,7 position (CHM)

Cath Catholic

Cath Cathedral (ARC)

CATS credit accumulation transfer scheme

CATU Ceramic & Allied Trades Union (UNI)

CATV community antenna television (FPA)

CATV cable television

CaV canteen van (FRS)

Cav, cav cavalry (MIL)

CAV, Cur adv vult curia advisari vult (*Latin: the court wishes to consider the case*)

CAVES Committee for the Advancement of Virtue and Elimination of Sin (*KSA*)

CAWU Clerical & Administrative Workers' Union (UNI)

CAZRI Central Arid Zone Research Institute

CB cash book (COM)

CB Companion of the Most Honourable Order of the Bath (*not if GCB &/or KCB*)

CB Citizens' Band (FPA)

CB County Borough

Cb centre of buoyancy

CBD cash before delivery; central business district (COM)

CBE Commander of the Most Excellent Order of the British Empire (*not if GBE &/or KBE or DBE*)

CBI Confederation of British Industries (*formerly FBI*) (COM)

CBM Christian Blind Mission

CBM condition-based monitoring (SCI)

CBO Crinkley Bottom Observer (*local paper in Noel's Houseparty, BBC 1*) (FPA)

Cbp critical backing pressure (SCI)

CBR chemical, bacteriological & radiation (MIL)

CBS Columbia Broadcasting System (MUS)

CBS central battery system (SCI)

CBSA Clay Bird Shooting Association

CBSO City of Birmingham Symphony Orchestra (MUS)

CBT computer-based training

CBT compulsory basic training (*for learner motorcycle riders*)

CBT cognitive behaviour therapy

CC credit note (COM)

CC cardboard city (PRP)

CC cellular confinement (PRP)

CC City Council; County Council(lor)

CC Challenge Certificate

Cc carbon copy; copies (COM)

CCA Cable Communications Association (COM)

CCA Canadian Curling Association (SPR)

CCAB Consultative Committee of Accounting Bodies

CCASG Co-operative Council for the Arab States of the Gulf

CCC Club Cricket Conference (SPR)

CCCBR Central Council of Church Bell-Ringers

CCCS Consumer Credit Counselling Service (*0113 297 0121*)

CCD charge-coupled device (SCI)

CCE Concours Complet d'Équitation (3-day event rules) (SPR)

CCF Combined Cadet Force (MIL)

CCG Control Commission, Germany

CChem Chartered Chemist

CCI Comité Consultatif International

CCIF Comité Consultatif International Téléphonique (SCI)

CCIR Comité Consultatif International des Radiocommunications (SCI)

CCIT Comité Consultatif International Télégraphique (SCI)

CCITT Consultative Committee on International Telephony & Telegraphy (SCI)

CCJ County Court Judgment

CCL Christian Copyright Licencing

CCM counter counter measure (MIL)

CCO Conservative Central Office

CCP casualty collecting post (MIL)

CCPR Sports Arena at Colex Exhibition, Olympia, London, 1961 & 63 (SPR)

CCPR Central Council of Physical Recreation (SPR)

CCRA Commander Corps Royal Artillery

CCRC Criminal Cases Review Commission (PRP)

CCRCSM Chef Conférie Royale et Chevalière de Saint Michel (*Belgian Fencing Guild*) (SPR)

CCS casualty clearing station (MIL)

CCT Churches' Conservation Trust

CCT computer-controlled teletext (SCI)

Cct circuit (SCI)

CCW Curriculum Council of Wales

CCWNA Certificate of Competence in Workplace Noise Assessment (*IOA award*) (SCI)

CD Canadian Forces Decoration

CD carried down (COM)

CD compact disc

CD Conference on Disarmament

CD Corps Diplomatique

Cd command (*paper*)

Cd cum dividend (*Latin: with dividend*) (COM)

Cd cash discount (COM)

CDC call-directing code (SCI)

CDD Courses, Diplomas & Degrees

CDE Conference on Confidence- & Security-Building & Disarmament in Europe

CDE compact disc erasable (SCI)

CDF Children's Defense Fund (*US version of NSPCC*)

CDF Congregation for the Defence of the Faith (*formerly Curia*)

CDG Charles de Gaulle Airport (*Paris*)

CD-I compact disc interactive (FPA)

CDM Cadbury's Dairy Milk (F&D)

CDNA Community & District Nursing Association (UNI)

CDNA complementary DNA (SCI)

CDP Community Development Project

Cdr Commander (MIL)

CDR compact disc recordable (SCI)

Cdre Commodore

CD-ROM compact disc read-only memory (SCI)

CD-RW Philips re-writeable CD

CDT Craft, Design, Technology (*NC subject*)

CDV compact video disc (FPA)

CDW collision damage waiver

CE Conseil de l'Entente

CE Common Entrance examination

CE Chief Executive

CE Chief Engineer

CE Civil Engineer

CE, C of E Church of England

CEA Central Electricity Authority

Cecil B De Mille Blount (*US film producer, 1881–1959*)

CEED Council for Energy Efficiency Development (COM)

Ceefax pronounced as 'see facts' – BBC's teletext presentation (SCI)

CEGB Central Electricity Generating Board (*formed in 1957*) (COM)

CEI Chartered Engineering Institutes (COM)

Cel, cell celluloid (SCI)

CEMA Council for the Encouragement of Music and the Arts

CEMS Church of England Men's Society

CEN Cambridge Evening News (FPA)

CEN,CELELEC Commission Européenne de Normalisation Electrique European (*French: Committee for Electrotechnical Standardisation*)

CEng Chartered Engineer (COM)

CENM Certificate in Environmental Noise Measurement (IOA award) (SCI)

CENTO, Cento Central Treaty Organisation

CEO Chief Executive Officer (COM)

CEO Chief Education Officer

CEP circular error probable/ central engineer park (MIL)

CEPS Central European Pipeline System (MIL)

CER Closer Economic Relations (*Australia & NZ*)

CERN Conseil Européenne pour la Recherche Nucléaire (*now Organisation Européen pour la Recherche Nucléaire, but still known as CERN*)

CES Clothing Exchange Store (PRP)

Cestr Bishop of Chester

CET common external tariff (COM)

CET combat engineer tractor (MIL)

CETS Church of England Temperance Society

CF carried forward, cost & freight (COM)

Cf confer (*Latin: compare*)

CF Chaplain to the Forces

Cf calfskin (FPA)

CF cold feed (ARC)

CF cystic fibrosis

CF&HE College of Further & Higher Education

CFA Cat Fanciers' Association (*America's largest cat association, also encompassing Canada & Japan*)

CFBAC Central Fire Brigade's Advisory Council (FRS)

CFC Computer Film Company (SCI)

CFC chlorofluorocarbon (CHM)

CFD compact floppy disc (SCI)

CFD computational fluid dynamics (SCI)

CFE College of Further Education

CFE Conventional Forces in Europe (MIL)

CFF Cat Fanciers' Federation (*USA*)

CFI, Cfi, cfi cost, freight & insurance (COM)

CFMU Central Flow Management Unit (air traffic)

CFO Chief Fire Officer (FRS)

CFP Common Fisheries Policy

CFR engine Co-operative Fuel Research Committee engine (*a specially designed standardised engine in which the knock-proneness or detonating tendency of volatile liquid fuels is determined under controlled conditions and specified as an octane number*) (SCI)

CFS Chelsea Flower Show

CFT Campaign for Freedom from Tobacco (*ASH relaunched*)

CG Captain General

CG Chaplain General

CG coastguard

CG Coldstream Guards

CG Consul General

Cg limits the forward and aft positions within which the resultant weight of an aircraft and its load must lie if balance and control are to be maintained

Cg, c of g centre of gravity (SCI)

CGA Country Gentlemen's Association

CGBR Central Government Borrowing Requirement

CGC Conspicuous Gallantry Cross (MIL)

CGGB Composers' Guild of Great Britain (MUS)

CGH Cape of Good Hope

CGLI City & Guilds of London Institute

CGM Conspicuous Gallantry Medal (*Navy & flying*)

CGS Chief of General Staff (MIL)

CGSWD Company of Gold & Silver Wyre Drawers (UNI)

CGT Capital Gains Tax (COM)

CGT Confédération Générale du Travail (*French Trade Union*) (UNI)

CGT Member of Cégétist

CGT Building where Evita's coffin was kept in Argentina

CGU Commercial Union and General Accident

CH Companion of Honour

CH Club House

Ch Chapter

CH Member of the Order of Companions of Honour

CH, ch Custom House

Ch, Chq, Cq cheque (COM)

Chanc Chancellor; Chancery

Chap Chaplain

Chap St J Chaplain of the Order of St John of Jerusalem

CHAPS Clearing House Automated Payment System

Char cal Charles Calthrop (*charcal = jackal, hence the Day of the Jackal*)

CHB central heating boiler

ChB Bachelor of Surgery

CHC Christchurch (*New Zealand airport*)

ChCh Christ Church (*Oxford, aka the House*)

ChColl Christ's College

ChE Chemical Engineer

Chem chemical; chemist; chemistry (SCI)

Chg charge (COM)

CHIME Churches' Initiative in Musical Education (MUS)

Chin China; Chinese

CHIPS Clearing House Inter-Payment System

CHIRP confidential human incidents reporting programme (*RAF Institute of Medicine*) (MIL)

CHM Master of Surgery

CHM, CHMn Chairman (*ie one who takes the chair - please avoid calling him or her 'the chair'*)

CI Lady of the Imperial Order of the Crown of India

CI civic instruction (*a school class in Dr Zhivago*) (FPA)

CI Channel Islands

CIA Central Intelligence Agency

CIAD Central Institute of Art and Design

CIB Criminal Investigation Branch

CIB Complaints Investigation Bureau

CIBSE Chartered Institution of Building Services Engineers (*estd 1897, Royal Charter 1976*) (ARC)

CIC Capital Issues Committee (COM)

CIC Chief Inspector of Constabularies

CICA Criminal Injuries Compensation Award

CICA Construction Industry Computer Association

CICAB Criminal Injuries Compensation Appeals Board

Cicestr Bishop of Chichester

CID Criminal Investigation Department

CIE Companion of the Order of the Indian Empire

CIE Companion of the Most Eminent Order of the Indian Empire (*not if GCIE &/or KCIE*)

Cie Compagnie (*French: Company*) (MUS)

CIE Commission Internationale d'Eclairage (*formed to study problems of illumination*) (ARC)

CIE co-ordinates set of colour co-ordinates specifying proportions of three theoretical additive primary colours required to produce any hue (ARC)

CIF carriage insurance forward (COM)

CIF charged in full (COM)

CIF&C cost, insurance, freight & commission (COM)

CIF&I cost, insurance, freight & interest (COM)

CIF, cif cost, insurance & freight (COM)

CIFC&I cost, insurance, freight, commission & interest (COM)

CIFE Colleges & Institutes of Further Education

Cig, ciggy cigarette

CIGS Chief of the Imperial General Staff (formerly in GB) (MIL)

CIM computer integrated manufacture (COM)

CIM computer input on microfilm (SCI)

CIM International Mini-Basketball Committee (SPR)

CIMarE Companion of the Institute of Marine Engineers

CIMechE Companion of the Institute of Mechanical Engineers

CIN Charts' Information Network (MUS)

C-in-C, C in C Commander in Chief

CIO Congress of Industrial Organisations (*US*) (COM)

CIOR Interallied Confederation of Reserve Officers (COM)

CIP BL Cataloguing in Publication (FPA)

CIPFA Chartered Institute of Public Finance and Accountancy

CIPS Chartered Institute of Purchasing & Supply (COM)

CIPW a quantitative scheme of rock classification based on the comparison of norms; devised by American petrologists Cross, Iddings, Pirsson & Washington

Cir circus

Circ circa

Circs circumstances

CIRE Co-operative for American Remittances to Europe

CIS Co-operative Insurance Society (COM)

CIS Commonwealth of Independent States

CIS Central Intelligence Services

CISC complex instruction set computer (SCI)

CISSE Chairman of the International Society for the Shy and Embarrassed (*Two Ronnies TV sketch*)

CISWO Coal Industry Social Welfare Scheme

CIT cash in transit

CIT Crime Investigation Team

CIT civilian instructor/trainer (PRP)

Cit cited

Cit citizen

Cit citadel (ARC)

CITB The Construction Industry Training Board

CITES Convention on International Trade in Endangered Species (*pronounced Sy-teas*)

CIU chemical incident unit (FRS)

Civ civil

Civ civilian

CIV City Imperial Volunteers

CIVV Commission Internationale Vol à Voile (*gliding – part of FAI*) (SPR)

CIWEM Chartered Institution of Water & Environmental Management (*estd 1895, Royal Charter 1995*)

CIWF Compassion in World Farming

CJ Chief Justice

CJM Congregation of Jesus and Mary

CK Citizen Kane (FPA)

CKD completely knocked down (*NZ – a car imported in parts*)

Cl Clerk

Cl Clergyman

CL centre stage left (FPA)

Cl cloth

CL, CLitt Companion of Literature

CLA Country Landowners' Association

CLA Copyright Licensing Agency (FPA)

CLAC Combined Life Assurance Company (COM)

CLAIT computer literacy & information technology

Class-A amplifier thermionic valve amplifier in which the polarising voltages are adjusted for complete operation on the linear portions of the curves of the valves without grid current (SCI)

Class-AB amplifier thermionic valve amplifier in which the valve grid bias is so adjusted that the operation is intermediate between classes A and B (SCI)

Class-B amplifier thermionic valve amplifier in which the grid bias is adjusted to give the lower cut-off in the anode current (SCI)

Class-C amplifier thermionic valve amplifier in which the grid bias is greatly in excess of class-B and in which the anode output power becomes proportional to the anode voltage for a given grid excitation (SCI)

CLB Church Lads' Brigade

CLC The Cheltenham Ladies' College

CLÉ Cumann Leabhar Fhoilsitheoir na hiram (*Irish writers' circle*)

Cleckheckmondsedge Portmanteau name for Yorkshire conurbation of Cleckheaton, Heckmondwike and Liversedge, south of Bradford

CLIC Cancer and Leukæmia in Children

CLJ Commander of the Order of St Lazarus of Jerusalem

CLJWG City of London Joint Working Group

Cllr councillor

CLLS City of London Law Society

CLR Cockpit Leadership Resource

CLS continuous linked settlement

Cm cras mane (*Latin: tomorrow morning*)

CM 'CM' wrote a remarkably detailed letter about a telegraph using static electricity to the Scots Magazine in 1753. Both Charles Marshall and Charles Morrison have been suggested, and rejected, as the author of this letter. Our proposal is Dr Cromwell Mortimer, a friend of the Stephen Gray (*c.*1617–1736) who laid the foundations of electrical science, and designed a telegraph using static electricity. On his deathbed, Gray dictated his last paper to the Royal Society to Cromwell Mortimer, so the latter was surely familiar with Gray's telegraph.

CM Chirurgiae Magister (*Latin: Master of Surgery*)

CM Canada Medal (*see* M du C)

CM counter measure

CM&GLAS Clerical, Medical & General Life Assurance Society (COM)

CMA Communication Managers Association (UNI)

CMAO Central Mines Action Office (*UN sponsored*) (MIL)

CMAS Confédération Mondiale des Activités Subaquatiques (*French: World Underwater Federation*) (SPR)

CMCRC Classic Motorcycle Racing Club

Cmd command (FRS)

Cmdr Commander

CME Chicago Mercantile Exchange (*US futures exchange*)

CME continuing medical education

CMEA, Comecon Council for Mutual Economic Assistance (*USSR, disbanded 1991*)

CMF Citizen Military Forces (*Australia*) (MIL)

CMG Companion of the Most Distinguished Order of St Michael & St George (*not if GCMG &/or KCMG or DCMG*)

CMG course made good (*maritime GPS data*) (NAV)

CMJ Church's Ministry among Jewish people

CML Council of Mortgage Lenders (COM)

Cml commercial (COM)

CMO Central Moneymarkets Office

CMOS complementary metal-oxide semiconductor/silicon (SCI)

CMP Cumbrian Mountain Pullman (*on the Settle-Carlisle Line*)

CMS Church Missionary Society

CMT Country Music Television (FPA)

CMU Monuron, a weedkiller (CHM)

CMYK cyan, magenta, yellow & black (*'process' colours*) (SCI)

CN credit note; consignment note; circular note (COM)

Cn cras nocte (*Latin: tomorrow night*)

CNA Certified Normal Accommodation (PRP)

CNAA Council for National Academic Awards

CNAR compound net annual rate (COM)

CND Campaign for Nuclear Disarmament

CNES Centre National d'Études Spatiales (*French space agency*)

CNHC Churches' National Housing Coalition

CNN Cable News Network (FPA)

CNN Chicken Noodle News

CNRS Centre National de la Recherche Scientifique (*French: National Centre for Scientific Research*)

CO conscientious objector (MIL)

CO Commanding Officer

Co, Coy Company (COM)

COAST Cambridge Optical Aperture Synthesis Telescope (*winning the Institute of Physics Guthrie Medal for Prof John Baldwin*) (SCI)

COBOL common business-oriented language (SCI)

COBRA Computerised Bibliographic Records Actions (FPA)

COBRA movement influential Parisian-based group of artists from Copenhagen, Brussels & Amsterdam (FPA)

COD cash on delivery (*Post Office service discontinued when rascals sent unsolicited goods, or even dummy packages*) (COM)

COD collect on delivery (*USA*)

COD crusty old devil (ex-AYM)

Co-D Co-Defendant (PRP)

Cod, cod codex (FPA)

CODASYL Conference on Data Systems Languages (SCI)

Cof$ Church of Scientology

CofA Certificate of Airworthiness

CofC Chamber of Commerce (COM)

CofE Church of England

COG course over ground (*maritime GPS data*) (NAV)

COHSE Confederation of Health Service Employees (*became UNISON*) (UNI)

COI Central Office of Information (*was MOI*)

COIF Charities' Official Investment Fund

COIS coccygeal-olecranar indistinguishability syndrome (*an inability to distinguish the medial arm-joint from the fundament*)

Cojack coat-jacket (designerspeak)

Col colour

Col Colonel

Col column (FPA)

Coll collection

Colloq colloquial(ly)

Colregs *see* IRPCS (NAV)

Col-Sergt Colour-Sergeant

Com commerce; commercial; committee (COM)

Com comedy; comic

Com Commander

Com Commodore (COM)

Computer output on microfilm (SCI)

Com company; commercial organisation (*Internet domain name*)

Com, commie Communist

COMARE Committee on Medical Aspects of Radiation in the Environment

Comb combining

Comd Command; Commander (MIL)

Comdg commanding (MIL)

Comdr commander (MIL)

Comdt commandant (MIL)

Comecon Council for Mutual Economic Assistance

COMINT Communications Intelligence (MIL)

Comintern Communist International (POL)

Comm O Communications Officer (FRS)

Comp comparative; compare; complete; compound; comprehensive; comprising; compiler; compositor

Comp rat composite ration (MIL)

CompIEE Companion of the Institution of Electrical Engineers

Comr Commissioner

COMSAT Communications Satellite Corporation (SCI)

COMSEN Communications Centre Co-ordinate (MIL)

Comy-Gen Commissary-General

Con conformist

Con control (FRS)

Con confidence trick

Con concern; conclusion; connection; consolidated; continued

Con convict

Con cr contra credit (COM)

Con Inv contra invoice (COM)

Con, con contra (*Latin: against*)

Con, Cons Conservative (POL)

Con, Cons Consul

Conc concentrated (SCI)

Condo condominium

Cong Congress; Congressional

Cong Congregational

Cong congregation

Cons consigned; consignment; consolidated; consulting (COM)

Cons consecrated

Cons consonant

Cons, cons constitution(al)

Cons, constr construction (ARC)

Cont containing; continued; contents

Cont continent(al)

Contd continued (FPA)

Contr contraction

Contrib contributor; contribution (FPA)

COP Certificate of Proficiency (*NZ*)

Cop policeman

COPE Committee of (*Medical*) Publication Ethics

COPS Cognitive Processing System (*computer-based knowledge-tester for children*)

COPS City of Peterborough Swimmers

Cor Coroner

Cor corner (ARC)

CORE Congress of Racial Equality (*USA*)

CORGI Confederation/Council of Registered Gas Installers (COM)

Corol, coroll corollary

Corp Corporation; Corporal

Corr Mem Corresponding Member

Correl correlative

CORSO Council of Organisations for Relief Services Overseas (*NZ*)

COS cash on shipment (COM)

COS Chief of Staff

COSC Swiss Official Chronometer Testing Institute (MIL)

COSLA Convention of Scottish Local Authorities

COTS Childlessness Overcome Through Surrogacy

CoU Coalition Unionist

COV crossover value (SCI)

Coy Company (MIL)

CP community programme

CP Court of Probate

CP Common Prayer

CP Communist Party (POL)

CP Country Party (*Australia*) (POL)

Cp compare

CP command post (MIL)

CP Canadian Press (FPA)

CP corporal punishment (*genre of erotic fiction*) (FPA)

Cp chemically pure (SCI)

CP crank position

CP close protection/command post (MIL)

CP/M control program monitor (SCI)

CPA Certified Public Accountant (COM)

CPA cyproterone acteate (CHM)

CPAS Church Pastoral Aid Society

CPC Certificate Of Professional Competence (PRP)

CPC chronology protection conjecture (*prevents time travel*) (SCI)

CPD continuing professional development (*engineering*) (SCI)

Cpd compound (SCI)

CPF Canine Partners For Independence (*helpful dogs*)

CPI consumer price index (COM)

Cpi characters per inch (FPA)

CPL Calendar of Papal Letters

Cpl Corporal

CPM College of St Paul & St Mary (*Gloucester*)

CPM Colonial Police Medal for Gallantry

CPN Community Psychiatric Nurse (PRP)

CPO Chief Petty Officer; Command Pay Office (MIL)

CPP current purchasing power (COM)

CPP Cambodian Peoples' Party

CPR cardio-pulmonary resuscitation

CPRE Council for the Protection/Preservation of Rural England

CPS Crown Prosecution Service (PRP)

Cps characters per second (SCI)

CPSA Civil & Public Services Association (UNI)

CPU Central Processor Unit (SCI)

CPVE Certificate of Pre-Vocational Education

CQ charge of quarters (MIL)

CQMS Company Quartermaster Sergeant (MIL)

CQSW Certificate of Qualification in Social Work

CR Company's risk (COM)

CR Community of the Resurrection

CR centre stage right (FPA)

Cr credit; creditor; Crown; created

Cr, Cllr Councillor

CRA Christian Research Association

CRAC Careers Research Advisory Centre

CRAFT Co-operation Research Action For Technology (SCI)

CRD Conservative Research Department (POL)

CRE Council/Commission for Racial Equality

Cres crescent

Crim criminal

CRINE Cost-reduction Initialising the New Era

CRIS Common Rail Interface System

CRIS Crime Reporting Information System

Crit criticism

CRIT Campaign for Real Intelligence

CRO Criminal Records Office

CRO Community Relations Officer

CRO cathode-ray oscilloscope (SCI)

CRP Central Reserve Police

CRT cathode-ray tube (SCI)

CRT composite rate tax (COM)

CRT Countryside Restoration Trust

Cryst crystalline (SCI)

CS capital stock (COM)

CS Chartered Surveyor

CS Christian Science; Christian Scientist

CS Civil Service; Civil Servant

CS Community Service (PRP)

CS Custody Sergeant (PRP)

Cs case

CS gas orthochlorobenzal malonitrile, a gas used for controlling civil disturbances invented by the Americans Ben Carson & Roger Staughton (CHM)

CS, cs Court of Session

CSA Ceskoslovenske Aerolinie

CSA Child Support Agency

CSBM confidence & security-building measures

CSC Civil Service Commission

CSC Customer Services Committee

CSC Conspicuous Service Cross

CSCE Conference on Security & Co-operation in Europe (*led to OSCE*)

CSDs Central Securities Depositories

CSE Certificate of Secondary Education

CSE Combined Services Entertainments

CSEU Confederation of Shipbuilding & Engineering Unions (UNI)

CSF cerebro spinal fluid

CSH called subscriber held (SCI)

CSI Companion of the Most Excellent Order of the Star of India (*not if GCSI &/or KCSI*)

CSIO Concours de Saut International Officiel (international showjumping rules) (SPR)

CSIR Commonwealth Council for Scientific and Industrial Research

CSIRO Commonwealth Scientific & Industrial Research Organisation (*Australia*)

CSJD Community of St John the Divine

CSLA Community Sports Leader Award (PRP)

CSM Company Sergeant Major

CSM corn-soya-milk (F&D)

CSMTS Card Setting Machine Tenders Society (UNI)

CSMV Community of St Mary the Virgin

CSO Central Selling Organisation (*world diamond marketers controlled by – you've guessed it – de Beers*) (COM)

CSO Community Service Order (PRP)

CSO colour separation overlay (*image superimposition technique*) (FPA)

CSP Chartered Society of Physiotherapy (UNI)

CSP cognitive skills programme (PRP)

CSR Colonial Sugar Refining Company (*Australia*) (COM)

CSR cab secure radio

CSS Certificate of Social Service

CSSA Computing Services and Software Association

CSSB Civil Service Selection Board

CSSG Combat Service Support Group (*The Black Adders*) (MIL)

CSSR RC Church - Congregatio Sanctissimi Redemptoris (*Latin: Congregation of the Most Holy Redeemer*)

CST Council of Science and Technology

CstJ Commander of the Order of St John of Jerusalem

CSU Civil Service Union (UNI)

CSV Community Service Volunteer

CSWIP Certification Scheme for Welding & Inspection Personnel (*TWI award*) (SCI)

CSYS Certificate of Sixth-Year Studies

Ct Court

Ct(s)

Certificate(s)

CT2 Cordless Telephone 2 (SCI)

CTA Chaplain Territorial Army

CTC City Technology College

CTC Cyclists' Touring Club (SPR)

CTC cut, twirl and curl (*tea processing method to ensure its strength and give maximum 'cuppage'*) (F&D)

CTC machine a device for breaking the leaves of tea into small particles (F&D)

CTH City Technology Holdings (COM)

CTM cordless terminal mobility (SCI)

CTM chicken tikka masala (F&D)

CTMO Community Trade-Marks Office

CTO cancelled to order

CTR Central Transport Rental (*formerly Tiphook*) (COM)

CTR controlled thermonuclear research (SCI)

CTR2 Channel Tunnel Route 2

CTR3 Channel Tunnel Route 3 (via Redhill to London)

CTSA Channel Tunnel Safety Authority

CTT capital transfer tax (COM)

CTV Canadian Television Network Limited (FPA)

CU Customs Union

CU Cambridge University

CU control unit (FRS)

CUAC Cambridge University Athletic Club

CUAFC Cambridge University Association Football Club

CUBC Cambridge University Boat Club (SPR)

CUBG Cambridge University Botanic Garden

CUCC Cambridge University Cricket Club

CUCD Council of University Classics Departments

CUFC Cambridge University Football Club

CUFOS Centre for UFO Studies

CuL De SAc Cuban Liberty & Democratic Solidarity Act

Cum div cumulative dividend (COM)

CUP Cambridge University Press (FPA)

CURFC Cambridge University Rugby Football Club

Curia *See* CDF

CUSO Canadian University Services Overseas

CUTS computer users' tape system (SCI)

CV cellular vehicle (PRP)

CV curriculum vitae (*Latin: the course of one's life*)

CV Cross of Valour (*Canada*) (MIL)

CV Cheval-Vapeur (*French*) or Pferdestärke (*German*) (*PS*) (*metric unit of horse-power, = 75kg m/s, 735 5W or 1 986hp*) (SCI)

CV combat vehicles (MIL)

CVA Creditors' Voluntary Agreement/Arrangement (COM)

CVD Central Vehicle Depot (MIL)

CVO Commander of the Royal Victorian Order (not if GCVO &/or KCVO or DCVO)

CVR cockpit voice recorder

CVR(T) or (W) combat vehicle reconnaissance tracked or wheeled

CVS Council for Voluntary Service

CVT continuously variable transmission

CW chemical weapons; chemical warfare (MIL)

CWA Country Women's Association

Cwlth Commonwealth

CWN City Women's Network

CWO, cwo cash with order (COM)

CWS Co-operative Wholesale Society (COM)

CWT complete waste of time

CWU Communications Workers Union (*Post Office union*) (UNI)

CYDS Can You Do Something (*helping the homeless*)

CYFA Church Youth Fellowships Association

Cyl cylinder; cylindrical

CYMK cyan, yellow, magenta & black (*process colours for 4-colour printing*) (FPA)

CYS Canterbury and York Society

CYSA Community & Youth Service Association (COM)

CYWU The Community & Youth Workers Union (UNI)

D

D Government Department

D dominus (*Latin: Lord*)

D Dutch

D Duke; Duchess; Don (*Spanish title*)

D deuterium (*heavy hydrogen*) (CHM)

D diamond(s) (*cards*)

D date; day

D depart(s)

D daughter

D- dextro- (*Latin: rotatory*) (SCI)

D unm died unmarried

D W Griffith David (*Llewelyn*) Wark (*US film director*)

D&B dandelion & burdock (F&D)

D&C discipline & complaints (PRP)

D&D drunk & disorderly (PRP)

D&G Dolce & Gabbana (*designer clothes*)

D, deg degree

D, dir Director

DA days after acceptance (COM)

DA duck's arse (*a haircut giving that appearance from the rear, explained to Granny as 'district attorney'*)

DA Diploma of Art

DA District Attorney (*USA*)

DA&QMG Deputy Adjutant and Quartermaster General

DAA Divisional Administrative Area (MIL)

DAA&QMG Deputy Assistant Adjutant and Quartermaster General

DAAG Deputy Assistant Adjutant General

DAB digital audio broadcasting (SCI)

DAC Defence Animal Centre

DAC digital-to-analogue converter (SCI)

DACG Deputy Assistant Chaplain General

DACO Deputy Assistant Chief Officer (FRS)

DAD Deputy Assistant Director

DADMS Deputy Assistant Director of Medical Services

DADOS Deputy Assistant Director of Ordnance Services

DADQ Deputy Assistant Director of Quartering

DADST Deputy Assistant Director of Supplies and Transport

DAG Deputy Adjutant General

DALR dry adiabatic lapse rate (SCI)

DAMN Drawstrings Are Much Nicer (*campaign to bring back non-elasticated pyjama bottoms*)

DANC Diploma in Acoustics & Noise Control (SCI)

DANTE Delivery of Advanced Network Technology to Europe

DAQMG Deputy Assistant Quartermaster General

DAR Daughters of the American Revolution (*USA*)

DARE Drug Abuse Resistance Education

DART digital advanced radio for trains (*GSM-based train communication*)

DARYL Date Analysing Robert Youth Lifeform (*US PG film 1985*)

DASc Doctor in Agricultural Sciences

DASH drone antisubmarine helicopter (MIL)

Dat dative

DAT digital audio tape (SCI)

DB daybook (COM)

dBA, dBB, dBC agreed curves of relative response against frequency for weighting the readings of sound level meters to meet practical situations. The dBA curve approximates to the human ear (SCI)

DBD dry-blanch-dry process (F&D)

DBE Dame Commander of the Most Excellent Order of the British Empire (*not if GBE*)

DBFO design, build, finance & operate (COM)

DBMS database management system (SCI)

DBS direct broadcast by satellite (SCI)

DC Detention Centre (PRP)

DC District Commissioner

DC District Council

DC Divisional Commander (FRS)

DC downstage centre (FPA)

Dc double column (FPA)

Dc double crown (FPA)

DC dimensional control (SCI)

DC direct current (SCI)

DCAS Deputy Chief of the Air Staff

DCB Dame Commander of the Most Honourable Order of the Bath (*not if GCB*)

DCC digital compact cassette (MUS)

DCF discounted cash flow (COM)

DCF deal-cased frame (ARC)

DCG Deputy Chaplain General

DCGS Deputy Chief of the General Staff

DCh Doctor Chirurgiae (Latin: Doctor of Surgery)

DCH Diploma in Child Health

DCI Detective Chief Inspector

DCIGS Deputy Chief of the Imperial General Staff

DCL Distillers' Company Ltd (COM)

DCL Doctor of Civil Law

DCLI Duke of Cornwall's Light Infantry

DCM Distinguished Conduct Medal (*Royal West African Frontier Force & King's African Rifles*)

DCM design, construction and management

DCMG Dame Commander of the Most Distinguished Order of St Michael & St George (*not if GCMG*)

DCMS Department of Culture, Media and Sport

DCnL Doctor of Canon Law

DCO Deputy Chief Officer (FRS)

DCR Discretionary Conditional Release (PRP)

DCRA Dominion of Canada Rifle Association (SPR)

DCS Doctor of Commercial Sciences

DCT discrete cosine transform (SCI)

DCU damage control unit (FRS)

DCVO Dame Commander of the Royal Victorian Order (*not if GCVO*)

DD days after date (COM)

DD direct debit (COM)

DD Doctor of Divinity

DD&Shpg dock dues & shipping (COM)

DDC Deputy Divisional Commander (FRS)

DDG drop dead gorgeous (*the late Princess of Wales on her eldest son*)

DDGM drop dead gorgeous man

DDIY don't do it yourself

DDL Deputy Director of Labour

DDMI Deputy Director of Military Intelligence

DDMS Deputy Director of Medical Sciences

DDNI Deputy Director of Naval Intelligence

DDO Diocesan Director of Ordinands

DDPH Diploma in Dental Public Health

DDPS Deputy Director of Personal Services (Naval)

DDRA Deputy Director Royal Artillery

DDS Doctor of Dental Surgery

DDSc Doctor of Dental Science

DDST Deputy Director of Supplies and Transport

Ddt deduct

DDT dichloro-diphenyl-trichlorethane (CHM)

DDU Drug Dependency Unit (PRP)

DDVP 2,2-dichlorovynyl dimethyl phosphate (*an insecticide*) (CHM)

DE, DoE Department of Employment (*now DfEE*)

DEA Development Education Association

Deb debenture (COM)

DEC Digital Equipment Company (COM)

Dec declaration; declension; declination; decrease

Dec, Decd, decd deceased

Decon U decontamination unit (FRS)

DECT digital European cordless telephone (SCI)

DEDS Danish Seaways

Def defective; deferred; definite; definition; defence

Deg degree

Del delegate

Del delineavit (*Latin: he/she drew it*) (FPA)

Del, deld delivered (COM)

Dele delete; cancel

DEM Diploma in Engineering Management (SCI)

Dem, demo demonstrate; demonstration

DEng Doctor of Engineering

DEOVR Duke of Edinburgh's own Volunteer Rifles

Dep deposition (PRP)

Dep departs; departure; deponent; deposed; deposit; depot

Dep deputy

Dep, dept, dpt department

DEPN Divisional Engineers' Professional Network (SCI)

Der derivative; derivation

DERA Defence Experimental Research Agency (MIL)

DERA Defence Evaluation Research Evaluation

DERV diesel-engined road vehicle (diesel oil)

DES Department of Education & Science (*now DfEE*)

Des res desirable residence

DèsL Docteur ès Lettres (*Doctor of Letters*)

DèsSc Docteur ès Sciences (*Doctor of Science*)

Det detached (MIL)

DETR Department of the Environment, Transport and the Regions (*formerly Dept of Transport*)

DEW line distant early warning line (MIL)

DF Defender of the Faith

DF direction finder (NAV)

DF defensive fire (MIL)

DFC Distinguished Flying Cross

DFD meat dark, firm, dry meat (F&D)

DfEE Department for Education & Employment (*DoE + DES*)

DFM Distinguished Flying Medal

DFmr Deputy Firemaster (*Scotland*) (FRS)

DFs DF118 (*brand name of a drug misused as a narcotic*) (PRP)

Dft draft (COM)

DG Deutsche Grammophon (COM)

DG Dei gratia (*Latin: by the grace of God*)

DG Deo gratias (*Latin: thanks be to God*)

DG Director-General

DGAA Distressed Gentlefolk's Aid Association

DGDP Diploma in General Dental Practice

DGII Directorate General II of the European Commission (*Economic and Financial Affairs*)

DGM Division General Manager (COM)

DGMS Director-General of Medical Services

DGMW Director-General of Military Works

DGO declared geographical origin (F&D)

DGP Director-General of Personnel

DGPS differential GPS (NAV)

DGR Dante Gabriel Rossetti (*poet & painter 1828–82*)

DGStJ Dame of Grace of the Order St John of Jerusalem

DGXV Directorate-General XV of the European Commission (*Financial Services etc*)

DGXXIV Directorate-General XXIV of the European Commission (*Consumer Policy*)

DH Department of Health

DH David Herbert (*Lawrence, British novelist 1885-1930*)

DH double-hung (ARC)

DH de Havilland

DH(C) drop-head (coupé)

DHA docosahexaenoic acid (*in fish oils*) (F&D)

DHL Doctor of Hebrew Literature

DHT deep humiliating trouble

Dia, diam diameter

Dial dialect

DIANE Direct Information Access Network for Europe (SCI)

Dict dictation; dictator

DIDO (*see* BEPO) (SCI)

Dif differential (SCI)

Diff different; difference

Dig digger (*Australian or NZ soldier*) (MIL)

DIG Deputy Inspector General

DIH Diploma in Industrial Health

DIMM double/dual in-line memory module (SCI)

DIN do it now (Sir Paul McCartney's watchword, inherited from his father)

DIN Deutsche Institut Für Normung (*a standards organisation eg DIN connector*)

DING, Ding double income, no girl-friend (Rugby Union player who has turned professional without giving up the day job)

DINK dual income, no kids

DINKY dual income, no kids – yet

DIO Dominion International Opera (MUS)

Dioc Diocese; Diocesan

Dip Mus Ed RSAM Diploma in Musical Education from the Royal Scottish Academy of Music (MUS)

Dip RSAM Diploma from the Royal Scottish Academy of Music (MUS)

Dip, dip Diploma

DipAD Diploma in Art & Design

DipChemEng Diploma in Chemical Engineering

DipCom Diploma of Commerce

DipEd Diploma in Education

DipHE Diploma in Higher Education

DipSW Diploma in Social Work

DipTech Diploma in Technology

Dis discount (COM)

Dis marriage dissolved

Disc discovered

DISH diffuse idiopathic skeletal hyprostosis (*eating to much protein causes the vertebrae to fuse – Friar Tuck Syndrome*)

Diss dissolved

Dist distance; district

Dist distinguish(ed); distant

DISTAFF directing staff (MIL)

DisTP Distinction Town Planning

Distr distributor; distribution

Div dividend; division; divided (COM)

Div divorced

Div division; divisional (FRS)

Div division (MIL)

Div HQ Divisional Headquarters (FRS)

DIY do it yourself

DJ disc jockey (FPA)

DJ dinner jacket

Dj dust jacket (FPA)

DJStJ Dame of Justice of the Order of St John of Jerusalem

Dk dark; deck; dock

DK Denmark

DL de-luxe

DL Deputy-Lieutenant

DL downstage left (FPA)

DLA Disability Living Allowance

D-layer the lowest layer or region of absorbing ionisation, up to 90km above the earth's surface

DLC Diploma, Loughborough College

DLI Durham Light Infantry

DLit, Doctor of Letters

DLitt Doctor of Literature

DLO Dead Letter Office

DLO Diploma in Laryngology and Otology

DLP Discretionary Lifer Panel (PRP)

DLPT Discretionary Lifer Panel Tribunal (PRP)

Dlr dealer

DLT Dave Lee Travis

DLT Darton Longman Todd (FPA)

DLVA Driver & Vehicle Licencing Agency

DM database management (SCI)

DM disconnecting manhole (ARC)

DM's Doc Marten's (*footwear*)

DMA divisional maintenance area (MIL)

DMD digital micromirror device

DMDT methoxychlor – used in weed killer (CHM)

DME distance measuring equipment

DMF dimethylformamide (CHM)

DMF decayed, missing, filled (dentistry)

DMFC direct methanol fuel cell

DMFO eflornithine (CHM)

DMG Deutsche Morgan Grenfell (COM)

DMI Director of Military Intelligence

Dml demolition (MIL)

DMO Drug-Misusing Offender (PRP)

DMR Diploma in Medical Radiology

DMRE Diploma in Medical Radiology and Electrology

DMS Director of Medical Sciences

DMS Diploma of Management Studies

DMS dimethyl sulphide (*the gas that gives the sea its distinctive smell*) (CHM)

DMSO dimethyl sulphoxide (CHM)

DMT Director of Military Training

DMTT Dazomet – used as fungicide & weed killer. (CHM)

DMus Doctor of Music (MUS)

DMZ demilitarized zone (MIL)

DN debit note (COM)

DNA deoxyribonucleic acid (SCI)

DNA did not attend

DNA National Dyslexia Association

DNAP, DNSAP, DNOSAP insecticide & fungicide (CHM)

DNC, DNOC Dinitro-o-cresol (*2-methyl-4,9-dinitro (1-hydroxybenzene); insecticide and herbicide*) (CHM)

DNH Department of National Heritage

DNI Director of Naval Intelligence

DNS Department for National Savings

DNV Det Norske Veritas

DO delivery order (COM)

DO Divisional Officer (FRS)

Do ditto (Latin: the same)

DO Doctor of Optometry

DO Doctor of Osteopathy

DO dissolved oxygan (SCI)

DO Denominación de Origen (*Spanish wine classification*) (F&D)

DO, D/O drawing office (COM)

DOB, dob date of birth

DoC Deacon of the Chapel

DOC Denominazione di Origine Controllata (*Italian wine classification*) (F&D)

DOC District Officer Commanding

Doc, doc Doctor

DocEng Doctor of Engineering

DOCG Denominazione di Origine Controllata e Garantita (*Italian wine classification*) (F&D)

DOD Department of Defense (*USA*) (MIL)

DOD drop on demand (*ink jet printhead*)

DoE Department of the Environment

DOF doddering old fool

DOHC double overhead camshaft

DOL Doctor of Oriental Learning

DOM Deo optimo maximo (*Latin: to God, the best, the greatest*)

Dom domain; domestic

DOM Deo omnium magister (*Latin: God the Master of All*)

DOM dirty old man

Dom Dominican

Dom Dominus (*Latin: Lord*)

DOMS Diploma in Ophthalmic Medicine and Surgery

DOR drop on request

Dorothy L Sayers Leigh (*English writer 1893-1957*)

DORTA damage only road traffic accident

DOS disk operating system (SCI)

DOSAAF Dobrovol'noye Obshchestvo Sodeystviya Armii, Aviatsii i Flotu (*Russian: Voluntary Society for Collaboration with the Army, Air Force and Navy*) (SPR)

DOT directly observed therapy

DOVAP DOppler Velocity And Position (MIL)

Dow Dowager

DP detained person

DP displaced person(s)

DP data processing

DPA Data Protection Act

DPA Diploma in Public Administration

DPA Discharged Prisoners' Aid

DPB Dental Practice Board

DPC damp proof course (ARC)

DPF Dental Practices' Formulary

DPH Diploma in Public Health

DPh, DPhil Doctor of Philosophy

Dpi dots per inch (SCI)

DPIC Death Penalty Information Centre

DPM Diploma in Psychological Medicine

DPM damp proof membrane

DpP documents against payment (COM)

DPP Director of Public Prosecutions

DPS Dead Poets' Society (*in an American boys' version of Marcia Blane's HSG, with Robin Williams as the Maggie Smith figure; carpe diem*) (FPA)

DPS Director of Personal Services (Naval)

DPT Dental Panoramic Tomograph

DPU Disability Programmes Unit (*BBC*) (FPA)

DPW Department of Public Works

DQMG Deputy Quartermaster General

Dr Doctor

DR downstage right (FPA)

DR dead reckoning

DR Democratic Republic

DRA Director Royal Artillery

DRAC Director Royal Armoured Corps

DRAM dynamic random-access memory (SCI)

DRC Dartford River Crossing

DRIP dividend re-investment program (COM)

DRO Dental Reference Officer

DRV dietary reference values (F&D)

DS day's sight (COM)

DS deciduous shrub

DS direct support; dressing station (MIL)

DSA Driving Standards' Agency

DSc Doctor of Science DSC Distinguished Service Cross

DScA Docteur en Sciences Agricoles (*French: Doctor of Agricultural Sciences*)

DSCD digital service control document (SCI)

DSD Director Staff Duties

DSE display screen equipment (SCI)

DSIR Department of Scientific & Industrial Research (*NZ*)

DSL double-shearleg crane (SCI)

DSM Distinguished Service Medal

DSM Deputy Stage Manager (FPA)

DSM Divisional Sergeant Major

DSM/DSM-I/DSM-II/DSM-III Diagnostic and Statistical Manual of Mental Diseases

DSO Companion of the Distinguished Service Order

DSORG data set organisation (SCI)

DSP Director of Selection of Personnel

DSP Docteur en Sciences Politiques (*Canada*) (*French: Doctor of Political Science*)

Dsp decessit sine prole (*Latin: died without issue*)

Dspm decessit sine prole mascula (*Latin: died without male issue*)

Dspms decessit sine prole mascula superstite (*Latin: without surviving male issue*)

Dsps decessit sine prole superstire (*Latin : died without surviving issue*)

DSRV deep submergence rescue vehicle

DSS Director of Social Services

DSS Department of Social Security

DST dedicated search team (*swoop squad/team equipped to search for drugs & other contraband*) (PRP)

DST Director of Supplies and Transport

DStJ Dame of the Order of St John of Jerusalem

DSV deep sea vessel

DSW Department of Social Welfare (*NZ*)

DT deciduous tree

DTB Deutsche Terminbörse (*Frankfurt futures exchange*)

DTD Dekoratie Voor Trouwe Dienst (*decoration for devoted service*)

DTG date time group (MIL)

DTH direct to home (COM)

DTh, DTheol Doctor of Theology

DThPT Diploma in Theory and Practice of Teaching

DTI Department of Trade & Industry

DTIC dicarbazine; an anti-cancer drug (CHM)

DTM Diploma in Tropical Medicine

DTMI Directorate of Torpedoes and Mining (*Investigation*)

DTP desk-top publishing

DTPA diethylene triamine pentaacetic acid (CHM)

DTR diffusion-transfer reversal (*process in which an emulsion is developed with a solution containing silver halide solvent while in contact with another layer which is not light-sensitive and to which unexposed silver halides dissolved by the developer are transferred, forming a positive image thereon by reaction with the chemicals of which it is composed*) (FPA)

DTT digital terrestrial television

Du Duke

DUBS Durham University Business School

DUKW pronounced 'duck', an amphibious WWII US Army vehicle, happily named from its factory code letters D = boat, U = lorry, KW = lorry chassis

DUMP downwardly-mobile urban middle-class professional

Dunelm Bishop of Durham

DUP Democratic Unionist Party (POL)

DUP Docteur de l'Université Paris (*French: Doctor of the University of Paris*)

Durcam Durham & Cambridge

DV domestic violence (PRP)

DV Deo volente (*Latin: God willing*)

DVD digital video disk; digital versatile disk (SCI)

DVH Diploma in Veterinary Hygiene

DVI Dust Veil Index (*re volcano eruptions*)

DVLC Driver & Vehicle Licensing Centre (*Now DVLA*)

DVM Doctor of Veterinary Medicine

DVP Delivery Versus Payment (*see* PVP)

DVSM Diploma in Veterinary State Medicine

DVST direct video storage tube (SCI)

DW dead weight (COM)

Dw dust wrapper (FPA)

DWEM dead white European male

Dwight D Eisenhower David (*US politician, 1890–1969*)

Dy delivery (COM)

DZ dropping zone (MIL)

E

E ecstasy (*an illegal drug*)

E Earl

E eldest

E- epi- (*containing a condensed double aromatic nucleus substituted in the 1,6 positions, substituted on the fifth carbon atom*) (CHM)

E–EEEEE US men's shoe fitting width

E A Freeman Edward Augustus (*1823-92*)

E Nesbit Edith (*British children's author, 1858-1924*)

E&M Exchange & Mart (FPA)

E&M electricity & magnetism (SCI)

E&OE errors & omissions excepted (COM)

E, Eng England; English

E/Hi elementary/high-school (*target market for textbook*)

E17 a pop group

E3 Electronic Entertainment Expo (*Los Angeles 1996*) (FPA)

EA Enterprise Agency

EA Environmental Assessment (SCI)

Ea each

EA, EAL Eastern Airlines Inc

EABF Entertainment Artists' Benevolent Fund (MUS)

EAM Ethniko Apelentherotiko Metopo (*Greek: National Liberation Front (in WWII)*) (MIL)

EAP East Africa Protectorate

EAPAA East Anglian Pig Advisors Association

EAR experimental & recent (*music in the USA*) (MUS)

EAR expired air respiration

EARS electronic attendance recognition system (SCI)

EARSS Electronic Attendance Registration System for Schools

EASCO East African Common Services Organization

Eb eastbound (NAV)

EBA English Bowling Association (*lawn bowls*) (SPR)

EBA ECU Banking Association (*see ECU*)

EBC eastbound carriageway (*see NBC, SBC and WBC*)

EBDIC, EBCDIC extended binary-coded decimal interchange code (SCI)

EBF English Bowling Federation (SPR)

EBF European Banking Federation

EBIT earnings before interest & tax (COM)

EBITDA earnings before interest & tax, depreciation & amortisation (*of intangibles, such as good will*) (COM)

Eblan Eblanensis (*of Dublin*)

E-boat enemy torpedo boat (MIL)

Ebor Eboracensis (*Latin: (Archbishop) of York*)

EBRD European Bank for Reconstruction & Development (COM)

EBU European Boxing Union (SPR)

EBYS eyes bigger than your stomach

EC Engineering Council (SCI)

EC European Community

EC East Central (*postal district*)

ECA Economic Co-operation Administration

ECAN extended control area network

ECB England & Wales Cricket Board (*replaced TCCB 1 January 97*) (SPR)

ECB European Central Bank

ECC external cardiac compression

Eccl, eccles ecclesiastic(al)

ECCM electronic counter measure (MIL)

ECDIS electronic charting display information system (NAV)

ECE external combustion engine (*Stirling engine*) (SCI)

Ech echelon (MIL)

ECM electronic countermeasures (MIL)

ECOFIN Council of Finance Ministers of the European Union

Econ economic; economics; economist

ECOWAS Economic Community of West African States

ECS European Communications Satellite

ECSC European Coal & Steel Community

ECTU European Confederation of Trades Unions (COM)

ECU English Church Union

ECU, ecu European Currency Union (*in the EU*)

ECUSA Episcopal Church in the United States of America (*1789*)

ECV earned community visit (PRP)

ED Consolidated Edison Company of New York (COM)

ED evening duties (PRP)

ED efficiency decoration (*instituted 1930 for officers of Commonwealth or Colonial Auxiliary Military Forces*)

Ed edited; editor; edition (FPA)

EDC European Defence Community (MIL)

EDDS electronic digital delivery service

EDFM earthworm-digested farmyard manure

EDH Enrolled Dental Hygienist

EDM electrical discharge machining (COM)

EDN Europe des Nations (*anti-Maastricht group*)

Edn education

Edn edition

Ednl educational

EDP electronic data processing (SCI)

EDP emergency defence plan (MIL)

EDR earliest date of release (PRP)

EDSAC electronic delay storage automatic calculator (SCI)

EDTA ethylene diamine tetra-acetic acid (CHM)

Edu educational establishment (*Internet domain name*)

Educ, educ educated; educated at

EDVAC electronic discrete variable automatic calculator (SCI)

EE electrical engineer(ing) (SCI)

EE east end (ARC)

E-e eine (*German: a (an*)

EE & MP Envoy Extraordinary & Minister Plenipotentiary

EEC electronic engine control

EEC European Economic Community

EEF Engineering Employers' Federation (SCI)

EEIA East of England Investment Agency

EEO Equal Employment Opportunity

EEOC Equal Employment Opportunity Commission (*US agency enforcing non-discriminatory hiring policies*)

EEPROM electrically-erasable programmable read-only memory (SCI)

EES extended electrode stickout (*welding*) (SCI)

EETPU Electrical, Electronic, Telecommunication and Plumbing Union EF east front

EF Benson Edward Frederic (*British writer, 1867-1940*)

EFA En Famille Agency (COM)

EFA Eton Fives Association (SPR)

EFC Employment Focus Course (PRP)

EFCT Einstein Family Correspondence Trust (an example of relativity?) (FPA)

EFDSA English Folk Dance & Song Association (MUS)

EFL English as a foreign language

EFT electronic funds transfer (SCI)

EFTA European Free Trade Association

EFTPOS electronic funds transfer at point of sale (SCI)

EFTU Engineering & Fastener Trade Union (UNI)

Eg exempli gratia (*Latin: for example*)

EGM extraordinary general meeting

EGM Empire Gallantry Medal

EGT exhaust gas temperature

EHO Environmental Health Officer

EI East India; East Indies

EIA Environmental Impact Assessment (SCI)

EIA Environmental Investigation Agency

EIB European Investment Bank (COM)

EIBA English Indoor Bowling Association (SPR)

EIC education infrastructure contribution (*local Section Government payment 106*)

EICS East India Company's Service

EinC Engineer-in-Chief

EIP Ethical Investments Policy (*Church Commissioners 1948*)

EIP examination in public (*of a structure plan*)

EIS Educational Institute of Scotland (UNI)

EISA extended industry standard architecture

EJU European Judo Union (SPR)

EK Eastman Kodak Company (*when George Eastman was seeking a name for his camera company, a friend told him that a name with 'k' in it would ensure sales - so he used two of them*) (COM)

EK Edward Kirke

EKCO E K Cole Ltd (COM)

EL early & late season

El Al Israel Airlines

ELDA European Laser Disc Association (SCI)

ELDO European Launcher Development Organisation (MIL)

Elec electrical (SCI)

ELG emergency lifting gear (FRS)

Elien Bishop of Ely

E-list escape list (*of prisoners likely to try*) (PRP)

ELN (*Colombian*) National Liberation Army

ELO Electric Light Orchestra (MUS)

ELR environment lapse rate

ELS electronic lodgment system (for feeding information to the taxman) (SCI)

Elsie electronic letter sorting and indicating equipment

ELSPA European Leisure Software Publishers' Association (FPA)

ELU English Lacrosse Union (SPR)

E-m einem (*German: to a (an)*)

EMA Engineers & Managers Association (UNI)

EMA East Midlands Airport

E-Man prisoner who has escaped, or attempted to do so (PRP)

Emb embarkation (MIL)

EMB Empire Marketing Board EMC effective minimum complement (*of staff to run prison*) (PRP)

Emcee, emcee MC (Master of Ceremonies)

EMCF European Monetary Corporation Fund (COM)

EMD electromechanical disruption (SCI)

EME East Midlands Electricity (COM)

EME Electrical and Mechanical Engineers (MIL)

EMF European Monetary Fund

EMG electromyogram; electromyograph (SCI)

EMI Electric & Musical Industries (*EMI is now its official name, see BMG*) (COM)

EMI European Monetary Institute (COM)

EMI electromagnetic interference (SCI)

Emi experiments in musical intelligence (*Santa Cruz University program for writing works 'in the style of'*)

EMMAS exorbitant mortgage, might attempt suicide

EMP electromagnetic pulse; electromagnetic propulsion (MIL)

EMS European Monetary System

EMTAD express message to all districts

En enemy (MIL)

EN Enrolled Nurse (PRP)

EN empty nester

EN English Nature (SCI)

E-n einen (*German: a (an)*)

Enc enclosed; enclosure

Enc Brit, EB Encyclopaedia Britannica (FPA)

Enc Jud, EJ Encyclopaedia Judaica (FPA)

Ency Brit Encyclopædia Britannica

ENEA European Nuclear Energy Agency

Eng, engr engineer; engineering, engraver (SCI)

EngS in engerem Sinne (*German: more strictly taken*)

EngTech Engineering Technician (SCI)

ENIAC electronic numerical integrator & computer (SCI)

ENO English National Opera (MUS)

ENP Emergency Nurse Practitioner

ENSA Entertainments National Service Association (FPA)

E-number European (F&D)

EO Executive Order (*issued by the President of the United States*)

EO Education Officer (MIL)

EO electro-optical (SCI)

EOBD European On-Board Diagnostics

EOD explosive ordnance disposal (MIL)

EOG electroculogram

EOKA Ethniki Organòsis Kipriakou Agonos (*Greek: National Organisation of Cypriot Struggle*) (MIL)

EoM end of message

EON Everything or Nothing Film Production (*Company set up by Harry Saltzman and Albert 'Cubby' Broccoli 1960*) (FPA)

EORU European Ozone Research Unit (SCI)

EOT extra oral traction

EP existing prison (PRP)

EP European Parliament

EP emotional pornography

EP extended-play record (*45rpm*) (MUS)

Ep end papers (FPA)

EPA Enduring Power Of Attorney

EPA educational priority area

EPA Environmental Protection Agency (SCI)

EPC European Patent Convention

EPC European political co-operation

EPC European Parliamentary Constituency (*71 proposed by BCE*)

EPCOT experimental prototype community of tomorrow (*EPCOT Center = theme park adjacent to Walt Disney World*) (SCI)

EPD earliest parole date (PRP)

EPE Elvis Presley Enterprises (FPA)

EPI echo-planar imaging (SCI)

Epi- (*containing a condensed double aromatic nucleus substituted in the 1,6 positions*) (CHM)

Epi- containing an intra-molecular bridge (CHM)

EPIRB emergency position indicating radio beacon (*floating beacon emits signal on emergency frequencies for up to 5 days*) (NAV)

EPNS electroplated nickel silver (SCI)

EPO European Patent Office

EPOD European Platform for Optical Discs (SCI)

EPOS electronic point of sale (SCI)

EPR electron paramagnetic resonance (SCI)

EPROM electrically-programmable read-only memory (SCI)

EPRUC English Professional Rugby Union Clubs (SPR)

EPS encapsulated PostScript (SCI)

EPS Eurostar Passenger Services

EPSRC Engineering & Physics Research Council (SCI)

Eq equal; equivalent

Eqpt equipment (MIL)

EQUIS european quality improvement system

EQUITY British Actors Equity Association (UNI)

Equiv equivalent

ER external relations (COM)

ER Elizabeth Regina (Latin: Queen Elizabeth)

ER everybody's randy

Er elder

E-r einer (*German: of/to a (an)*))

ERA Employment Rights Act 1996 (COM)

ERA equal rights amendment

ERA earned runs average (*baseball*) (SPR)

ERA English Racing Automobiles

ERC ever-ready case (*for a camera*) (SCI)

ERD emergency reserve decoration (*Army*)

ERD extended-reach drilling (SCI)

ERDE *see* RARDE

ERDF European Regional Development Fund

ERIC Enurensis Resource and Information Centre

ERIC Educational Resources (*was Research*) Information Center (*US data-dissemination agency*)

ERISA Employee Retirement Income Security Act (US)

Erk aircraftman or naval rating

ERM exchange rate mechanism

ERNIE, Ernie electronic random number indicating equipment (SCI)

ERP early release of prisoners (PRP)

ERP European recovery programme

ERS Economic Research Service (*US Dept of Agriculture Agency*)

ERSPA English Rights Scotland (*Protection Agency*)

ERTA Economic Recovery Tax Act 1981 (*US*)

ERTMS European Rail Traffic Management System

Erw electric resistance welded (*style of tube much used in heat exchangers*) (SCI)

ES evergreen shrub

ES Edison screwcap (SCI)

ESA European Space Agency

ESA Educational Supplies Association

ESA environmentally-sensitive areas (SCI)

ESAS European Scandinavian Airlines System

ESC Economic & Social Council (UN)

Esc escape

ESCB European System of Central Banks (COM)

ESCO Educational, Scientific & Cultural Organisation

ESF European Social Fund

ESL English as a second language (PRP)

ESLMSD employment service labour market system database

ESN educationally sub-normal; education special needs (*the latter is PC, but doesn't necessarily mean the same thing as the former*)

ESO exhaust-gas oxygen

ESO Europeans Settlement Office

ESOP employee stock ownership plan (COM)

ESP extrasensory perception (*pseudoscientific wishful thinking*)

Esp especially

ESPRIT European Strategic Programme of Research & Development in Information Technology

Esq Esquire (*in Mediaeval England, a knight's attendant; now a male title - not to be used with Mr! - used chiefly in correspondence*)

ESR electric sun roof

ESRC Economic and Social Research Council

ESRO European Space Research Organisation (*now ESA*)

ESSO Standard Oil (*Ess-O; US: Exxon*) (COM)

EST emergency/salvage tender (FRS)

Est estate; estimate; estimated est, estab, estd established

ESU English-speaking Union

ET emergency tender (FRS)

ET evergreen tree

ET extraterrestrial (SCI)

ET elapsed time (*drag racing*) (SPR)

Et ethyl (-C_2H_5 *radical*) (CHM)

Et etwas (*German: something*)

ET essential tremor (*the most common movement disorder in humans, affecting 10% of those over 65*)

Et al et alibi (*Latin: and elsewhere*) et alii (*Latin: among others*)

Et seq et sequens (*Latin: and the following*)

ETA expected/estimated time of arrival

ETA Euzkadi ta Azkatsuna (*Basque: Basque Nation & Liberty, nationalist-terrorist group*) (MIL)

Etc, etc, &c et cetera (*Latin: and the rest*)

ETH (*Switzerland*) Eidgenössische Technische Hochschule (*German: Federal Institute of Technology*)

ETH extraterrestrial hypothesis (SCI)

ETO European Theater of Operations (*WWII*) (MIL)

EtOH ethyl alcohol (*also medical interm for a drunk*) (CHM)

ETP executive training programme (COM)

ETPS Empire Test Pilots' School (*Boscombe Down*) (MIL)

ETS Educational Testing Service (US)

ETS endoscopic transthoracic sympathieotomy (operation to combat blushing)

ETSI European Telecommunications Standards Institute (SCI)

ETUC European Trade Union Confederation (COM)

ETX end of text (SCI)

EUA executive unit of account (COM)

EURATOM, Euratom European Atomic Energy Commission

EURECA European Retrievable Carrier

EUREKA European Research Co-operation Agency

EurIng Européen Ingénieur (SCI)

Euro N-CAT new car assessment test

Eurochambers Association of European Chambers of Commerce & Industry

Eurostat Eurostat Statistical Office of the European Communities (*sometimes SOEC*)

EUW European Union of Women

EV extended visit (PRP)

EV exposure value

EVA extra-vehicular activity (SCI)

EVA English Volleyball Association (SPR)

EVAK Edmond Vaughan & Arthur Knott (*signature for their joint artistic works*)

EW early warning; electronic warfare (MIL)

EWBA English Women's Bowling Association (*lawn bowls*) (SPR)

EWBC Elizabethan Women's Bowling Council (*Australia - lawn bowls*) (SPR)

EWBF English Women's Bowling Federation (*lawn bowls*) (SPR)

EWI Expert Witnesses' Institute (1996)

EWIBA English Women's Indoor Bowling Association (SPR)

EWO Educational Welfare Officer

EWR Newark, New Jersey airport

EWT elsewhere taken (*ie taken into account elsewhere*) (ARC)

Ex examination; examined; example; exchange; executed; except; extra (*Latin: outside*)

Ex exercise (MIL)

Ex person's former partner

Ex & ct excavate & cart away (ARC)

Ex in ex interest (COM)

Ex Tele exchange telephone (FRS)

Ex, exc except; exception; excursion

Ex, exec executive

Ex, exp express

Ex. sur. tr. & ct. excavate surface trenches & cart away (ARC)

Exc Excellency

Exc excellent

Exch exchange

Excl excluding; exclusive; exclaim

EXE external combustion engine (*eg the Stirling engine*) (SCI)

Exec executive; executor; executrix

Exon Bishop of Exeter

Exor executor

Exp experiment(al); expenses; expired; exporter

Ext extinct; extract; extension; external; extra

EYC express yourself clearly

EZ enterprise zone

F

F failure

F false (*as in T or F?*)

F Fellow

F fridge/freezer

F Fellow of

F fiction (FPA)

F filial generation (*inheritance*) (SCI)

F face; flat (ARC)

F first class (air fare)

F fahrenheit

F- military aircraft fighter(*US*) (MIL)

F display type of radar display, used with directional antenna, in which the target appears as a bright spot which is off-centre when the aim is incorrect. (MIL)

F Plan fibre plan (*diet*) (F&D)

F Scott Fitzgerald Francis (*US novelist, 1896–1940*)

F&M Fortnum & Mason (COM)

F/ full upper denture

F/F full upper and lower denture

F1 Formula 1 motor racing

F1 hybrid first generation (*plant breeding cross*) (SCI)

FA from above (ARC)

FA Football Association (SPR)

FA, fa Fanny Adams (*see* SFA)

FAA Fellow of the Australian Academy (*of Science*)

FAA Fleet Air Arm (MIL)

FAA Film Artistes' Association (FPA)

FAA Federal Aviation Administration (US)

FAAS Fellow of the American Academy of Arts and Sciences

FABLE for a better life with epilepsy

Fabye Family By Choice Community (*founded at Kew by the psychoanalyst Catherine Gainsburg; parenting shared by men and women*)

FAC Friends' Ambulance Corps (MIL)

FAC forward air controller (MIL)

Fac faculty

Fac factor; factory; facsimile

FACCA Fellow of the Association of Certified and Corporate Accountants

FACD Fellow of the American College of Dentistry

FACE Fellow of the Australian College of Education

FACI Fellow of the Australian Chemical Institute

FACP Fellow of American College of Physicians

FACS Fellow of American College of Surgeons

FACT Federation Against Copyright Theft (FPA)

FAGE Fluorescence Assay By Gas Expansion (*for pollution studies*)

FAGI false alarm good intent

FAGS Fellow of the American Geographical Society

FAHA Fellow of the Australian Academy of Humanities

Fahr fahrenheit

FAI Fédération Aéronautique Internationale (*French: International Aeronautical Federation (flying and ballooning*) (SPR)

FAIT Families Against Intimidation & Terror (*NZ*)

FAM false alarm malicious

FAM Free & Accepted Masons

Fam familiarisation

Fam familiar; family

Fan fanatic

Fannie Mae *see* FNMA

FANY First Aid Nursing Yeomanry

FAO Food & Agriculture Organisation (*UN*)

Fao for the attention of

FAPHA Fellow American Public Health Association

FAQ fair average quality (COM)

FarELF Far East Land Forces

FAS Funding Agency for Schools

FAS Fellow of the Auctioneers' Institute

FAS fat and stupid (*in the north*); fickle and smelly (*in the south*)

FAS, fas free alongside ship

FASB Financial Accounting Standards Board (*of the American Institute of Certified Public Accountants*) (COM)

FASSA Fellow of the Academy of Social Sciences in Australia

FAST Federation Against Software Theft (SCI)

FAST RM system for sorting unmachinable items

FAT file allocation tables

FAVL fleet-wide automatic vehicle locations (*London Transport system*)

FAWN Farm Animal Welfare Network (originally Chickens' Lib 1970s)

FAX, fax facsimile (*transmission*)

FBA Fellow of the British Academy

FBAA Fellow of the British Association of Accountants

FBCS Federation of British Craft Societies

FBF feel-bad factor (*see* CFS)

FBF Frankfurt Bookfair (FPA)

FBHI Fellow of the British Horological Institute

FBI Federal Bureau of Investigation (US)

FBIM Fellow of the British Institute of Management

FBOA Fellow of the British Optical Association

FBOU Fellow of the British Ornithologists Union

FBP foam branch pipe (FRS)

FBPsS Fellow of British Psychology Society

FBR fast-breeder reactor (SCI)

FBritIRE Fellow of the British Institution of Radio Engineers

FBS Fellow of the Botanical Society

FBSA Foreign Banks and Securities Houses Association

FBSI Fellow of the Boot and Shoe Industry

FBSM Fellow of the Birmingham School of Music (MUS)

FBU Fire Brigades Union (UNI)

FBW fly-by-wire (MIL)

FC front cover (*publishing*) (FPA)

FCA Fellow of the Institute of Chartered Accountants

FCA Federation of Civil Engineers (SCI)

FCA Federation of Commodity Associations

FCC Firearms Consultative Committee

FCC Federal Communications Commission (*US broadcasting regulator*) (FPA)

FCC Foreign Compensation Commission

FCC Foundation for Credit Counselling (*0800 138 111*)

FCCA Fellow of the Chartered Association of Certified Accountants

FCCS Fellow of the Corporation of Certified Secretaries

FCD feline cognitive dysfunction

FCGI Fellow of the City & Guilds Institute

FCH Fellow of Coopers Hill College

FChs Fellow of the Society of Chiropodists

FCI Fédération Colombophile Internationale (*pigeon racing*) (SPR)

FCIA Fellow of the Corporation of Insurance Agents

FCIArb Chartered Institute of Arbitrators

FCIB Fellow of the Chartered Institute of Bankers

FCIB Fellow of the Corporation of Insurance Brokers

FCIBS Fellow of the Chartered Institution of Building-Services Engineers

FCIBSE Fellow of the Chartered Institute of Building Services Engineers

FCIC Fellow of the Canadian Institute of Chemisty

FCII Fellow of the Chartered Insurance Institute

FCIPA Fellow of the Chartered Institute of Patent Agents

FCIS Fellow of the Chartered Institute of Secretaries & Administrators

FCIT Fellow of the Chartered Institute of Transport

F-class insulation a class of insulating material which is assigned a temperature of 155°C (ARC)

FCMA Fellow of the Institute of Cost & Management Accountants

FCO Foreign and Commonwealth Office

FCO fire control officer (FRS)

FCOP fire control operator (FRS)

FCP Fellow of the College of Preceptors

FCS Fellow of the Chemical Society

FCST Fellow of the College of Speech Therapists

FCT federal capital territory

FCTB Fellow of the College of Teachers of the Blind

FCWA Fellow of the Institute of Cost and Works Accountants

FD Fire Department

FD fidei defensor (*Latin: Defender of the Faith*)

FDA Association of First Division Civil Servants (UNI)

FDA Food & Drug Administration (*US food & pharmaceuticals overseer*) (F&D)

FDD flight data display

FDI Fédération Dentaire Internationale (*French: International Denture Federation*)

F-diagram the cumulative residence time distribution in a continuous flow system plotted on dimensionless co-ordinates (SCI)

FDIC Federal Deposit Insurance Corporation (*US bank account insurance agency – see* FSLIC) (COM)

FDN Nicaraguan Democratic Front (POL)

Fdn foundation

FDO Fighter Defence Officer (*directing planes on board ship*)

FDR Franklin Delano Roosevelt (*1882–1945; US President 1933–45*)

FDR flight data recorder (*black box*)

FDS fax deprivation syndrome (*in TV sitcom*) (FPA)

FDS feminine deodorant spray (*US brand name*)

FDS Fellow in Dental Surgery

FDSCR Friends of Dorothy Society of Change Ringers (*homosexual & bisexual group*)

FDX, Fedex Federal Express Corporation (COM)

FEANI Fédération Européenne d'Associations Nationales d'Ingénieures (*French: European Federation of National Associations of Engineers*) (SCI)

FEBA forward edge of the battle area (MIL)

FEC Federal Elections Commission (*US agency*)

Fec fecit (*Latin: he/she made*)

Fed an FBI agent (*USA*)

Fed Federal Reserve Board

FEDLINK Federal Library & Information Network (*US*) (FPA)

FEE Fédération des Experts-Comptable Européene

FEI Fédération Équestre International (*French: International Equestrian Federation*) (SPR)

FEIN Federal Employer Identification Number (*US*)

FEIS Fellow of the Educational Institute of Scotland

Fem female; feminine

FEng Fellow of the Fellowship of Engineering

FERMILAB Fermi National Accelerator Laboratory (*US physics research facility, Batavia IL*) (SCI)

FES Fellow of the Entomological Society

FES Fellow of the Ethnological Society

FESH Federation of Ethical Stage Hypnotists

FET familial essential tremor (*FET1 - a gene identified in Icelanders*)

FEU fire experimental unit (FRS)

Ff firefighter (FRS)

Ff following (pages) (FPA)

FF field force

FFA Future Farmers of America

FFA Fellow of the Faculty of Actuaries

FFA Fédération Française d'Athlétisme (*French: French Athletics Federation*) (SPR)

FFARCS Fellow of the Faculty of Anaesthetists, Royal College of Surgeons

FFAS Fellow of the Faculty of Architects & Surveyors

FFB Fédération Française de Boxe (*French: French Boxing Federation*) (SPR)

FFEI Fujifilm Electronic Imaging Ltd

FFEPW Federation of Far Eastern Prisoners of War (MIL)

FFF Free French Forces

FFHom Fellow of the Faculty of Homoeopathy

FFI French Forces of the Interior

FFLT Fédération Française de Lawn Tennis (*French: French Lawn Tennis Federation*) (SPR)

FFN full-frontal nudity (FPA)

FFPJP Fédération Française de Pétanque et Jeu Provençal (*French: French Federation for Pétanque and Provincial Games*) (SPR)

FFPS Fellow of the Royal Faculty of Physicians and Surgeons

FFR Fédération Française de Rugby (*French: French Rugby Federation*) (SPR)

FFSc Fellow of the Faculty of Sciences

FG foam generator (FRS)

FGA Fellow of the Gemmological Association

FGA fighter ground attack (MIL)

FGBP freshly ground black pepper (F&D)

FGC full gold crown (dentistry)

FGI Fellow of the Institute of Certified Grocers

FGS Fellow of the Geological Society

FGSM Fellow of the Guildhall School of Music & Drama (MUS)

FGWP freshly ground white pepper (F&D)

FHA Federal Highway Administration (US)

FHA Future Homemakers of America

FHAS Fellow of the Highland and Agricultural Society of Scotland

FHB family hold back (*catering for unexpected guests – or some culinary disaster*)

FHLMC Federal Home Loan Mortgage Corporation (*Freddie Mac*)

FHM For Him Magazine

FHR food hygiene regulations (F&D)

FHS Fellow of the Heraldry Society

FHSM Fellow of the Institute of Health Service Management

FHW Freeman, Hardy & Willis (*in receivership 1 June 1996*) (COM)

FHWC Fellow of Heriot-Watt College, Edinburgh

FI Falkland Islands

FI Inst Fellow of the Imperial Institute

FIA Fédération Internationale de l'Automobile (*French: International Automobile Federation*) (SPR)

FIAA&S Fellow of the Incorporated Association of Architects and Surveyors

FIAeS Fellow of the Institute of Aeronautical Sciences

FIArb Fellow of the Institute of Arbitrators

FIAS Fellow of the Institute of Aeronautical Sciences (US)

FIAS Family Insurance Advisory Services Ltd

FIB Fellow of the Institute of Bankers

FIBA Fédération Internationale de Basketball Amateur (*French: International Amateur Basketball Federation*) (SPR)

FIBD Fellow of the Institute of British Decorators

FIBiol Fellow of the Institute of Biology

FIBP Fellow of the Institute of British Photographers

FIC Fellow of the Institute of Chemistry (*see* FRIC)

FICA Federal Insurance Contributions Act

FICE Fellow of the Institution of Civil Engineers

FICS Fellow of the Institution of Chartered Shipbrokers

FID Fellow of the Institute of Directors

Fid Def, FID DEF, fid def fidei defensor (*Latin: defender of the faith*)

FIE Fédération Internationale d'Escrime (*French: International Fencing Federation*) (SPR)

FIEE Fellow of the Institution of Electrical Engineers

FIEONA Fuel Injection Equipment Open Network Association

FIERE Fellow of the Institution of Electronic & Radio Engineers

FIES Fellow of the Illuminating Engineering Society

FIF Fédération Internationale de Pétanque (*French: International Pétanque Federation*) (SPR)

FIF Forward in Faith

FIFA Fédération Internationale de Football Association (French: International Federation of Football Associations) (SPR)

FIFO first in, first out (*redundancy and computer memory*) – *see* FILO, LILO (SCI)

Fig, fig figure

FIGCM Fellow of the Incorporated Guild of Church Musicans

FIH Fédération Internationale de Hockey (*French: International Hockey Federation*) (SPR)

FIH Fédération Internationale de Hockey sur Gazon (*French: International Grass Hockey Federation*) (SPR)

FIIA Fellow of the Institute of Industrial Administration

FIK Fédération Internationale de Korfbal (*French: International Korfbal (type of handball) Federation*) (SPR)

FIL Fellow of the Institute of Linguists

FILA Fédération Internationale des Lutte Amateur (*French: International Federation of Amateur Wrestlers*) (SPR)

FILO first in, last out – *see* FIFO, LILO (SCI)

FILTH failed in London, try Hong Kong (*cracker joke*)

FIM Fellow of the Institute of Metals

FIM Fédération Internationale Motocycliste (*French: International Motorcyclists' Federation*) (SPR)

FIMBRA Financial Intermediaries, Managers & Brokers Regulatory Association (*see* PIA) (COM)

FIMI Fellow of the Institute of the Motor Industry

FIMM Fellow of the Institution of Mining & Metallurgy

FIMT Fellow of the Institute of the Motor Trade

Fin finish

FIN Fellow of the Institute of Navigation

FINA Fédération Internationale de Natation Amateur (*French: International Amateur Swimming Association*) (SPR)

FInstF Fellow of the Institute of Fuel

FInstMet Fellow of the Institute of Metals

FInstP Fellow of the Institute of Physics

FInstPet Fellow of the Institute of Petroleum

FInstPl Fellow of the Institute of Patentees (*Incorporated*)

FInstW Fellow of the Institute of Welding

FIO Fellow of the Institute of Ophthalmic Opticians

FIOB Fellow of the Institute of Builders

FIP fairly important person

FIPV Federación Internacional de Pelota Vasca (*Spain*) (SPR)

FIQ Fédération Internationale des Quilleurs (*French: International 10-pin bowling Federation*) (SPR)

FIQS Fellow of the Institute of Quantity Surveyors

FIRA (Ind) Fellow of the Institute of Railway Auditors and Accountants (*India*)

FIRE Fellow of the Institution of Radio Engineers

FIRI Fellow of the Institution of the Rubber Industry

First D first diploma

FIS Fellow of the Institute of Statisticians

FIS Fédération Internationale de Ski (*French: International Ski Federation*) (SPR)

FISA Fédération Internationale des Sociétés d'Aviron (*French: International Rowing Federation*) (SPR)

FISB Fédération Internationale de Skibob (*French: International Bobsleigh Federation*) (SPR)

FISE Fellow of the Institution of Sanitary Engineers

FIT Fire Investigation Team (FRS)

FITA Fédération Internationale de Tir à l'Arc (*French: International Archery Federation*) (SPR)

FIU Fire Investigation Unit

FIU Framed Investigation Unit

FIWM Fellow of the Institution of Work Managers

FJ Sir Martin Furnival Jones (*1912–97; DG MI5 1965–72*) (MIL)

FJAP fixed action pattern

FJI Fellow of the Institute of Journalists

FKC Fellow of Kings College (*London*)

FL Flight Lieutenant

Fl flyleaf (FPA)

Fl, flor floruit (*Latin: he/she flourished (at such & such a date)*)

FLA Fellow of the Library Association

FLA Finance and Leasing Association

FLAA Fellow of the Association of Certified and Corporate Accountants

FLAG Food Labelling Agenda Group

FLAS Fellow of the Land Agents Society

Flav flavus (*Latin: yellow*)

FLCM Fellow of the London College of Music

Flem Flemish

FLET forward location enemy troops (MIL)

FLHS Fellow of the London Historical Society

FLIR forward-looking infrared (MIL)

FLNKS Front de Libération National Kanake Socialiste (*in New Caledonia*) (POL)

Flojo Florence Griffith-Joyner (*US gold medal sprinter 1959-1998*)

FLOP foreign lazy overseas plonker (*epithet for non-British officers at Sandhurst following alleged malpractices*)

FLOT forward location own troops (MIL)

FLP Financial Law Panel

FLS Fellow of the Linnean Society

FM Foreign Minister; Foreign Ministry

FM Field Marshal (MIL)

FM frequency modulation (FPA)

Fm, fr from

FMCG fast-moving consumer goods (COM)

FME Forensic Medical Examiner (*police surgeon*)

FMEP friction mean effective pressure (*IMEP – BMEP*)

Fmm formation (MIL)

Fmr Firemaster (*Scotland*) (FRS)

Fmr farmer

FMRAAM future medium-range air-to-air missile (MIL)

FMS flexible manufacturing system (COM)

Fn night or off-peak accommodation in first-class

FNF Friday night fracas (PRP)

FNI Fellow of the National Institute of Sciences in India

FNMA Federal National Mortgage Association (*US 'Fanny Mae'*)

FO Foreign Office

FO Flying Officer

FO Field Officer

Fo folio (FPA)

Foaf friend of a friend

FOB free on board (COM)

FOB, fob faecal occult blood (*sign of colorectal cancer*)

FOBAA Flag Officer British assault area

FOC free of charge (COM)

FoC Father of the Chapel

FOCC Flight Operations Control Center (*NASA*) (SCI)

FOCUS Financial Outstation Central Unified System (*accounting*) (PRP)

FOD foreign object damage (*and hence the material which causes it. The RAF officer who toured RAF stations to assess FOD risks was known as the MOD FOD BOD. The Jordanian desert was 'defodded' for the land-speed record attempt 1996*) (MIL)

FOE Fraternal Order of Eagles (*US*)

FoE Friends of the Earth

FOH, FoH front of house (*entertainment – interface with public*) (FPA)

FOI freedom of information

FOIA Freedom of Information Act (*US*)

FOIC flag officer in charge

FOL federation of labour (*NZ*)

Fol followed; following

Fol folium (*Latin: leaf*) (FPA)

Folg following

FONT Friends of the National Trust

FOO forward observation officer (MIL)

FOP Friendship Oil Pipeline (*Eastern Europe*) (COM)

FOP Fraternal Order of Police

FOR free on rail (COM)

For forestry; foreign

FOREST Forestry Sectional Research Technology (SCI)

FORTRAN, Fortran formula translation (SCI)

FOT False or True (*children's TV programme*) (FPA)

FoT foam tender (FRS)

FOW first open water (*after the winter freeze*) (NAV)

FP false pretences (PRP)

FP fire prevention (FRS)

FP fireplace (ARC)

Fp fine point

Fp frontispiece (FPA)

Fp freezing point (SCI)

FPA flight path angle

FPA Family Planning Association

FPC fish protein concentrate (*a food additive*) (F&D)

FPD free prize draw

FPFSG Federation of Prisoners' Families' Support Groups (PRP)

FPhS Fellow of the Philosophical Society

FPO Fire Prevention Officer (FRS)

FPS Fellow of the Pharmaceutical Society

FPSO vessel floating production storage & offloading vessel (SCI)

FPWP Female Prisoners' Welfare Project (PRP)

Fr frater (*Latin: brother*)

Fr Frau (*German: Mrs*)

Fr Father

Fr fragment

FR France

FR Hort S Fellow of the Royal Horticultural Society

FR Mets Fellow of the Royal Meteorological Society

FRACP Fellow of the Royal Australasian College of Physicians

FRACS Fellow of the Royal Australasian College of Surgeons

FRAD Fellow of the Royal Academy of Dancing

FRAeS Fellow of the Royal Aeronautical Society

FRAHS Fellow of the Royal Australian Historical Society

FRAI Fellow of the Royal Anthropological Institute

FRAIA Fellow of the Royal Australian Institute of Architects

FRAM Fellow of the Royal Academy of Music (MUS)

FRAS Fellow of the Royal Astronomical Society

FRB Federal Reserve Bank/Board (*US monetary control agency*) (COM)

FRBS Fellow of the Royal Society of British Sculptors

FRCGP Fellow of the Royal College of General Practitioners

FRCM Fellow of the Royal College of Music (MUS)

FRCN Fellow of The Royal College of Nursing

FRCO Fellow of the Royal College of Organists

FRCO-CHM Fellow of the Royal College of Organists – Choirmaster (MUS)

FRCOG Fellow of the Royal College of Obstetricians & Gynaecologists

FRCP Fellow of the Royal College of Physicians

FRCPath Fellow of the Royal College of Pathologists

FRCPE Fellow of the Royal College of Physicians, Edinburgh

FRCPGlas Fellow of the Royal College of Physicians & Surgeons of Glasgow

FRCPI Fellow of the Royal College of Physicians, Ireland

FRCPsych Fellow of the Royal College of Psychiatrists

FRCR Fellow of the Royal College of Radiologists

FRCS Fellow of the Royal College of Surgeons (*England*)

FRCS Ed Fellow of the Royal College of Surgeons of Edinburgh

FRCS Eng Fellow of the Royal College of Surgeons of England

FRCS I Fellow of the Royal College of Surgeons in Ireland

FRCSGlas Royal College of Physicians and Surgeons, Glasgow

FRCVS Fellow of the Royal College of Veterinary Surgeons

FREconS Fellow of the Royal Economic Society

Freddie Mac *see* FHLMC

Frelimo Frente de Libertação de Moçambique (*Portuguese: Mozambique Liberation Front*)

FREPS(G) Fellow of Royal Faculty of Physicians and Surgeons (*London*)

Freq frequent(ly)

FRES Fellow of Royal Empire Society; Fellow of the Royal Entomological Society of London

Fretilin an East Timorese Radical Independence Movement

FRGS Fellow of the Royal Geographical Society

FRHistS Fellow of the Royal Historical Society

FRHortS, FRHS Fellow of the Royal Horticultural Society

FRI Fellow of the Royal Institution

FRIAS Fellow of the Royal Incorporation of Architects of Scotland

FRIBA Fellow of the Royal Institute of British Architects

FRIC (*formerly FIC*) Fellow of Royal Institute of Chemistry

FRICS Fellow of the Royal Institute of Chartered Surveyors

FRIH Fellow of Royal Institute of Horticulture (*NZ*)

FRIPHH Fellow of the Royal Institute of Public Health and Hygiene

Fris, Frs Frisian

Frl Fräulein (*German: Miss*)

FRMCM Fellow of the Royal Manchester College of Music (MUS)

FRMetS Fellow of the Royal Meteorological Society

FRMS Fellow of the Royal Microscopical Society

FRNS Fellow of the Royal Numismatic Society

FRNSA Fellow of the Royal Naval School of Architects

FROG for relief of glaucoma

FRPS Fellow of the Royal Photographic Society

FRPSL Fellow of the Royal Philatelic Society, London

FRS Fellow of the Royal Society

FRSA Fellow of the Royal Society of Arts

FRSAI Fellow of the Royal Society of Antiquaries of Ireland

FRSanI Fellow of the Royal Sanitary Institute

FRSC Fellow of the Royal Society of Chemistry

FRSE Fellow of the Royal Society of Edinburgh

FRSGS Fellow of the Royal Scottish Geographical Society

FRSL Fellow of the Royal Society of Literature

FRSM Fellow of Royal Society of Medicine

FRSNZ Fellow of the Royal Society of New Zealand

FRSSA Fellow of Royal Society of South Africa

FRST Fellow of the Royal Society of Teachers

FRSTM&H Fellow of Royal Society of Tropical Medicine and Hygiene

Frt freight (COM)

FRT forward repair team (MIL)

Frt fwd freight forward (COM)

Frt ppd freight prepaid (COM)

FRTPI Fellow of the Royal Town Planning Institute

Frug (*verb*) fund raising under the guise (*of carrying out a survey – see* sug) (COM)

Frugger (*noun*) one who frugs (COM)

FRVIA Fellow of the Royal Victorian Institute of Architects

FRZSScot Fellow of the Royal Zoological Society of Scotland

FS fire safety (FRS)

FS factor of safety (SCI)

Fs semi (*Latin: half*)

FSA formal safety assessment (COM)

FSA Forensic Science Agency

FSA Fellow of the Society of Antiquaries

FSA food service assistant (F&D)

FSA Football Supporters Association

FSAA Fellow of the Society of Incorporated Accountants and Auditors

FSAM Fellow of the Society of Art Masters

FSArc Fellow of the Society of Architects (*merged with RIBA 1925*)

FSAScot Fellow of the Society of Antiquaries of Scotland

FSASM Fellow of the South Australian School of Mines

FSAVC free standing AVC

FSB Federation of Small Businesses (UNI)

FSC Fire Service College (FRS)

FSD focus-skin distance (SCI)

FSD full scale deflection (SCI)

FSE Fellow of the Society of Engineers

FSEB Fire Services Examination Board (FRS)

FSGT Fellow of the Society of Glass Technology

FSH family & social history

FSH full service history

FSI Fellow of the Surveyors' Institution

FSI Fellow of the Royal Institution of Chartered Surveyors (*changed August 1947 to FRICS*)

FSIA Fellow of the Society of Industrial Artists

FSLIC Federal Savings & Loan Insurance Corporation (*US insuring agency; see* FDIC) (COM)

FSMA Fellow of the Incorporated Sales Managers' Association

FSNAG fascinating sensitive new-age guy

FSO Foreign Service Officer (*in US Department of State*)

FSO Friars' Society Orchestra (MUS)

FSO Future sound of London

FSP food safety panel (F&D)

FSR Flying Saucer Review (SCI)

FSS Fellow of the Royal Statistical Society

FSScA Fellow of the Society of Science and Art, London

FST front suspended tow (*for broken down or accident vehicles*)

FSVA Fellow of the Society of Valuers & Auctioneers

FT full term (PRP)

Ft fort

Ft fiat (*Latin: let it be made*)

FTA failed/failure to arrive (PRP)

FTA Future Teachers of America

FTAI French Territory of Afars & Issas (*now Djibouti*)

FTC Federal Trade Commission (*US agency enforcing anti-trust laws, fair advertising, labelling etc*)

FTCD Fellow of Trinity College, Dublin

FTCL Fellow of Trinity College of Music, London (MUS)

FTD Florists' Transworld Delivery (COM)

FTD fastest time of day

FTE full-time employee (or equivalent; eg two halves) (COM)

FTE full-time education (PRP)

FTI Financial Times Index (COM)

FTI Fellow of the Textile Institute

FTII Fellow of the Taxation Institute Inc

FTP file transfer protocol (SCI)

FTR failed/failure to return (PRP)

FTr foam trailer (FRS)

FTS failed/failure to surrender (PRP)

FTSC Fellow of the Tonic Sol-fa College (MUS)

FTZ Federal/Foreign Trade Zone (*US duty-free zones*)

FUP forming up point/place (MIL)

Fur furlongs

Fut future

FWB front-wheel brakes

FWD four/front wheel drive

Fwd, fwd forward

F-word euphemism for the word 'f***'

FWP Federal Writers' Project (*New Deal writers' program; produced series of US travel guides*) (FPA)

FX effects (FPA)

FYROM Former Yugoslav Republic of Macedonia

FZS Fellow of the Zoological Society

G

G&S Gilbert & Sullivan

G&S glue(d) & screw(ed) (ARC)

G&W Gulf & Western Industries (COM)

G, Ger, Gy German; Germany

G,g gauges

G20 Group of 20

GA General Accident (COM)

GA Gamblers Anonymous (PRP)

GA General Assembly (*UN*)

GA general average; General Assembly

GA general anaesthetic

GA Henty George Alfred (*English author (boys' adventures) 1832–1902*)

GAA Gay Activists' Alliance

GAA Gaelic Athletic Association (*hurling, Gaelic football, handball & rounders - does not now cater for athletics*) (SPR)

GAAP generally accepted accounting principles (COM)

GABA gamma-aminobutyric acid (CHM)

GAC Government Art Collection

GAD Government Actuary's Department

GAGGLE General Association of Gleeful Gooselovers Everywhere (*celebrating garden (as in garden gnome) geese*)

GAL Spanish anti-terrorist liberation group (MIL)

Gal gallery (FPA)

Galv galvanic; galvanise(d); galvanism;

GAO General Accounting Office (*US Congress investigative body*)

GAR Grand Army of the Republic (*US Civil War veterans' union*) (MIL)

GAS George Augustus (Henry) Sala (1828–95)

GATT General Agreement on Tariffs & Trade

GATX General American Transportation Corporation (*GATX now official*)

GAU Gay Academic Union

Gaz gazette; gazetteer (FPA)

GB, Gr Brit, Gt B Great Britain

GBA Gurkha Brigade Association (MIL)

GBAT Graduate Business Administration Test

GBE Knight (*or Dame*) Grand Cross of the Most Excellent Order of the British Empire

GBF gay black female

GBH grievous bodily harm (PRP)

GBM gay black male

GBP Great British Public

GBS George Bernard Shaw (*Irish writer, 1856–1950*)

GBSM Graduate of the Birmingham School of Music (MUS)

GC George Cross

GC great circle; gyrocompass (NAV)

GCA ground control approach

GCAS ground collision avoidance system

GCB Knight Grand Cross of the Most Honourable Order of the Bath

GCC Gulf Co-operation Council (*Bahrain, KSA, Kuwait, Oman, Qatar & UAE*)

GCCS Government Code & Cipher School

GCE General Certificate of Education

GCH Knight Grand Cross of Hanover

GCHQ Government Communications Headquarters

GCIE Knight Grand Commander of the Most Eminent Order of the Indian Empire

GCLH Grand Cross of the Legion of Honour

GCLJ Knight Grand Cross of the Order of St Lazarus of Jerusalem

GCMG Knight (*or Dame*) Grand Cross of the Most Distinguished Order of St Michael & St George

GCMPC General Chairman & Member of the Pickwick Club (*ie Samuel Pickwick*) (FPA)

GCP good chemical practice (SCI)

GCSE General Certificate of Secondary Education

GCSI Knight Grand Commander of the Most Excellent Order of the Star of India

GCStJ Bailiff or Dame Grand Cross of the Most Venerable Order of the Hospital of St John of Jerusalem

GCT Game Conservancy Trust (SPR)

GCVO Knight (*or Dame*) Grand Cross of the Royal Victorian Order

Gd granddaughter

GDC General Dental Council

GDP gross domestic product (COM)

GDP general defence plan (MIL)

GDR German Democratic Republic (E Germany)

Gds goods (COM)

GE General Electric Company (US) (COM)

GE German

GEAES General Electric Aircraft Engineering Services

GEC General Electric Company (UK) (COM)

Gen general

Gen gender; general(ly); generic; genitive

Gen genus (SCI)

Gent gentleman

GEPAN aka SEPRA – French UFO Group (SCI)

Ger gerund

Ges Gesellschaft

Gestapo Geheime Staatspolizei (*German: Secret State Police, NAZI organisation*) (MIL)

GF General Foods Corporation (COM)

GF girl Friday

GFCO Group Fire Control Officer (FRS)

GFS gardening from scratch (FPA)

GFS Girls' Friendly Society

GG Girl Guides (now Guides)

GG Governor General

Ggd great granddaughter

GGF Glass & Glazing Federation (UNI)

Ggs Gegensatz (*German: antonym*)

Ggs great grandson

GGSM Graduate of the Guildhall School of Music & Drama (MUS)

GH Lewes George Henry (1817–78)

GH, GHQ General Headquarters (MIL)

GHA Greenwich hour angle (*at pole, made by meridian of heavenly body with the Greenwich meridian, always measured west*) (NAV)

GHB gamma hydroxy butyrate (*for body-building and a gay aphrodisiac; commonly called GBH; liquid ecstasy*) (PRP)

GI general infantryman (MIL)

GI gold inlay

GI, GI Joe enlisted soldier in US army, from the army term 'government issue' applied to kit and equipment (MIL)

Gib Gibraltar

GIC glass ionomer cement

GIGO garbage in, garbage out (SCI)

GILOC gravity induced loss of consciousness (*see* G-LOC)

GIMechE Graduate of the Institution of Mechanical Engineers

G-in-C General Officer-in-Chief

Ginnie Mae *see* GNMA

GIP glazed imitation par(CHM)ent (FPA)

GIS geographical information system (NAV)

GIT genetic interest group

Gk Greek

GKC Gilbert Keith Chesterton (*English writer, 1874–1936*)

GKN Guest Keen & Nettlefolds (COM)

Gl glass; gloss (ARC)

GL Grand Lodge (*Masonic*)

GLAAD Gay and Lesbian Alliance Against Defamation

GLAM greying, leisured, affluent, middle-aged

GLB Girls' Life Brigade

GLC Greater London Council

GLCC Greater London County Council

GLF Gay Liberation Front (*1960s pioneer homosexual rights' groups, now defunct*)

G-LOC gravitation loss of consciousness (*see* GILOC)

GLP good laboratory practice (SCI)

GLR Greater London Radio (FPA)

Glt gilt (FPA)

GM grant maintained (school)

GM George Medal (MIL)

GM Grand Master (chess) (SPR)

G-M counter Geiger-Muller counter (SCI)

G-man FBI agent (*USA*); Political Detective (*Irish*)

GMAT general management administration test

GMB General, Municipal, Boilermakers (*amalgamation of two former Unions: GMBATU & GMWU*) (UNI)

GMB Grand Master Bowman

GMBATU General, Municipal, Boilermakers & Allied Trades Union (UNI)

GmbH Gesellschaft mit beschrankter Haftung (COM)

GMC general management committee (COM)

Gmc Germanic

GMDSS global maritime distress & safety system (NAV)

GMIE Grand Master of the Order of the Indian Empire

GMLS Gardener Merchant Leisure Services

GMMG Grand Master of St Michael and St George

GMMR great man-made river (*Libyan irrigation project*)

GMMRA Great Man-made River Authority (*GSLPAJ (Libya) project to extract fresh water from aquifers*)

GMMRUA Great Man-made River Utilisation Authority

GMO genetically modified organism

GMP good manufacturing practice (F&D)

GMR Greater Manchester Radio (FPA)

GMS grant maintained school/status

GMS general maintenance system

GMSI Grand Master of the Star of India

GMWU General & Municipal Workers Union (UNI)

GN grid north (NAV)

GNAS Grand National Archery Society (SPR)

GNMA Government National Mortgage Association (*'Ginnie Mae'*)

GNP gross national product (COM)

Gnr gunner (MIL)

GNS Gannett News Service (*US*) (COM)

GNVQ general national vocational qualification

GO gym officer/orderly (PRP)

GO general order (MIL)

GOAD good order & discipline (PRP)

Gob good ordinary brand (SCI)

GOC General Officer Commanding (MIL)

GOC-in-C General Officer Commanding-In-Chief

GO-GEOID Gondwana geoscientific indexing database

GOK God only knows

GOM God's own medicine (= *morphine*) (PRP)

GOM Grand Old Man (originally applied to William Ewart Gladstone 1809-98)

GONG Global Oscillation Network Group (*studies vibrations in the Sun*) (SCI)

GOOD get out of debt (*a GOOD job – 'you wouldn't dream of not quitting when the debt is repaid'*)

GOP Grand old party (*US Republicans*)

GORA Great Ouse River Authority (*now Anglia Water*)

Goth gothic

Gov Governor

Gov Government organisation (*Internet domain name*)

Gov, Govt Government

GP graduated pension (COM)

GP Gray Panthers (*US senior citizens' group*)

GP Gallup poll

GP Grand prix (*French: big prize*)

GP parental guidance suggested (movie rating; now PG) (FPA)

GP general practitioner

Gp Capt Group Captain

GPA Government procurement agreement

GPA grade point average

GPC global personal communicator (SCI)

GPDO General Permitted Development Order

GPDST Girls' Public Day School Trust

GPM graduated payment mortgage (COM)

GPMG general purpose machine gun (MIL)

GPMU Graphical, Paper & Media Union (*was NATSOPA, then NGA*) (UNI)

GPO Government Printing Office (*US THO analog*)

GPO General Post Office (*later, The Post Office*)

GPS general problem solver

GPS Great Public Schools (*Australia*)

GPS global positioning system (NAV)

GQ general quarters (MIL)

GQ Gentlemen's Quarterly (FPA)

GQT Gardeners' Question Time

GR Georgius Rex (*Latin: King George*)

GR Greece

Gr grade

Gr Greek

Gr wt gross weight (COM)

GRA Greyhound Racing Association (SPR)

GRACE group routing & charging equipment (SCI)

Grad graduate; graduated

GramSch grammar school

GRAS generally recognised as safe (*FDA food-additive rating*) (F&D)

GRB gamma-ray burst (*from deep space*)

GRE graduate record examination

Green S food colour known as Wool green S (F&D)

GRFGS Gloucestershire Root, Fruit and Grain Society (*founded in 1863 to settle – some say – an argument between farmers as to who grew the better swedes*)

GRNN goods return notification number

GROLIES Guardian reader of limited intelligence in an ethnic skirt

GRP glass(fibre)-reinforced plastic (SCI)

GR-S Government rubber-styrene (*synthetic rubber developed in the US during WWII*) (SCI)

GRSM Graduate of the Royal Schools of Music (MUS)

GRT gross registered tonnage

GRU Glavnoye Razvedyvatel'noye Upravleniye (*Russian: Centra Intelligence Office*) (MIL)

GRUMP grown-up urban mature professional

Gs grandson

GSA General Services Administration (*US property management agency*)

GSA Girl Scouts of America

GSA Guildford School of Acting

GSL general sales licence (COM)

GSLP guaranteed student loan program (*US*)

GSLPAJ Great Socialist Libyan People's Arab Jamariyah

GSM Guildhall School of Music & Drama (MUS)

GSM global system for mobile telecommunications (*agreed standard*) (SCI)

GSM, gsm grams per square metre (*measure of weight of paper or card*) (FPA)

GSO general staff officer (MIL)

GSOH, gsoh good sense of humour

GSPP global shared productivity program (*Levi's two-for-one millennium salary program*) (COM)

G-string skimpy pubic covering

G-suit, anti-G suit pressurised suit for high-speed aircraft or space crew

GT Goodyear Tire & Rubber Company (COM)

GT gran turismo (*high performance luxury sports car*)

GTA Graduate Teaching Assistant

GTC good till cancelled (COM)

GTC General Teaching Council (*Scotland*)

GTCL Graduate of Trinity College of Music, London (MUS)

Gtd guaranteed (COM)

GTE General Telephone & Electronics Corporation (*US; now official*) (COM)

GTF glucose tolerance factor (F&D)

GTG good time girl

GTI, GTi gran turismo Injection (*sports car*)

GTN General Telephone Network (SCI)

GTO gran turismo omologato (*Italian: certified for grand touring*)

GUC Grand Union Canal

GUG/GUM Genito-Urinary Clinic/Unit (PRP)

GUI graphical user interface (SCI)

GULO General Union of Loom Overlookers (UNI)

GULP Grenada United Labour Party (*Sir Eric Gairy (1922–97) founded the Manual, Maritime and Menial Workers' Union, from which in 1950 he organised Grenada's first political party, then left learning GULP*)

GUS Great Universal Stores (COM)

GUT grand unified theory (SCI)

Guv governor (*informal term for senior colleague*)

GVA Geneva (*Swiss airport*)

GVN Government of Vietnam

GWF gay white female

GWM gay white male

GWP gift with purchase (*bribe for cosmetic consumers*) (COM)

GWSD Guild of Weavers, Spinners & Dyers (UNI)

GWTW Gone with the Wind (*book & film*) (FPA)

Gy Gray (*SI unit for ionizing radiation = 1J/kg*) (F&D)

GYE Guinness yeast extract (F&D)

Gyro gyrocompass; gyroscope (NAV)

H

H heroin (PRP)

H House (*of Representatives, US*)

H highly commended

H with another letter: US military search & rescue aircraft

H heart(s) (*cards*)

H US airfare: coach economy discounted

H & D curve Hurter & Driffield curve (SCI)

H & D number emulsion speed (SCI)

H E Bates Herbert Ernest (*British novelist, 1905–74*)

H G Wells Herbert George (*English Novelist, 1866–1946*)

H&C heroin & cocaine taken together (PRP)

H&C, h&c hot & cold

H&Q Harpers & Queen (FPA)

H&V heating and ventilating/ ventilation (ARC)

H2S an airborne centimetric radar system.

HA hardy annual

HA home address

HA Housing Authority

HABS historic American building survey (*collection held at US Library of Congress*) (FPA)

HAC Honourable Artillery Company

HAL heuristically programmed algorithmic computer (*2001: A Space Odyssey; the letters H-A-L are one removed from I-B-M*)

HALCA an orbiting radiotelescope

HALOW help and advice line (*for prisoners*) (PRP)

HAPS honey & peanut butter sandwich (F&D)

HARC Heritage Arms Rescue Committee (*saving babies from bathwater disposal*)

HARC Houston Advanced Research Centre (SCI)

Harry S Truman 1884–1972; US president 1945–52; adopted the S in accordance with American name-initial-name principle; hence called in derision 'Harry S-for-nothing Truman'

Harv Harvard

HB House Bill (*US government*)

HB hard black (*pencil*) (FPA)

HB half back (*US football*) (SPR)

Hb symbol for a molecule of haemoglobin minus the iron atom (SCI)

HBC history; Historical Book Club (FPA)

HBC Hudson Bay Company

HBI housebreaking implements (PRP)

HBM Her/His Britannic Majesty ('s)

HBMS His/Her Britannic Majesty's Service/Ship (MIL)

HBN a range of potent weedkillers (CHM)

HBO Home Box Office (*a division of TWEC*) (FPA)

H-bomb hydrogen bomb (MIL)

Hc honoris causa

HC, HofC House of Commons

HCC Health Care Centre (PRP)

HCF highest common factor

HCF Honorary Chaplain to the Forces

HCHASC House of Commons Home Affairs Select Committee

HCL high cost of living (COM)

HCM His/Her Catholic Majesty

HCM hypertrophic cardio-myopathy

HCO Health Care Officer (PRP)

HCO Hackney Carriage Office

HCPI harmonised consumer price index

HCR House concurrent resolution (*US government*)

HCSA Hospital Consultants & Specialists Association (UNI)

HCSP Health Care Service For Prisoners (PRP)

HD hot date

HD Hilda Doolittle (*poet, 1886–1961*)

HD hard disk (SCI)

HD hyperactivity disorder

HDD head-down display (SCI)

HDO harbour defence only (MIL)

HDO water in which an appreciable proportion of ordinary hydrogen is replaced by deuterium (CHM)

HDRA Henry Doubleday Research Association

HDTV high-definition television (SCI)

HE high explosive (MIL)

HE His/Her Excellence

HE His/Her Eminence

HE high energy (SCI)

H E Monro Harold Edward (*English poet, founded* Poetry Review, *1879–1932*)

HEAT high explosive anti tank (MIL)

Heb Hebrew

HECS home energy conservation strategy

HEFC Higher Education Funding Council

HEGOS heated exhaust gas oxygen sensor

HEH His/Her Exalted Highness

HEIC Honourable East India Company

HEICS Honourable East India Company's Service

Heir app heir apparent

Heir-pres heir presumptive

Hel helicopter (MIL)

HEL high energy laser (SCI)

HELP help establish lasting peace

HEM hybrid electromagnetic (*wave*) (SCI)

He–Ne laser helium–neon laser (SCI)

HEOD dieldrin – a widely used contact insecticide such as mothproofing of carpets & furnishings (CHM)

HEPA high efficiency particulate air

HER human error rate

HERA Hadron electron ring accelerator (SCI)

HES house exchange system (SCI)

HESH high explosive squash head (MIL)

HETP height equivalent to a theoretical plate (*a measure of the separation efficiency of a distillation column*) (SCI)

HEW US department of Health, Education & Welfare (*now replaced by the Departments of Education and Health & Human Services*)

HF high frequency (SCI)

HFARA Honorary Foreign Associate of the Royal Academy

HFC Household Finance Corporation

HFCS high-fructose corn syrup (F&D)

HFL highly-flammable liquid (SCI)

HFMA Healthcare Financial Management Association

HFS heated front screen

HG His/Her Grace

HG Home Guard

HG The Hundred Group

H G Wells Herbert George (*English writer, 1866–1946*)

HGMPRC Human Genome Mapping Project Resource Centre

HGO/SGO he's/she's getting old (*surprise at photograph or TV appearance cf IHO/ISO, THWD*) (FPA)

HGV heavy goods vehicle (*taxation class*)

HH His/Her Highness

HH His Holiness (*the Pope*)

Hh hands high (*1 hand (equine decimetre) = 4 inches*)

H H Munro Hector Hugh (*pen name Saki – Scottish humorous writer 1870–1916*)

HHA half-hardy annual

Hhd hogshead

HHDN an insecticide (CHM)

HHH husband holds the handbag

HHS US Department of Health & Human Services

HI height of instrument

HICAS high capacity actively controlled suspension

Hi-fi high fidelity (SCI)

Hi-Fi, hifi high fidelity (*reproduction*) (MUS)

HIGNFY Have I Got News For You (FPA)

HIH His/Her Imperial Highness

HIM His/Her Imperial Majesty

HIS hic iacet sepultus (*Latin: here lies buried*)

HIVI husband is a village idiot

HJS hic jacet sepultus (*Latin: here lies buried - see* HSE)

HK Hong Kong

HKCC Hong Kong Cricket Club (SPR)

HKW The history of the King's Works (ARC)

HL hose-layer (FRS)

HL high line

HLB hydrophilic–lipophilic balance (*in emulsifying agents*) (SCI)

HLCA hill livestock compensatory allowances

HLED home leave eligibility date (PRP)

HLI Highland Light Infantry

HM His/Her Majesty('s)

HM Headmaster

HMAS Her/His Majesty's Australian Ship (MIL)

HMC His/Her Majesty's Customs

HMC Headmasters' Conference

HMCG His/Her Majesty's Coastguard (now TCA) (NAV)

HMCIP His/Her Majesty's Chief Inspector of Prisons (PRP)

HMCS His/Her Majesty's Canadian Ship

HMD hatches, matches & dispatches (*see* BMD)

HMD hydraulic mean depth

HMG His/Her Majesty's Government

HMHS His/Her Majesty's Hospital Ship

HMI His/Her Majesty's Inspector/ate

HMIP His/Her Majesty's Inspector of Pollution

HML His/Her Majesty's Lieutenant

HMO house of multiple occupation

HMP His/Her Majesty's Prison (PRP)

HMRI His/Her Majesty's Railway Inspectorate

HMS His/Her Majesty's Service/ Ship (MIL)

HMSO His/Her Majesty's Stationery Office (*government printer & publisher – became TSO 1 October 1996*)

HMT HM Treasury

HMV His Master's Voice (*heard by Nipper*) (MUS)

HMY Her Majesty's Yacht (*Britannia*) (MIL)

HNC Higher National Certificate

HND Higher National Diploma

HNW head, nut & washer (ARC)

HO Home Office

HO Head Office

Ho house

HOAI Home Office Addicts' Index (PRP)

HOBGOBLIN Help! Our budget's gone beyond the limits of our income

HOBO hopeful, optimistic box owner

HofC House of Commons

HOHO hopeful, optimistic home owner

HOLMES Home Office Large Major Enquiry System (*it's a police computer, Watson*)

HOMINTERN London's network of homosexual politicians and diplomats

Hon Honourable (*title*); honorary (*unpaid*)

Hon ARCM Honorary Associate of the Royal College of Music (MUS)

Hon FRAM Honorary Fellow of the Royal Academy of Music (MUS)

Hon FRCM Honorary Fellow of the Royal College of Music (MUS)

Hon FTCL Honorary Fellow of Trinity College of Music, London (MUS)

Hon FTSC Honorary Fellow of the Tonic Sol-fa College (MUS)

Hon GSM Honorary Graduate of the Guildhall School of Music & Drama (MUS)

Hon RAM Honorary Member of the Royal Academy of Music (MUS)

Hon RCM Honorary Member of the Royal College of Music (MUS)

Hon TCL Honorary Member of Trinity College of Music, London (MUS)

HOR(&P)U Home Office Research (& Planning) Unit

HOTAS hands on throttle & stick

HOTYS Horse Of The Year Show (*annual Wembley event*) (SPR)

How howitzer

HP hydraulic platform (FRS)

HP hire-purchase

HP high pressure (SCI)

HP sauce Houses of Parliament sauce (*a brown sauce*) (F&D)

HP, hp horsepower (SCI)

HPA Heritage Preservation Association (*GA, USA, to retain, eg, the words 'darkie' & 'massa' in songs*) (FPA)

HPA Hurlingham Polo Association (SPR)

H-paper Hochstadter paper (*coated on one side with aluminium foil, the composite sheet being perforated to allow oil to flow freely*) (SCI)

HPF hexafluorphosphoric acid (CHM)

H-plane the plane containing the magnetic vector H in electromagnetic waves (SCI)

HPS highest possible score (*shooting*) (SPR)

HQ headquarters (*note back-formation 'to headquart'*)

HR home rule

HR House of Representatives (*USA*)

HR home run (baseball) (SPR)

HR holiday route

H-radar navigation system in which an aircraft interrogates 2 ground stations for distance.

HRCA Honorary Royal Cambrian Academician

HRDA high-rate deposit account (COM)

HRE Holy Roman Emperor

HRE Holy Roman Empire

HRH His/Her Royal Highness

HRHA Honorary Member of the Royal Hibernian Academy

HRI Holy Roman Empire

HRI Honorary Member of the Royal Institute of Painters in Watercolours

HROI Honorary Member of the Royal Institute of Oil Painters

HRR Henley Royal Regatta (SPR)

HRSA Honorary Member of the Royal Scottish Academy

HRSW Honorary Member of the Royal Scottish Watercolour Society

HRW heated rear window

HS Home Secretary

HS high school

HS hospital ship (MIL)

HS Hawker-Siddeley

HS&F huntin', shootin' & fishin' (*antiquarian book category*) (FPA)

HS/HT harmonised system/harmonised tariff

HSBC Hong Kong and Shanghai Banking Corporation

HSD horizontal situation display (NAV)

HSE Health & Safety Executive

HSE hic sepultus est (*Latin: here lies buried - see* HJS)

HSG high school for girls

HSH His/Her Serene Highness

HSL cable with H-paper wrapping and lead sheath (SCI)

HSM His/Her Serene Majesty

HSrep Health & Safety Representative (FRS)

HST Hubble space telescope (SCI)

HSV high-sided vehicle

HT hybrid tea (rose)

HT high tension (SCI)

HTB Holy Trinity, Brompton

HTML hypertext mark-up language (SCI)

HTO water in which an appreciable proportion of ordinary hydrogen is replaced by tritium (CHM)

HTR high temperature reactor

Hts height(s)

HTS heat transfer salt (CHM)

HTTP hypertext transfer protocol (SCI)

HTU height of transfer unit (*measure of the separating efficiency of packed columns for mass transfer operations*) (SCI)

HTV Harlech Television (FPA)

HUAC House Un-American Activities Committee (*US Congress*)

HUD US Department of Housing & Urban Development

HUD head-up display

Hum humanity; humanities (*classics*)

HVM hyper velocity missile (MIL)

HW high water (*tide*)

H-wave *see* TE-wave (SCI)

HWM high water mark (NAV)

HX high expansion foam (FRS)

Hy heavy

H-Y Harvard-Yale

Hyp hypothesis; hypothetical

I

I International

I Institute

I moment of inertia (SCI)

I current (SCI)

I isospin (SCI)

I Island(s) (NAV)

I Independence; Independent

I inter-state highway (*US*)

I Imperator or Imperatrix; Emperor or Empress

i interest (COM)

i intransitive

i- iso- (*containing a branched hydrocarbon chain*) (CHM)

I neutrons those possessing such energy as to undergo resonance absorption by iodine (SCI)

I signal in the NTSC colour TV system, that corresponding to the wideband axis of the chrominance signal (SCI)

i/c in charge (MIL)

I/O input/output (SCI)

I-500 Indianapolis 500-mile motor race (SPR)

IA Indian Army

Ia Iowa (*US*)

IAA indoleacetic acid (*plant hormone*) (SCI)

IAAF International American Athletic Federation (SPR)

IAAS Incorporated Association of Architects and Surveyors

IAB International Association of Bookkeepers (COM)

IAC Institute of Amateur Cinematographers

IAD Internal Affairs Department

IADB Inter-American Development Bank (COM)

IAE Institution of Agricultural Engineers (*estd 1938, inc 1960*) (SCI)

IAEA International Atomic Energy Agency

IAF Indian Air Force (MIL)

IAHM Incorporated Association of Headmasters

IAOC Indian Army Ordnance Corps

IARO Indian Army Reserve of Officers

IARU International Amateur Radio Union (FPA)

IAS Institute of Advanced Studies (*Princeton, NJ*) (SCI)

IAS indicated airspeed

IASC International Accounting Standards Committee

IATA International Air Transport Association

IB, ib, Ibid, or ibid ibidem (*Latin: in the same place*)

IBA Independent Broadcasting Authority (*see ITA*) (FPA)

IBA International Boxing Association (*−1939*) (SPR)

IBB International Bowling Board (*lawn bowls*) (SPR)

IBC, ibc inside back cover (*publishing*) (FPA)

IBF Institute of British Foundrymen (*estd 1904, Royal Charter 1921*) (UNI)

IBF International Badminton Federation (SPR)

IBF International Bobsleigh Federation (SPR)

IBM International Business Machines (*Corporation*) (COM)

IBM International Brotherhood of Musicians

IBM, ICBM intercontinental ballistic missile (MIL)

IBRA International Bible-Reading Association

IBRD International Bank for Reconstruction & Development (*UN affiliate*) (COM)

IC internal communications (COM)

IC Imperial College (*London*)

IC immediate constituent

IC imum coeli (*Latin: astrological horizon's lowest point*)

IC internal-combustion (SCI)

IC integrated circuit (SCI)

IC information content (SCI)

IC international 10sq m sailing canoe (SPR)

IC engine *see* ICE (SCI)

ICA Institute of Contemporary Arts (FPA)

ICA International Colour Association

ICAA Invalid Children's Aid Association

ICAEW Institute of Chartered Accountants in England and Wales

ICAN atmosphere International Commission for Air Navigation atmosphere (*superseded by Standard Atmosphere*)

ICAO International Civil Aviation Organisation (*UN affiliate*)

ICBM inter-continental ballistic missile

ICC Interstate Commerce Commission (*US transport regulator*)

ICC International Consensus Committee

ICC International Cricket Conference (SPR)

ICCF International Cycle Polo Federation (SPR)

ICCF International Correspondence Chess Federation

ICCNL International Committee of Chairmen of National Libraries (FPA)

ICD-9 International Classification of Diseases

ICE Institution of Civil Engineers (*estd 1818, Royal Charter 1828*) (SCI)

ICE internal combustion engine (SCI)

Icel Icelandic

ICER Independent Commission on Electoral Reform

ICF International Canoe Federation (SPR)

ICF International Curling Federation (SPR)

ICFC Industrial & Commercial Finance Corporation (*became 3i*) (COM)

ICFTU International Confederation of Free Trade Unions (COM)

IChemE Institution of Chemical Engineers (*UK's senior professional engineering organisation; estd 1822, Royal Charter 1828*) (SCI)

ichth icthyology (SCI)

ICI Imperial Chemicals Industries

ICJ International Court of Justice (*UN affiliate*)

ICL International Computers Ltd (SCI)

ICO Interim Care Order (PRP)

ICRC International Committee of the Red Cross

ICS Indian Civil Service

ICSDs International Central Securities Depositories (*eg Euroclear and Cedel*)

ICSI intra-cytoplasmic sperm injection (*one egg, one sperm*)

ICSSTIS International Commission for the Supervision of Standards of Telephone Information Services (SCI)

ICSTIS Independent Committee for the Supervision of Telephone Information Services (SCI)

ICW interrupted continuous waves (SCI)

ID Intelligence Department

ID identity; identification (*pronounced 'eye-dee'*)

Id ibidem (*Latin: in the same place*)

id idem (*Latin: the same*)

ID, id inside/internal diameter (SCI)

IDA International Development Association (*UN affiliate*)

IDA Institute of Domestic Arts

IDB illicit diamond buying (*Republic of South Africa*) (COM)

IDC Industrial Development Certificate (COM)

idc completed a course at, or served for a year on the staff of, The Imperial Defence College

IDF intermediate distribution frame (SCI)

IDFA Infant & Dietetic Foods Association (F&D)

IDN in Dei nomine (*Latin: in the name of God*)

IDP integrated data processing (SCI)

IDPR inmate development pre-release (*preparation programme*) (PRP)

IDS International Dendrology Society

IDSM Indian Distinguished Service Medal

IE Indo-European (FPA)

IE&T Institute of Engineers & Technicians (SCI)

ie, i.e. id est (*Latin: that is*)

IEA International Energy Agency

IEAM Institute of Entertainment and Arts Management

IEC International Energy Commission (*forgotten water-powered car begetter*) (COM)

IECC Integrated Electronic Control Centre

IED Institution of Engineering Designers (*estd 1945, incorporated 1974*) (SCI)

IEE Institution of Electrical Engineers (*estd 1871, Royal Charter 1921*) (SCI)

IEEIE Institution of Electronics & Electrical Incorporated Engineers (SCI)

IEng Incorporated Engineer (SCI)

IEPS incentives and earned privileges scheme (PRP)

IERSM International Earth Rotation Service Monitors

IES Indian Educational Service

IESS International Encyclopaedia of the Social Sciences (FPA)

IET Institute of Engineers & Technicians (*estd 1948*) (SCI)

IF, if intermediate frequency (SCI)

IFA Independent Financial Adviser (COM)

IFA Institute of Financial Accountants (COM)

IFAA International Flight Attendants' Association (COM)

IFAD International Fund for Agricultural Development (*UN affiliate*)

IFAL International Federation of Amateur Lacrosse (SPR)

IFC, ifc inside front cover (*publishing*) (FPA)

IFF identification, friend or foe (*early radar*) (MIL)

IFF, iff if, and only if (SCI)

IFIF International Forum for Internal Freedom (*Timothy Leary*)

IFM International Association of Food Manufacturers (F&D)

IFMA Institutional Fund Manager's Association

IFMC International Folk Music Council (MUS)

Ifor implementation force (*Bosnia*) (MIL)

IFR Instrument Flight Rules

IFR Instrument Flying Regulations

IFS Institute for Fiscal Studies (COM)

IFS information fatigue syndrome (SCI)

IFS Irish Free State (*now Republic of Ireland*)

IFSLYC International Federation of Sand and Land Yacht Clubs (SPR)

IFWHA International Federation of Women's Hockey Associations (SPR)

IG Indo-Germanic (FPA)

IG Inspector General

IGA Independent Grocers' Alliance Distributing Company (COM)

IGB inner German border (MIL)

IGBM International Agency of Breast Feeding Minority

IGC Inter-Governmental Conference (*Europe every two years*)

IGE Institution of Gas Engineers (*estd 1863, Royal Charter 1929*) (SCI)

IGF International Gymnastics Federation (SPR)

IGFET insulated-gate field-effect transistor (SCI)

IGHAR International Group for Historic Aircraft Recovery

ign ignites; ignition

ign ignotus (Latin: unknown)

IGV inlet guide vanes (SCI)

IGY International Geophysical Year

IH International Harvester (*now Navistar*) (COM)

IH Indo-Hittite (FPA)

IHC intellectually handicapped child (*NZ*)

IHF International Handball Federation (SPR)

IHIE Institute of Highway Incorporated Engineers (SCI)

IHO/ISO isn't he/she old (*surprise at photograph or TV appearance cf HGO/SGO, THWD*) (FPA)

IHP International House of Pancakes (*restaurant chain*) (COM)

ihp indicated horse power (SCI)

IHS in hoc signo (*Latin: in this sign (you will conquer); revelation of the Sign of the Cross to the Roman Emperor Constantine before entering battle*)

IHS immersion heater switch

IHS Iesus Hominum Salvator (*Latin: Jesus the Saviour of Mankind*)

IHT Inheritance Tax (COM)

II image intensifier (MIL)

IIEE Institution of Incorporated Executive Engineers (*estd 1987*) (SCI)

IIHF International Ice Hockey Federation (SPR)

IIP Institute of Incorporated Photographers (UNI)

IJF International Judo Federation (SPR)

IJP ink-jet printer

Ike Dwight D Eisenhower David (*1890–1972*) (*US general & Republican president 1953–61*)

IKEA Idioten kaufen eben alles (*German joke: some fools will buy anything*)

IKF International Kendo Federation (SPR)

IKP internet keyed payments (SCI)

ILA International Longshoremen's Association (UNI)

ILE Institution of Lighting Engineers (*estd 1923, incorporated 1924*) (SCI)

ILEA Inner London Education Authority

ILF International Luge Federation (SPR)

ILF Independent Living Fund (*for the disabled*)

ILGWU International Ladies' Garment Workers' Union (UNI)

ill, illo, illus illustrated; illustration (FPA)

ILLINET Illinois Library & Information Network (FPA)

illum illuminating (MIL)

ILO International Labour Organisation (*UN affiliate*) (UNI)

ILP Independent Labour Party

ILPA International League for the Protection of Horses

ILPH International League for the Protection of Horses

ILS instrument landing system

ILT infectious laryngotracheitis

ILTF International Lawn Tennis Federation (SPR)

ILU Institute of London Underwriters

ILY I love you

ILYVD I love you very dearly

IM Institute of Materials (*estd 1869, Royal Charters 1899 & 1975*) (SCI)

IMA International Music Association

IMAW International Mo(u)lders' & Allied Workers' Union (UNI)

IMC Institute of Measurement & Control (*estd as SIT 1944, Royal Charter 1975*) (SCI)

IMC Infrastructure Maintenance Company

IMC instrument meteorological conditions

IMCO International Maritime Consultative Organisation (*UN affiliate*)

IME Institute of Marine Engineers (*estd 1889, Royal Charter 1933, supplemental Charter 1973*) (SCI)

IME Institution of Mining Engineers (*estd 1889, Royal Charter 1915*) (SCI)

IMEA Incorporated Municipal Electrical Association

IMechE Institution of Mechanical Engineers (*estd 1847, Royal Charter 1930*) (SCI)

IMechIE Institution of Mechanical Incorporated Engineers (estd 1988) (SCI)

IMEP indicated mean effective pressure (*BMEP + FMEP*)

IMF International Monetary Fund (*UN affiliate*)

IMF International Myeloma Foundation

IMHO in my humble opinion

IMI Imperial Metal Industries

IMinE Institute of Mining Engineers

IMM International Money Market (*at the Chicago Mercantile Exchange*) (COM)

IMM Institution of Mining & Metallurgy (*estd 1892, Royal Charter 1915*) (SCI)

IMMTA International Money Markets Trading Association

IMMTS Indian Mercantile Marine Training Ship

IMO International Maritime Organisation (NAV)

IMP integrated mail processor

Imp Imperator; Imperatrix (*Latin: Emperor; Empress*)

imp import; importer (COM)

imp imprimatur

imp imperfect; imperial; imperative; impersonal; important

imp impression (FPA)

impf, imperf imperfect

IMR inmate medical record (PRP)

IMRO Investment Management Regulatory Organisation (COM)

IMS Indian Medical Service

IMS International Musicological Society (MUS)

IMS information management system (SCI)

IMSA International Motor Sports Association (SPR)

IMunE Institution of Municipal Engineers

IN Indian Navy

IN intelligent networking

In loc in loco (*Latin: in its place*)

in loc cit in loco citato (*Latin: in the place cited*) (FPA)

INA Institution of Naval Architects

INAROE Angolan Institute for the Removal of Explosive Objects (MIL)

inbd inboard

Inc incorporated

inc income (COM)

inc include; included; including; inclusive; increase; incomplete

incl includes; including

Incog incognito; unknown; unrecognised; in secret

IND in nomine Dei (*Latin: in the name of God*)

Ind Independent

Ind India

ind industry; industrial (COM)

ind independent; independence; indirect; indicative

ind index (FPA)

Ind Imp Indiae Imperator/rix (*Latin: Emperor/ess of India*)

indef indefinite

indic indicative; indicator; indicating

Indie The Independent (*newspaper*) (FPA)

INDOEX Indian Ocean Experiment (*meteorology*)

induc induction

INE Institution of Nuclear Engineers (*estd 1959*) (SCI)

INF intermediate-range nuclear forces (MIL)

INF international nuclear force

inf inferior; infra; infinitive; information

Inf, inf Infantry (MIL)

inf, infl influence

info information

INH into nearest hedgerow

init initial

Inkel International Nickel

INLA Irish National Liberation Army (POL)

INLORS inner London orbital route studies

Inmarsat International Maritime Satellite Organisation

INN Independent News Network (FPA)

inorg inorganic (SCI)

INQ index of nutritional quality (F&D)

INRI Iesus Nazarenus Rex Iudaeorum (*Latin: Jesus of Nazareth, King of the Jews*)

INS Immigration & Naturalization Service (*US agency*)

INS International News Service (FPA)

ins insurance; insured (COM)

ins insulated; insulation

ins, insp, Insp Inspector

insp inspect(ed)

inst instant(aneous); instrument(al); institute; institution

InstCE Institution of Civil Engineers

InstMM Institution of Mining and Metallurgy

InstP Institute of Physics (*estd 1918, Royal Charter 1970*) (SCI)

int interest (COM)

int interpreter

int interior; internal (ARC)

Int, int intelligence (MIL)

Int, int, intl international

Integer The Intelligent and Green Housing Project

INTELSAT International Tele-communications Satellite ' (SCI)

intens intensifier; intensive; intensified

inter intermediate

intercom intercommunications system (SCI)

interj interjection

Interpol International Police Organisation

interrog interrogate; interrogation; interrogative

intr intransitive

intr, introd introductory; introduction

INTSUM intelligence summary (MIL)

INTUC Indian National Trade Union Congress (COM)

INUCOSM it's no use crying over spilt milk (*don't worry, it was an inucosm*)

Inv invenit (*Latin: he designed*)

inv invoice (COM)

inv invention; invented

inv inventor

INVEST I'm not very speakable to

invt, invty inventory

IO Intelligence Officer (MIL)

IOA Institute of Acoustics (*estd 1974 from InstP Acoustics Group + BAS*) (SCI)

IOC initial/interim operational capability (MIL)

IOC International Olympics Committee (SPR)

IOE Institute of Energy (*estd 1929, Royal Charter 1946*) (SCI)

IOE inlet over exhaust

IOF International Orienteering Federation (SPR)

IOGT Independent Order of Good Templars

IOM Indian Order of Merit (*Military Division or Civil Division*)

IoM Isle of Man

IOOF Independent Order of Oddfellows

IOP Institute of Painters in Oil Colours

IOS Isles of Scilly

IOU I owe you

IoW Isle of Wight

IP International Paper Company (COM)

IP in possession (PRP)

IP Internet protocol (SCI)

IP injured party (*victim*)

IP(R) intellectual property (*rights*) (COM)

IP, IoP Institute of Plumbing (*estd 1906*) (UNI)

IPA International Police Association

IPA International Phonetic Alphabet (FPA)

IPA India Pale Ale (F&D)

IPC International Publishing Company (COM)

IPC, IPPC isopropyl n-phenyl-carbamate (a herbicide) (CHM)

IPD Institute of Personnel Development (COM)

IPE Institution of Plant Engineers (*estd 1946*) (SCI)

IPEMB (*see* BES) (SCI)

IPG Independent Publishers' Guild (FPA)

iph impressions per hour (FPA)

IPM Institute of Personnel Management (COM)

IPMA International Primary Markets Association

IPMS Institution of Professionals, Managers & Specialists (UNI)

IPPR Institute for Public Policy Research

IPR individual performance review (COM)

IPRS inmate personal record system (PRP)

IPS ingress protection standard (SCI)

IPT thermometers thermometers conforming to Institute of Petroleum technologists' standards (SCI)

IPV inter-prison visit (PRP)

Iq, iq idem quod (*Latin: the same as*)

IQA Institute of Quality Assurance (*founded 1919, incorporated 1922*) (COM)

I-Queue mail non-junk e-mail

IR Inland Revenue (COM)

IR infrared (SCI)

Ir Irish

IRA Individual Retirement Account (COM)

IRA Irish Republican Army (POL)

IRAS Infrared Astronomy Satellite (SCI)

IRB Industrial Revenue Board (COM)

IRB Irish Republican Brotherhood (POL)

IRBM intermediate range ballistic missile (MIL)

IRC International Revenue Code (*US tax laws*)

IRC International Red Cross (MIL)

IRC Innovation Relay Centre (SCI)

IRDA Industrial Research & Development Authority

Ire Ireland

IRFO International Road Freight Office

IRG Indian Resources Group

IRG immediate replenishment group (MIL)

IRIS infrared intruder system

IRIS from the Greek goddess, but advertised as 'It runs in silence' (*British car marque 1905–13*)

IRM innate releasing mechanism

IRN Independent Radio News

IRO Inland Revenue Office(r) (COM)

IRO International Refugee Organisation

IRPCS International Rules for Prevention of Collisions at Sea (*COLREGS*) (NAV)

irreg irregular; irregularly

IRS Internal Revenue Service (*US treasury agency*)

IRSF International Roller Skating Federation (SPR)

IRSP Irish Republican Socialist Party (POL)

IRSTS infrared search & track system (SCI)

IRTE Institute of Road Transport Engineers (*estd 1945*)

IRU Irish Rugby Union (SPR)

IS International Society of Sculptors, Painters and Gravers

IS internal security (MIL)

IS&DN Illustrated Sporting & Dramatic News (FPA)

ISA Independent Savings Account

ISBN International Standard Book Number(ing) (*not ISBN number*) (FPA)

ISBNs bar codes (*library*)

ISC Indian Staff Corps

ISCC Isles of Scilly Steamship Company Ltd (COM)

ISCM International Society for Contemporary Music (MUS)

ISD international subscriber dialling (SCI)

ISDA International Swaps and Derivatives Association

ISDN integrated services digital network (SCI)

ISDT International Six Days Trial (*motorcycles*) (SPR)

ISE Indian Service of Engineers

ISF International Softball Federation (SPR)

ISF International Surfing Federation (SPR)

ISIN International Securities Identification Number

ISM Incorporated Society of Musicians (MUS)

ISM Incorporated Society of Museums

ISMA International Securities Markets Association

ISO Companion of the Imperial Service Order

ISO International Standards Organisation

ISO Imperial Service Order

ISO International Space Observatory

ISO rating film speed (FPA)

ISOS integrated software on silicon

Isoworg International Society for World Government (*1971 thriller by the Earl of Portland*) (FPA)

ISP internet service provider (SCI)

ISPA Internet Service Providers' Association (SCI)

ISRF International Squash Rackets Federation (SPR)

ISSN International Standard Serial Number(ing) (*periodicals*) (FPA)

ISTC Iron & Steel Trades Confederation (UNI)

Isth, isth isthmus

IStructE Institution of Structural Engineers (*estd 1908, Royal Charter 1934*) (SCI)

ISU International Skating Union (SPR)

ISU International Shooting Union (SPR)

IT Italy (MIL)

IT information technology (SCI)

IT Indian Territory (*US*)

It Italy; Italian

ITA Independent Television Authority (*became IBA 1990*) (FPA)

ITA International Trampolining Association (SPR)

ITA, ita Initial Teaching Alphabet (FPA)

Ital Italian

ital italic (*type*) (FPA)

ITC investment tax credit (*US*) (COM)

ITC Independent Television Commission (FPA)

Iter international thermonuclear experimental reactor

ITM inch trim moment (*moment to change trim one inch*)

ITMA Institute of Trade Marks Agents

ITMA It's That Man Again (*WW2 weekly comedy radio show featuring Tommy Handley – who came to be looked upon as 'that man', though it originally referred to Adolf Hitler*) (FPA)

ITN Independent Television News

ITO International Trade Organisation (COM)

ITSA Information Technology Services Agency (SCI)

ITT International Telephone & Telegraph Corporation (COM)

ITT immersed tube tunnel (*subsea equivalent of cut-and-cover*) (SCI)

ITTF International Table Tennis Federation (SPR)

ITU International Telecommunications Union (*US affiliate*) (COM)

ITV Independent Television (FPA)

ITV interactive television (FPA)

ITWF International Tug-of-War Federation (SPR)

IUHS Independent Union of Halifax Staff (UNI)

IUKEA Inside UK Enterprise Awards

IUMA Internet underground music archive (MUS)

IUPAC International Union of Pure & Applied Chemistry

iv initial velocity (SCI)

IVB Invalidity Benefit

IVF International Volleyball Federation (SPR)

ivr instantaneous velocity of reaction (SCI)

IW isotopic weight (SCI)

IW individual weapon (MIL)

IWA Inland Waterways Authority

IWA Institute of World Affairs

IWC International Whaling Commission

IWF International Weightlifting Federation (SPR)

IWM Imperial War Museum (MIL)

IWMA International Working Men's Association (COM)

IWO Institution of Water Officers (*estd 1945*)

IWS International Wool Secretariat (COM)

IWW Industrial Workers of the World ('*Wobblies*') (COM)

IWW International Workers of the World (COM)

IX ion exchange (SCI)

IY Imperial Yeomanry

IYDLAOTMTFOAHABM If you don't like anything on the menu, then f off and have a big Mac (*at the foot of the menu at The Talkhouse, Stanton St John, Oxford*)

IYRU International Yacht Racing Union (SPR)

IZ I Zingari (*cricket club*)

J

J journal (FPA)

J joule(s) (SCI)

J current density (SCI)

J yellow in names of dyestuffs (CHM)

J jack

J US airfare business class premium

j jemand (*German: somebody*)

J A M Whistler James Abbott McNeill (*US artist, 1834–1903*)

J B Priestley John Boynton (*English novelist, 1894–1984*)

J C Bach Johann Christian (*German composer, 1735–1782*)

J C F Bach Johann Christoph Friedrich (*German composer, 1732–95*)

J D Salinger Jerome David (*US writer, 1919–*)

J display modified A display with circular time base (SCI)

J Edgar Hoover John (*US lawyer & director of FBI, 1895–1972*)

J M W Turner Joseph Mallord William (*English painter, 1775–1851*)

J R R Tolkien John Ronald Reuel (*English author, 1892–1973*)

J S Bach Johann Sebastian
(*German composer, 1685–1750*)

J, JJ Judge; Judges

J, JJ Justice; Justices

JA joint account (COM)

JA Junior Achievement (US)

JA Judge Advocate

J-acid intermediate for dyestuffs
(CHM)

JAG Judge Advocate General (MIL)

JAL Japan Air Lines

JAMS Journal of the American
Musicological Society (MUS)

J-antenna dipole fed and matched
at the end of 1/4-wavelength line
(SCI)

JAP Jewish American Prince/Princess

JAP JA Prestwich

JAPE joke analysis production
engine (*computer program shown
on BBC's Tomorrows World*)

Jas James

JASNA Jane Austen Society of
North America (FPA)

JAT Jugoslovenski Aerotransport

JATO jet-assisted take off

JATP Jazz at the Philharmonic
(MUS)

Jaycees Junior Chamber of
Commerce (*see* JCC) (COM)

JBAA Journal of the British
Archaeological Association (FPA)

JC Job Club (PRP)

JC Jesus Christ

JC Julius Caesar

JC Jockey Club (SPR)

JCAEU Joint Committee on
Appliances, Equipment &
Uniform (FRS)

J-carrier system broadband
carrier telephony system (SCI)

JCB Joseph Cyril Bamford
(*manufacturer of JCBs*)

JCC Junior Chamber of Commerce
(*now officially JAYCEES*) (COM)

JCD Doctor of Canon Law (*Latin:
Juris Canonici Doctor*)

JCD Doctor of Civil Law (Latin:
Juris Civilis Doctor)

JCFBC Joint Committee on Fire
Brigade Communications (FRS)

JCFBO Joint Committee on Fire
Brigade Operations (FRS)

JCI JAYCEES International (COM)

JCJDMU Jewel Case & Jewellery
Display Makers' Union (*1894–
1996*) (UNI)

JCL job control language (SCI)

JCR Junior Common Room

JCS Joint Chiefs of Staff (MIL)

jct, uctn junction

JD juris/jurum doctor (*Latin:
Doctor of Jurisprudence/Laws*)

JD juvenile delinquent

JDL Jewish Defense League (US
action group)

Jerome K Jerome Klapka (*author of
Three Men in a Boat, 1859–1927*)

Jes Jesus

JESSI Joint European Submicron
Silicon Initiative

JET Joint European Torus (SCI)

JET Scheme Jobs, Education &
Training Scheme (*Australian
Government*)

JFET junction field effect
transistor (SCI)

JFf Junior Firefighter (FRS)

JFK John Fitzgerald Kennedy

JFPC Joint Fire Prevention
Committee (FRS)

JG, jg jolly good

JHQ Joint Headquarters (MIL)

Jhr Jonkheer

JICTAR Joint Industry Committee
for Television Advertising
Research (FPA)

JIT just in time

JJ Sir Joseph John Thomson (*1856–1940; physicist and discoverer of the electron, 1897*)

JJ Judges

JJ Justices

JKG John Kenneth Galbraith (*US economist, 1908–*)

jls Journals

j-m jemandem (*German: to somebody*)

j-n jemanden (German: somebody (accusative))

jnd just noticeable difference

JOCO Journal of Canine Obedience

Joh or Jno John

JOY Jubilee Outreach Yorkshire

JP Justice of the Peace

Jp Japan(ese)

JPC Joint Pensions Committee (FRS)

JPEG Joint Photographic Experts Group (FPA)

JPL Jet Propulsion Laboratories

JPL John Player League (*cricket*) (SPR)

JPT jet pipe temperature (SCI)

JR Judge's Remand (PRP)

JR John Ross Ewing Jr (*ruthless character in TV series Dallas*)

JRDF joint rapid deployment force (MIL)

j-s jemandes (*German: of somebody*)

JSA Job Seekers' Allowance

jsc qualified at a Junior Staff Course, or the equivalent, 1942–46

JSCP joint strategic capabilities plan (MIL)

JSD Doctor of Juristic Science

jssc Joint Services Staff Course

JSSL Joint Services School for Languages

JSSU Joint Services Signals Unit (MIL)

jt joint

JTC Joint Training Committee (FRS)

JUB jack-up barge (SCI)

JUD juris utriusque doctor (*Latin: Doctor of Canon & Civil Law*)

JUGFET junction-gate field effect transistor (SCI)

JUMPER Joint Unit for Minorities Policy & Research

Jun Junior

Jun Opt Junior Optime

JV joint venture (COM)

JVP Sri Lankan Left-wing Peoples' Liberation Front

JWT J Walter Thompson (*an advertising agency*) (COM)

JWV Jewish War Veterans

JY Jimmy Young

K

K khat (*catha edulis, a drug*) (PRP)

K kindergarten

K equilibrium constant (SCI)

K kaon; K-meson (SCI)

K unit of 1024 words, bits or bytes (*distinguish from k = 1,000*) (SCI)

K US airfare: thrift

k kilo (*of drugs*) (PRP)

k Boltzmann constant (SCI)

k radius of gyration (SCI)

k velocity constant of a chemical reaction (SCI)

k mass transfer coefficient (SCI)

K computer Kitchen (*home-made by George Stibitz 1937*) (SCI)

K ration emergency rations in WW2 (*after Ancel Keys*) (MIL)

K/T boundary cretaceous/tertiary boundary

K2 the world's second highest mountain 8611m (28,200ft), in the Karakoram Range on the Kashmir–Xinjiang Uygir AR border – also called Mount Godwin Austen

K9 Star Wars dog robot (*canine*) (FPA)

KA Knight of the Order of Australia

K-acid an intermediate in dyestuff manufacture (SCI)

KAMP (*US police reports*) known as male prostitutes

Kans Kansas (*US*)

KANU Kenya African National Union

KAR King's African Rifles (MIL)

KB knockback (PRP)

KB King's Bench

KB Knight Bachelor

KB, kbyte 1,024 bytes (SCI)

KBE Knight Commander of the Most Excellent Order of the British Empire (*not if GBE*)

Kbit 1,024 bits (SCI)

KBS knowledge-based system (SCI)

KC King's Counsel

KC Kansas City

KC, KofC Knights of Columbus (*US fraternal organisation*)

KCB Knight Commander of the Most Honourable Order of the Bath (not if GCB)

KCC Commander of Order of Crown, Belgian and Congo Free State

KCH King's College Hospital

KCH Knight Commander of Hanover

KCH Honorary Chaplain to the King

KCIE Knight Commander of the Most Eminent Order of the Indian Empire (*not if GCIE*)

KCL King's College, London

KCLJ Knight Commander of the Order of St Lazarus of Jerusalem (*not if GCLJ*)

KCMG Knight Commander of the Most Distinguished Order of St Michael & St George (*not if GCMG*)

KCR Kimmidge Cross Roads (*Dublin*)

KCSG Knight Commander of St Gregory

KCSI Knight Commander of the Most Excellent Order of the Star of India (*not if GCSI*)

KCSS Knight Commander of St Silvester

KCVO Knight Commander of the Royal Victorian Order (*not if GCVO*)

KD knocked down (*machinery in parts*) (COM)

KDF Kraft durch Freude (*German: strength through joy*) (POL)

KDG King's Dragoon Guards

KE kinetic energy (SCI)

Keb Keble College, Oxford

KEH King Edward's Horse

Kelpra Studio silkscreen printmakers founded by Chris Prater & Rose Kelby (FPA)

Ken Dodd PHD prepares hot dinners

KF&R Knight, Frank & Rutley (*now Knight Frank*) (COM)

KFAT [National Union of] Knitwear, Footwear and Apparel Trades

KFC Kentucky Fried Chicken (F&D)

KG Knight of the Most Noble Order of the Garter (*not ladies of the Order*)

KGB Komitet Gosudarstvennoye Bezhopaznosti (*Russian: Committee of State Security – Russian secret police*) (MIL)

KGStJ Knight of Grace, Order of St John of Jerusalem

KHDS Honorary Dental Surgeon to the King

KHNS Honorary Nursing Sister to the King

KHP Honorary Physician to the King

KHS Honorary Surgeon to the King

KHS Knight of the Holy Sepulchre

KIA killed in action (MIL)

KICC Kingsway International Christian Centre (*East London Evangelical Church*)

KiH Kaisar-i-Hind (Emperor of India; medal)

KISS keep it simple, stupid (*superseded by keep it short & simple*)

KJV King James' Version (of the Bible) (FPA)

KKIA King Khalid International Airport (*Kingdom of Saudi Arabia*)

KKK Ku Klux Klan (*Greek: kuklos – circle*)

KL Kuala Lumpur

KLJ Knight of the Order of St Lazarus of Jerusalem

KLM Koninklijke Luchtvaart Maatschappij (*Royal Dutch Airlines*)

Kmeson kaon (SCI)

kn US airfare: night/off-peak thrift discounted

KO Coca-Cola Company (COM)

KO knock(ed) out (SPR)

KORR King's Own Royal Regiment

KOSB King's Own Scottish Borderers (*not to be called 'Cosby'*) (MIL)

KOYLI King's Own Yorkshire Light Infantry (*not to be called 'Coyly'*) (MIL)

KP Knights of Pythias

KP Knight of the Order of St Patrick

KP Kitchen Police (*USA*) (MIL)

KPD Kommunistische Partei Deutschlands (*German Communist Party*) (POL)

KPFSM King's Police & Fire Services Medal for Gallantry

KPI key performance indicator

KPM King's Police Medal

KRL knowledge representation language (SCI)

KR-law *see* CR-law

KRR King's Royal Rifles

KRRC King's Royal Rifle Corps

KSA Kingdom of Saudi Arabia

KSG Knight of St Gregory

KSLI King's Shropshire Light Infantry

KStJ Knight of the Order of St John of Jerusalem

KT Knight of the Most Ancient & Most Noble Order of the Thistle (*not ladies of the order*)

Kt Knight

KWIC keyword in context (SCI)

KWOC keyword out of contaxt (SCI)

KYTV spoof TV station, based on jelly (FPA)

L

L loss (COM)

L Lodge

L Labour (*Socialist*) (POL)

L live

L large

L learner driver

L Licentiate (*in titles*)

L angular momentum (SCI)

L symbol for molar latent heat (SCI)

L symbol for Avogadro constant (SCI)

L inductor, self-inductance (SCI)

L latent heat (SCI)

L Linnaeus (SCI)

L symbol for molar conductance (SCI)

L symbol for Ao at infinite dilution (SCI)

L lunch (F&D)

L lift

L US air fare: thrift discounted

l symbol for specific latent heat per gramme (SCI)

l symbol for mean free path of molecules (SCI)

l (with subscript) equivalent ionic conductance, 'mobility' (SCI)

l lepton number (SCI)

l radioactive decay constant (SCI)

l mean free path (SCI)

l laevorotatory (*rotating the plane of polarisation of a polarised ray of light to the left*) (CHM)

L display a radar display in which the target appears as two horizontal pulses, left and right from a central vertical time base, varying in amplitude according to accuracy of aim (NAV)

L ès L Licencié ès lettres

L Mus LCM Licentiate in Music, London College of Music (MUS)

L Mus TCL Licentiate in Music, Trinity College of Music, London (MUS)

L of C Lines of Communication

L T low tension (SCI)

L, l league; left; length; line; low; link

L, l leaf (SCI)

L, l lake

L, l, lib liber (*Latin: book*) (FPA)

L, Lat Latin (FPA)

L, lg, lge large

L, lgth length (SCI)

L, Lib Liberal

L/Cpl Lance-Corporal (MIL)

L/P letterpress (FPA)

L/R left/right

L'pool Liverpool

L4 light 4-wheel drive vehicle (FRS)

LA lesbian activities (PRP)

LA Local Authority

LA Legislative Assembly

LA Library Association

LA local agent

LA Los Angeles (CA)

LA local anaesthetic

LAB Laboratories for Applied Biology Ltd (COM)

Lab Labrador

lab labour; laboratory

LAC leading aircraftman (MIL)

LACW leading aircraftwoman (MIL)

LAD Light Aid Detachment (*Reme*) (MIL)

LAES Latin American Economic System (*aka SELA*) (COM)

laevo- left (*Latin: laevus (prefix)*) (CHM)

LAFTA Latin-American Free Trade Area pre-1981 (*now LAIA*)

LAIA Latin-American Integration Association (*formerly LAFTA*)

LAID comedians get – laughter affected infective disease/ laughter addicted inferiority disease

LA-LA land Los Angeles area

lam laminated

LAMDA London Academy of Music & Dramatic Arts (FPA)

LAN local area network (SCI)

Lancs Lancashire

LANDSAT land satellite (*producing terrestrial images*) (SCI)

lang language (SCI)

LAPADA The Association of Art and Antique Dealers (FPA)

LAPD Los Angeles Police Department

LAS Las Vegas (NV)

Laser light amplification by stimulated emission of radiation (SCI)

LASMO London & Scottish Marine Oil (COM)

Lat latitude

LAUTRO Life Assurance & Unit Trust Regulatory Organisation (*see* P/A) (COM)

lav lavatory

LB local battery (SCI)

LB linebacker (*American football*) (SPR)

lb s t static thrust (SCI)

L-band radio-frequency band between 390 & 1550MHz (FPA)

LBB/W locks, bolts & bars/ windows (PRP)

LBC London Brick Company (COM)

LBC large bayonet cap (SCI)

LBCM Licentiate of the Bandsmen's College of Music (MUS)

LBD little black dress

LBF London Bookfair (FPA)

LBJ Lyndon Baines Johnson (*1908– 73 USA president, 1963–69*)

LBMA London Bullion Market Association

lb-mol pound-mol (*the mass of compound equal to its molecular weight in pounds (obsolete)*) (SCI)

LBO leveraged buyout (*pronounced to rhyme with feather-edged*) (COM)

LBO last but one

LBS Little Black Sambo (FPA)

LBV late bottled vintage (F&D)

LBW, lbw leg before wicket (cricket) (SPR)

LC letter of credit (COM)

LC Library of Congress (*Washington DC*) (FPA)

lc lower case (FPA)

lc left centre (FPA)

LC coupling inductor output load of an amplifier circuit is connected through a capacitor to the input of another circuit (SCI)

lc, loc cit loco citato (*Latin: in the place cited*)

LCC London County Council (*pre GLC*)

LCC linear cutting cord (*aircraft escape aid – see* MDC) (MIL)

LCCIEB London Chamber of Commerce and Industry Exams Board (*and an associated publishing house*)

LCD liquid crystal display (SCI)

LCDLVC Library of Congress Digital Library Visitors' Center (FPA)

LCF London College of Fashion

LCH London Clearing House

LCh Licentiatus Chirurgiae (*Latin: Licentiate in Surgery*)

LCJ Lord Chief Justice

LCL less than carload lot (COM)

LCM landing craft, mechanised/ medium (*US Navy*) (MIL)

LCN load classification number

LCP Licentiate of the College of Preceptors

LCT landing craft, tank (*US Navy*) (MIL)

LD Liberal Democrat

ld load (COM)

ld lead (FPA)

LDDC London Docklands Development Corporation

Ldg leading

LDiv Licentiate in Divinity

LDMA London Discount Market Association

LDR latest date of release (*now SED*) (PRP)

LDS laus Deo semper (*Latin: praise be to God for ever*)

LDS Latter-Day Saint(s) (*Church of Jesus Christ of; Mormons*)

LDS Licentiate of Dental Surgery

LDV Local Defence Volunteers (*later the Home Guard*)

LEA Local Education Authority

lea league

lea leather

LED licence expiry date (PRP)

LED light-emitting diode (SCI)

led ledger (COM)

LEFTA Lower Esk Freemen's Tidal Association

Leg legislature; legislation

leg legal

leg legate

Legco Legislative Council

LEL Letitia Elizabeth Landon (*poet, novelist and mild scandaleuse, 1802–38. Afterwards Mrs Maclean*)

LEM Lunar Excursion Module (SCI)

LEN Ligue Européenne de Natation (*French: European Swimming League*) (SPR)

LEO low earth orbit (SCI)

LEO Lyons Electronic Office (SCI)

LEP large electron-positron collider (SCI)

lepido- prefix (*Greek lepis, lepidos; a scale*) (SCI)

LEPRA Leprosy Relief Association

LET linear energy transfer (*the linear rate of energy dissipation by particulate or RM radiation while penetrating absorbing media*) (SCI)

LETS Local Exchange Trading Scheme (COM)

leuco- leuko- prefix from Greek leukos, white (SCI)

lex lexicon (FPA)

lexicog lexicographer; lexicography; lexicographical (FPA)

LF scam long firm scam (*obtaining goods without paying therefor*) (PRP)

LFA less-favoured areas

LFA London Football Association (SPR)

LFCOp Leading Fire Control Operator (FRS)

LFf Leading Firefighter (FRS)

L-forms morphological variants developed from large bodies by prolonged exposure to various treatments (SCI)

LFPS Licentiate of the Faculty of Physicians and Surgeons

LFT live fire trial

LG liquid gold (*amyl nitrite*) (PRP)

LG David Lloyd George (1863–1945; British Prime Minister 1916–22)

LG Literary Guild (FPA)

LG low German (FPA)

LG Life Guards

LGCM Lesbian & Gay Christian Movement

LGF light gasworks feedstock (*deprecated term for low flash-point petroleum distillates which are unsuitable for use in ICEs*) *see* LPF (SCI)

LGSM Licentiate of the Guildhall School of Music & Drama (MUS)

LGU Ladies' Golf Union

LGV light goods vehicle (*taxation class*)

LH Lufthansa (*German airline*)

LH, lh left hand

LHA local hour angle (*distance of the local celestial meridian west of Greenwich*) (NAV)

LHD Litterarum Humaniorum Doctor (*Latin: Doctor of Humane Letters*)

LHD, lhd left-hand drive

L-head petrol-engine cylinder head carrying the inlet & exhaust valves in a pocket at one side (SCI)

LHS left-hand side

LI Light Infantry (MIL)

Lib Liberal (POL)

lib liberty (PRP)

lib library; librarian

LIBA London Investment Banking Association

Lib-Dem Liberal Democrat (POL)

LIBID London inter-bank bid rate

LIBOR London inter-bank offered rate

Lic Licenciado (*Spanish: Lawyer*)

Lic Med Licentiate in Medicine

Lic S Licentiate in Surgery

Lic. Med Licentiate of Medicine

LIDS local inmate database system (PRP)

Lieut, Lt Lieutenant (MIL)

LIFE European Environment Fund

LIFO last in, first out (*redundancy & computer memory*) (SCI)

LILO last in, last out (*redundancy & computer memory*) (SCI)

LIMP London information meetings pilot (*trial scheme for saving marriages*)

LIMS Laboratory Information Management Service (COM)

LINC Language in the National Curriculum (*Government-sponsored educational project 1989–91 under Professor Ronald Carter*)

Linear A an ancient system of writing (FPA)

Linear B an ancient system of writing (FPA)

LINX London Internet Exchange (*documents*)

LIPA Liverpool Institute of Performing Arts (FPA)

LIRMA London International Insurance and Reinsurance Market Association

L-iron a structural member of wrought-iron or rolled steel, having an L-shaped cross section (*angle iron*) (SCI)

LISA London International School of Acting (FPA)

LISP list processing (SCI)

LIST library & information selective targeting (FPA)

Lit Hum Literae Humaniores (*Latin: Faculty of classics and philosophy, Oxford*)

LitB, LittB Litterarum Baccalaureus (*Latin: Bachelor of Letters, Bachelor of Literature*)

LitD, LittD Litterarum Doctor (*Latin: Doctor of Letters, Doctor of Literature*)

lith lithograph; lithography (FPA)

lithol lithology

LJ Library Journal (FPA)

LJ(J) Lord Justice(s)

LL legal letter (PRP)

LL Lord Lieutenant

LL low Latin; late Latin (FPA)

LL Lloyd's of London

ll lines (FPA)

LLA Ladies' Lacrosse Association (SPR)

LLA Lady Literate in Arts

LLAD low level air defence (MIL)

LLB Legum Baccalaureus (*Latin: Bachelor of Laws*)

LLC Leica Leitz Camera

LLCM Licentiate of the London College of Music (MUS)

LLCM (TD) Licentiate of the London College of Music (*Teaching Diploma*) (MUS)

LLD Legum Doctor (*Latin: Doctor of Laws*)

L-leucine colourless flakes formed by the decomposition of albuminous substances. Amino acid essential for maintenance of growth in rats (CHM)

LLL Licentiate in Laws

LLM Legum Magister (*Latin: Master of Laws*)

LLO Lifer Liaison Officer (PRP)

LM Licentiate of Midwifery

LMBC Lady Margaret Boat Club

LMCC Licentiate of Medical Council of Canada

LMF lacking/lack of moral fibre (*one-time military term for cowardice, now replaced by counselling and compensation*) (MIL)

LMG light machine gun (MIL)

LMH Lady Margaret Hall (*aka London, Midland & Hottish*)

LMP lemon meringue pie (F&D)

LMS Local Management Of Schools

LMS level measuring set (SCI)

LMSSA Licentiate in Medicine & Surgery, Society of Apothecaries

LMU Lifer Management Unit (PRP)

LMVD Licenced Motor Vehicle Dealer

Ln linen

LNat Liberal National

LNG liquefied natural gas (SCI)

LNLC Ladies' Naval Luncheon Club (MIL)

LNSM Local Non-Stipendiary Minister

LO liaison officer (MIL)

LOA length overall (NAV)

LOB left on base (*baseball*) (SPR)

LOB lift of body (prams)

loc locating (MIL)

loc cit loco citato (*Latin: in the place cited*) (FPA)

LOFIT London Organised Fraud Investigation Team (*the 'DHS SAS' targeting organised Housing Benefit fraud*)

LOFTE line orientated flight training exercises (*in a simulator*)

log logarithm

log logistic (MIL)

log dec logarithmic decrement (SCI)

Loisada Latino contraction of Manhattan's Lower East Side

LOLNAD little old lady with no actual disease

LOMBARD loads of money but a right dickhead

Londin Bishop of London

Long longitude

longi- prefix (*Latin longus: long*) (SCI)

Lonrho London & Rhodesia Mining and Land Company

LOP loss of privileges (PRP)

LOP line of position (*a bearing or other indication that a vessel is on a particular line*) (NAV)

LOPE Live on Planet Earth (*youth service*)

loq loquitur (*Latin: he/she speaks*)

lorac-A system with a master & 2 slave radio stations (NAV)

lorac-B system A with the addition of a reference radio station (NAV)

LORAN long range navigational system (*measures differences in time of radio signals from widely dispersed stations – accurate to within 200m*) (NAV)

LOT Polskie Linie Lotnicze (*Polish Airlines*)

LOX, lox liquid oxygen (CHM)

LP Lord Provost

LP long-playing record (*33rpm*) (MUS)

LP large portly

LP compressor low-pressure compressor (SCI)

LP stage low-pressure turbine stage (SCI)

LP turbine low-pressure turbine (SCI)

LP, lp low pressure (SCI)

LPA The London Academy of Performing Arts (FPA)

LPF light petroleum feedstock (*same as LGF*) (SCI)

LPG liquefied petroleum gas (*eg propane & butane*) (CHM)

L-plate (red L) learner driver sign

LPO London Philharmonic Orchestra (MUS)

LPP light portable pump (*below 1600 lpm*) (FRS)

LPS Lord Privy Seal

LPTB London Passenger Transport Board

LR left rear

LR living room

LRA Lord's Resistance Army (*Northern Uganda*)

LRAM Licentiate of the Royal Academy of Music (MUS)

LRATGW long range anti tank guided weapon (MIL)

LRC Local Review Committee (PRP)

LRCPE Licentiate Royal College of Physicians, Edinburgh

LRCS Licentiate of the Royal College of Surgeons

LRCSE Licentiate of the Royal College of Surgeons, Edinburgh

LRCVS Licentiate of the Royal College of Veterinary Surgeons

L-rest lathe rest used in hand turning shaped like an inverted L (SCI)

LRFPS Licentiate of the Royal Faculty of Physicians and Surgeons

LRIBA Licentiate Royal Institute of British Architects

LRINF longer-range nuclear forces (MIL)

LRS London Research Station (*of British Gas*) (COM)

LRSC Licentiate of the Royal Society of Chemistry

LS, ls locus sigilli (*Latin: place of seal*)

LSA Licentiate of the Society of Apothecaries

LSAT Law School Admissions Test

LSB least significant bit (SCI)

LSD lysergic acid diethylamide (PRP)

LSD League for Spiritual Discovery (*Timothy Leary*)

LSD landing-ship, dock (*US Navy*) (MIL)

Lsd librae, solidi, denarii (*Latin: pounds, (£), shillings and pence*)

LSE London School of Economics

LSE London Stock Exchange

L-section section or half-section of a wave filter, having one shunt and one series arm (SCI)

LSI large scale integration (SCI)

LSO London Symphony Orchestra (MUS)

LST landing-ship, tank (*US Navy*) (MIL)

LSW light support weapon (MIL)

LSWS London Society for Women's Service (*formerly Suffrage – non-militant organisation led by Dame Millicent Fawcett*)

LSZ limited speed zone (*NZ*)

LT London Transport (COM)

LT low-tension

Lt Cdr Lieutenant Commander (MIL)

LT Col, Lt Col Lieutenant Colonel

Lt Gen Lieutenant General

Lt Gov Lieutenant Governor

Lt, Lieut Lieutenant

LTA Lawn Tennis Association (SPR)

LTC Leaseway Transportation Corporation (COM)

LTC Lawn Tennis Club (SPR)

LTCL Licentiate of Trinity College of Music, London (MUS)

Ltd Limited (*Liability Company*) (COM)

LTh Licentiate in Theology

LTI long-term inmate (PRP)

LTNS long time no see

LTRB Long Term Review Board (PRP)

LTSC Licentiate of the Tonic Sol-fa College (MUS)

LTU Luft Transport Union

LTV Ling-Temco-Vaught (COM)

LU lighting unit (FRS)

LU loudness unit (SCI)

lug lugsail

LUL London Underground Limited

LUOTC London University Officers' Training Corps

Luth Lutheran

LUTr lighting unit trailer (FRS)

Luxair Société Luxembourgeoise de Navigation Aérienne

LV luncheon voucher

LVFF Lloyds Forces Volunteer Fund (MIL)

LVIS low vision intensifier system (SCI)

LVMH Louis Vuitton Moët Hennessy (*French luxury goods conglomerate*) (COM)

LVO Lieutenant of the Royal Victorian Order (*not if GCVO &/ or KCVO or DCVO &/or CVO*)

LW long wave (SCI)

LW low water (tide) (NAV)

LWB long wheelbase

LWE long white envelope (*in competition circles, usually contains notification of success*)

LWL load waterline (NAV)

LWL, lwl length (at) waterline

LWM low water mark

LWT London Weekend Television (FPA)

LX low expansion foam (FRS)

LXX septuagint (FPA)

LZ loading zone (MIL)

M

M morphine (PRP)

M member

M master

M middle

M microwave

M Majesty

M Marquis

m male

M member (*in titles*)

M Monsieur (*French: Mr*)

M em (*width of square type body*) (FPA)

M mature audience (*over 15 in Australia*) (FPA)

M moment of force (SCI)

M Messier's Catalogue of stars & nebulae; an entry therein (SCI)

M general symbol for a metal or an electropositive radical (SCI)

M relative molecular mass (SCI)

M modulus (SCI)

M medi(a)eval

M mach

m mass (SCI)

m molality (SCI)

m meridian (SCI)

m- mesa- (CHM)

m- meta- (*containing a benzeze nucleus substituted in the 1, 3 positions*) (CHM)

M and Ms drugs in pill form (PRP)

M Brit IRE Member of the British Institute of Radio Engineers

M curve relationship between the refractive modulus& height above the earth's surface (SCI)

M display radar A display in which a pedestal signal is manipulated by a control calibrated in distance along the baseline until it meets the horizontal of the target break (NAV)

M du C Médaille du Canada (*French: Canada Medal – French-speaking Canadians (see* CM)*)

M Inst CE Member of the Institute of Civil Engineers

m m f magnetomotive force (SCI)

m p melting point (SCI)

M Q metol-quinol or metol-hydroquinone developers (SCI)

M to F Monday to Friday (PRP)

M&B May & Baker (COM)

M&G Marine and General

M&S Marks & Spencer (COM)

M&W Moore & Wright (*toolmakers*) (COM)

M&W Morecambe & Wise (*comedians*) (FPA)

M, m mutual inductance (SCI)

m, masc masculine

M, Mc, Mac son of (*prefix in Irish Gaelic & Scottish names*)

M, MM Monsieur/Messieurs (*French: Sir(s)*)

M/N ratio in radiation chemistry, the ion yield (SCI)

M-1 rifle semi-automatic weapon (MIL)

M-1000 American motor race (SPR)

MA Master of Arts MA Museums' Association (FPA)

Ma, ma mother

MAAF Mediterranean Allied Air Forces

MAAS Member of the American Academy of Arts and Sciences

MAB Metropolitan Asylums Board

MAC multiplexed analogue component (FPA)

Maced Macedonia(n)

mach machine; machinery

mach machinist

MACHO massive compact halo objects (SCI)

MAD mutual assured destruction (*USA*) (MIL)

MAD Mothers Against Death (*'neater' writes Ben Elton in his* Popcorn *than 'against violence and murder. But that would have spelt MAVAM'*) (FPA)

Madag Madagascar; Malagasy

MAEE Marine Aircraft Experimental Establishment

MAFF Ministry of Agriculture, Fisheries & Food

MAG *Museums & Galleries (Magazine)* (FPA)

mag magazine (FPA)

mag magnet; magnetic; magnetism (SCI)

mag magneto

MAG Mines Advisory Group

MAG MAG International Consultants

Magd Magdalen; Magdalene

MAgr Master of Agriculture

MAI Magister in Arte Ingeniaria (*Latin: Master of Engineering*)

maint maintain (MIL)

Maj major

Mal Malaya(n)

MALAYA my anxious lips await your arrival

MAM, mam maximum authorised mass (SCI)

Man Manila (FPA)

MAO monoamine oxidise inhibitor

MAOT mobile air operations team (MIL)

MAOU Member of the American Ornithologists' Union

MAP Ministry of Aircraft production

MAPLES Melanoma and Pigmented Lesion Evaluation Study

MAR microanalytical reagent (*a standard of purity which indicates that a reagent is suitable for use in microanalysis*) (CHM)

mar maritime

MArch Master of Architecture

marg marginal

marg, marge margarine (F&D)

Marq Marquis; Marquess

MARS Modern Architectural Research Association

Marv Marvetol (*children's laxative sometimes mixed with cocaine*) (PRP)

MARV manoeuvrable re-entry vehicle (SCI)

MAS Motorscaf i Anti-Sommergibili (*Italian motorboat*)

MASCE Member of the American Society of Civil Engineers

MASER molecular amplification by stimulated emission of radiation (SCI)

MASH Mobile Army Surgical Hospital (MIL)

MASME Member of the American Society of Mechanical Engineers

MASTA Mechanical Advisory Service for Travellers Abroad

MAT motivational analysis test

mat matrix (FPA)

mat material (MIL)

mat matinée (FPA)

max maximum

MAXL maximum potential licence period (PRP)

MAYC Methodist Associating Youth Clubs

MB Medal of Bravery (*Canada*)

MB Bachelor of Medicine

MB megabyte (SCI)

MB/D Medicinae Baccalaureus/Doctor (*Latin: Bachelor/Doctor of Medicine*)

MB/D Musicae Baccalaureus/Doctor (*Latin: Bachelor/Doctor of Music*)

MBA Master of Business Administration

MBD minimum brain damage

MBE Member of the Most Excellent Order of the British Empire (*not if GBE &/or KBE or DBE &/or CBE &/or OBE*)

MBI management buy-in (COM)

MBO management buy-out (COM)

MBO management by objectives (COM)

MBOU Member of the British Ornithologists' Union

MBT main battle tank (MIL)

MBU, M&BU Mother & Baby Unit (PRP)

MC Member of Congress (*USA*)

MC Master Of Ceremonies

MC medium capacity (*bomb*) (MIL)

MC Military Cross (MIL)

MC medium coeli (*Latin: mid-heaven*) (SCI)

MCA Manchester Cruising Association (NAV)

MCB miniature circuit breaker (SCI)

MCC Marylebone Cricket Club (SPR)

MCD Movement for Christian Democracy

MCDOA Minewarfare & Clearance Diving Officers' Association (MIL)

MCE Master of Civil Engineering

MCh Master of Surgery

MChD Master of Dental Surgery

MCMES Member of Civil and Mechanical Engineers Society

MCMV mine counter measures vessels

MCom Master of Commerce

MConsE Member of the Association of Consulting Engineers

MCP male chauvinist pig

MCP, MCPA a selective weedkiller (CHM)

MCPB a weedkiller (CHM)

MCPS Mechanical Copyright Protection Society (COM)

MCR Monte Carlo Rally (SPR)

Mcrit critical Mach number

MCS Madras Civil Service

MCT Minack Chronicles Trust (*20-acre Cornish animal & nature sanctuary established by author Derek Tangye (1912–96)*)

MD managing director (COM)

MD mentally deficient

MD Doctor of Medicine (*see* MB)

MDB multi therapy di Bella (*controversial cancer treatment from the Italian retired Professor Luigi di Bella*)

MDC miniature detonating cord (*to blow away aircraft cockpit canopy prior to ejection*) (MIL)

MDC Max Delbruck Centre (*for muscular medicine, Berlin*)

m-derived network electric wave-filter element which is derived from a normal (constant K) element by transformation, the aim being to obtain more desirable impedance character-istics than is possible in the prototype (SCI)

MDF main distribution frame (SCI)

MDS Master of Dental Surgery

MDS, MMDS multipoint microwave distribution system (FPA)

mdse merchandise (COM)

MDT mandatory drugs testing (PRP)

MDU Medical Defence Union

ME Methodist Episcopal

Me meter point

Me Maître (*French: master*)

ME most excellent (*in titles*)

ME mechanical engineer

ME mining engineer

ME middle English (FPA)

ME marine engineer (SCI)

Me methyl (*-CH3 radical, as in 'synthesis by the methyl-ethyl-futile method'*) (CHM)

Me general symbol for metal (CHM)

m-e meine (*German: my*)

MEC Member of the Executive Council

MECC Middle East Council of Churches

mech mechanical; mechanism; mechanic; mechanics; mechanical

MEcon master of economics

MED Municipal Electricity Department (*NZ*)

MEd master of education

Med Mediterranean region

med medical (MIL)

MEF Middle East Force

mega one million times

MEGO my eyes glaze over (*Christopher South, BBC Radio Cambridgeshire*)

MEIC Member of the Engineering Institute of Canada

MEK methyl ethyl ketone (CHM)

MELF Middle East Land Forces

Mem, memo memorandum

MEMS micro-electro-mechanical systems

MENC Music Educators' National Conference (MUS)

MEng master of engineering

MEP Member of the European Parliament

MEP Mars Exploration Programme

MEPC Metropolitan Estate & Property Committee

mer meridian (SCI)

MES medium Edison screw-cap (*an ES having a diameter of approximately 1 in & approximately 7 threads per in*) (SCI)

MESAN Mouvement pour l'Evolution Sociale de l'Afrique

Messrs plural of Mr

MET Memory Enhancement Technology

Met Metropolitan Police (PRP)

met metaphysics

met metaphor

Met Metropolitan Opera House (*New York*) (MUS)

met meteorology; meteorological (SCI)

met metropolitan (SCI)

Met Mus Metropolitan Museum (*New York*)

meta- prefix (Greek: meta - after) (CHM)

Meth Methodist

MEWP mobile elevated working platform

MF machine-finished (*paper which has been surfaced while on the paper-making machine*) (COM)

MF middle French (FPA)

MF resin melamine-formaldehyde resin (SCI)

MFC mortar fire controller (MIL)

mfd manufactured (COM)

mfg manufacturing (COM)

MFGB Miners' Federation of Great Britain

MFGC Mensa Foundation for Gifted Children

MFH Master of Foxhounds

MFH missing from home

MFI Monetary Financial Institution

MFN most favoured nation

mfr manufacture(r) (COM)

MFS minimum flying speed

MG machine-glazed paper (*made on an MG, or Yankee, machine*) (COM)

MG machine gun (MIL)

MG make good (ARC)

MG Morris Garages

MGA Mushroom Growers' Association (COM)

MGAM Morgan Grenfell Asset Management (COM)

MGB Ministerstvo gosudarstvennoi bezopasnosti (*Russian: Ministry of State Security 1946–54*)

MGDC Morgan Grenfell Development Capital (COM)

MGM Metro-Goldwin-Meyer

MGN Mirror Group Newspapers (COM)

MGOC MG Owners' Club

Mgr manager (COM)

Mgr Monseigneur (*French*)

Mgr, Msgr Monsignor (*Italian*)

MH Master of Harriers

MHA Member of the House of Assembly (*Australia, Canada & Newfoundland*)

MHA Mental Health Act

MHD magnetohydrodynamic(s) (SCI)

MHG middle High German (FPA)

MHR Member of the House of Representatives (*USA & Australia*)

MHS Meat Hygiene Service

MI military intelligence (MIL)

MI British E Member of the Institute of British Engineers

MILocoE Member of the Institution of Locomotive Engineers

MIMarE Member of the Institute of Marine Engineers

MI.Mech.E Member of the Institute of Mechanical Engineers

MI.Min.E Member of the Institute of Mining Engineers

MI.Mun.E Member of the Institution of Municipal Engineers

MI5 Security Service (MIL)

MI6 Secret Intelligence Service (MIL)

MIA Murrumbidgee Irrigation Area (Australia)

MIAE Member of the Institution of Automobile Engineers

MIAeE Member of the Institute of Aeronautical Engineers

MIAS Member of the Institute of Aeronautical Science

MIB man/men in black (FPA)

MIBOS measurement of ingratiatory behaviours in organisational settings (*creep factor*) (COM)

MIC mobile incident centre

MIC Mountain Instructor's Certificate (SPR)

MIC minimum inhibitory concentration

MICE *see* MInstCE

MICEI Member of the Institution of Civil Engineers of Ireland

MIChemE Member of the Institution of Chemical Engineers

MICR magnetic ink character recognition (SCI)

micro one-millionth part

MICV mechanised infantry combat vehicle

mid middle

Mid midshipman (MIL)

MIDAS missile defence alarm system (MIL)

MIDI musical instrument digital interface (MUS)

MIE (Ind) Member of the Institution of Engineers, India

MIEA Member of the Institution of Engineers, Australia

MIEE Member of the Institution of Electrical Engineers

MIEI Member of the Institute of Engineering Inspection

MIESS Member of the Institution of Engineers and Shipbuilders, Scotland

MIEX Member of the Institute of Export

MIF milk in first (*supposed, but thermodynamically questionable, class indicator*)

MIG mortgage indemnity guarantee (COM)

MiG Mikoyan & Gurevich (*designers of Russian fighter plane*) (MIL)

MIG welding metal inert gas welding (SCI)

mil militia (MIL)

MIL malfunction indicator light

mil, milit military (MIL)

milli one-thousandth part

Mil-Specs military specifications issued in the USA which lay down basic requirements to be observed by design teams in the development of aircraft. (MIL)

MIMM Member of the Institution of Mining and Metallurgy

MIMO multiple input, multiple output

MIMunE Member of the Institute of Municipal Engineers

Min Ministry

min minimum

min mining

Min Minister

min mineralogy; mineralogical (SCI)

MINA Member of the Institution of Naval Architects

MINL minimum licence period (PRP)

MInstCE Member of the Institution of Civil Engineers (*changed February 1946 to MICE*)

MInstGasE Member of the Institution of Gas Engineers

MInstHE Member of the Institution of Highway Engineers

MInstME Member of the Institution of Mining Engineers

MInstMet Member of the Institute of Metals

MInstPet Member of the Institute of Petroleum

MInstPI Member of the Institute of Patentees and Inventors

MInstRA Member of the Institute of Registered Architects

MInstT Member of the Institute of Transport

MInstW Member of the Institute of Welding

MInstWE Member of the Institute of Water Engineers

MIOSH Member of the Institute of Occupational Safety and Health

MIP Monthly Investment Plan; Maximum Investment Plan (COM)

MIPE *see* MIProdE

MIProdE Member of the Institute of Production Engineers (*formerly MIPE*)

MIPS million instructions per second (SCI)

MIR micropower impulse radar (MIL)

MIRA Motor Industries' Research Association

MIRAS mortgage interest relief at source (COM)

MIRTE Member of the Institute of Road Transport Engineers

MIRV multiple independently targeted re-entry vehicle (SCI)

MIS management information system (COM)

MIS materials information service (SCI)

misc miscellaneous; miscellany

MISI Member of the Iron and Steel Institute

MISO multiple input, single output

MIStructE Member of the Institution of Structural Engineers

MIT Massachusetts Institute of Technology

MJI Member of the Institute of Journalists

MJIE Member of the Junior Institute of Engineers

MJS Member of the Japan Society

Mk mark

MKSA system metre-kilogram-second-ampère system (SCI)

mkt market (COM)

ML mediaeval Latin (FPA)

MLA Member of the Legislative Assembly

MLA Modern Language Association (*USA*) (FPA)

MLC Meat & Livestock Commission

MLC Member of the Legislative Council (*Australia & India*)

MLF multilateral (*nuclear*) force (MIL)

MLG middle Low German (FPA)

MLitt Master of Letters

Mlle(s) Mademoiselle (*plural: Mesdemoiselles*) (*French: Miss*)

MLO military liaison officer

MLR minimum lending rate (COM)

MLS Member of the Japan Society

mm mutatis mutandis (*Latin: the necessary change having been made*)

MM Messieurs (*French equivalent of Messrs*)

MM Military Medal (MIL)

MM Melody Maker (MUS)

MMA monomethyl aniline (*an anti-knock agent*) (CHM)

MMB Milk Marketing Board (*now Milk Marque*)

MMC Monopolies & Mergers Commission (COM)

MME Montessori Method of Education Mme(s)

Mme. Madame (Mesdames) (*French: Mrs*)

MMF Motor Manufacturers' Federation

MMH medication misuse headache (*headache caused by taking drugs to cure headaches – a vicious circle*)

MMI man-machine interface (SCI)

MMI management of medical innovation

MMIHS Megacystis Microcolon Intestinal Hypoperistalsis Syndrome (*very rare condition where under body cannot absorb food*)

MMM Member of the Order of Military Merit (MIL)

MMM overlay a special material on which an impression of the entire letterpress form is taken and which, after heat treatment, becomes a mechanical overlay (FPA)

MMSA Master of the Midwifery Society of Apothecaries

MMus Master of Music (MUS)

Mn Merchant Navy (MIL)

MN magnetic north (NAV)

m-n meinen (*German: my*)

MNA Member of the National Assembly (*in Quebec, Canada*)

MNAD multi-national airmobile division (MIL)

MNAS Member of the National Academy of Sciences

MND A Midsummer Night's Dream (FPA)

MO money order; mail order (COM)

MO medical officer

mo modus operandi (*Latin: way of working – particularly of committing a crime*)

MO medical orderly

mo moulded (ARC)

MoA Memorandum of Association (COM)

MOB man overboard (*man embraces woman*)

mob mobilisation (MIL)

Mob Con mobilising control (FRS)

Mob O mobilising officer (FRS)

MOBA Museum of Bad Art (*Boston, MA*)

MOBO awards for music of black origin (MUS)

MoC Mother of the Chapel

MoD Ministry of Defence

modem modulator-demodulator (SCI)

Mods Honour Moderations (*Oxford University*)

MOG material other than grapes (*Australian winemaking*) (F&D)

MOH medical officer of health

MOI Ministry of Information (*now COI*)

mol mole (SCI)

mol molecule; molecular (SCI)

mol wt molecular weight (SCI)

MOM Member in Orthodontics

MOMI Museum of the Moving Image (FPA)

MOMIMTS Military & Orchestral Musical Instrument Makers Trade Society (UNI)

mon monetary (COM)

Mona Lisa Mine & Onshore North Sea Acquisition for Lithpospheric Royal Ymary Seismic Wave

Monte Montevideo (*Uruguay; whence the best exported sheepskins became known as 'the full monte'*)

MOPA method of physical action (*acting technique known as 'the method' in development by Konstantin Staniskavski (1863–1938), co-founder of the Moscow Art Theatre 1897*) (FPA)

MOPIES multiple original prints (*cf copies*)

MOR middle-of-the-road (FPA)

mor Morocco (*binding – 'Like Webster's Dictionary, we're Morocco bound – song from the Crosby–Hope–Lamour film* The Road to Morocco) (FPA)

MORI Market Opinion Research International (COM)

morph, morphol morphology; morphological (SCI)

MOS mail-order sales

MOS metal oxide semiconductor (SCI)

Mosa mobile social alarm (*BT 'spy phone'*)

Most Rev Most Reverend

MoT Ministry of Transport

MOT, MoT moment of truth

MoU memorandum of understanding (COM)

MovO movement order (MIL)

MP Metropolitan Police

MP Mounted Police

MP Member of Parliament (POL)

MP Military Police(man) (MIL)

MP mile post

mp melting point (SCI)

MPAG Maxwell Pensioners' Action Group (COM)

MPC multimedia personal computer (SCI)

MPD magnetoplasmadynamic (SCI)

MPDS monitored professional development scheme (*for would-be chartered engineers*) (COM)

MPEG Motion Picture Experts Group (FPA)

MPG main professional grade

MPh, MPhil Master of Philosophy

MPLA Movimento Popular de Libertacão de Angola (*Portuguese: Popular Movement for the Liberation of Angola*) (POL)

MPO Managerial & Professional Officers (UNI)

MPP Member of the Provincial Parliament (*Ontario, Canada*)

MPS Member of the Philological Society

MPS Member of the Physical Society

MPT Modern Poetry in Translation (*founded by Ted Hughes & Daniel Weissbort, 1966*) (FPA)

MPV multi-purpose vehicle

MPW Mander Portman Woodward (*Independent Sixth-form Colleges*)

MPW Marco Pierre White (chef)

MQ *see* PQ developer

MR motivational research (COM)

MR Master of the Rolls

m-r meiner (*German: of/to my*)

Mr Big head of a large organisation, especially criminal

Mr W H Shakespearean dedicatee; to 'Mr W H the onlie begetter of these insuing sonnets' (*possibly William, Lord Herbert, later Earl of Pembroke, or Henry Wriothesly, Earl of Southampton – or even William himself*)

Mr, Messrs Mister(s)

MRA Ministry for Rural Affairs

MRA moral re-armament

MRAO Mullard Radioastronomy Observatory (SCI)

MRAS Member of the Royal Asiatic Society

MRBM medium-range ballistic missile (MIL)

MRC Medical Research Council

MRCA multi-role combat aircraft (MIL)

MRCOG Member of the Royal College of Obstetricians and Gynæcologists

MRCP Member of the Royal College of Physicians

MRCPE Member of the Royal College of Physicians, Edinburgh

MRCS Member of the Royal College of Surgeons

MRCSE Member of the Royal College of Surgeons, Edinburgh

MRCVS Member of the Royal College of Veterinary Surgeons

MRD Member in Restorative Dentistry

MREmpS Member of the Royal Empire Society

MRG moisture-retaining gel

MRIA Member of the Royal Irish Academy

MRIAI Member of the Royal Institute of Architects of Ireland

MRLP Monster Raving Loony Party (POL)

MRM machine/mechanically recovered meat (F&D)

m-RNA a shortlived, transient form of RNA (SCI)

MRP Mouvement Républicain Populaire (*French: Popular Republican Movement*) (POL)

MRPharmS Member of the Royal Pharmaceutical Society

MRS Midlands Research Station (*of British Gas*) (COM)

Mrs Mistress (*a married woman, or professional title for cook, housekeeper*)

MRS magnetic resonance spectroscopy (SCI)

MRSanI Member of the Royal Sanitary Institute

MRSC Member of the Royal Society of Chemistry

MRST Member of the Royal Society of Teachers (MUS)

MRTA Tupac Amaru Revolutionary Movement (*rebels who besieged Japanese Ambassador's residence in Lima, Peru 17 December 96 to 22 April 97*) (POL)

MRUSI Member of the Royal United Service Institution

MS *see* Mil-Specs

MS Master of Science

MS memoriae sacrum (*Latin: sacred to the memory of*)

MS Master of Surgery

Ms Miss or Mrs (*to avoid marital status distinction*)

MS mass spectrometry (SCI)

MS mile stone

MS motor ship

MS(S), ms(s) manuscript(s) (*even when referring to a typescript*) (FPA)

MS,MSS manuscript; manuscripts

MSA Mutual Security Agency (COM)

MSA Marine Safety Agency (COM)

MSA particle-size analyser (SCI)

MSA Motor Sports' Association

MSA Marine Safety Agency

MSAE Member of the Society of Automotive Engineers (*America*)

MSALAS Medical Sickness Annuity & Life Assurance Society (COM)

MSAutE Member of the Society of Automobile Engineers

msb most significant bit (SCI)

MSc Master of Science

MSC a method of system building developed in UK combining structural steelwork with in-situ concrete floors with a galvanised sheet metal deck, clad with prefabricated sheets of various materials (ARC)

MSCA Metropolitan Swimming Clubs Association (*became ASAGB*) (SPR)

MSD Merck Sharp & Dohme (COM)

MSD multi-sensor display (SCI)

MSD Microsoft System Diagnostics

MSD licence music, singing & dancing licence (FPA)

MS-DOS Microsoft Disk-Operating System ™ (SCI)

MSF Manufacturing, Science & Finance Union (UNI)

MSG Miners' Support Group (UNI)

MSG monosodium glutamate (F&D)

MSG meteosat second generation

Msgr Monsignor

MSI Movimento Sociale Italiano (*Italian Social Movement*) (POL)

MSI medium scale integration (SCI)

MSIA Member of the Society of Industrial Artists

MSL mean sea level

msl missile (MIL)

MSM Medal for Meritorious Service (*Navy before 20 July 1928*)

MSM mirror - signal - manoeuvre (driving)

MSN Microsoft Network (SCI)

MSOM Monmouthshire School of Mines

MSP Manic Street Preachers (*pop band*)

MSPCG Most Sparsely Populated Councils Group

MSR Member of the Society of Radiographers

Ms-Th mesothorium (CHM)

MSW Master of Solid Work

MSW magnetic surface wave (SCI)

M-synchronisation flash-synchronised shutters which, when released, can close an electrical circuit for firing flash. M operates at the moment when the shutter is fully open – *see* X-synchronisation (SCI)

MT medical transfer (PRP)

Mt Rev, Mt Revd Most Reverend

MTA maximum time aloft

MTAG Mission Theological Advisory Group

MTB motor torpedo boat (MIL)

MTBF mean time between failures (SCI)

MTech Master of Technology

mtg meeting

mtg, mtge mortgage (COM)

MTh Master of Theology

MTI moving target indicator (SCI)

MTNA Music Teachers National Association (*US*) (MUS)

MTPI Member of the Town Planning Institute

MTRA Machine Tools Research Association (COM)

MTTA Machine Tool Traders' Association (COM)

MTV Music Television (FPA)

MTX Mobile Telephone Exchange (SCI)

MU Mothers' Union (COM)

MU Musicians Union (UNI)

MUF maximum usable frequency (SCI)

MUFON Mutual UFO Network (SCI)

MUFTI minimum use of force tactical intervention (PRP)

mun municipal

mus music; musical (FPA)

Mus museum; museo etc

MusB/D Bachelor/Doctor of Music (*See* MB/D)

MusM Master of Music

MV military vigilance (MIL)

MV muzzle velocity (MIL)

MV merchant vessel; motor vessel

MVD Ministerstvo vnutrennikh del (*Russian: Ministry of Internal Affairs*)

MVO Member of the Royal Victorian Order (*not if GCVO &/or KCVO or DCVO &/or CVO &/or LVO*)

MVS Master of Veterinary Surgery

MVSc Master of Veterinary Science

MVSN Milizia Volontaria per la Sicurezza Nazionale (*Italian Voluntary Militia for National Security*) (POL)

MW mid week booking

MW Master of Wines (F&D)

MW medium wave

MWB Metropolitan Water Board (COM)

M-wire metre wire (*over which the operation of the calling subscriber's meter is controlled*) (SCI)

MX medium expansion foam (FRS)

MY motor yacht

MYOB mind your own business

MZ monozygotic twin

N

N neutral

N National(ist)

n natus (*Latin: born*)

n note

n nominative

N en (*width half height of type body*) (FPA)

N Norse (FPA)

n neutrino (SCI)

n nephew

n- normal (CHM)

N display a radar K display whose target produces two breaks on the horizontal time base; the direction proportional to the relative amplitude of the breaks, and the range indicated by a calibrated control which moves a pedestal signal to coincide with the breaks (SCI)

N, n new

n, neut neuter

N, noun noun

n, num, nos number(s)

N/SVQ National/Scottish Vocational Qualification

NA not applicable (COM)

NA Narcotics Anonymous (PRP)

NA neutral axis (SCI)

NA – PADA National Association of Parents Against Drug Abuse

NAA National Aeronautic Association

NAACP National Association for the Advancement of Colored People (*founded with Liberal Rights 1909*)

NAAFI, Naafi Navy, Army & Air Force Institute (MIL)

NAAH Notable Artist and Historian

NABC National Association of Boys' Clubs

NABISCO National Biscuit Company (COM)

NAC National Advisory Council

NACAB National Association of Citizens Advice Bureaux

NACO National Association of Co-operative Officials (UNI)

NACODS National Association of Colliery Overmen, Deputies & Shotfirers (UNI)

NACRO National Association for the Care & Resettlement of Offenders (PRP)

NACSS National Approval Council for Security Systems

NAD nicotinamide adenine dinucleotide (*coenzyme employed as acceptor of electrons from a substrate*) (SCI)

NADFAS National Association of Decorative & Fine Art Societies (FPA)

NADGE NATO Air Defence Ground Environment (MIL)

NADPAS National Association of Discharged Prisoners' Aid Association

NAFAS National Association of Flower Arranging Societies

NAFPATPAMNFPG National Association for Promoting Acronyms to Provide a Memorable Name for Pressure Groups

NAFTA New Zealand & Australian Free Trade Agreement

NAG National Acquisitions Group (FPA)

NAGM National Association of Glove Manufacturers (COM)

NAHT National Association of Head Teachers

NAK negative acknowledgement (SCI)

NaK sodium (Na)-potassium (K) (*alloy molten at room temperature used as a coolant for liquid-metal reactor*) (CHM)

NAL non-associated labour (PRP)

NALC National Association of Local Councils

NALGO National and Local Government Officers' Association (*now UNISON*)

NALHM National Association of Licensed House Managers (UNI)

NAM National Army Museum (MIL)

NAMBLA North American Man-Boy Love Association

NAO National Audit Office

napalm naphthene and palmitate (*used in flamethrowers*) (CHM)

NAPF National Association of Pension Funds

NAPO National Association of Probation Officers (UNI)

NAPT National Association for the Prevention of Tuberculosis

NAPV National Association of Prison Visitors (PRP)

NAR Nuclei di Azioni Rivoluzionaria (*Italian: Armed Revolutionary Nuclei*) (POL)

Narco The Narcotics Squad (PRP)

NASA National Aeronautical & Space Administration (SCI)

NASCAR American National Association for Stock-Car Auto Racing (SPR)

NASO National Adult School Organisation (*emerged in Nottingham 1798; founded by Quaker Samuel Fox and Methodist William Singleton*)

NASP non-acoustic sensor platform

NASUWT National Association of Schoolmasters/Union of Women Teachers (UNI)

NATE National Association for the Teaching of English

NATFHE National Association of Teachers in Further & Higher Education (*The University & College Lecturers Union*)

NATO National Association of Theater Owners (*US*) (FPA)

NATO North Atlantic Treaty Organisation

NATS National Air Traffic Services

NatSci natural sciences

NATSOPA National Society of Operative Printers, Graphical & Media Personnel (*became NGA; now GPMU*) (UNI) (NAV)

net asset value (COM)

nav naval (MIL)

nav navigable; navigation; navigator (SCI)

Navtex telex warning system being developed by IMO (NAV)

NAWT National Animal Welfare Trust

Nazi *see* NSDAP (POL)

nb northbound (NAV)

NB New Brunswick

NB nota bene (*Latin: note well*)

NBA net book agreement (FPA)

NBA National Basketball Association (*USA*) (SPR)

NBC northbound carriageway (*see* SBS, EBC and WBC)

NBC Nuclear, Biological and Chemical Warfare (MIL)

NBC (suit) nuclear, biological, chemical (suit) (MIL)

NBL National Book League (*was National Book Council*)

NBM nil by mouth/no bowel movement

NBPA National Back Pain Association

NC national curriculum

NC&SS National Cactus & Succulent Society

NCA news & current affairs (FPA)

NCAA National Collegiate Athletic Association (*USA*) (SPR)

NCB National Coal Board (*now British Coal Corporation*) (COM)

NCB National Central Bank

NCBA National Cattlemans' Beef Association

NCC National Consumer Council

NCC Network Central Council

NCCL National Council for Civil Liberties

NCCPG National Council for the Conservation of Plants & Gardens

NCDT National Council for Drama Training (FPA)

NCF National Coaching Federation (SPR)

NCI new community instrument (*for borrowing & lending*)

NCIS National Criminal Investigation Service

NCLC National Council of Labour Colleges

NCO Non-Commissioned Officer (MIL)

NCPGW nothing can possibly go wrong

NCPM National Centre for Popular Music (*Sheffield*) (MUS)

NCPTA National Confederation of PTAs

NCR National Cash Register Co Ltd (COM)

NCR no carbon required (*trade term for office stationery with copying microcapsules incorporated*)

NCS National Crime Squad

NCSA National Center for Supercomputing Applications (SCI)

NCSS National Council of Social Service (*of which the uncrowned King Edward VIII was Patron when he said at Dowlais (18 November 36) 'These steelworks brought these men here. Something must be done to see that they stay here – working'*)

NCT National Childbirth Trust

NCTU Northern Carpet Trades Union (UNI)

NCU National Cyclists' Union

ND Nouvelle Droite (*French: New Right*) (POL)

nd no date

NDA National Diploma in Agriculture

NDB non-directional beacon (NAV)

NDD National Diploma in Dairying

NDP Net Domestic Product (COM)

NDT non-destructive testing (SCI)

NE Nuclear Electric (*see BE and SN*) (COM)

NEAC New English Art Club

NEAC National Entertainments Agents' Council

NEB New English Bible

NEBDN National Examining Board for Dental Nurses

NEBOSH Diploma 0171 412 7331

NEC National Executive Committee (PRP)

NEC National Executive Council

NEC National Exhibition Centre (*Birmingham*)

nec necessary (MIL)

NECInst North East Institution of Engineers and Shipbuilders

NEDC National Economic Development Council

NEG, neg negative

negs child neglect (PRP)

NEI Northern Engineering Industries (COM)

NEIDS north east interim data system

NELLY no one ever loved like you

Nem Con, nem con nemine contradicente (*Latin: no one contradicts, ie everyone in favour*)

Nem Dis, nem dis nemine dissentiente (*Latin: no person disagreeing ie unanimously*)

nemby nembutal (PRP)

nemp non-nuclear electro-magnetic pulse (*death-ray for automobiles*) (SCI)

NEPO new entrant prison officer (PRP)

NERC National Electronics Research Council (*body proposed by Lord Mountbatten (to secure a large salary for himself as chairman)*) (SCI)

NERC Natural Environment Research Council

nes not elsewhere specified

NESA panel non-electrostatic shield formulation 'A' (*a laminated glass windshield panel which is heated by electric current to combat icing*) (SCI)

NESTA National Endowment for Science, Technology and the Arts

Net, Nett netto (*Italian: free from all deductions*)

NEWT not environmentally worse than (*planning criterion*)

NF no funds (COM)

NF National Front (POL)

NF Norman French (FPA)

NFA no fixed abode (PRP)

NFA/B normal for Andover/Bridgewater

NFC National Freight Consortium (COM)

NFCA National Foster Care Association

NFFF National Federation of Fish Fryers (UNI)

NFH National Federation of Hairdressers (COM)

NFL National Football League (*USA*) (SPR)

NFLA Nuclear-free Local Authorities

NFS normal for Selby

NFS National Fire Service

NFT National Film Theatre (FPA)

NFU National Farmers' Union (UNI)

NFWI National Federation of Women's Institutes

NG National Guard (*USA*) (MIL)

NG National Gallery (London) (FPA)

NG narrow gap (welding) (SCI)

NG, ng no good

NGA National Graphical Association (*was NATSOPA; now GPMU*) (UNI)

NGC New General Catalogue [of nebulae & clusters of stars] (SCI)

NGH National Group on Homeworking

NGk New Greek (FPA)

NGL natural gas liquids

NGL nionoglycerine (CHM)

NGO non-governmental organisation

NGO non-gazetted officer (*India*) (MIL)

NGRC National Greyhound Racing Club Ltd (SPR)

NGST new generation space telescope (*NASA design*)

NGTE rigid rotor a helicopter self-propelling rotor system which uses the jet flap principle to obtain high lift coefficients (SCI)

NHER national home energy rating

NHL National Hockey League (*USA - ice*) (SPR)

NHLF National Heritage Lottery Fund

NHMF National Heritage Memorial Fund (FPA)

NHPA National Horseshoe Pitching Association (*USA*) (SPR)

NHRA National Hot-Rod Association (SPR)

NI national insurance

NI Northern Ireland

ni night

NIAB National Institute of Agricultural Botany

NIC national insurance contributions (COM)

NIC nominal index card (PRP)

nicad nickel-cadmium (*electric battery*) (SCI)

NICAM near-instantaneous companded audio multiplex (MUS)

NID naval intelligence division

NID National Institute for the Deaf

NIFES National Industrial Fuel Efficiency Service (COM)

NIH not invented here

NIH National Industry of Health

NII Nuclear Installations Inspectorate

NIMBY not in my back yard

NiMH nickel metal hydride (CHM)

NIMQ not in my queue (*said when refusing tasks through being overloaded – pronounced nim-queue*) (COM)

NIMTO not in my term of office

NIRC National Industrial Relations Court

NIREX Nuclear Industry Radioactive Waste Executive

NIRNS National Institute for Research in Nuclear Science

NIRV new international readers versions

NISW National Institute of Social Workers

NIV new international version (*of the Bible*) (FPA)

NKA National Karting Association (SPR)

NKGB Narodny Komissariat Gosudarstvennoi Bezopasnosti (*Russian: People's Commissariat of State Security – Soviet Agency 1943–46 – see* KGB)

NKRF National Kidney Research Fellowship

NKVD Narodny Komissariat Vnutrennikh Del (*Russian People's Commissariat of Internal Affairs – Soviet Agency 1934–46*) (*See* OGPU)

NL Netherlands

NL no liability (*Australia*) (COM)

nl non licet (*Latin: it is not permitted*)

nl non liquet (*Latin: it is not clear*)

NL new Latin (FPA)

nl new line (FPA)

NLB non-linear behaviour (SCI)

NLBD National League of the Blind & Disabled (UNI)

NLC National Liberal Club

NLD National League for Democracy

NLF National Liberal Federation

NLH National Harmonic League

NLL National Lending Library (FPA)

NLLST National Lending Library for Science & Technology (FPA)

NLP Neuro-Linguistic Programming

NLS National Library of Scotland (FPA)

NLSI National Library of Science & Invention (FPA)

NLW National Library of Wales (FPA)

NME New Musical Express (MUS)

NMEC New Millennium Experience Company (*Dome Providers*)

nmi no middle initial

NMM National Maritime Museum (FPA)

NMPFT National Museum of Photography, Film & Television (FPA)

NMR nuclear magnetic resonance (SCI)

NMSI National Museum of Science & Industry (*The Science Museum*) (FPA)

NN noise network (*see* RPQC)

NN nepoznato (*Bosnian: not known*)

n-n junction junction between crystals of n-type semiconductors, having different electrical properties (SCI)

NNP net national product (COM)

NNTR no need to return

NO Norway

No, no numero (*number(s)*)

NOAA [US] National Oceanic and Atmospheric Administration

NOC not our class

NODE New Oxford Dictionary of English (*pronounced NODDY*)

NOISE nurses' observational scale for inpatient evaluation

NOJ New Orleans Jazzband (MUS)

NOK next of kin

NOL next on list

nol pros nolle prosequi (*Latin: do not pursue/prosecute*)

nom nominative; nominal

Non seq non sequitur (*Latin: it does not follow*)

NOP national opinion poll(s) (COM)

NORK New Orleans Rhythm Kings (MUS)

norm normal

Norm Norman

NORTHAG Northern Army Group (MIL)

Norvic Bishop of Norwich

NORWEB North West Electricity Board (COM)

NORWICH (k)nickers off ready when I come home

NOS not off sanctions (PRP)

NOS Nine o'clock Service

NOS National Osteoporosis Society

Noton Northampton

NOW new opportunities for women

np nisi prius (*Latin: unless previously*)

NP noun phrase

np new paragraph (FPA)

np no place for publication (FPA)

n-p junction a semiconductor junction with electron and hole conductivities on respective sides of the junction (SCI)

NP, np Notary Public

NP, NPA N-1-naphthylphthalamic acid (naptalam, a weedkiller) (CHM)

NPA Newspaper Publishers' Association (FPA)

NPA National Pistol Association

NPD new product development (COM)

NPD Nationaldemokratische Partei Deutschlands (*German: National Democratic Party of Germany*) (POL)

NPD north polar distance (SCI)

NPG National Portrait Gallery (*London*) (FPA)

n-p-i-n transistor similar to n-p-n transistor, with a layer of intrinsic semiconductor between base and collector to extend high-frequency range (SCI)

NPL National Physical Laboratory (*founded by the Royal Society in 1900 as a national authority for establishing basic units (mass, length, time, resistance, frequency, radioactivity &c*)) (SCI)

n-p-n transistor a junction transistor with a thin slice of p-type forming the base between two pieces of n-type semiconductor (SCI)

NPP net primary production (farming)

NPV net present value (COM)

NPV no par value (COM)

NQOCD not quite our class, darling

NQUD not quite us, darling

nr near

NRA National Recovery Administration (*US*)

NRA National Rounders Association (SPR)

NRA British National Rifle Association (SPR)

NRD national registered designer

NRDC National Research Development Corporation (COM)

NRM National Railway Museum (*York*) (FPA)

NRME notched, returned and mitred ends (ARC)

NRN National Radio Network

NRPB National Radiological Protection Board

NRRA National Romany Rights Association

NRT Nicotine Replacement Therapy

NRV net realisable value (COM)

NS not sufficient/satisfactory

NS non-smoker

ns new series

ns not specified

NS nuclear ship (MIL)

NS National Service (MIL)

NS Nova Scotia

NS new style in the calendar (*of Great Britain after 1752*)

ns Graduate of Royal Naval Staff College, Greenwich

NSA National Security Agency (*was SIS*) (MIL)

NSA National Skating Association (SPR)

NSAGB National Skating Association of Great Britain

NSC National Security Council (*USA*)

NSC National Sporting Club (SPR)

NSDAP Nationalsozialistische Deutsche Arbeiterpartei (*German: National Socialist German Workers' Party - the Nazis*) (POL)

NSF not sufficient funds (COM)

NSF! not so fast!

NSG non-statutory guidelines (*on NC*)

NSGC National Socialist Glider Club (*Nazi organisation putting more emphasis on marching than on gliding*)

NSIT not safe in taxis

NSP non-smoker preferred

NSPCC National Society for the Prevention of Cruelty to Children

NSRA National Small-Bore Rifle Association (SPR)

NSS national surveillance scheme

NSSAAL National Survey of Sexual Attitudes & Lifestyles

NSSR National Savings Stock Register

NSU motorbike (SPR)

NSW New South Wales (Australia)

NT New Testament

NT national teacher (Ireland)

NT National Trust (FPA)

NT National Theatre (FPA)

NT north transept (ARC)

NT no trump(s)

NT Northern Territory (*Australia*)

nt wt net weight (COM)

NTI noise transmission impairment (SCI)

NTP, ntp normal temperature & pressure (*now STP*) (SCI)

NTR nothing to report (MIL)

N-truss also called Whipple-Murphy truss, Linville truss, Pratt truss

NTS National Trust for Scotland

NTS not to scale (*on plans*)

NTSB National Transportation Safety Board

NTSC National Television System Committee (SCI)

n-type semiconductor one in which the electron conduction (negative) exceeds the hole conduction (absence of electrons), the donor impurity predominating

NU Norwich Union (COM)

NU number unobtainable (SCI)

NUAAW National Union of Agricultural & Allied Workers (UNI)

NUCPS National Union of Civil & Public Servants (UNI)

NUDAGO National Union of Domestic Appliances & General Operatives (UNI)

NUIW National Union of Insurance Workers (UNI)

NUJ National Union of Journalists (UNI)

NUKFAT National Union of Knitwear, Footwear & Apparel Trades (UNI)

NULMW National Union of Lock & Metal Workers (UNI)

NUM National Union of Mineworkers (UNI)

NUMAST National Union of Marine, Aviation & Shipping Transport Officers (UNI)

NUP NU Policy

NUPE National Union of Public Employees (*now UNISON*)

NUR National Union of Railwaymen (UNI)

NUS National Union of Students (UNI)

NUS National Union of Seamen (UNI)

NUT National Union of Teachers (UNI)

NuT Newcastle upon Tyne

NUTN National Union of Trained Nurses

NUWW National Union of Women Workers

NV, nv naamlose vennootschap (*Dutch plc*) (COM)

nvg not very good

NVG night-vision goggles (SCI)

NVH noise, vibration & harshness (SCI)

NVLA National Viewers' & Listeners' Association (FPA)

NVM nonvolatile matter (SCI)

NVOD near-video-on-demand (FPA)

NVQ national vocational qualification

NW narrow width(s) (ARC)

NWCTU National Women's Christian Temperance Union

NWFP North-West Frontier Province

NWP North-Western Provinces

NWT North West Territory

NWT North-Western Territories

NY New York

NYAC New York Athletic Club (SPR)

NYC New York City (SCI)

NYK not yet known (MIL)

NYO National Youth Orchestra (MUS)

NYPD New York Police Department

NYR National Year of Reading

NYTLC New York Taxi & Limousine Commission (*US regulator; saviour of Wallace & Gromit*)

NZ Neue Zeitschift für Musik (*German music magazine*) (MUS)

NZ New Zealand

NZBA New Zealand Bowling Association (*lawn bowls*) (SPR)

NZBC New Zealand Broadcasting Corporation (FPA)

NZCC New Zealand Croquet Council (SPR)

NZCER New Zealand Council for Educational Research

NZEF New Zealand Expeditionary Force (*WWI*) (MIL)

NZEFIP New Zealand Expeditionary Force in the Pacific (*WWII*) (MIL)

NZEI New Zealand Educational Institute

NZF New Zealand flatworm

NZLR New Zealand Law Reports

NZRFL New Zealand Rugby Football League (SPR)

NZRFU New Zealand Rugby Football Union

NZRN New Zealand Registered Nurse

O

O opium (PRP)

o only; order

o ohne (*German: without*)

O osten (*German: east*)

O ouest (*French: west*)

o- ortho- (*containing a benzene nucleus substituted in the 1, 2 positions*) (CHM)

O – oxygen atom attached to radical (CHM)

o d only daughter

o g, og own goal

O Henry William Sydney Porter (*US writer, 1862–1910*)

O J Simpson Orenthal James (*notorious for overlong televised murder trial*)

o s only son

O St J Officer, Order of St John of Jerusalem

O&M organisation & method (COM)

O&M operation & maintenance (SCI)

O&O Oriental and Occidental (*Steamship Co*)

O&Y Olympia & York (*Construction Company*) (COM)

O, o old

O/D overdrive

o/w otherwise

OA the Order of Australia

OAP old age pensioner (= *Senior Citizen*)

OAPEC Organisation of Arab Petroleum-Exporting Countries

OAS Organisation of African States

OAS Organisation Armée Sécrète (*French: Secret Army Organisation*) (POL)

OAS Organisation de l'Armée Secrète (*Algeria early 1960s*) (MIL)

OAS Organization of American States

OAU Organization of African Unity

OB Old Boy (*of a school, for example*)

OB Order of Burma (*for gallantry &/or distinguished service*)

ob ordinary building (*NZ grade of timber*) (ARC)

Ob obiit (*Latin: he/she died*)

OBD on-board diagnostics

OBE Officer of the Most Excellent Order of the British Empire (*not if GBE &/or KBE or DBE &/or CBE*)

OBE other buggers' efforts

OBE other by-pass efforts (*Institute of Landscape Art*)

OBG old but good

OBI Order of British India

obj objection

obj object

obl oblong; oblique

OBM ordnance bench mark

OBN order of the brown nose

obs obscure

obs observation

obs obsolete

Obs, obs observation; observatory (SCI)

OC overcharge (COM)

OC Old Carthusian

OC officer commanding (MIL)

OCAM Organisation Commune Africaine et Mauricienne

OCAS Organization of Central American States (*aka ODECA*)

OCAU observation, classification and allocation unit (PRP)

occas occasional(ly)

OCF officiating chaplain to the forces

OCPP Oliphaur copper pitting propensity

OCR optical character reader/ recognition (SCI)

OCS Officer Candidate School (MIL)

OCTU Officer Cadet Training Unit

OCU operational conversion unit (MIL)

OD overdraft; overdrawn; on demand (COM)

OD overdose (PRP)

OD old Dutch (*marriage partner of long standing*)

OD officer of the day (MIL)

OD overseas delivery

OD, od olive drab (MIL)

OD, od outside diameter (SCI)

ODA overseas development administration

ODECA Organización de Estados Centroamericanos (*aka OCAS*)

Odeon OD entertains our nations (*from Odeion amphitheatre – chain of cinemas built by Oscar Deutsch & Co in 30s*)

ODESSA Organisation der Ehemaligen SS-Angehörigen (*German: Organisation for Former Members of the SS*) (POL)

ODIHR Office for Democratic Institutions & Human Rights

ODWE Oxford Dictionary for Writers and Editors

OE old Etonian

OE old English (FPA)

OE, oe omissions excepted (COM)

OECD Organisation for Economic Co-operation & Development (*formerly OEEC*)

OED Oxford English Dictionary (FPA)

OEEC Organisation of European Economic Co-operation (*now OECD*) (COM)

OEIC open ended investment company

OEM original equipment manufacturer (COM)

OF old French (FPA)

off offer; office; official; officer

OFFER, Offer Office of Electricity Regulation

OFGAS, Ofgas Office of Gas Supply

OFHC oxygen-free high-conductivity copper (SCI)

OFI Office of Federal Investigation

OFM Ordo Fratrum Minorum (*Latin: Order of Minor Friars – the Franciscans*)

OFris old Frisian (FPA)

OFSTED, Ofsted Office for Standards in Education

OFT Office of Fair Trading

OFTEL, Oftel Office of Telecommunications

OFWAT, Ofwat Office of Water Services

OG old girl

OG Officer of the Guard (MIL)

OG ogee (*a shape of moulding*) (ARC)

OG original gum

OGPU Obyedinyonnoye Gosudarstvennoye Politi-cheskoye Upravleniye (*Russian: United State Political Administr-ation – Soviet State Security System 1923–34 – see NKVD*)

OGS old git syndrome

OH old Harrovian

OH overall height

OHC overhead camshaft

OHG old High German (FPA)

OHMS On His/Her Majesty's Service

OHP overhead projector (COM)

OHV overhead valve engine

OIC Organisation of the Islamic Conference

OIC officer-in-charge

OIC officer in the case

oil red O an acid monoazo (*a fat stain*) (CHM)

OIRO offers in the region of (*house adverts*)

OJ Orenthal James Simpson

OJ orange juice (F&D)

OK signifying acknowledgement, or something in good condition. Variously from (1) Orl Korrect; (2) Choctaw okeh = it is so; (3) Obadiah Kelly, freight agent; (4) aux quais; but (5) probably referring to the OK Club founded 1840 by supporters of US President Martin Van Buren, born at Old Kinderhook

OL ordinary letter (PRP)

OL overall length

OL old Leysian

OLE object linking & embedding (SCI)

O-level ordinary level examination (*became GCSE*)

OLG old Low German (FPA)

OLIC on-line inspection centre (*of British Gas*) (COM)

OM Member of the Order of Merit

Om Ostmark

OMI Oblate of Mary Immaculate

OMM Officer of the Order of Military Merit

OMP oblique musical philosopher (*Ivor Cutler of y'Wup OMP*)

OMR optical mark recognition (SCI)

OMS Organisation Mondiale de la Santé (*French: World Health Organization*)

ON Ordre Nouveau (*French: New Order*) (POL)

ON old Norse (FPA)

OND Opera Nazionale Dopolavoro (*Italian: National After-Work Leisure Organisation*) (POL)

OND Ordinary National Diploma

ono or nearest offer (*spotted: £700 ono; no offers*)

ONS Office for National Statistics

OOP object-oriented programming (SCI)

OP own protection (PRP)

OP Ordo Praedicatorum (*Latin: Order of Preachers – the Dominicans*)

op operator

OP old Persean

OP observation post (MIL)

op cit opere citato (*Latin: in the work cited*) (FPA)

OP, op out of print (FPA)

op, opp opposite

OPAS Occupational Pensions Advisory Service (COM)

OPC, opc ordinary Portland Cement (ARC)

OPCS Office of Population Censuses and Surveys

OPEC Organisation of Petroleum Exporting Countries

OPG Dental Panoramic Tomograph

OPIEM Older People in Europe Week

opO operational order (MIL)

OPP film orientated polypropene film (*biaxially stretched to improve its physical properties, widely used*) *in packaging because of its high gloss, clarity, impact strength and low moisture permeability*) (SCI)

OPRAF Office of Passenger Rail Franchising

opt optative; optimum; optional

opt optician

OPTI over-mortgaged, post-Thatcherite individual

OR operations research (COM)

or owner's risk (COM)

OR other ranks (MIL)

OR or (*a logical operation*) (SCI)

ORB omnidirectional radio beacon (NAV)

ORBAT order of battle (MIL)

ORC Offshore Racing Council (*attacking wolf-in-sheep's-clothing yachts*) (NAV)

ORC Orange River Colony

ORCHID one recent child, heavily in debt

ord ordinance

ord ordinary

ord order (MIL)

ORD optical rotatory dispersion (SCI)

ord ordinal (SCI)

ord, ordn ordnance (MIL)

org organisation; organised

org organic (SCI)

ORI Office of Research Integrity (*US watchdog*)

orig origin; original(ly)

ORTF Office de Radiodiffusion-Télévision Française (*France – former state radio and television service*) (MUS)

Orth Orthodox

ORV off-road vehicle

OS outstanding; out of stock (COM)

OS old school

OS ordinary seaman

os only son

OS old Saxon (FPA)

OS one side (ARC)

OS outsize

OS ordnance survey

OS old style in the calendar (*of Great Britain before 1752*)

OS&M operation support & maintenance (SCI)

OS&W oak, sunk & weathered (ARC)

OS, os old series

OSA Official Secrets Act (PRP)

OSA Order of Saint Augustine

OSB Order of Saint Benedict

OSCA Out-of-School Childcare Association

OSCE Organisation for Security and Co-operation in Europe (*grew out of mid-70s East–West Forum ESCE*)

OSD Order of Saint Dominic

OSF Order of Saint Francis

OSFC [of the] Order of St Francis, Capuchin

OSL optically stimulated learning

OSNC Orient Steam Navigation Co

OSRD Office of Scientific Research and Development

OSS Office of Strategic Services (MIL)

OSS Open Spaces Society

OSS outside the solar system (SCI)

OST Office of Science & Technology (COM)

OSTI Office for Scientific & Technical Information

OStJ Officer of the Order of St John of Jerusalem

OT overtime

OT occupational therapist

OT overland telegraph (*Australia*) (SCI)

OTC over the counter

OTC Officers' Training Corps
OTE on target earnings (COM)
OU Open University
OU Oxford University
OUAC Oxford University Athletic Club
OUAFC Oxford University Association Football Club
OUBC Oxford University Boat Club (SPR)
OUCC Oxford University Cricket Club
OUDS Oxford University Dramatic Society
OUP Oxford University Press
OURFC Oxford University Rugby Football Club
OUSA Open University Students' Association
OV open visit (PRP)
OV open vent (ARC)
ovno or very near offer
OVRA Opera di Vigilanza e Repressione Antifascista (*Italian Organisation for Vigilance & Repression of Anti-Fascism*) (POL)
OW overall width
Oxon Oxoniensis (*Latin: of Oxford*)

P

P Pastor
P perennial
P pump with 9m or 10.5m ladder (FRS)
p per
p post (after)
p pro (*Latin: in favour of*)
P President
P Priest
P Prince
p population
P parental generation (SCI)
p proton (SCI)

p pipe (ARC)
P Post Office
P page (*pp – pages*)
p piano (*Latin: softly*)
P public information (*info*) (MIL)
p- primary (*the functional group attached to a -CH2 group*) (CHM)
p- pros- (*containing a condensed double aromatic nucleus substituted in the 2,3 positions*) (CHM)
p- para- (*containing a benzene nucleus substituted in the 1,4 positions*) (CHM)
P D James Phyllis Dorothy (*English author, 1920–*)
P display PPI unit map display produced by intensity modulation of a rotating radial sweep (NAV)
P G Wodehouse Pelham Grenville (*English/US novelist, 1881–1975*)
P gas one based on argon, used for gas-flow counting (CHM)
P&G Procter & Gamble (*NB: not Proctor*) (COM)
P&L profit & loss (COM)
P&O Peninsular & Oriental (COM)
P&OSNCo Peninsular and Oriental Steam Navigation Co
p&p postage & packing (COM)
P&P pay & privileges (PRP)
P&S pepper & salt (F&D)
P&S proposed & seconded
P, p, pp page(s)
p, part participle
P/E ratio price/earnings ratio (COM)
p/w per week (COM)
PA purchasing agent (COM)
PA private account (COM)
PA particular average (COM)
PA Press Association (COM)
pa per annum (*Latin: through the year*) (COM)

PA prison auxiliary (PRP)

PA Power of Attorney

PA public address (system)

PA publicity agent

PA personal assistant

PA post adjutant

PA public agent

PA press agent

Pa father

PA Publishers' Association (FPA)

PA personal appearance (FPA)

PAAAFE patients' authority alternative appropriate facilities elsewhere

PABX private automatic branch exchange (SCI)

PAC Penal Affairs Consortium (PRP)

PAC Pan-African Congress

pac passed the final examination of the Advanced Class, The Military College of Science

PACE Police & Criminal Evidence Act (1984)

PACE Property Advisors to the Civil Estate

PAFO pissed & fell over

PAG Pan-American Games (SPR)

PAGAD People Against Gangsterism & Drugs (*South African vigilante group*)

PAGAN people against goodness & normalcy

PAH polycyclic aromatic hydro-carbons (CHM)

PAIN Prisoners' Advice & Information Network (PRP)

PAIN Parents Against Injustice (*those falsely accused of abuse*)

PAL phase alternative line (*the development of the NTSC colour TV system adopted by most west European broadcasting systems, the major exception being France (see* SECAM)) (FPA)

PamPAC Pamela Harriman's Political Action Committee (*raising funds for the US Democrats*)

PAMRA Performing Artists' Media Rights Association

PANS pretty amazing new services (*telephony – see* POTS) (SCI)

PAO principal administration officer (FRS)

PAPA Professional Authors and Publishers' Association

PAQ Position Analysis Question-naire (*McCormick Jeanneret & Meacham 1962*) (COM)

PAR parole assessment report (PRP)

par paragraph (FPA)

PAR planed all round (*of timber; now PSE*) (ARC)

PAR precision-approach radar (NAV)

par Parish

Par C Parian Cement (ARC)

par, parens parenthesis/es ( ) (FPA)

Park Bench telegraphic address of Dorothy Parker & Robert Benchley

Parl Agt Parliamentary Agent

parl proc parliamentary procedure

part particular

PAS prisoners' advice service (PRP)

PAS para-aminosalicylic acid (CHM)

PAs rock climbing boots named after Pierre Allain

PAS power-assisted steering

PAS reaction periodic acid (*Schiff*) (SCI)

PASI Professional Associate of the Chartered Surveyors' Institution (*changed August 1947 to ARCS*)

pat(d) patent; patented
PATA Pacific Travel Association
PAU Pan American Union
pav pavlova (*Australia & NZ*) (F&D)
PAX private automatic exchange (SCI)
pax passengers
PAYE pay as you earn
payt payment (COM)
PB prayer book (FPA)
PB personal best
PBA paralysis by analysis
PBAB please bring a bottle (F&D)
PBC porcelain bonded crown
PBX private branch exchange (SCI)
PC petty cash; price current (COM)
pc price (COM)
PC previous convictions (PRP)
PC Parish Council (*not to be confused with the PCC, as it is in Dibley*)
PC police constable (FRS)
PC Privy Council(lor) (*does it standing up*) (POL)
PC politically correct
PC Prince Consort
PC Parish Councillor
PC Parish Clerk
PC past commander
PC Progressive Conservative (*Canada*)
PC prompt corner (FPA)
PC personal computer (SCI)
PC people carrier
pc per centum (*Latin: in the hundred*)
PC, pc postcard
pc, pcs piece(s)
PCAS Polytechnics Central Admission System
PCB printed circuit board (SCI)
PCB polychlorinated biphenyl (CHM)

PCC Parochial Church Council (*different from the Parish Council except, apparently, in Dibley*)
PCCU Psychiatric Criminal Care Unit (PRP)
PCD pitch-circle diameter (SCI)
PCE pyrometric cone equivalent (SCI)
PCF Parliamentary Christian Fellowship
PCF Party Communiste Français (*French: French Communist Party*) (POL)
PCFC Polytechnics' & Colleges' Funding Council
PCI Partito Comunista Italiano (*Italian: Communist Party*) (POL)
PCI peripheral component inter-connect (*type of expansion slot*)
PCL power-train check lamp
PCM per calendar month
PCM pulse code modulation (SCI)
PCMO principal colonial medical officer
PCN Personnel Certification in Non-destructive Testing (*TWI award*) (SCI)
PCN personal communications network (SCI)
PCNB pentachloronitrobenzene (*quintozene, used as a fungicide*) (CHM)
PCO prison custody officer (PRP)
PCP phencyclidine™ (*angel dust*)
PCQ Please Charleston Quietly
PCR Production & Casting Report (FPA)
PCR polymerase chain reaction (SCI)
PCR Production and Casting Report (*weekly perfoming-arts briefing*)
PCS *Porpoise* Carrier service (*red and blue flag flown on submarine*

mine layer Porpoise *on return to England after running supplies to Malta 1942*)

PCT personal construct theory – Kelly

PCU prisoner casework unit (*dealing with Prisoners' requests & complaints above prison level*) (PRP)

PCV public carrying vehicle

pd paid (COM)

PD pretty disgusting (PRP)

PD Police Department (*USA*)

pd potential difference (SCI)

PDA postdeflection acceleration (SCI)

PDC programme delivery control (SCI)

PDE professional development in education PDF portable document format (SCI)

PDI pre-delivery inspection

PDMS postal direct marketing service (COM)

PDP personal development plan (COM)

PDQ pretty damn quick

PDR personal development review (COM)

PDR price-dividend ratio (COM)

PDS prison disciplinary system (PRP)

PDS Partei Demokratischen Sozialismus (*German: Party of Democratic Socialism*) (POL)

PDS Partito Democratico della Sinistra (*Italian: Democratic Party of the Left*) (POL)

PDSA People's Dispensary for Sick Animals

PDT pre-driver training

PDU Personality Disorder Unit

PE Protestant Episcopal

PE presiding elder

PE physical education

PE, pe printer's error (FPA)

PEC photoelectric cell (SCI)

PEC Plain English Campaign

PECUSA Protestant Episcopal Church in the United States of America

PED parole eligibility date (PRP)

PED polymer engineering directive

ped pedal

ped pedestal (ARC)

PEI, PEIO, PEO physical education instructor; instructing officer; officer (PRP)

pekabid people everyone else knows about but I don't

PEM partial eclipse of the moon (SCI)

PEN International Association of Poets, Playwrights, Editors, Essayists & Novelists (FPA)

Pentriburg Bishop of Peterborough

PEP personal empowerment programme (PRP)

PEP political & economic planning

PER Professional Employment Register (COM)

per person

perf perforated; perforation (FPA)

perf, pf perfect (FPA)

perfin perforated with initials (*now SPIF*)

perm permutation

PERME Propchant Experimental Rocket Motor Establishment (*see* RARDE)

pers person; personal

PERT programme evaluation & review technique (*a management control tool for project organising & continuous assessment*) (COM)

pert pertaining

perv sexual pervert

PES partial eclipse of the sun (SCI)

Pest Pressure for Economic and Social Toryism

PET Prisoners' Education Trust (PRP)

PeTA People for the Ethical Treatment of Animals

PETN pentaerythritol tetranitrate (*a detonating explosive*) (CHM)

PF Patriotic Front (POL)

pf preferred

pf power factor (SCI)

PF plain face (ARC)

PF resins phenol formaldehyde (methanol) resins (SCI)

PFA Professional Footballers Association (UNI)

PFA pre-family adult PFCO principal fire control officer (FRS)

PFD personal flotation device (*lifebelt*) (NAV)

PFF prisoners' families & friends (PRP)

PFI private finance initiative PFI&R part fill in & ram (ARC)

PFN Parti des Forces Nouvelles (*French: Party of New Forces*) (POL)

PFR Partito Fascista Repubblicano (*Italian: Fascist Republican Party*) (POL)

PG postgraduate

PG Parti Québecois (*Canada*) (POL)

PG paying guest; professional guest

PG video classification – parental guidance advised (FPA)

PGA Prison Governors' Association

PGA British Professional Golfers' Association (SPR)

PGAA Professional Golfers' Association of America (SPR)

PGCE Post Graduate Certificate of Education

PGOM Poor great old man (*Paul Erdös, mathematician (1913–96)*

styled himself thus when his mother died – he also added the initials LD (*living dead*) when he became 60, and AD (*archaeological discovery*) at 65)

PGR parental guidance recommended (*Australia*) (FPA)

Ph the phenyl radical C6H5- (CHM)

pH potential of hydrogen

PH Public House

pH value potential of hydrogen (*a measure of acidity or alkalinity of a solution; a logarithmic index for the hydrogen ion concentration in an aqueous solution. pH 7 is neutral; <7 is acid; >7 is alkali*) (SCI)

ph, phr phrase

Phar, phar, Pharm, pharm pharmacist

PhD Doctor of Philosophy

PHI permanent health insurance (COM)

phil philosophy

philol philology; philological (FPA)

PHLEGM The People's Hayfever Listener Examiner Gazette Magazine (*a magazine for hayfever sufferers – Ben Elton Gasping 1990*) (FPA)

phonol phonology (FPA)

phot, photog photograph; photographic; photography (SCI)

photog photographer

photom photometry (SCI)

PIA Personal Investment Authority (*replaced FIMBRA & LAUTRO July 1994*) (COM)

PIAT project integrity assurance team (COM)

PIAT platoon infantry anti-tank (*weapon*) (MIL)

PIB polyisobutylene or polybutene (SCI)

PIBS permanent interest-bearing shares (COM)

PICA publishing in the Cambridge area

PICAO Provisional International Civil Aviation Organisation

PICS Platform for Internet Content Selection (SCI)

pict pictorial (FPA)

PID Political Intelligence Department (*of the FO*)

PIDC proportional integral differential controller

PIE period of interruption of employment

PIGS procedures, information, guidance & standards (COM)

PILOH pay in lieu of holiday (COM)

PIN personal identification number (*used at EFTOS – please not 'PIN number'*) (COM)

PIN pain in the neck

p-i-n p-type, intrinsic, n-type (SCI)

PIN or p-i-n diode a semiconductor p-n diode with a layer of intrinsic semiconductor incorporated between the p & n junctions, used as an RF switching element (SCI)

pinx pinxit (*Latin: he/she painted it*) (FPA)

PIP People's Independent Party

PIR passive infrared detector (SCI)

PIT passive immune therapy

PJC porcelain jacket crown

PJs pyjamas

Pk park

pk park; peak

pkg package; packing

PKK Kurdish Workers' Party

PKP group associated with the Kurds

PKU phenylketonuria

PL pump with 13.5m ladder (FRS)

PL Pluto (SCI)

pl place

Pl, pl(s) plural(s)

Pl, plat platoon (MIL)

PL/1 programming language 1 (SCI)

pl/s plate/s (FPA)

PLA Port of London Authority (COM)

PLA People's Liberation Army (*China*)

PLA private light aircraft

PLASA Professional Lighting and Sound Association

plat plateau

PLC Plain Language Commission

PLC, plc Public Limited Company (COM)

PLCWTWU Power Loom Carpet Weavers & Textile Workers Union (UNI)

Plen plenipotentiary

PLG private light goods (*vehicle taxation class*)

PLJ™ Pure Lemon Juice (F&D)

PLO Palestine Liberation Organisation

PLP prison link project (PRP)

PLP Parliamentary Labour Party (POL)

PLR public lending right (FPA)

PLUTO pipeline under the ocean (MIL)

pm premium (COM)

PM Prime Minister (POL)

PM past master

PM paymaster

PM postmaster

PM provost marshal (MIL)

pm post meridiem (*Latin: after noon*)

PMB Potato Marketing Board

PMBX private manual branch exchange (*knitting piano*) (SCI)

PMC Peterborough Motor Club

pmfji pardon me for joining in (*netspeak*)

PMG paymaster general

PMG postmaster general

PMG provost marshal general (MIL)

PMID pick me, I'm desperate

PMO Pathfinder Mission Operations

PMO principal medical officer

PMPO peak music power output

PMPQ professional & management position questionnaire (Mitchell & McCormick 1979) (COM)

PMRAFNS Princess Mary's Royal Air Force Nursing Service (MIL)

PMRC Parents' Musical Research Centre (campaigning to ban broadcasts of songs with explicit sex & violence) (FPA)

PMS pre-menstrual syndrome

PMT photomechanical transfer (*formerly a bromide – a B&W photograph made by the bromide process*) (FPA)

PMTS predetermined motion time system (*work measurement technique*) (COM)

PMU Population Management Unit (PRP)

PMX private manual exchange (SCI)

PN promissory note (COM)

p-n junction boundary between n-type semiconductors, having marked rectifying characteristics, used in diodes, photocells, transistors etc (SCI)

PNB personal needs break (*'being excused' – at the comfort station*) (COM)

PNC Police National Computer

PNF Partito Nazionale Fascista (*Italian: National Fascist Party*) (POL)

PNG persona non grata (*Latin: an unacceptable or unwelcome person; a diplomat who is unacceptable to the sovereign or government to whom he/she is accredited*)

PNG passive night goggles (MIL)

PNG Papua New Guinea

p-n-i-p transistor similar to p-n-p transistor with a layer of an intrinsic semiconductor (germanium of high purity) between the base and the collector to extend the HF range (SCI)

p-n-p transistor a junction transistor in which a thin slice of n-type is sandwiched between slices of p-type, & amplification arises from hole conduction controlled by the electric field in the n-type slice (SCI)

PNR point of no return (SCI)

PNS Principal Nursing Sister (PRP)

PO postal order (COM)

PO personnel officer (COM)

PO pilot officer

PO Philharmonic Orchestra (MUS)

PO Portugal

PO post office

PO almost invariably principal officer especially in speech (PRP)

PO perspiration odour

PO petty officer

PO box post office box (switchable resistors) (SCI)

PO bridge post office bridge (*instrument for measuring/testing electrical resistance*) (SCI)

PO, Pat Off Patent Office (COM)

po, potty pot de chambre (*French: chamber pot*)

POA price on application

POA Prison Officers Association (UNI)

POB post office box

POC potential officer cadet (MIL)

POCL Post Office Counters Ltd

POD pay on delivery (COM)

POE port of entry (COM)

POE port of embarkation (MIL)

POETS day piss off early, tomorrow's Saturday

POEU Post Office Engineers Union (UNI)

PoI police (FRS)

POL petroleum, oil & lubricants (MIL)

pol, polit politics; political

POLA Port of London Authority

POLAND please open lovingly and never destroy

poly polytechnic

pom Prisoner of His/Her Majesty (*traditionally, but the Australian National Dictionary suggests it's a shortening of 'pomegranate', itself a corruption of 'immigrant'*)

PONA person of no account (*ie not on the Internet*)

POP post office preferred (*envelope size*) (COM)

pop popular

pop population

POP printing-out paper (*a photographic paper which produces an image on printing and which needs only fixing, no development. Obsolete for general use but sometimes used for proofing*) (SCI)

POPP prison officer in a private prison (PRP)

POPS Partners of Prisoners & Families Support Group (PRP)

POS point of sale (COM)

pos position; positive

POSEIDON perfectly ordinary system for entering inventions and discoveries on the net

POSH port out(ward), starboard home (*supposed to be the better sides of a cruise-liner, hence the cabins were more expensive, and 'POSH' would be chalked on the luggage*)

poss possession; possessive

poss, possy possibly

POSSLQ persons of opposite sex sharing living quarters (*pronounced possil-queue*)

POST point of sales terminal (COM)

POT Post Office Tower

pot potential; potentiometer (SCI)

POTS plain old telephone services (*see* PANS) (SCI)

POUT prison officer under training (PRP)

pov point of view

POW Prisoner Outreach Work (PRP)

POW, PoW Prince of Wales

POW, PoW prisoner of war (MIL)

PP prepaid (COM)

pp past participle

PP Parish Priest

PP past president

pp printed pages (FPA)

p-p junction one between p-type crystals having different electrical properties (SCI)

pp, per pro per procurationem (*Latin: on behalf of, by proxy, by delegation to, through the agency of*)

PP, pp parcel post

PPA Prison Parole Assessment (PRP)

PPA Pre-School Playgroups Association

PPA Phoebe Persis Allen (*1931–96; OUP head of desk editing 1969–86*) (FPA)

PPA prescription priority authority

PPC professional personnel consultant (COM)

PPC pour prendre congé (*French: to take leave*)

PPC plain plaster cornice (ARC)

PPCLI Princess Patricia's Canadian Light Infantry

ppd post-paid (COM)

ppd prepaid

PPE philosophy politics & economics

PPE personal protective equipment

PPF Parti Populaire Français (*French: Popular French Party*) (POL)

PPG planning policy guidance

PPI Partito Popolare Italiano (*Italian Popular Party*) (POL)

PPI plan position indicator (NAV)

ppi picks per inch (*textiles*) (SCI)

PPL Phonographic Performance Ltd (*collecting and distributing royalties*) (FPA)

PPL Private Pilot's Licence

P-plate (green P) optional indication of recent driving-test pass

ppm parts per million (SCI)

PPM, ppm peak programme meter (FPA)

PPnined assaulted – possibly with PP9 battery in a sock (PRP)

PPP purchasing power parity (COM)

PPP Private-Public Partnerships

PPPPPP planning & performance prevent piss poor performance

PPQ bar pterygopalatoquadrate bar (*the rod forming the upper jaw in cartilaginous fish*) (SCI)

ppr, p pr present participle

PPRA Past President of the Royal Academy

PPRR Performance Planning & Review Record (PRP)

PPRS preferred planning reporting system (PRP)

PPS personal/parliamentary private secretary (POL)

PPS post-polio syndrome

pps post postscriptum (*Latin: after postscript*)

PPSS post pee skirt syndrome

ppt precipitate (SCI)

PPTA Post-primary Teachers Association (*NZ*)

PPU Peace Pledge Union (*sells white poppies*) (POL)

PPV pay per view (FPA)

PQ parliamentary question

pq previous question

PQ Province of Quebec

PQ developer pyrazolidone & hydroquinone (*compound with characteristics similar to MQ*) (SCI)

PR public relations (COM)

pr price; preferred; preference (COM)

PR Prison riot (PRP)

PR proportional representation

PR public relations

PR Peter Rabbit (*put your chin up so mother can button up to your neck – from a Beatrix Potter illustration*)

pr pair(s)

Pr Priest

Pr Prince

pr paper (FPA)

pr printed (FPA)

Pr propyl (*-C3H7 radical*) (CHM)

pr, pron pronoun; pronounce(d); pronunciation

PRA President of the Royal Academy (FPA)

PRA Picture Research Association (*formerly spread*)

PRAM parameter RAM (SCI)

PRAMS processing asset management system (COM)

PRB Pre-Raphaelite Brotherhood (*first appeared on their work at the RA 1849*) (FPA)

PRBS pseudo random binary sequence (SCI)

Preb Prebendary

prec preceding

precon previous conviction (PRP)

pred predicate

pref prefatory; preference; preferred

pref prefix

pref preface (FPA)

prep preparatory

prep preparation

prep preposition

PRES pre-release employment scheme (PRP)

pres presidential

Pres president

pret, pt preterite

PRF pulse repetition frequency (SCI)

PRIA President of the Royal Irish Academy

priv private

priv privative

PRO Public Records Office (COM)

pro professional

pro prostitute

PRO Public Relations Officer

pro tem pro tempore (*Latin: for the time being, temporary*)

prob probable; probably; problem

proc proceedings

proc procedure; process

prod produce; product; production (COM)

Prof, prof professor

prog progress; progressive

Prog, prog programme (SCI)

prole proletarian

PROM programmable read only memory (SCI)

prom promenade; promontory

PROMIS processing management information system (COM)

pron pronominal

pron pronounced; pronunciation

prop property (COM)

PROP preservation of the rights of prisoners (*now called PROP*) (PRP)

prop propeller

prop proposition

prop property (ARC)

prop, propr proprietor (COM)

Prot Protectorate

Prot Protestant

prov provincial; provisional

Prov Provost

Prov Provençal

Prov, prov province

Provo provincial

provos Provisional IRA

prox proximo (*Latin: of the next month*) (COM)

Prox acc proxime accessit (*Latin: next in order of merit to the winner, or a very close second*) (PRP)

performance-related pay (COM)

PRR post-recall release (PRP)

PRS Performing Rights Society (*GB*) (MUS)

PRS President of the Royal Society

PRSE President of the Royal Society of Edinburgh

PRST please return some time

PRT Petroleum Revenue Tax (COM)

PRT Prison Reform Trust (PRP)

PRWS President Royal Society of Painters in Water Colours

PS private secretary (COM)

PS police sergeant

PS personal service

PS post scriptum (*Latin: after the writing*)

PS phrase structure

ps pieces

PS prompt side (FPA)

PS Pferdestärke = cheval-vapeur (CV) (*metric unit of horse-power, = 75kg m.s-1, 735·5W or 1·986hp*) (SCI)

PS passenger steamer

Ps & Qs pleases & thank-yous

PSA Property Services Agency

PSA Police Superintendents' Association

PSA Public Service Association (*NZ*)

PSA Public Securities Association (*New York*)

psa graduate of RAF Staff College

PSBR public sector borrowing requirement (COM)

PSC permanent stressing cable (SCI)

psc passed staff college

PSD past sell-by date

PSDB Police Scientific Development Branch

PSDS Prison Service Drug Strategy (PRP)

PSE personal & social education

PSE pre-stamped envelope (*philately*)

PSE planed square edge (*of timber; was PAR*) (ARC)

pseud pseudonym

PSF Parti Social Français (*French Social Party*) (POL)

PSG phrase structure grammar

PSI professional services income (COM)

PSI Partito Socialista Italiano (*Italian Socialist Party*) (POL)

PSIF Prison Service Industries & Farming (PRP)

PSK phase shift keying (SCI)

PSL private sector liquidity (COM)

PSLA Pre-school Learning Alliance

psm Passed School Of Music (*Certificate of the Royal Military School of Music*) (MUS)

PSNC Pacific Steam Navigation Company

PSPA Pre-School Play Apparatus (PC toys)

PSPG phase-shifting pulse gate (*machine devised by composer Steve Reich (b 1936) which demonstrated that his music is not as mechanical as is sometimes supposed*) (MUS)

PSPSV Pre-school Playgroup Support Visitor

PSR pre-sentence report (PRP)

PSRA Persil stain release agent (*despots dalmatians?*) (COM)

PSTCU Public Services Tax & Commerce Union

PSTN public switched telephone network (SCI)

PSV public service vehicle (*taxation class for bus or coach*)

psycho psychopath

PT purchase tax (COM)

PT part time (PRP)

PT physical training

pt pro tempore (*Latin: for the time being*)

pt past tense

PT pupil teacher

pt patient

pt point (FPA)

PT postal telegraph (SCI)

pt(s) payment(s) (COM)

pt(s) part(s)

pt(s) point(s)

Pt(s), pt(s) port(s)

PTA Passenger Transport Authority (COM)

PTA preferential trade area (COM)

PTA Parent–Teacher Association

PTB patrol torpedo boat (*USA, now MTB*) (MIL)

PTC phenylthiocarbamide (CHM)

PTD package travel directive

Ptd A pointed arch (ARC)

PTE part-time education (PRP)

Pte private (MIL)

PTE Passenger Transport Executive

Pte, Pvt private

PTFCE polytrifluorochloroethane

PTFE polytetrafluoroethane

ptg printing (FPA)

PTN public telephone network (SCI)

PTO public telecommunications operator(s) (SCI)

PTO power take-off

PTO, pto please turn over (FPA)

PTR printer (SCI)

PTT post telephone & telegraph administration (COM)

Pty proprietary (*denoting Private Limited Company (Australia, NZ & RSA)*) (COM)

p-type semiconductor one in which the hole conduction (absence of electrons) exceeds the electron conduction, the acceptor impurity predominating (SCI)

pub public

pub, publ publisher; published; publishing; publication (FPA)

PUD pushing up daisies

PUFFIN pedestrian user-friendly intelligent crossing

pug pugilist

PUK Patriotic Union of Kurdistan

pulsar pulsating radio star (SCI)

PUP Progressive Unionist Party (POL)

PUVA psoralen + ultraviolet A (SCI)

PV parole violator (PRP)

PV porcelain veneer

PVA polyvinyl acetate; polyvinyl alcohol (SCI)

PVC polyvinyl chloride (SCI)

PVM Prisons Video Magazine (PRP)

PVM Publius Virgilius Maro (*the Roman poet Virgil/Vergil*)

PVO privileged visiting order (PRP)

PVP payment versus payment (*See* DVP)

PVS persistent vegetative state

PW policewoman

PWA person with AIDS

PWD Public Works Department (*roads, buildings, Government Railways, telegraphs, etc*)

PWE pre-warfare executive (MIL)

P-wire private (*or guard or 3rd wire of the three which constitute a channel through an exchange*) (SCI)

PWLB Public Works Loan Board

PWO Prince of Wales's Own Regiment (MIL)

PWR pressurised-water reactor (SCI)

PWS Prisoners' Wives' Service

PX Post Exchange (*US equivalent of Naafi*) (MIL)

PX private exchange (SCI)

Py pyridine (*a nucleus*) (CHM)

PYO pick your own (*labour-saving fruit-farmer's device where additionally the customer exercises quality control and cannot, therefore, subsequently complain*)

PZT photographic zenith tube (SCI)

Q

Q Queen

Q Sir Arthur Quiller-Couch (*British novelist, 1863-1944*)

Q boat unmarked police car (PRP)

Q code an internationally understood code established by ICAO, consisting of groups or letters which represent interrogatory phrases used in various aircraft flight operations

q e quod est (*Latin: which is*)

q l quantum libet (*Latin: as much as you please*)

q t quiet; secretly

Q(ops) quartering (*operations*)

Q, q, qu, ques question

Q, Qlty quality

Q, Qm Quartermaster

q, qr, quart quarterly (FPA)

q, qy query

Q$_{10}$ the ratio of the rate of progress of any reaction or process, at a given temperature, to the rate at a temperature 10° lower-temperature coefficient (SCI)

QAIMNS Queen Alexandra's Imperial Military Nursing Service

QALAS Qualified Associate Land Agents' Society

QALY quality of life adjusted years

QANTAS Queensland & Northern Territories Aerial Services

QANTAS quite a nice trip; all survived

QARANC Queen Alexandra's Royal Army Nursing Corps (MIL)

QARNNS Queen Alexandra's Royal Naval Nursing Service (MIL)

QB Queen's Bench

QbA Qualitätswein bestimmter Anbaugebiet (*German wine classification*) (F&D)

Q-band frequency band used in radar (SCI)

QBD Queen's Bench Division

QC quality control(ler) (COM)

QC Queen's Counsel

QCA Qualifications and Curriculum Authority

QCD quantum chromodynamics (SCI)

QCO queer as a clockwork orange

QE Queen's Evidence (PRP)

QED quod erat demonstrandum (*Latin: which was to be demonstrated*)

QED quantum electrodynamics (SCI)

QEF quod erat faciendum (*Latin: which was to be done*)

QF quick-firing (MIL)

QFD quantum flavourdynamics (SCI)

q-feel a term given (because of the use of q in a relative equation) to a device which applies an artificial force on the control column of a power-controlled aircraft proportional to the aerodynamic loads on the control surfaces, thereby simulating the natural 'feel' of the aircraft throughout its speed range (SCI)

QFSM Queen's Fire Service Medal for Gallantry

QFT Quantum Field Theory (SCI)

qg quarter girth (SCI)

Q-gas one based on helium widely used in gas-flow counting (CHM)

QGM Queen's Gallantry Medal

QHC Queen's Honorary Chaplain

QHDS Queen's Honorary Dental Surgeon

QHF Quintus Horatius Flaccus (*Roman poet Horace*)

QHNS Queen's Honorary Nursing Sister

QHP Queen's Honorary Physician

QHS Queen's Honorary Surgeon

QIPS quality improvement projects (COM)

QM Quartermaster

QMAAC Queen Mary's Army Auxiliary Corps

QMC Queen Mary College

QMC Quartermaster Corps (MIL)

QMG Quartermaster General

QmP Qualitätswein mit Prädikat (*German wine classification*) (F&D)

QMS Quartermaster Sergeant

QMV quality majority vote (POL)

QPD Quality Paperbacks Direct (COM)

QPM Queen's Police Medal

Q-point the static operating point for a valve or transistor (SCI)

QPP amplifier quiescent push-pull amplifier (SCI)

qpq quid pro quo (*Latin: something for something*)

QPR Queen's Park Rangers

qq questions

qqv quae vide (*Latin: which see – pl*)

Qr quarter

QRADS Quick Reaction Alert Defence System

QS Quarter Sessions

QS quick sweep (ARC)

QS Quantity Surveyor (ARC)

Q-ship query-ship (*with concealed guns*) (MIL)

QSM Queen's Service Medal (*NZ*)

QSO Queen's Service Order (*NZ*)

QSO quasi-stellar object (SCI)

QT quiet (*on the QT*)

qto quarto (*original size folded twice at right angles*) (FPA)

qty quantity (FPA)

Quacker Qualifications & National Curriculum Authority (*March 1997; a late-night sitting in the House of Lords, and the Bishop of Ripon asked if the 'National' could be dropped for technical reasons, whereupon Lord Morris observed 'It will now be called Quacker rather than Quanker'*)

QUANGO Quasi-Autonomous Non-/National Government(al) Organisation (*both forms are found but there is a world of difference between them*)

Quanker see Quacker

Quant Suff quantum sufficit (*Latin: a sufficient Quantity*)

quasar quas(i-stellar) (*radio source*)

QUB Queen's University, Belfast

QUI Queen's University in Ireland

QUICK quality, understanding, integrity, creativity, knowledge (COM)

QV qui vive

qv quod vide (*Latin: which see*)

Q-value quantity of energy released in a given nuclear reaction, normally expressed in MeV, but occasionally in atomic mass units (SCI)

QVC quality, value & convenience (*TV shopping channel*) (FPA)

qwerty indicates the standard English keyboard (*from the first six keys*) (*see* azerty)

qy query

R

R Rex/Regina (*Latin: king/queen; the Crown in a court case*)

R Rabbi

R Rector

R Response (*Christian liturgy*)

R Republican (POL)

R Royal

R restricted exhibition (*unsuitable under 18*) (FPA)

R an organic hydrocarbon radical, especially an alkyl radical (CHM)

R render (ARC)

r rare; ruled

r recipe (F&D)

R Reaumur

r- racemic (CHM)

r a m relative atomic mass (SCI)

R D Blackmore Richard Dodderidge (*author of Lorna Doone and 13 other novels: 1825–1900*)

R H Barham Revd Richard Harris (*English humourist: 1788–1845*)

R H Benson Robert Hugh (1871–1914)

r m m relative molecular mass (SCI)

R of O Reserves of Officers

R, in chromotography, the ratio of distance moved by a particular solute to that moved by the solvent front (SCI)

R&A Royal & Ancient Golf Club, St Andrews

R&B rhythm & blues (MUS)

R&C Reckitt & Colman (COM)

R&C request & complaint (PRP)

R&D research & development (COM)

R&R rape & robbery (PRP)

R&R rest & relaxation

R, Reg Regina (*Latin: Queen*)

R, Regd registered (COM)

R/D refer to drawer (*bankspeak for no money in the account*) (COM)

R2D2 robot in Star Wars (FPA)

RA robustus archistratalis (region in bird's brain concerned with song)

RA Royal Academician

RA Royal Academy (FPA)

RA right ascension (*the angle at the pole between the equinoctial colure and the hour circle through the body whose coordinates are being measured*) (SCI)

ra-, Rd radio- (*the radioactive isotope of an element*) (CHM)

RAAF Royal Australian Air Force (*was AFC*)

RAAMC Royal Australian Army Medical Corps

RABI Royal Agricultural Benevolent Institution

RAC Royal Armoured Corps (MIL)

RAC Royal Automobile Club

RAC Royal Agricultural College

RAC MSA Royal Automobile Club Motor Sports Association

R-acid used in preparation of azo-dyes for wool (CHM)

RACP Royal Australasian College of Physicians

RACS Royal Australasian College of Surgeons

rad radio (PRP)

rad radical

rad radiator (ARC)

RAD Royal Academy of Dancing

RADA Royal Academy of Dramatic Art

radar radio direction and ranging (MIL)

RADC Royal Army Dental Corps

RADI Register of Approved Driving Instructors (COM)

RAE Royal Aircraft Establishment (MIL)

RAE Royal Aerospace Establishment

RAEC Royal Army Educational Corps (*was AEC*)

RaEm radium emanation (radon) (CHM)

RAeS Royal Aeronautical Society (*estd 1866, Royal Charter 1949*)

RAF Royal Air Force (*not to be called 'Raff', formed 1 April 1918 from merger of RFC + RNAS*) (MIL)

RAFO Reserve of Air Force Officers

RAFRO Royal Air Force Reserve of Officers

RAFVR Royal Air Force Volunteer Reserve (MIL)

RAG boat owned by Messrs Rigden, Anderson & Gann, divers of Whitstable

RAGC Royal & Ancient Golf Club (SPR)

RAHS Royal Australian Historical Society

RAI Radio Audizioni Italiana (*now Radiotelevisione Italiana*) (FPA)

RAIA Royal Australian Institute of Architects

RAKE Radio Activated Key Entry [Committee] (*investigating motor car security*)

RAM Rothschild Asset Management (COM)

RAM Royal Academy of Music, London (MUS)

RAM random access memory (SCI)

ram relative atomic mass (*see* at wt) (SCI)

RAMC Royal Army Medical Corps

RAN Royal Australian Navy (MIL)

RANVR Royal Australian Naval Volunteer Reserve

RAOC Royal Army Ordnance Corps

RAP rocket assisted projectile (MIL)

RAP Regimental Aid Post

RAPC Royal Army Pay Corps

RAPT Rehabilitation for Addicted Prisoners Trust (*was ADT*) (PRP)

RAR Royal Australian Regiment (MIL)

RARDE Royal Armaments Research & Development Establishment (*was ERDE, became PERME*)

RARO Regular Army Reserve of Officers

RAS Royal Astronomical Society (SCI)

RAS Royal Agricultural Society

RAS reticular activating system

RAS, RAeS Royal Aeronautical Society

RASB Rolling Stock Acceptance Board

RASC Royal Army Service Corps (*now RCT*) (MIL)

RASE Royal Agricultural Society of England

RAT repossessed and terrified

RAT ram-air turbine (SCI)

RAT rope access technician (*abseiler working on the Millenium Dome*)

rat ratatouille (F&D)

RATO rocket-assisted take off (SCI)

RATOG rocket-assisted take off gear (SCI)

RAuxAF Royal Auxiliary Air Force

RB- Reconnaissance Bomber (MIL)

RBA Royal Society of British Artists

RBA Member of the Royal Society of British Artists

RBC Royal British Colonial Society of Artists

RBE relative biological effectiveness (SCI)

RBI runs batted in (*baseball*) (SPR)

RBL Royal British Legion (MIL)

RBOC Refined Bell Operating Company

RBS Royal Society of British Sculptors

RBSA Royal Birmingham Society of Artists

RBT random breath testing

RC Remand Centre (PRP)

RC Red Cross

RC Roman Catholic

RC Reserve Corps (MIL)

RC rough cutting (ARC)

R-C coupling resistance-capacitance coupling (SCI)

RC, rc reinforced concrete (ARC)

RCA Royal Canadian Academy

RCA Royal College of Art

RCA Rodeo Cowboys Association (SPR)

RCA Radio Corporation of America

RCAF Royal Canadian Air Force (MIL)

RCCC Royal Canadian Curling Club (SPR)

RCCC Royal Caledonian Curling Club (SPR)

RCD residual current device (SCI)

rcd received (COM)

RCD radio carbon dating

RCDS Royal College of Defence Studies (MIL)

R-cells in the larvae of some diptera, cells in the ring gland which are probably homologous with the prothoracic glands of other insects (SCI)

RCFU Reactive Crime Fighting Unit

R(CHM) Royal Commission on Historical Monuments

R(CHM)E Royal Commission on Historical Monuments in England (ARC)

RCI reliability-centred inventory (SCI)

RCL Revised Common Lectionary (*alternative service book*)

RCM Royal College of Music, London (MUS)

RCM reliability-centred maintenance (SCI)

RCMP Royal Canadian Mounted Police (*was RNWMP*)

RCN Royal Canadian Navy (MIL)

RCNC Royal Corps of Naval Constructors

RCNVR Royal Canadian Naval Volunteer Reserve

RCO Royal College of Organists

RCOG Royal College of Obstetricians and Gynæcologists

rcpt, rect, rept receipt (COM)

RCS Royal Corps of Signals (MIL)

RCS(I) Royal College of Surgeons (of Ireland)

RCT running call telephone (FRS)

RCT Royal Corps of Transport (*formerly RASC*) (MIL)

rct recruit

RCTC Royal Calcutta Turf Club (SPR)

RCUC Redundant Churches' Users' Committee

RCZ rear combat zone (MIL)

RD refer to drawer (COM)

RD Decoration for Officers of the Royal Naval Reserve

RD Região Demarcada (*Portuguese wine classification*) (F&D)

RD Rural Delivery (*NZ*)

Rd road

rd rendered (COM)

rd round
RdAc radioactinium (CHM)
RDC Rural District Council (*pre-1974*)
RDF radio direction finder (*navigation system for finding position from intersection of radio bearings from known transmitters*) (NAV)
RDI Royal Designer for Industry
RDN Registered Dental Nurse
RDS radio data system (*retunes car radio & collects traffic news*)
RDS radio date system (*for self-timing*)
RDSSMR radio date system for self-timing & message reception
RdTh radiothorium (CHM)
RDX Research Department Explosive (*cyclonite*) (CHM)
RE Religious Education
RE Reformed Episcopal
RE Right Excellent
Rear-Adm Rear Admiral
reb rebel
rebro rebroadcast (MIL)
REC Regional Electricity Company
rec recovery (MIL)
recap recapitulation
recce reconnaissance (MIL)
recd received
REconS Royal Economic Society
Rect Rector; Rectory
red reduce(d)
redupl reduplicate; reduplication
ref reference; reformed
ref with reference to
ref referee
refl reflection; reflective
Reg Regent
reg register; registered; registry; regular; regulation

reg Registrar
reg Regulator
reg Regiment (MIL)
Reg Prof, RP Regis Professor
Regt Regiment (MIL)
rehab rehabilitation
REKR Royal East Kent Regiment (*The Buffs*) (MIL)
rel released
rel relating; related
rel religion; religious
rel relative
REM rapid eye movement (SCI)
REM a pop group (MUS)
REME Royal Electrical & Mechanical Engineers ('*Reemy*' *acceptable*) (MIL)
REP die Republikaner (*German: The Republican Party*) (POL)
Rep representative; Republican (*USA*) (POL)
rep reputation
rep reporter
rep repertory (FPA)
rep, repp representative
rep, repr reprint(ed) (FPA)
rep, rept, rpt report; reported
Rep, Repub Republic; Republican
Repo repossession
repr represent; represented
req request; required; requisition
RERO Royal Engineers Reserve of Officers
Res, res research; reserve(d); residence; resides; resigned; resolution; resident
resp Respondent
resp respective(ly)
RET resolution enhancement technology
Ret retained (FRS)

ret, retd retain(ed); retired; return(ed)

rev revenue (COM)

rev reverse(d); review; revise; revision; revolution; revolve; revolving

Rev(d) Reverend

RF radio frequency (SCI)

RF- reconnaissance fighter (MIL)

RF heating radio-frequency heating (*microwaves*) (F&D)

RFA Royal Field Artillery

RFC Royal Flying Corps (MIL)

RFC Rugby Football Club (SPR)

RFE Radio Free Europe (FPA)

RFH Royal Festival Hall (MUS)

RFI radio-frequency interference (SCI)

RFL Road Fund Licence

RFO Regional Flood Office

RFQ request for quotation (COM)

RFS render, float & set (ARC)

rft reinforcement (MIL)

RFU Rugby Football Union (SPR)

RGA Royal Garrison Artillery

RGB red, green & blue (*monitor*) (SCI)

RGJA Repertory Grid Job Analysis (*Smith, Gregg & Andrews 1989*) (COM)

RGN Registered General Nurse

RGO Royal Greenwich Observatory (*Greenwich-Herstmonceux-Cambridge*) (SCI)

RGS Royal Geographical Society

RH Royal Highness

RH Royal Hospital (MIL)

rH value Log10 of the reciprocal of hydrogen pressure which would produce same electrode potential as that of a given oxidation-reduction system, in a solution of the same pH value (SCI)

RHA Road Haulage Association (UNI)

RHA Royal Horse Artillery (MIL)

RHA Regional Health Authority

RHD, rhd right-hand drive

rheo rheostat (SCI)

rhet rhetoric

RHG Royal Horse Guards (MIL)

RHortS Royal Horticultural Society

RHQ Regimental Headquarters (MIL)

RHR Royal Highland Regiment

RHS Royal Historical Society

RHS Royal Humane Society

RHS right-hand side

RHS Royal Horticultural Society

RHT Racecourse Holdings Trust

RI religious instruction

RI Royal Institution

RI Regina et Imperatrix (*Latin: Queen & Empress*)

RI Rex et Imperator (*Latin: King & Emperor*)

RIA Royal Irish Academy

RIAA curve Record Industry Association of America curve (SCI)

RIAM Royal Irish Academy of Music

RIASC Royal Indian Army Service Corps

RIB rubber inflatable boat (MIL)

RIB rigid-hull inflatable boat (NAV)

RIB Royal Institute for the Blind

RIBA Royal Institute of British Architects (*see* FSArc) (ARC)

RIBI Rotary International in Great Britain and Ireland

RIC remand in custody; rest in cell (PRP)

RIC Royal Irish Constabulary

RICS Royal Institute of Chartered Surveyors (ARC)

RIDDOR Reporting of Injuries, Diseases and Dangerous Occurrences Regulations 1995

RIE Recognised Investment Exchanges (COM)

RIF Royal Irish Fusiliers

rigid PVC PVC in its unplasticised form used chiefly for corrosion-resistant applications such as chemical pipework (SCI)

RIIE Royal Institute of International Engineers

RIM Royal Indian Marine

RIN Royal Indian Navy

RINA Royal Institution of Naval Architects (estd 1860, Charter of Incorporation 1910, Supplemental Charter 1960) (MIL)

RIP barricade- penetration device used by police

RIP requiescat/requiescant in pace (*Latin: may he, she or they rest in peace*)

RIP resin-in-pulp (SCI)

RISC reduced instruction set (SCI)

RKP Routledge & Kegan Paul (FPA)

RL Rugby League

RLED Resettlement Licence Eligibility Date (PRP)

RLIB Rugby League International Board (SPR)

RLS Robert Louis (Balfour) Stevenson (*Scottish writer 1850–1894*)

RLV Reusable Launch Vehicle (*Lockheed Martin VentureStar*) (SCI)

RM (Ian) Robert Maxwell (*British Publisher 1923–91, originally Robert Hoch, born in Slovakia*)

RM Royal Marines (MIL)

RM Royal Mail

rm ream(s) (FPA)

rm room(s) (F&D)

RMA rear maintenance area (MIL)

RMA Royal Military Academy (*Sandhurst*)

RMC Royal Military College, Sandhurst (*now incorporating Royal Military Academy*)

RMCM Royal Manchester College of Music (MUS)

RMetS Royal Meteorological Society

RMIF Retail Motor Industry Federation

RMLI Royal Marine Light Infantry

RMN Registered Mental Nurse

RMO Resident Medical Officer(s)

RMP Royal Military Policeman (MIL)

RMPA Royal Medico-Psychological Association

RMS Royal Mail Service

RMS Royal Microscopical Society

RMS Royal Mail Steamer/Ship

RMS Royal Society of Miniature Painters

RMT National Union of Rail, Maritime & Transport Workers (UNI)

RN Royal Navy

RN Registered Nurse

RNA ribonucleic acid (SCI)

RNA Romantic Novelists' Association (FPA)

RNAS Royal Naval Air Service(s) (MIL)

RNAS Royal Naval Air Station (MIL)

RNCM Royal Northern College of Music, Manchester (MUS)

RNEC Royal Navy Engineering College (*HMS* Thunderer, Manadon, Plymouth) (MIL)

RNLI Royal National Lifeboat Institution

RNP Rassemblement National Populaire (*French: National Popular Rally*) (POL)

RNR Royal Naval Reserve (MIL)

RNVR Royal Navy Volunteer Reserve (MIL)

RNVSR Royal Naval Volunteer Supplementary Reserve

RNWMP Royal Northwest Mounted Police (*now RCMP*)

RNXS Royal Naval Auxiliary Service

RNZAF Royal New Zealand Air Force (MIL)

RNZN Royal New Zealand Navy

RO Retired Officer (MIL)

RO Radio Orchestra (MUS)

RO roll-on closure (method of sealing bottles) (F&D)

RO registered owner (vehicle)

Ro recto (*on the right hand page*)

ROC Royal Observer Corps (MIL)

RoCoCo Romsey Community Car Option (*Cambridge Scheme*)

Roffen Bishop of Rochester

ROHCG Royal Opera House, Covent Garden (MUS)

ROI Royal Institute of Oil Painters

ROK Republic of Korea

Rom romance (FPA)

rom roman (*as opposed to italic*) (FPA)

ROM read-only memory (*computer*)

ROM Retail Operations Manager

Rom Cath Roman Catholic

ROMP radical office moving policy

RON reality or nothing (*from Dennis Potter* – Cold Lazarus) (FPA)

Roneo rotary neostyle (*single-cylinder stencil duplicator*) (FPA)

ROP run of paper (*ie advert may be set anywhere in the paper*) (FPA)

RORC Royal Ocean Racing Club (NAV)

RORO roll on, roll off

ro-ro roll on, roll off (PRP)

Rosco Rolling-Stock Company

ROSL Royal Over-Seas League

ROSLA raising of the school-leaving age

RoSPA Royal Society for the Prevention of Accidents

ROTI record of taped interview

ROV remotely operated vehicle

Roy Royal

RP Reformed Presbyterian

RP received pronunciation

RP Regis Professor

RP Royal Society of Portrait Painters

RPA Radiation Protection Adviser

RPB recognised professional bodies (COM)

RPC Royal Pioneer Corps (MIL)

RPG report program generator (SCI)

RPI Retail Price Index (COM)

RPM Retail Price Maintenance (COM)

rpm revolutions per minute (SCI)

RPO Royal Philharmonic Orchestra (MUS)

RPQC Right to Peace & Quiet Campaign (*founded Valerie Gibson MBE; relaunched September 1996 as the NN*)

RPRA Royal Pigeon Racing Association (SPR)

RPS Royal Photographic Society

RPV remotely piloted vehicle

RR right rear

RR Right Reverend

RR road racing (SPR)

RR alloys properly Hiduminium RR alloys (*a series of alloys of aluminium with small additions of Cu, Ni, Mg & Si*) (SCI)

RR Lyrae variables variable stars with periods of less than one day (SCI)

RRC Member of the Royal Red Cross

RRLO Race Relations Liaison Officer (PRP)

RRMT Race Relations Management Team (PRP)

RRP recommended retail price (COM)

RS Royal Society

RSA Royal Sun Alliance (COM)

RSA Royal School of Artillery (MIL)

RSA Royal Scottish Academy

RSA Royal Scottish Academician

RSA Royal Society of Arts

RSA Returned Services Association (*NZ*) (MIL)

RSA Republic of South Africa

RSA Rollright Stones Appeal

RSAI Royal Society of Antiquaries of Ireland

RSanI Royal Sanitary Institute

RSC Royal Society of Chemistry

RSC Royal Shakespeare Company (FPA)

RSCN Registered Sick Children's Nurse

RSD reflex sympathetic dystrophy (*affects nerves and can make joints swell and feel sensitive*)

RSDA Road Surface Dressing Association (*founded 1942*)

RSE Royal Society of Edinburgh

RSF rough sunk face (ARC)

RSFSR Russian Soviet Federative Socialist Republic (*now no more*)

RSG Rate Support Grant

RSG Regional Seat of Government

RSGB Radio Society of Great Britain

RSGS Royal Scottish Geographical Society

RSI Government's Rough Sleepers' Initiative

RSIN Rural Stress Information Network

RSJ rolled steel joist (ARC)

RSL Royal Society of Literature

RSL Returned Services League (*Australia*) (MIL)

RSM Royal Society of Medicine

RSM Regimental Sergeant Major (MIL)

RSME Royal School of Mechanical Engineering (MIL)

RSNZ Royal Society of New Zealand

RSO Radio Symphony Orchestra (MUS)

RSO Rural Sub-Office; Railway Sub-Office

RSPB Royal Society for the Protection of Birds

RSPCA Royal Society for the Prevention of Cruelty to Animals

RSPP Royal Society of Portrait Painters (FPA)

RSSAILA Returned Sailors, Soldiers and Airmen's Imperial League of Australia

RSVP répondez, s'il vous plaît (*French: please reply*)

RSW (Member of the) Royal Scottish Society of Painters in Watercolours

RSWP remember send wedding present

RT radio telephone (FRS)

RT Radio Times (FPA)

RT radio telegraphy; radio telephony (SCI)

Rt Hon Right Honourable

Rt Revd Right Reverend (*of a Bishop*)

RTA Radio Telecommunication Agency

RTB Richard Thomas & Baldwins Ltd (COM)

RTC round table conference (COM)

RTC Road Transport Corporation (*India*) (COM)

RTD, R&TD Research & Technological Development (SCI)

RTE Radio Telefís Éireann (FPA)

RTFF real-time flood forecasting

RTFM Deutsch catalogue (of the works of Schubert)

RTFM read the f***ing manual (*computer problem solved by those in the know – 'you've got a spot of RTFM there', see also RTMS*) (SCI)

RTGS real-time gross settlement

RTI Reflective Technology Interface (*Manchester reflective clothing company*) (COM)

RTM Rotterdam (*Netherlands airport*)

RTM ready to move (MIL)

RTMS read the manual, stupid (SCI)

RTO Railway Transport Officer

RTOS realtime operating system (SCI)

RTPI Royal Town Planning Institute

RTR Royal Tank Regiment

RTS Royal Television Society (FPA)

RTS Royal Toxophilite Society (*archery*) (SPR)

RTS Religious Tract Society

RTT, RRTY radioteletype (SCI)

RTU ready to use (*accommodation in Cat C & D prisons to meet overcrowding*) (PRP)

RTU return to unit (MIL)

RTV rocket test vehicle (SCI)

RTZ Rio Tinto Zinc (COM)

RU Rugby Union

RUBSSO Rossendale Union of Boot, Shoe & Slipper Operatives (UNI)

RUC Royal Ulster Constabulary

RUFC Rugby Union Football Club (SPR)

RUG Really Useful Group

RUG restricted users group (SCI)

RUI Royal University of Ireland

RUMP remarried upwardly mobile person

RUR Royal Ulster Rifles (MIL)

RUR Rossum's Universal Robots (FPA)

Rus Russian

RUSI Royal United Service Institution

RV Revised Version (*of the Bible*)

RV radiator valve (ARC)

R-value % decrease in density of reactor fuel for 1% burn-up (SCI)

RVM Royal Victorian Medal

RVO Royal Victorian Order

RW Right Worshipful

RW Right Worthy

RWA Race Walking Association (SPR)

RWB rear-wheel brakes

RWD, rwd rear-wheel drive

RWE Radar Warfare Establishment (*Foulsham*) (MIL)

RWF Royal Welsh Fusiliers (MIL)

RWG rainwater goods (ARC)

RWHA Royal Warrant Holders' Association

RWHS Royal Windsor Horse Show

R-wire ring wire (*in the cord circuit on a telephone switchboard, the wire connected to ring contacts on terminating plugs, and eventually the B-wire of subscriber's line*) (SCI)

RWP rainwater pipe (ARC)

RWS (Member of the) Royal Society of Painters in Water Colour

RWV robbery with violence (PRP)

RWYC Royal Western Yacht Club

RX (*radio*) receiver (SCI)

R-Y signal component of colour TV chrominance signal Combined with luminance (Y) signal it gives primary red component (SCI)

RYA Royal Yachting Association (SPR)

RYM Report of the Friends of York Minster

RYS Royal Yacht Squadron

S

S Senate

S socius (*Latin: fellow of*)

S society

S Socialist (POL)

S south

S sache (*German: thing*)

S shower

S satisfactory

S Signor

S black in names of dyestuffs (CHM)

S spade(s) (*cards*)

s succeeded

s siehe (*German: see*)

s see; semi; sign(ed); succeed(ed)

s singular

s substantive

s son

s sire

s second

s solidus (*Latin: shilling*)

s- secondary (*substituted on a carbon atom which is linked to two other carbon atoms*) (CHM)

s- syn- (*containing the corresponding radicals on the same side of the plane of a double bond between a carbon & a nitrogen atom or between two nitrogen atoms*) (CHM)

S & B slash & burn (*a method of clearing virgin forest*)

S I T spontaneous ignition temperature (SCI)

S level Special level (*of GCE/GCSE taken with A level; was Scholarship level*)

S L-type cable separate lead-type cable (*each core has its own lead sheath; a fourth lead sheath encloses them*) (SCI)

s o b son of a bitch or sonofabitch (*USA & Canada*)

S wave secondary seismic wave

S&F shopping & f***ing (*genre of novel*) (FPA)

S&M sales & marketing (COM)

S&P Save & Prosper (*Investment Company*) (COM)

S&P salt & pepper

S, San santa; santo; são (saint)

S, Sax Saxon (FPA)

S, sch school

s, semi semi-detached (ARC)

S, SS Saint(s)

s-, sym- symmetrically substituted (CHM)

S/N curve stress-number curve (SCI)

S/N ratio signal-to-noise ratio (SCI)

S/N ratio speech-to-noise ratio (SCI)

s/s same size (FPA)

S4C Sianel 4 Cymru (*Wales*) (FPA)

SA Sociedad Anónima (*Spanish limited company*) (COM)

SA Société Anonyme (*French limited company*) (COM)

SA Salvation Army

SA Sturmabteilung (*German: Storm Troopers – Nazi terrorist militia*) (POL)

sa sub anno (*Latin: under the year*)

SA, sa sex appeal

SAA South African Airways

SAAB Société d'Avions Adolphe Bernard

SAAF South African Air Force

SAB self-appointed busybody

SABA South African Bowling Association (*lawn bowls*) (SPR)

SABC South African Broadcasting Corporation (FPA)

SABENA Société Anonyme Belge d'Exploitation de la Navigation Aérienne (*Belgian World Airlines*)

SAC Senior Aircraftman (MIL)

SAC Strategic Air Command (*USA*) (MIL)

SAC Service d'Action Civique

SACA South African Croquet Association (SPR)

SACEUR Supreme Allied Commander Europe (MIL)

S-acid an intermediate in dyestuffs manufacture (CHM)

SACSEA Supreme Allied Command SE Asia

SACU Scottish AutoCycle Union (SPR)

SAD spurious acronym diploma

SAD seasonal affective disorder

SADCC South African Development Co-ordination Conference

SADG Société de Architectes Diplômés par le Gouvernmente

SADS Schedules for Affective Disorders in Schizophrenia

SAE Society of Automotive Engineers (*US; gives name to a motor oil viscosity scale*) (SCI)

SAE stamped addressed envelope; self-addressed envelope

SAF Société Aéronautique Française

SAG Société d'Automobiles à Genève

SAGA send a granny away

SAGE Stage section of Help the Aged

SAL Society of Asian Languages

sal saloon

SALIGIA Superbia, Avaritia, Luxuria, Invidia, Gula, Ira, Acedia (*Latin: acronym for the seven deadly sins*)

SALLY Small-scale Alternative Location Licence (*for local radio*)

Salop Shropshire

SALR saturated adiabatic lapse rate

SAM share appreciation mortgage (COM)

SAM social accounting matrix

SAM surface-to-air missile (MIL)

SAMBO sam (ozaschchita) b(ez) o(ruzia) (*type of wrestling using judo techniques, originating in Russia*)

SAMM Support after Murder & Manslaughter

SAMO same old shit (*coined by Jean-Michel Basquiat and Al Diaz, New York City, May 1978 – 'a tool for mocking bogusness'*)

SAMS South American Missionary Society

SAN styrene & acrylonitrile copolymer (SCI)

SAND Société Anonyme Nieuport-Delage

sanger, sarnie sandwich (F&D)

SANM Societa Anomina Nieuport-Macchi

SANROC South African Non-Racial Olympics Committee

SAO serious arrestable offence (PRP)

SAO Senior Arboricultural Officer

SAP Societa Anonima Piaggio

SAR Staff Appraisal Report (COM)

SARFB South African Rugby Football Board (SPR)

SARshack Search & Rescue shack

SARTOR Standards and Routes to Registration as an engineer (SCI)

Sarum Bishop of Salisbury

SAS Special Air Service (MIL)

SAS speed, aggression & surprise (MIL)

SAS Survive at School (*Henderson Funfax series*) (FPA)

SAS Shearer & Sheringham (England Strikers)

SASE self-addressed stamped envelope (*US equivalent of SAE*)

SASH Students Against Sexual Harassment

SASHT Shut Awards for Stupid Human Tricks (*hand in hand with the Danish Awards for contributions to the gene pool through self sacrifice*)

SASO Senior Air Staff Officer

SASU Suicide Awareness Support Unit (PRP)

Sat Saturn (SCI)

SATAN system administrators' tool for analysing networks (*for detecting security flaws*) (SCI)

SATC situation assessment and tactical control (MIL)

SATS School Standards Assessment Test Papers

SAU Special Auxiliary Unit (*of the Home Guard*)

SAV stock at valuation (COM)

sav saveloy (*Australia & NZ*) (F&D)

SAW surface acoustic wave (SCI)

Sax Saxony

SB simultaneous broadcasting (FPA)

sb substantive

sb southbound (NAV)

SB alloy a resistance material having a low temperature coefficient of resistance (SCI)

SBA Scottish Bowling Association (*lawn bowls*) (SPR)

SBA standard beam approach (NAV)

SBAC Society of British Aerospace Companies (COM)

SBAC Society of British Aircraft Constructors

SBC small bayonet cap (SCI)

SBC southbound carriageway (*see EBC, NBC and WBC*)

SBD sell-by date (F&D)

SBDSPCF Society for the Prevention of Cruelty to Food (*mooted by Raymond Postgate and emerging as the Good Food Guide, 1951*) (F&D)

SBFD Society of British Fight Directors (on stage)

SBIS Stanford Binet Intelligence Scale SBP spirit special boiling-point spirit (SCI)

SBS Special Boat Service (*see SAS*) (MIL)

SBS sick building syndrome (ARC)

SBU Strategic Business Unit (COM)

SC Star of Courage (*Canada*)

SC School Certificate (*Australia & NZ*)

SC self catering

SC Signal Corps (MIL)

SC spontaneous combustion

SC Supreme Champion

sc scilicet (*Latin from scire licet : namely, it is permitted to know*)

sc scale; scene; science

sc small capitals (FPA)

sc scene (FPA)

sc screw (SCI)

SCA Society for Creative Anachronism

SCA Specialist Cheesemakers' Association

SCAA Schools Curriculum & Assessment Authority

SCAO Senior Civil Affairs Officer

SCAPA Society for Checking the Abuses of Public Advertising

scc single cotton-covered (*wire*) (SCI)

SCCA Sports Car Club of America (SPR)

ScD Scientiae Doctor (*Latin: Doctor of Science*)

SCDA Standing Conference on Drugs Abuse

SCE Scottish Certificate of Education

SCF Senior Chaplain to the Forces

SCFBAC Scottish Central fire Brigade's Advisory Council (FRS)

schizo schizophrenic

SCID severe combined immunodeficiency disease

sci-fi science fiction (genre) (FPA)

SCL Student in Civil Law

SCM Student Christian Movement

SCM State Certified Midwife

SCM standard mean chord (*navigation*)

SCOT Scottish Canadian Oil & Transportation (COM)

SCOTVEC Scottish Vocational Education Council

SCP single-cell protein (SCI)

SCP service control power (routes your dialled number)

SCPS Society of Civil & Public Servants

SCR senior common room

SCR silicon controlled rectifier (SCI)

Script scriptural

SCS Serious Crime Squad (PRP)

SCSI small computer system interface (SCI)

SCTA Southern California Timing Association (*hot-rod*) (SPR)

sculp sculptor; sculptress

sculp sculpture (ARC)

sculpt sculpsit (*Latin: he/she sculpted*) (FPA)

Sculpt sculptor

SCY vehicle registration for Isles of Scilly (*Truro*)

SD spin dryer

sd sine die (*Latin: without a day (being fixed); indefinitely*)

sd sense datum; sound

SD syringe driver

SDA Scottish Development Agency (COM)

SDB Salesian of Don Bosco

SDC Society for the Divine Compassion (*founded in 1884*)

SDD School of Dressmaking & Design

SDF Social Democratic Federation

SDF Sudan Defence Force

SDI Strategic Defense Initiative (MIL)

SDLP Social Democratic & Labour Party (POL)

SDO Senior Divisional Officer (FRS)

SDP social, domestic, pleasure (*private car classification*) (COM)

SDP Social Democratic Party (POL)

SDRs special drawing rights (COM)

SDWW self defence with weapons

SE special equipment

s-e seine (*German: his, one's*)

SEA South-East Asia

SEAC School Examination & Assessment Council

SEALF South-East Asia Land Forces

SEALS Sea, Air & Land Service (*commandos*) (MIL)

SEAQ Stock Exchange automated quotation (COM)

SEATO South-East Asia Treaty Organisation

SEC Securities & Exchange Commission (*America's leading financial regulator*) (COM)

sec secondary; sector

sec, sect section

sec, secy, sec'y secretary

SECAM Séquential couleur à memoire (*colour TV broadcasting system used in France and Russia* (*see* PAL) (FPA)

secs seconal (*a barbiturate*) (PRP)

SED sentence expiry date (was LDR) (PRP)

SED Scottish Education Department

SEEK Science and Engineering Experiments for Kids

SEF self-elevating framework (ARC)

SEFI sequential electronic fuel injection

seg segregation block/unit (PRP)

SELA Systema Economico Latino-Americana (*aka LAES*) (COM)

SELNEC South-East Lancashire, North-East Cheshire

sel-sync selective synchronization (FPA)

Selw Selwyn College, Cambridge

SEM Society for Ethnomusicology 1955 (MUS)

SEN State Enrolled Nurse (superseded)

Sen, sen Senator

sen, snr senior

SEP Smallpox Eradication Programme

sep separate

sep sepal (SCI)

SEPRA *See* GEPAN

seq sequel (FPA)

seq(q) sequens (sequentia) (*Latin: the following*)

ser serial; series

ser sermon

SERC Science of Engineering Research Council

SERCS South-East Regional Crime Squad

SERENDIP Search for Extra-terrestrial Radio Emissions from Nearby Developed Intelligent Populations

SERM selection oestrogen receptor modulator

SERPS State Earnings Related Pension Scheme

SES *see* 2,4-DES (CHM)

SESA Support for Exhibitions and Services Abroad (*DTI Grant Scheme*)

SESO Senior Equipment Staff Officer

SET Selective Employment Tax (COM)

SET Supported Employment & Training

SEWMAR Sewer Mapping System

SF, sf science fiction (*genre*) (FPA)

SFA sweet Fanny Adams

SFCOp Senior Fire Control Operator (FRS)

SFEP Society of Freelance Editors & Proofreaders

SFIO Section Française de l'Internationale Ouvrière (*French Section of the Workers' International*) (POL)

SFO Superannuation Funds Officer (COM)

SFO Serious Fraud Office (1988)

SFor stabilisation force (MIL)

SFPO Senior Fire Prevention Officer (FRS)

SFR stand on fork and reach (*forklift truck features*)

SFTA Society of Film & Television Arts (*see* BAFTA *and* BFA) (FPA)

SFTL Small Firms' Trading Loan (COM)

SFTRC Small Firms' Training Resource Centre (COM)

SFU Signals Flying Unit (MIL)

SFU Scottish Football Union (*rugby*) (SPR)

SG Solicitor General

SG Super Gran

SG, sing singular

sg, sp gr specific gravity (SCI)

SGA Scottish Games Association (SPR)

sgd signed

SGHWR steam-generated heavy-water reactor (SCI)

SGI Sports Grounds Initiatives

Sgl Signal; Signalman (MIL)

SGM Special General Meeting

SGM Sea Gallantry Medal (*for saving life at sea*)

SGO Sports & Games Officer (PRP)

SGR Scientists for Global Responsibility

Sgt Sergeant

SH support helicopters (MIL)

sh, shr share (COM)

SHAEF Supreme Headquarters Allied Expeditionary Force

SHAPE Supreme Headquarters Allied Powers, Europe (MIL)

SHCGB Siberian Husky Club of Great Britain

SHE Springfields 97 Horticultural Exhibition

SHF, shf superhigh frequency

SHM simple harmonic motion (SCI)

shpt shipment (COM)

SHU Super Heavy User

SI Système Internationale d'Unités (*French: International System of Units*)

SI Statutory Instrument

SI Secret Intelligence (*within OSS*)

SIAI Societa Indrovolanti Alta Italia

SIB Securities & Investments Board (COM)

SIB Special Investigation Branch (MIL)

Sic so written

SICA Signalling Infrastructure Condition Assessment

SID standard instrument departure (NAV)

SIFE Security Intelligence Far East

Sig, sig signature

Sig, sig Signor; Signore

SIM subscriber identity module (*as in mobile phone*) (SCI)

SIMB Société Industrielle des Métaux et du Bois

SIMEX Singapore International Monetary Exchange (COM)

SIMM single in-line memory module (SCI)

SIMNOO single income new married owner occupier

SIMO single input multiple output

simp simpleton (*USA*)

SIMR seriously ill for medical research

simul simultaneous

SINBAD single income, no boy-friend and desperate

SINGLE sexy, intelligent, naughty, generous, loving, exciting

Sinopec China Petro-chemical Corporation (COM)

SINS ship's inertial navigation system (NAV)

SIO Senior Investigating Officer

SIPRI Stockholm International Peace Research Institute

SIPS side-impact protection system (*Volvo feature*)

SIPT Strikemaster instrument protection trainer

Sir J M Barrie James Matthew (*Scottish dramatist and novelist, 1860–1937*)

SIRB Swedish Institute for Race Biology (*Dissolved eugenics organisation*)

SIS Signals Intelligence Service (*became NSA*) (MIL)

sis sister

SISO single input, single output

SISTER Special Institute for Science & Technology Education & Research

sit situation (MIL)

SIT Society of Instrument Technology (*estd 1944, see* IMC) (SCI)

SITCOM single income, two children, oppressive mortgage

sitcom situation comedy (FPA)

sitrep situation report (MIL)

SIU School Improvement Unit

SIW Self-Inflicted Wound (*a Wilfred Owen poem*)

SJ Society of Jesus

SJ soldered joint (ARC)

SJC Supreme Judicial Court

SJD Scientiae Juridicae Doctor (*Latin: Doctor of Juridical Science*)

SJT Stephen Joseph Theatre, Scarborough (*Alan Ayckbourn's 'local'*)

Skr, Skt Sanskrit (FPA)

SL special letter (PRP)

SL Solicitor at Law

SL short lengths (ARC)

SLA second language acquisition

SLA State Liquor Agency (*New York*)

SLBM submarine-launched ballistic missile (MIL)

SLCM sea-launched cruise missile (MIL)

SLD Social & Liberal Democratic Party (*Northern Ireland*) (POL)

sld sailed; sealed; sold

SLI specific language improvement

SLOA Steam Locomotive Operators' Association

SLR single lens reflex (*camera*) (SCI)

SLR self loading rifle (MIL)

SM Stage Manager (FPA)

SM School of Meditation

s-m seinem (*German: to his/one's*)

SM, Sgt Maj Sergeant Major

SMA Society of Marine Artists

SMART Special Measures Action Reform Team

SMART Stop Motor Crime and Ring Today (*Crime Stoppers Motor Crime Campaign*)

SMART Shocking Mainstream Adolescent into Resisting Temptation (*plan of Sheriff for Arpaio of Phoenix, Arizona to prevent delinquency*)

SMASH Steeple Morden After School & Holiday Club

SMATV small master antenna television/satellite master antenna television (FPA)

SMC Substances Misuse Co-ordinator (PRP)

SMD surface mounted device (SCI)

SMEs small & medium-sized enterprises (COM)

SMG sub machine gun (MIL)

SMILE St Mary's Immediate and Long-term Equipment

SMIRE Senior Member Institution of Radio Engineers (*New York*)

smk smoke

SMM Society of Motor Manufacturers

SMO Senior Medical Officer (PRP)

Smops School of Maritime Operations (*HMS Dryad, Southwick Park*)

SMP Statutory Maternity Pay

SMPE Society of Motion Picture Engineers (*a standard for soundtracks on sub-standard cinematograph film in which the sound-track is located on the left-hand side of the picture as normally projected on the screen, as contrasted with the DIN standard, at one time in considerable use in Europe, which places the sound-track on the right-hand side. In each type the sound-track replaces one set of sprocket holes on the side of the film*) (FPA)

SMRC Society of Miniature Rifle Clubs (SPR)

SMRV Sea Mammal Research Unit

SMV stolen motor vehicle

SN Scottish Nuclear (*See* BE)

sn sein (*German: be (verb)*)

s-n seinen (*German: his, one's*)

SNAG sensitive new-age guy

SNAGG sensitive new-age garbage guts

SNARLER services no longer required (*sacking*)

SNC Shergottite, Nakhlite & Chassignite; group of Martian meteorites named for their respective points of impact (SCI)

SNCC Student Non-violent (later National) Coordinating Committee (*USA*)

SNCF Société Nationale des Chemins de Fer (*French railway system*) (COM)

SNCO Senior Non Commissioned Officer (MIL)

SNES Super Nintendo Entertainment System (SPR)

SNG synthetic natural gas (CHM)

SNHS School of Natural Health Sciences (*Batley, Yorkshire*)

SNO Scottish National Opera (MUS)

SNP Scottish Nationalist Party (POL)

SO Shipping Order (COM)

SO Seller's Option (COM)

SO Stationery Office (COM)

SO Senior Officer (PRP)

SO Staff Officer (FRS)

SO Special Order

SO Symphony Orchestra (MUS)

SOAP Samuel Wilberforce, Bishop of Oxford (1845–69) was known as 'Soapy Sam'. He commissioned a building from the architect A W N Pugin, and some wag suggested that the collaboration should be incised in stone – SOAP (Samuel Oxoniensis; Augustus Pugin)

sob sonofabitch; silly old bugger

Soc, soc Socialist (POL)

Soc, soc Society

SOCA Submariners Old Comrades Association (MIL)

SOCO Scenes of Crime Officer

SOD, SODD start of day disk (SCI)

SOE Special Operations Executive (MIL)

SOE *See* EUROSTAT

SOED Shorter Oxford English Dictionary (FPA)

SOFA shifting offered furniture around

SOG speed over ground (*maritime GPS data*) (NAV)

SOGAT Society of Graphical & Allied Trades (UNI)

SOH sense of humour ('*I don't have a sense of humour' is an interesting conversation-stopper*)

SOHC single overhead camshaft

SOHO Solar and Heliospheric Observatory (*chosen also because it was a Mediaeval hunting cry*) (SCI)

sol soluble; solution (SCI)

Sol(r) Solicitor

SOLT Society of London Theatres (FPA)

SOM start of message (SCI)

SOP standard operating procedure (COM)

sop soprano

SoR Society of Radiographers (UNI)

SORN statutory off road notification

SOS save our souls (*a back-formation from the Morse* • • – – – • • •)

SOSUS sound surveillance system (MIL)

Soton Southampton

SOVA Society of Voluntary Associates (PRP)

Soweto South West Township

SP starting price/position (*horse racing*) (PRP)

SP Spain

SP single pole (SCI)

SP soil pipe (ARC)

SP small portly

Sp Spaniard; Spanish

Sp spirit (CHM)

SP self propelled/start point (MIL)

sp specific; specimen

sp spelling

sp gr specific gravity (SCI)

sp ht specific heat (SCI)

sp(p) species (SCI)

SP, sp sine prole (*Latin: without issue*)

sp, spec special

SPA Society for Popular Astronomy (SCI)

SPA Special Protection Agency (*for wildlife*) (SCI)

SpA Società per Azioni (*Italian: limited company*) (COM)

SPAG spelling, pronunciation & grammar

SPAM Society for the Publication of American Music (MUS)

SPAR Staff Planning & Reporting System (PRP)

SPASM Specific Person With Authority To Spend Money (*Zoë Fairbairn: Closing*) (FPA)

SPC South Pacific Commission

SPC Statistical Process Control (SCI)

SPCB State Pollution Control Board (SCI)

SPCC Society for the Prevention of Cruelty to Children

SPCK Society for Promoting Christian Knowledge

SPD Sozialdemokratische Partei Deutschlands (*German: Social Democratic Party of Germany*) (POL)

SPEA someone pushed the emergency alarm

SPEC South Pacific Bureau for Economic Co-operation

SPEC System Performance Evaluation Cooperative

spec speculation; speculative (*on spec*)

spec specific; specification (*pronounced speck by engineers and spess by architects*) (SCI)

Spectre Special Executive for Counter-Intelligence, Revenge & Extortion (*James Bond films*) (FPA)

Spesh speciality act

SPET single photon electron telemetry

SPF South Pacific Forum

SPF simple process factor (SCI)

SPF sun protection factor

SPG Society for the Propagation of the Gospel

spgr specific gravity

SPICE Special Programme of Initiative, Challenge & Excitement (*Manchester-based 18-80 activity organisation*)

Spidir spiritual direction

SPIV suspected persons & itinerant vagrants

SPNM Society for the Promotion of New Music (GB) (MUS)

SPO Senior Probation Officer (PRP)

SPO sausage, potato & onion (F&D)

SPOA Scottish Prison Officers Association (UNI)

SPOTS Sex Pistols on tour secretly/Sex Pistols on this stage (*'guerilla' tour of the group when persona non grata – 'Club Lafayette presents mystery group who will be known as the SPOTS'*) (MUS)

SPQR Senatus Populusque Romanus (*Latin: the Senate & People of Rome*)

SPRC Society for Prevention and Relief of Cancer

SPREd Society of Picture Researchers & Editors (*now PRA*)

SPSA Single-pitch Supervisor's Award (climbing) (SPR)

SPUD salary policy under discussion (COM)

SQ squint quoin (ARC)

sq sequence; square

sq(q) sequens/sequentia (*Latin: the following one(s)*)

SQBLA Scottish Quality Beef & Lamb Association (F&D)

SQL standard query language (SCI)

Sqn Squadron (MIL)

Sqn Ldr, S/Ldr Squadron Leader (MIL)

SR stage races (SPR)

Sr Sister

Sr Senior

Sr Señor

Sr Sir

s-r seiner (*German: of his*)

SRA satanic ritual abuse

SRA Shooters' Rights Association (SPR)

SRA Squash Rackets Association

Sra Señora; Segnora

SRAM static random-access memory (SCI)

SRC Science Research Council (SCI)

SRC Silverstone Racing Club

SRL Sleep Research Laboratory (*Loughborough University*)

SRM sample return mission

SRMC Southern Rhodesia Medical Corps

SRN State Registered Nurse (*now superseded*)

s-RNA soluble RNA (*a low molecular weight sequence of nucleic acids which serves as the adaptor between the m-RNA and the ribosome. It is visualised as having two ends, one for attaching to a specific amino acid, the other for attaching to its appropriate codon on the m-RNA. There are at least as many different species of s-RNA as there are amino-acids. Also called t-RNA*) (SCI)

SRO Self-Regulatory Organisation (COM)

SRO Statutory Rules & Orders (COM)

SRO standing room only

SRP Sozialistische Reichspartei (*German: Socialist Reich Party*) (POL)

SRP Society of Recorder Players (*1973*)

SRS safety restraint system

Srta Señorita (*Spanish*), Senhorita (*Portuguese*)

SRV surface recombination velocity (SCI)

SS Sunday School

SS Schutzstaffel (*German: protection squad*) (POL)

SS saints

Ss Santissima; Santissimo

ss suspended sentence (PRP)

ss semi (*Latin: half*)

s-s seines (*German: of one's*)

SS&AFA Soldiers Sailors and Airmens' Families Association

ss&sc lathe sliding, surfacing and screw-cutting lathe (*suitable for working on the periphery and on the end faces of workpieces & capable of cutting a screw thread using a single-point tool*) (SCI)

SS, S/S steamship

SSA standard spending assessment (COM)

SSB single sideband

SSC Solicitor to the Supreme Court (*Scotland*)

SSC Secondary School Certificate (*India*)

SSC supersonic car

SSCU Segregation Security & Care Unit (PRP)

SSD Social Services Department

SSF Society of St Francis (*formed in 1937*)

SSHA Scottish Special Housing Association

SSI Social Services Inspectorate

SSJE Society of St John the Evangelist

SSL secure socket layout (*web-encription protocol*) (SCI)

SSM surface-to-surface missile (MIL)

SSM Society of the Sacred Mission

SSM Supreme Sergeant Major

SSN severely subnormal

SSO Senior Staff Officer (FRS)

SSO Senior Supply Officer

SSP Statutory Sick Pay

ssp(p) subspecies (SCI)

SSR Soviet Socialist Republic

SSRC Social Science Research Council

SSS strict suicide supervision (PRP)

SSS standard scratch score (*golf*) (SPR)

SSS, 3S sweet and sour sauce

SSSI Site of Special Scientific Interest

SST supersonic transport/travel

SSTA Scottish Secondary Teachers Association (UNI)

SSU Special Secure Unit

SSVC Services Sound and Vision Corporation (MIL)

ST sawn timber (ARC)

ST surface trench (ARC)

ST south transept (ARC)

ST small thin

St Saint

st stet (*Latin: let it stand – to countermand a correction*)

st stanza

St Ex Stock Exchange (COM)

St, st street

St, st, stat Statute

sta, stat stationary

Staatl 23 Staatliche 23een music

Staatl Mus Staatliche Museen (MUS)

Staatsbib Staatsbibliothek (MUS)

stab a workman who receives a weekly wage is said to be 'on the establishment' as opposed to one who does piecework (ARC)

Stadtbib Stadtbibliothek

STAR Strategic Action in Rural Areas

STAR Society of Ticket Agents and Retailers (*combating sharp practice*)

START Strategic Arms Reduction Talks (MIL)

START Selling Sales Techniques & Resources Training (*Zoë Fairbairn: Closing*) (COM)

stat statim (*Latin: immediately*)

stat statutory

stat statue (ARC)

stbd starboard

STC State Trading Company (COM)

STC subject to contract

STCA short-term conflict alert (MIL)

STD Sacrae Theologiae Doctor (*Latin: Doctor of Sacred Theology*)

STD subscriber trunk dialling (SCI)

STD subscriber toll dialling (*NZ*) (SCI)

std standard

STE Society of Telecom Executives (UNI)

Ste Sainte (*female Saint*)

STEER Sustainable Transport and Environment for the Eastern Region

STEN, Sten Shepherd & Turpin (*designers*) + Enfield (*manufacturers of the weapon bearing the name*) (MIL)

steno stenographer (*USA & Canada*)

STEP Special Temporary Employment Programme

STEP Shell Technology Enterprise Programme

stge storage (COM)

Stip Stipend; Stipendiary stipe Stipendiary Magistrate

stk stock (COM)

STM Sacræ Theologiæ Magister (*Latin: Master of Sacred Theology*)

Stn station (FRS)

Stn O Station Officer (FRS)

STOL short take-off & landing (SCI)

stolly Stolichnaya vodka (F&D)

STOP stop, think, orientate, plan (*how to survive*)

STOVL short take-off & vertical landing (MIL)

STP, stp standard temperature & pressure (*a temperature of 0°C & a pressure of 101 325N/m2*) (*was NTP*)) (SCI)

Str Straße (*German: street*)

str straight

str strings; stringed (FPA)

str stroke oar

str steamer

STS space transportation system (SCI)

STSI Space Telescope Science Institute (*Baltimore*) (SCI)

STSO Senior Technical Staff Officer

STT secure transaction technology (SCI)

STUC Scottish Trades Union Congress (UNI)

STV Single Transferable Vote (COM)

STV Scottish Television

STX start of text (SCI)

sub subscription; substitute

sub subeditor (FPA)

sub sub-officer (Fire Brigade)

sub suburb(an)

sub subway

Sub Lt Sub-Lieutenant

Sub O Sub Officer (FRS)

subj subjunctive

suf, suff suffix

Suff Suffragan

suff sufficient

sug (verb) selling under the guise (*of doing a survey, etc; hence sugging, sugger etc; cf frug*) (COM)

SUNBAC Sutton Coldfield & North Birmingham Automobile Club

sup supply (COM)

sup supra (*Latin: above*); superlative

sup supine

sup ben Supplementary Benefit (COM)

sup, super superior

sup, suppl supplement; supplementary

super superseded; superfine; supernumerary

superl superlative

SUPLO Scottish Union of Power-Loom Overlookers (UNI)

Supp Res Supplementary Reserve (*of officers*)

supr supreme

surv Surveyor; surveying

susso sustenance (*Aussie slang for unemployment benefit, or the person receiving it*)

SV Sancta Virgo (*Latin: Holy Virgin*)

SV Sanctitas Vestra (*Latin: Your Holiness*)

sv sub verbo/voce (*Latin: under the entry; under the word*)

sv sailing vessel

SVC sententious Victorian crap (*over-syrupy art or literature*) (FPA)

SVQ Scottish Vocational Qualification

SVT, SWT sheer volume/weight of traffic (cause of jams, particularly on the M25)

SW short wave (SCI)

Sw Swedish

SWALK sealed with a loving kiss

SWAN Society for Wildlife Art of the Nations (FPA)

SWAPO South West Africa People's Organisation (POL)

SWAT special weapons & tactics (MIL)

SWAT steering wheel anti-theft (*device*)

SWD stoneware drain (ARC)

SWEB South West Electricity Board (COM)

SWELLS serious with energetic lifestyles

SWET Society of West End Theatres (FPA)

SWG standard wire gauge (SCI)

SWIFT Society for World-wide Interbank Funds Transfer

SWIP shared working in prisons (PRP)

SWL safe working load (*of lifting equipment*) (SCI)

SWOT strengths, weaknesses, opportunities & threats (COM)

SWR standing-wave ratio (*where standing & progressive waves are superimposed, the SWR is the ratio of the amplitudes at nodes & antinodes*) (SCI)

SWS Social Welsh and Sexy (*London group* (*also Welsh for Kiss*))

SWSWU Sheffield Wool Shear Workers Union (UNI)

SWWJ Society of Women Writers and Journalists

SY Steam Yacht

SYHA Scottish Youth Hostels Association

syl, syll syllable; syllabus

SYLK symbolic link (SCI)

sym symmetrical

Syn synonymous; synonym

synd syndicate

synop synopsis (FPA)

SYNTOS so you never tire of saying

SYP simple yet perfect

SYP Society of Young Publishers (FPA)

Syr Syrian

SYSCTLG system catalog (SCI)

T

T toilet

T surface tension (SCI)

T tritium (*very heavy hydrogen*) (CHM)

T telephone

T territory

T true (as in T or F?)

t tare (COM)

t tense

t transitive

t tenor

T – triple bond (*beginning on the corresponding carbon atom*) (CHM)

t – trans- (*containing the two radicals on opposite sides of the plane of a double bond or acrylic ring*) (CHM)

t – tertiary (*substituted on a carbon atom which is linked to three other carbon atoms*) (CHM)

T & G Transport & General Workers Union (UNI)

T I F telephone interference (*or influence*) factor (SCI)

T P turning point (*see* change point)

T S Eliot Thomas Stearns (*US/British poet, 1888–1965*)

T U traffic unit (*the measure of occupancy of telephonic apparatus during conversation. 1 TU = the use of 1 circuit for 1 minute or 1 hour*) (SCI)

T&AFA Territorial and Auxiliary Forces Association

T&B tit(s) & bum(s) (*genre of art*) (FPA)

T&C terms & conditions

T&F track & field (*athletics*) (SPR)

T&G tongue(d) & groove(d) (ARC)

TA Territorial Army (MIL)

TA Tactical Advisor (*firearms*)

TAA Trans-Australia Airlines

TAA Territorial Army Association

TAB Totalizator Agency Board (*Australia & NZ*) (COM)

tab tabulate; tabulator (COM)

tab table/list/chart

TAC Temporary Allocation Centre (PRP)

tac tactical (MIL)

TAC total allowable catch (F&D)

TACAN tactical air navigation

TACH Turban Action Committee against Helmets (*Sikh stand against compulsory crash-helmets, when Baldur Singh Chahal (1937–96) stood for Southall in the parliamentary election, February 1974. He polled 310 votes*)

TAD Thomas A Dorgan (*Hearst Newspapers cartoonist*)

TAF tactile air force

TAKA Teddy & Koala Association

TALK Transfer of African Language Knowledge (*South African language school*)

TAM telephone answering machine

tam tam-o'-shanter

TAMBA Twins And Multiple Birth Association

TAP training access point

TAP Thornton Adjustable Positioner

TAPS Television Arts Performance Showcase (FPA)

TARDIS Time & Relative Dimension in Space (*Dr Who's police-box*) (FPA)

TARGET Trans-European Automated Real-time Gross settlement Express Transfer System

TARM Tupac Amaru Revolutionary Movement (*held the Japanese Ambassadors resident in Lima, Peru 1996*)

TARO Territorial Army Reserve of Officers

TART that's all right, then (*reaction when hearing of some dreadful accident, which turns out to have happened a long way away*)

TAS true air speed (*the actual speed of an aircraft through the air, computed by correcting the indicated sidespeed for altitude, temperature, position error & compressibility effect*) (SCI)

TASCS The Automation Spares Control System (SCI)

TASM tactical air-to-surface missile (MIL)

Tassie Tasmania (*the State*); Tasmanian (*Person from Tasmania*)

TATT tired all the time

TB torpedo boat (MIL)

tb trial balance (COM)

TBA to be agreed/arranged

TBC total body crumble (*was the Doctor speaking of his car or a patient?*)

T-beam T-shaped beam forming part of the construction of a reinforced concrete floor (ARC)

TBL tits, bums and lips (*MRM used in sausages, etc*)

TBM tunnel-boring machine (SCI)

TBO or tbo time between overhauls (SCI)

TBS transmission-based signalling

TBT tri-n-butyl tin (*used in marine paints*) (CHM)

TC Training Centre (FRS)

TC Top Cat (FPA)

TCA tricarboxylic acid (CHM)

TCA The Coastguard Agency

T-CAS traffic collision avoidance system (*automatic control of cars*)

TCCA Theatres Critical Care and Anaesthesia

TCCB Test & County Cricket Board (*see* ECB) (SPR)

TCD Trinity College, Dublin

TCE total compass error

TCF Temporary Chaplain to the Forces

TCI to come in (COM)

TCI Telecommunications Inc (COM)

TCMF toroidal chamber with magnetic field

TCN third country national

TCNB 1,2,4,5-tetrachloro-3-nitrobenzene (*technazene, a fungicide*) (CHM)

TCP transmission control protocol (SCI)

TCP traffic control post

TCP trichlorphenol (CHM)

TCPA Town & Country Planning Act

TCV Tibetan Children's Village

TCV troop carrying vehicle (MIL)

TD Teachta Dála (Irish Gaelic: member of the Dáil) (POL)

TD Territorial Decoration (1908–30); Territorial Efficiency Decoration (*instituted 1930 for officers of Auxiliary Military Forces*)

TD technical drawing (SCI)

TD thwartship distance (*rowing*) (SPR)

TD, td touchdown

TDA taking & driving away (PRP)

TDC, tdc top dead centre (SCI)

TDI toluene-2, 4-di-isocyanate (CHM)

TDM Time-Division Multiplexing (SCI)

TDMA Time-Division Multiple Access (SCI)

TDS total dissolved solids (SCI)

TDT terrestrial digital television

TE, TEL, T E Lawrence (*Lawrence of Arabia*) Thomas Edward (*British archaeologist, soldier and writer 1888–1935. Also known as TE Shaw since 1923 and changed his name officially by deed poll in 1927. He would have been tickled to know that TE Shaw had no birth certificate and TE Lawrence had no death certificate.*)

TEC Training & Enterprise Council (COM)

tech Technical College (COM)

tech technical; technology (SCI)

ted teddy boy

TEDS Tenders Electronic Dialling System (COM)

TeeEmm Training Manual (*RAF – featuring P/O Prime*) (MIL)

TEETH tried everything else – try homeopathy

TEFL Teaching English as a Foreign Language (FPA)

TEG top edge gilt (FPA)

tehp total equivalent brake horsepower (SCI)

tel telegram; telephone; telegraphic (SCI)

TELCO The East London Community Organisation

teleran television radar air navigation

TEM total eclipse of the moon (SCI)

Temp temporary (FRS)

tems temazepam (PRP)

TEN Trans-European Network

TENS™ transcutaneous electrical nerve stimulation equipment

TEOTWAWKI The end of the world as we know it (*millennial phobia sweeps US*)

TEPP bis-O, O-diethylphosphoric anhydrate (*an insecticide, also tetraethyl pyrophosphate*) (CHM)

ter, terr territory

TES Times Educational Supplement (FPA)

TES total eclipse of the sun (SCI)

Tesco Tesco emerged in 1924, and is named from Jack Cohen (*knighted 1969*) and his first business partner T E Stockwell

TESL Teaching English as a Second Language (FPA)

TESSA Tax-Exempt Special Savings Account

TETRA Trans-European trunked radio (FPA)

TETRA terrestrial trunked radio (digital radio system)

TE-wave transverse electric wave (*having no component of electric force in the direction of transmission of electromagnetic waves along a waveguide Also known as H-wave (since it must have magnetic field component in direction of transmission)*) (SCI)

TE-wave transverse electric wave (*see* H-wave) (SCI)

Tex Texan

TF Bundy totally fickle but unfortunately not dead yet

TF Bundy totally f***ed but unfortunately not dead yet

TFIF, TFI Friday Thank Four It's Friday (*Channel 4 programme; some aver that Four is really f****) (FPA)

TFL Registration letters of Two Fat Ladies' motorcycle

TFN Tradepoint Financial Networks

TFR Territorial Forces Reserve

TFU tactical firearms unit

TG transformational grammar

Tg point transformation point (SCI)

TgAAT transgenic alpha-1 antitrypsin (*protein that may relieve cystic fibrosis*)

TGAT Task Group on Assessment & Testing (COM)

TGIF Thank God it's Friday

TGT turbine gas temperature (SCI)

tgt target (MIL)

TGWU Transport & General Workers Union (UNI)

TH Town Hall (Guildhall &c)

TH Huxley Thomas Henry (*English biologist, 1825–95*)

ThB Theologicae Baccalaureus (*Latin: Bachelor of Theology*)

THC Tourist Hotel Corporation (*NZ*) (F&D)

ThD Theologicae Doctor (*Latin: Doctor of Theology*)

The five Ks traditionally worn or carried by Sikhs, each possessing a symbolic importance: Kangha (comb – clean hair), Kara (steel bangle), Kesh (beard and uncut hair), Kirpan (short sword for protecting the weak), Kuccha (short trousers for ease of riding)

The Foure PP (ie the four Ps) The playe called the foure PP: A newe and very mery enterlude of A palmer, A pardoner, A potycary, A pedler. Made by John Heywood 1544 (FPA)

The HALO Trust Hazardous Areas Life Support Organisation (*set up by Lt-Col 'Mad Mitch' Mitchell (1925–96) to clear mines so that refugees can return home*) (MIL)

The MARS Group Modern Architectural Research (ARC)

theo theology; theological

theol theologian

theos theosophy; theosophical

THES Times Higher Education Supplement

THF Trust House Forte (COM)

THI temperature-humidity index (SCI)

THL terminal home leave (PRP)

THO *see* GPO

tho though

thro through

THT Terrence Higgins Trust (PRP)

THWD I thought he was dead (*surprise at photograph or TV appearance cf IHO, HGO*) (FPA)

THY Turk Hava Yollari

TI Tube Investments (COM)

TIALU thermal imagery and laser unit

TIC Tourist Information Centre

TIC(s) taken into consideration (*crimes to which a convicted person admits, but is not charged with, considered when sentence is passed*)

TIF telephone influence/interface factor (SCI)

TIFE Take it from 'ere (*BBC Light Programme pre-sitcom starring Jimmy Edwards, Dick Bentley & Joy Nichols*) (FPA)

TIFF tagged image file format (SCI)

TIGR Treasury Investment Growth Receipts (COM)

TINA there is no alternative (*short-lived nick-name for the then Mrs Thatcher after her making that pronouncement*)

TIR Transports Internationaux Routiers (*French: International Road Transport*)

TIR convention Geneva Convention on International Road Transport

TISWAS Today is Saturday – Wear a Smile (*Children's TV programme*) (FPA)

TITODO Tune in, turn on, drop out (*Timothy Leary*)

tk tank (MIL)

TKO technical knockout

TL thermal luminescence (*dating rocks*)

TL turntable ladder (FRS)

TLA three-letter abbreviation

TLEH true love & everlasting happiness

TLR twin-lens reflex (*camera*) (FPA)/ (SCI)

TLS Times Literary Supplement (FPA)

TM Transcendental Meditation

TM trade mark

TM Tracey meal (*prawn cocktail, steak, & BFG*) (F&D)

TMA Theatrical Management Association (FPA)

TML Trans-Manche Link

TMO telegraph money order (COM)

TMO two mouthfuls only (F&D)

TN trade name

TN true north (NAV)

Tn ton

TNC temporary non-compliance

tng training

TNT part of TNT International express delivery (COM)

TNT trinitrotoluene $((NO_3)_3\text{-}C_6H_2\text{-}CH_3)$ (CHM)

TO turnover (*unannounced search*) (PRP)

TO Transport Officer (FRS)

TOB tackling offending behaviour (PRP)

TOBI towed ocean bottom instrument (exploring the sea floor)

ToE The Theory of Everything (*ultimate theory of the Cosmos and everything in it*)

tog unit of quilt/duvet warmth

TOIL time off in lieu (PRP)

Tokamak toroidal chamber with magnetic field (*comes from toroidalnaya kameras aksialnym magnitnym polem*)

TOLS The Odeon, Leicester Square (FPA)

TONCHE Tory Campaign for Homosexual Equality

toot tutu (*NZ*)

topog topography; topographical

TOPS Training Opportunities Scheme (COM)

TOR, TsoR terms of reference (COM)

TOT time on target (MIL)

TOTP Top Of The Pops (FPA)

TP tall, portly

tp troop (MIL)

TPI tax & price index (COM)

TPI threads per inch (*the inverse of the pitch of a screw thread*) (SCI)

TPI tons per inch (*weight required to increase mean draft by one inch*)

TPM total productive maintenance (SCI)

TPO Tree Preservation Order/ Officer

TPOC transaction processing performance comment (SCI)

Tpr trooper (MIL)

TPS telephone preference service (SCI)

tpt transport (MIL)

TQM total quality management (COM)

tr translated; translation

tr translator

tr transpose (*printing*)

TR tube transmit-receive tube (SCI)

tr, treas Treasurer

TRA training-related activity (COM)

TRA Tennis & Rackets Association (SPR)

TRACE test equipment for rapid automatic check-out & evaluation (*computerised general purpose testing rig for aircraft electrical & electronic systems*) (SCI)

transf transferred (COM)

transl translator; translate(d)

TRBG thick, rich, brown gravy (F&D)

TRC Truth & Reconciliation Committee

TRC Thames Rowing Club

TRC Tithe Rent Charge

treas Treasurer; Treasury

TRF temporary release failure (PRP)

TRH Their Royal Highnesses

TRIC Television & Radio Industries Club (FPA)

TRIFFID three recent infants, and falling further into debt

TRIN Transport Research & Information Network

tripl triplicate (COM)

TriStar Lockheed model L-1011-500

TRL Transport Research Laboratory

t-RNA *See* s-RNA (SCI)

TRO Traffic Regulation Order

trop tropic(al)

TRV thermostatic radiator valve (ARC)

TS test solution (SCI)

TS(S)

typescript(s)

TSB Trustee Savings Bank (*now known supererogatorily as TSB Bank, & probably issuing PIN numbers*) (COM)

TSC transmitter start code (SCI)

TSD Tertiary of St Dominic

TSO Trading Standards Officer

TSO The Stationery Office (*privatised HMSO*) (FPA)

TSP textured soya protein (*trade name*) (F&D)

TSRA Tornado and Storm Research Associations

TSSA Transport Salaried Staffs Association (UNI)

TT telegraphic transfer (COM)

TT teetotal; teetotaller

TT Tourist Trophy (*motorcycle racing*) (SPR)

TT time trials (SPR)

TT tall, thin

TT tuberculin tested (F&D)

TTA to take away

TTFN ta ta for now (*one of Mrs Mopp's (Dorothy Summers) catchphrases in ITMA*) (FPA)

TTH to take home

TTK Tokamak Toroidalnaya Kameras

TTL temporary traffic lights

TTO to take out

TTP thermocytopenic purpura (*rare blood disorder*)

TTP trusted third party

TTT Tram & Trolleybus Trust (*Riga, Latvia*)

TTTV Tyne Tees TeleVision (FPA)

TU Trade Union (UNI)

TU transmission unit (SCI)

TU Turkey

TUA Telecommunications Users' Association (SCI)

TUBE totally unnecessary breast examination

TUC Trades Union Congress (UNI)

TULIP two used, leftover, insolvent parents

turps turpentine (CHM)

TV television; colour television

TVA Tennessee Valley Authority

TVA taxe valeur adjouté (*French VAT*)

TVEI technical & vocational educational initiative (COM)

TV-G US family viewing (FPA)

TVM television movie (FPA)

TV-M US mature viewing (FPA)

TVO tractor vapourising oil

TVP textured vegetable protein (*soya – may contain genetically-engineered material*) (F&D)

TVR television rating (FPA)

TVR marque after Trevor Wilkinson

TVRO television receive only (FPA)

TVV TV version (*of a film*) (FPA)

TVWB Thames Valley Water Board

TW antenna travelling-wave antenna (SCI)

TW3 That Was The Week That Was (*First satirical TV programme*) (FPA)

TWA TransWorld Airlines (*jocularly: try walking across*)

TWAIN technology without an important name (*scanner/digital camera transfer utility*)

TWC, TWOC, twocker taking (a vehicle) without consent; one who does so (*as in: ' 'ere – somebody's twocked me wheels'*) (PRP)

TWEC Time-Warner Entertainment Co (FPA)

TWI The Welding Institute (*established 1923; because it is now the 'World Centre for Materials Joining Technology' of which welding is but a part, it is now officially to be called TWI*) (SCI)

T-wire tip-wire (*connected to the tips of the plugs which terminate the cords of an operator's cord-circuit*) (SCI)

TWTWTW That Was The Week, That Was (*see* TW3) (FPA)

TWW Telewelly, Television for Wales & the West of England

TX (radio) transmitter (SCI)

TYC Thames Yacht Club

TYFYL, tyfyl thank you for your letter

typ, typw, typwr typewriter; typewritten

TYVM thank you very much

TZD towards zero defects (SCI)

☧ monogram for Christ – Greek: chi + rho – first 2 letters of Christos

☨ Christ (*Greek: chi + tau - first and last letters of Christos*)

U

U university

U Unionist (POL)

U united

U upper class

U Burmese: Mr

U universal (*film/video classification – suitable for all ages*) (FPA)

U urban test fuel consumption

u symbol for unit of unified scale of atomic & molecular weights based on the mass of the ^{12}C isotope of carbon being taken as 12 exactly, so the atomic mass unit = 1.660 x 10^{-27} kg. Adopted in 1960 by the International Unions of Pure & Applied Physics and Pure & Applied Chemistry (SCI)

u s ubi supra (*Latin: where mentioned above*)

U/S unserviceable (MIL)

U2 rock band (FPA)

U2 spy plane (MIL)

UA user area (SCI)

UAB Unemployment Assistance Board

UAE United Arab Emirates

UAM Afro-Malagasy Union

UAM underwater-to-air missile (MIL)

UART universal asynchronous receiver transmitter (SCI)

UAV uninhabited air vehicle (*pilotless aircraft*) (MIL)

UB40 index card used for unemployment benefit

UB40 rock band named after unemployment form (FPA)

U-boat Unterseeboot (*German: submarine*) (MIL)

UBR uniform business rate

UC University College

UC up stage centre (FPA)

U$_c$ universal (*video classification - suitable for all, especially children*) (FPA)

uc upper case (FPA)

UCAC Undeb Cenedlaethol Athrawon Cymru (*Welsh: Education – Teachers & Lecturers*) (UNI)

UCAS University and Colleges Admissions Service

UCATT Union of Construction, Allied Trades & Technicians (UNI)

UCCA Universities Central Council on Admissions (*now UCAS*)

UCD University College, Dublin

U-centre unit region of CRT phosphor, determined by an electron beam & perforated screen in establishing a colour TV image (SCI)

UCH University College Hospital (*London*)

UCI Union Cycliste Internationale (SPR)

UCL University College, London

UCLU University & College Lecturers' Union

UCNW University College of North Wales

UCP/21 hexahydro-2,7-dithio-1,3,6-thiadiazepine (*a fungicide*) (CHM)

UCSW University College of South Wales

UCW Union of Communication Workers (UNI)

UDA Ulster Defence Association (MIL)

UDC Urban District Council

UDF United Democratic Front (*South Africa*) (POL)

UDI Unilateral Declaration of Independence

UDM Union of Democratic Mineworkers (UNI)

UDP Unitary Development Plan

UDR Ulster Defence Regiment (MIL)

UE university entrance

UE unerupted

UEA University of East Anglia (*Norwich*)

UEFA Union of European Football Associations (SPR)

UF urea-formaldehyde (*used in manufacture of plastics*) (SCI)

UFAW, Ufaw Universities' Federation for Animal Welfare

UFC Universities' Funding Council

UFM Union Française de Marche (*French: French Race Walking Union*) (SPR)

UFO, ufo unidentified flying object

UGC University Grants Committee

UHB urban haute bourgeoisie

UHF ultra high frequency

UHT ultra-high-temperature (*sterilisation at 147°c*) (F&D)

UIT Union Internationale de Tir (*International Rifle Shooting Union*) (SPR)

UJD Utriusque Juris Doctor (*Latin: Doctor of Canon and Civil Law*)

UK United Kingdom

UKAEA UK Atomic Energy Authority

UKIP UK Independence Party (POL)

UKLF United Kingdom Land Forces (MIL)

UKMF United Kingdom Mobile Forces (MIL)

UKOL UK online (SCI)

UKOLIN UK Office for Library & Information Networks (FPA)

UKWGL UK Working Group on Landmines (MIL)

UL upstage left (FPA)

ULCC ultra-large crude carrier

ult ultimo (*Latin: of the last month*) (COM)

umd unmarried

UMDS *a headset from St Thomas's Hospital Sleep Hospital, shown on* Hot Gadgets *with Carol Vorderman*

UMIST University of Manchester Institute of Science & Technology

UNA United Nations Association

UNCHS United Nations Centre for Human Settlements

UNCIO United Nations Conference on International Organization

unclass unclassified (MIL)

UNCLE United Network Command for Law Enforcement (*fabrication, as in* The Man from UNCLE) (FPA)

UNCTAD United Nations Conference on Trade & Development

UN-DHA United Nations – Department of Human Affairs

UNDP United Nations Development Programme

UNDRO United Nations Disaster Relief Organisation

UNEF United Nations Emergency Force

UNEP United Nations Environment Programme

UNESCO United Nations Educational, Scientific and Cultural Organisation

UNFAO United Nations Food & Agriculture Organization

UNFPA United Nations Fund for Population Activities

UNHCR United Nations High Commissioner for Refugees

UNICEF United Nations Children's Funds

UNIDA United Nations International Development Association

UNIDO United Nations Industrial Development Organisation

UNIFAD United Nations Fund for Agricultural Development

UNIFC United Nations International Finance Co-operative

UNIFI does not at present stand for anything – however, Union & Finance are both in there. It is the new union of Barclays Bank Staff, formerly BGSU, soon to be opened to other finance groups (UNI)

UNISON Union for local government, health care, water, gas, electricity, further education, transport, housing associations etc workers formed 1 July 1993 from NALGO, NUPE & COHSE (UNI)

Unita National Union for the Total Independence of Angola

UNITAR United Nations Institute for Training & Research

UNITU United Nations International Telecommunication Union

Univ universalist

univ universal

Univ, univ university

UNIX™ multi-user multitasking operating system (SCI)

UNRRA United Nations Relief and Rehabilitation Administration

UNRWA United Nations Relief & Works Agency

UP United Press (COM)

UP Uttar Pradesh

UPI United Press International (COM)

U-PRAT unsociable person responsible for all the trouble

UPU universal postal union

UQ uomo qualunque (*Italian: the common man*)

UR upstage right (FPA)

URC United Reformed Church

URL universal resource locator (SCI)

UROD ultra-rapid opiate detoxification

urspr ursprünglich (*German: original(ly)*)

URTU United Road Transport Union (UNI)

US United States

US unseated rider

USA United States of America

USA United States Army (MIL)

USA unfortunately still alive

USAAF United States Army Air Force

USAC United States Auto Club (SPR)

USAEC United States Atomic Energy Commission (SCI)

USAF United States Air Force (MIL)

USARSA United States Amateur Roller Skating Association (SPR)

USB unit selection board (MIL)

USC University of Southern California

USCTA United States Court Tennis Association (SPR)

USDAW Union of Shop, Distributive & Allied Workers (UNI)

USDD United States Department of Defense (MIL)

USEPA United States Environmental Protection Agency (SCI)

USFSA Union des Sociétés Françaises de Sports Athlétiques (SPR)

USGA United States Golf Association (SPR)

USGS United States Geological Survey

USI unlawful sexual intercourse (PRP)

USM unlisted securities market (COM)

USMA United States Military Academy

USN United States Navy (MIL)

USNLTA United States National Lawn Tennis Association (SPR)

USNR United States Naval Reserve

USO United States Organisation

USP unique selling proposition (COM)

USPO United States Post Office

USROA United States Roller Skating Rink Operators Association (SPR)

USS United States Senate

USS united states ship

USS thread Sellers screw thread (*the USA standard thread with a profile angle of 600 & a flat crest made by cutting ¹/₈ off the thread height*) (SCI)

USSR Union of Soviet Socialists Republics

USW ultrashort wave (FPA)

usw und so weiter (*German: etc; and so on*)

USWLA United States Women's Lacrosse Association (SPR)

UT unauthorised taking (PRP)

UT chart contour chart giving, for a stated time, the world-wide values of an ionospheric characteristic such as the critical frequency

UTC under the counter

Ute utility truck (Australia)

UTV Ulster Television (FPA)

UTW Union of Textile Workers (UNI)

UU Ulster Unionist (POL)

UUP Ulster Unionists' Party (POL)

UV ultraviolet stamp (*on visitor's hand*) (PRP)

UV ultraviolet (SCI)

UVA ultraviolet-A (*accelerates skin ageing, and contributes to cancer*) (SCI)

uva und viele(s) andere (*German: and many others*)

UVB ultraviolet-B (*causes burning and cancer*) (SCI)

UVC ultraviolet-C (*filtered out by the earth's atmosphere, hence the importance of preserving the mix*) (SCI)

UVED under-vehicle explosive device (MIL)

UVF Ulster Volunteer Force (MIL)

uvm und viele(s) mehr (*German: and many more*)

UVO underwater vehicle for one

UWIST University of Wales Institute of Science & Technology

UXB unexploded bomb (MIL)

V

V visit (PRP)

V victory

V Viscount

V venerable

V very (*in titles*)

V vice (*in titles*)

v vide (*Latin: see*)

v versus (*Latin: against*)

v von; vom (*German: of, by, from*)

v verse; version

v occurrence of rock at ground surface (SCI)

V & A Victoria and Albert Museum

v a verb active

v aux auxiliary verb

v p verb passive

V Rev(d)

Very Reverend

v t verb transitive

V&V visions & values (PRP)

V, v very

V, v, vb verb

V, Ven Venerable

v, voc, vocat vocative

V1 decision velocity

V-1 German WWII flying bomb, or doodlebug (MIL)

V2 provisional name of Richard Branson's new record company, he having sold Virgin Records in 1992 (MUS)

V2 safe flying speed

V-2 German WWII rocket-powered bomb (MIL)

V6 V-shaped 6-cylinder ICE

V8 V-shaped 8-cylinder ICE

VA voluntary associate (PRP)

VA Vicar-Apostolic

VA Order of Victoria & Albert

VA Vice Admiral

VA Veterans' Administration (*USA*) (MIL)

VA volt-ampère (SCI)

VAB voice answer back (SCI)

vac vacation

vac vacuum cleaner

VAD Voluntary Aid Detachment (*or a nurse therefrom*) (MIL)

vag vagrant; vagrancy (PRP)

van short for advantage (*tennis in UK*)

var variable; variant; variation; variety; various

VAR, var visual-aural range (*navigational system giving mutually perpendicular courses, one displayed visually, the other aurally*) (SCI)

VAS video aiming system

VASI visual approach slope indicator (NAV)

VAT value added tax

Vat Vatican

VB verbal constituent

V-band frequency band 4.6 - 5.6 x 1010 Hz (SCI)

V-beam scanning by 'fan' beams, 1 vertical & the other 4 inclined – interval between reflections depends on target elevation (SCI)

VC volumetric control (PRP)

VC visiting committee (PRP)

VC Vice-Chairman

VC Vice Chancellor

VC Vice Consul

VC Vietcong

VC Victoria Cross

VC Vatican City

VCAS Vice-Chief on the Air Staff

VCC Veteran Car Club (SPR)

VCD vacuum contact drying (F&D)

V-chip for preventing children viewing violence (FPA)

V-chromosome one with two arms (SCI)

VCO voltage-controlled oscillator (SCI)

V-connection alternative name for open delta connection of two phases of a 3-phase AC system (SCI)

VCR video cassette recorder

VCR visual control room

VCT Victims of Crime Trust

VD Volunteer Officers' Decoration 1892–1908; India & Colonies 1894–1930; Colonial Auxiliary Forces Officers' Decoration 1899–1930

vd various dates

VDC Volunteer Defence Corps (MIL)

VDL Van Dieman's Land

VDQS vins délimités de qualité supérieure (*French wine classification*) (F&D)

VDSM Victoria Devoted Service Medal (*awarded only once – to John Brown*)

VDT visual display terminal (SCI)

Vdt Vini da Tavola (*Italian wine classification*) (F&D)

VDU video display unit (SCI)

VE viewing essential

veg vegetables (*as in meat & 2 veg*) (F&D)

veggie vegetarian

veh vehicle (MIL)

Ven venerable

Vent ventriloquist; ventriloquism

ver verse; version

verb sap, verb sat verbum sapienti satis (*Latin: a word is enough to the wise*)

Verdi Victor Emmanuel Re d'Italia (*patriotic acronym which could be shouted at performances of Nabucco without fear*) (MUS)

VERSE voluntary early retirement scheme (*1996*) (PRP)

vet veteran; veterinary surgeon; veterinarian

vet veteran (*USA & Canada*)

VF or v-f voice frequency telegraphy (SCI)

VFA Victorian Football Association (Australia) (SPR)

VFL Victorian Football League (*Australia – fl 1930s, 40s & 50s*) (SPR)

VFR visual flight rules

VG Vicar General

vg recorder vertical-gust recorder

VGA video graphics array (SCI)

vgc very good condition

vgl vergleiche (*German: compare*)

VGPI visual glide path indicator (NAV)

VGSOH very good sense of humour

vhc very highly commended

VHF very high frequency

VHS Honorary Surgeon to the Viceroy of India

VI volume indicator (SCI)

vi vide infra (*Latin: see below*)

vi verb intransitive

Vic Vicar

VIFF vector in forward flight (MIL)

VIN vehicle identification number

VIP very important person

VIR Victoria Imperatrix Regina (*Latin: Victoria, Empress & Queen*)

Virsa Village Retail Services Association (*founded in 1991 by Derek Smith 1932–97*)

Vis Viscount; Viscountess

VISIT Vacancies in Systems & Information Technology

VISTA Volunteers in Service to America

VIVA visual identity verification auditor

VIXEN vehicle information crossed with electronic notebook

viz videlicet (*Latin: namely*)

vizzo visit (PRP)

VJ video jockey (FPA)

VJ Vaucluse junior (*Australia*) yacht

VJC Victorian Jockey Club (*Australia*) (SPR)

VL vulgar Latin (FPA)

vl, VR varia lectio (*Latin: variant reading*)

VLA very large array (*a collection of 27 radio telescopes in New Mexico*)

VLCC very large crude carrier

VLF very low frequency (SCI)

VLS vapour-liquid-solid (SCI)

VLSI very large scale integration (SCI)

VLT very large telescope

VLV Voice of the Listener & Viewer (*formerly VOL*) (FPA)

V-man sinister man who chases you in dreams

VMC visual meteorological conditions

VMD Veterinariae Medicinae Doctor (*Latin: Doctor of Veterinary Medicine*)

VMG velocity made good (*maritime GPS data taking tide, current, leeway, boat speed and course sailed into account*) (NAV)

VMH Victoria Medal of Honour (*awarded by RHS*)

VO visiting order (PRP)

VO very old (*spirits*) (F&D)

Vo, vo verso (*on the left hand page*)

VOC volatile organic compounds (CHM)

vocab vocabulary

VOD video on demand (SCI)

VOL Voice of the Listener (*See* VLV) (FPA)

Vol volunteer (FRS)

vol volume (FPA)

vol volcano

VOR VHF omnidirectional range

VOR vehicle off the road

VOV Voice of the Viewer (FPA)

VP Vice-President (*pronounced 'veep'*) (COM)

VP vulnerable prisoner (PRP)

VP verb phrase

VP Vice President

VP vent pipe ((ARC))

VPI vapour phase inhibitor (SCI)

VPL visible panty line

VPP velocity production programme (*computer program correlates past performance & present information*) (NAV)

VPP virtually perfect pub (Carling lager advert) (F&D)

VPP virus pneumonia of pigs

VPP velocity prediction program (*yachting*)

VPU Vulnerable Prisoners' Unit (PRP)

VR voluntary redundancy (COM)

VR Victoria Regina (*Latin: Queen Victoria*)

VR Volunteer Reserve (MIL)

VR virtual reality (SCI)

VR velocity rotate (NAV)

vr tube voltage-regulator tube (SCI)

VRD Royal Naval Volunteer Reserve Officers' Decoration

VRI Victoria Regina et Imperatrix (*Latin: Victoria, Queen & Empress*)

VRML virtual reality modelling language (SCI)

VRO Vehicle Registration Office

VS Veterinary Surgeon

VS volumetric solution (SCI)

VS vertical speed

VS very special/superior

vs vide supra (*Latin: see above*)

VSA very small array (SCI)

vsb vestigial sideband (SCI)

VSCC Vintage Sports Car Club (SPR)

VSI vertical speed indicator (SCI)

VSO Voluntary Service Overseas

VSO Very Superior Old (*port, brandy*) (F&D)

VSOP Very Special/Superior Old Pale (*two extra years in barrel*) (F&D)

VSP Victor Sawden Pritchett

VSS vehicle speed sensor

VSV very slender vessel (*powerboat*)

VSWR voltage standing-wave radio (SCI)

VTB curve voltage/time-to-breakdown curve (SCI)

VTC Vocational Training Course (PRP)

VTOC volume table of contents (SCI)

VTOL vertical take-off & landing (SCI)

VTR videotape recorder/recording (FPA)

VTU voluntary testing unit (PRP)

VU volume unit (SCI)

Vulg vulgate (FPA)

vulg vulgar(ly)

vv vice versa (*Latin: with the order reversed*)

VVB Vehicle Valuation Bureau

VW Very Worshipful

VX a lethal nerve gas (*USA*) (MIL)

VYW Volunteer Youth Worker

VYWT Volunteer Youth Worker Training

W

W (Search) Warrant (PRP)

W warden

W Welsh (FPA)

W Wales

w with

w wife

w symbol for load per foot run or weight per cubic foot (SCI)

W B Yeats William Butler (Irish poet, 1871-1957)

w e f with effect from (COM)

W F Bach Wilhelm Friedmann (*German composer, 1710-84*)

W H Auden Wystan Hugh (US poet,1907-1973)

W I wrought iron (SCI)

W O Bentley Walter Owen (*British car manufacturer*)

W S Gilbert William Schwenk (English librettist, 1836-1911)

W Somerset Maugham William (*English writer, 1874-1965*)

W/B, WB, wb waybill

W/cdr Wing Commander

w/o without

W3, WWW world-wide web (SCI)

WAAAF Women's Auxiliary Australian Air Force (MIL)

WAAC Women's Army Auxiliary Corps

WAAC West African Airways Corporation

Waac Member of Women's Army Auxiliary Corps

WAAF Women's Auxiliary Air Force

Waaf Member of the Women's Auxiliary Air Force

WAGN we are going nowhere

WAIA World Association of Introduction Agencies

WAIC Wechsler Adult Intelligence Scale

WAIL wildlife acoustic information link

Wal Walloon

WAN wide area network (SCI)

WAPL William Arthur Philip Louis (*Prince William*)

WASP White Anglo-Saxon Protestant (*popularized by Digby Baltzell (1915-96), US historian & sociologist*)

WAT curves graphs relating to take-off & landing behaviour of an aeroplane. Their preparation & use is mandatory for British public transport (SCI)

WATCH Writers & their Copyright Holders (FPA)

WATCh What About The Children

WATCH, WATCh Women and the Church

WAVES, Waves Women Accepted for Volunteer Emergency Service (*USA*) (MIL)

WB World Bank (COM)

wb westbound (NAV)

wb water ballast

WBA World Boxing Association (SPR)

WBC westbound carriageway (*see* NBC, SBC and EBC)

WBC World Boxing Council

WBC Women's Boxing Commission

WBD World Book Day

WBO Western Buddhist Order

WC water closet

WC Sir Winston Leonard Spencer Churchill (*1874-1965, British Prime Minister 1940-45; 1951-55*)

WC William 'Bill' Charnock

wc without charge

WCA Water Companies Association (*for the tiddlers*)

WCC World Council of Churches

WCF World Congress of Faiths

W-chromosome the X-chromosome when the female is of the heterogametic sex (SCI)

WCMC World Conservation Monitoring Centre (*Huntingdon*) (SCI)

WCT World Tennis Championship (SPR)

WCT War Crimes Tribunal

WD Works Department

wd word

WD(s), wd(s) weekday(s) (PRP)

WDM World Development Movement

WE War Establishment (MIL) WE(s), we(s) weekend(s) (PRP)

WEA Workers' Educational Association

WEF World Economic Forum

wef with effect from

weitS in weiteren Sinne (*German: more widely taken*)

WET Water and Effluent Treatment

WEU Western European Union

WF west front (ARC)

wf wrong fount (*of type*) (FPA)

WFAGA Women's Farms & Gardens Association

WFB Works Fire Brigade (FRS)

WFF well-formed formula

WFM! Wait for me!

WFTU World Federation of Trade Unions (COM)

WG W G Grace (*cricketer (see* WGG))

WG, wg water gauge (SCI)

WGA Writers Guild of America

WGBA World Gut-Barging Association (*set up by Binkie Braithwaite, landlord of the Dandy Lion, Bradford-on-Avon 1996*) (SPR)

WGG William Gilbert Grace (*renowned English cricketer 1848–1915*)

WGGB The Writers Guild of Great Britain (UNI)

WGRF World Greyhound Racing Federation (SPR)

wh white

wh wheeled (MIL)

WHC World Handball Council (SPR)

whf wharf (COM)

WHM wife has means

WHO World Health Organisation

Whr watt-hour

WhSc Whitworth Scholar

whsle wholesale (COM)

WI Women's Institute

WI Welding Institute (SCI)

WI West Indies

WIB women in black

WIBF Women's International Boxing Federation

WIFE Womens' Institute for Football Education (US)

WIHRB Women's International Hockey Rules Board (SPR)

wilco [I] will comply [with]

William G Stewart Gladstone (*Presenter of Channel 4's 15 ~ 1*)

WIMP weakly interacting massive particle (SCI)

WIMP windows, icons, menus/mice, pointers

WIMP whinging incompetent malingering person (MIL)

Winton Bishop of Winchester

WIP Women in Prison (PRP)

WIP Women in publishing (*whose newsletter is called WIPlash*) (FPA)

WIPO, Wipo World Intellectual Property Organization (COM)

WIS Women's Information Service

WISC Wechsler Intelligence Scale for Children

WISE Women in Science & Engineering (SCI)

wk weak

wksp workshop (MIL)

WL, wl water line

WLA Women's Land Army (MIL)

WLA work-load assessment (SCI)

WLF Women's Liberal Federation

WLG Wellington Airport, New Zealand

WLL West London Line

WLM Women's Liberation Movement

WLTM would like to meet

WM washing machine

WMD Women in Marketing & Design (COM)

wmk watermark (FPA)

WMO World Meteorological Organization

WMR war maintenance reserve (MIL)

WNO Welsh National Opera (MUS)

WO written off (COM)

WO water officer (FRS)

WO warrant officer (MIL)

WO wireless operator

wo without; with respect to

WOAH World Organisation for Animal Health

WOF warrant of fitness (*NZ*)

WOG Winter Olympic Games (SPR)

wog wily oriental gentleman

WooHa pet name for HMS *Woodbridge Haven* (MIL)

WOOP well-off older person

WORA write once, run anywhere

WORM write once, read many (*times*) (SCI)

WOSB War Office Selection Board (MIL)

WOTS work opportunities through self-help

WOW waiting on weather (COM)

WP World People (*whom Donald Trump expects to inhabit Trump International, his 52-storey hotel condominium in New York*)

WP word processor; word processing (SCI)

WP weather permitting

WPB waste-paper basket; wegger-pegger

WPC woman police constable

wpm words per minute (COM)

WPPSI Wechsler Pre-school Primary Scale of Intelligence

WPRC Women Prisoners' Resource Centre (PRP)

WPS work profiling system (*Saville & Holdsworth 1988*) (COM)

WR western region

WRAAC Women's Royal Australian Army Corps (MIL)

WRAAF Women's Royal Australian Air Force (MIL)

WRAC Women's Royal Army Corps (MIL)

WRAF Women's Royal Air Force

WRANS Women's Royal Australian Naval Service (MIL)

WrC water carrier (FRS)

WrL water tender with 13.5m ladder (FRS)

WRNS Women's Royal Naval Service (MIL)

wrnt warrant

WrT water tender with 9m or 10.5m ladder (FRS)

WRVS Women's Royal Voluntary Service (*formerly WVS*)

WS Writer to the Signet (*old Scottish term for solicitor*)

WS workshops (FRS)

WSA Wine & Spirits Association (F&D)

WSA Water Services' Association

WSM World's Strongest Man (SPR)

WSPA World Society for Protection of Animals

WSPU Women's Social and Political Union

WT whole-time (FRS)

wt weight

WTGMT Whoops! There go my trousers (*farce genre*) (FPA)

WTN Worldwide Television News

WUW Welsh Union of Writers (FPA)

WVS Women's Voluntary Service (*see* WRVS)

WWCP walking wounded collection point (MIL)

WWF World Wildlife Fund (*now World Wide Fund for Nature*)

WWSU World Water Ski Union (SPR)

WWW world wide web (SCI)

Wy way

WYSIWYG what you see is what you get (SCI)

X

X Christ (*X is really the Greek: 'chi' - first letter of Christos. To speak of 'Xmas' is, strictly speaking, wrong*)

X an unknown person

X for adults only, an old film classification system (FPA)

X symbol for reactance (SCI)

X symbol for an electronegative atom or group, especially a halogen (CHM)

X cross (ARC)

X crossing (*as in roads or rivers*)

X specific location on map, as in X marks the spot

X's atmospherics, interfering or disturbing signals of natural origin

x-axis the longitudinal or roll axis of an aircraft (SCI)

X-back a conducting surface on the back of negative cinematograph film to eliminate scratches arising from the discharge of electric charges which are separated by friction on the film (FPA)

X-band frequency band widely used for 3cm radar, now designated Cx-band (SCI)

X-body an amorphous inclusion in a plant cell suffering from a virus disease (SCI)

xc ex coupon

X-chromosome one associated sex determination, usually occurring paired in the female, & alone in the male, zygote & cell (SCI)

X-cut special cut from a quartz crystal normal to the electric (X) axis (SCI)

XD ex-directory (SCI)

XD, xd ex dividend (COM)

X-disease bovine hyperkeratosis – a disease of cattle characterised by emaciation, loss of hair & thickening of the skin due to poisoning by chlorinated naphthalene compounds XF cross-fade (FPA)

x-height the height of lower case letters exclusive of extenders, varying between the extremes of small & large according to the design of the type face (FPA)

XL extra large

XMT transmit (SCI)

XMTR transmitter (SCI)

xn ex new (ie secondhand)

XO extra old

X-organ neurosecretory organ in the eye-stalks of certain crustaceans (SCI)

X-plates pair of electrodes in a CRT to which horizontal deflecting voltage is applied in accordance with cartesian coordinate system (SCI)

X-rays electromagnetic waves of short wavelength (around 10-3 – 1nm) produced when cathode rays impinge on matter) (SCI)

Xs ecstasy (PRP)

X-synchronisation flash-synchronised shutters which, when released, can close an electrical circuit for firing flash. X delays shutter opening, allowing certain flashbulbs to reach peak brightness at exposure – *see* M-synchronisation (SCI)

XTC ecstasy (an illegal drug)

XTE cross track error (*maritime GPS data*) (NAV)

X-tgd cross-tongued ((ARC))

X-wave the extraordinary component of an electro-magnetic wave (SCI)

XX retree (*slightly damaged paper from reams, R in USA*) (FPA)

Y

Y YMCA or YWCA

Y US air fare: coach economy

Y the phenyl radical C6H5- (CHM)

Y amphi- (*containing a condensed double aromatic nucleus substituted in the 2, 6 positions*) (CHM)

Y rectifier full-wave rectifier system for a 3-phase supply (SCI)

Y signal the monochromatic signal in colour TV which conveys the intelligence of brightness Combines with the 3 chromin-ance components to produce the 3 colour primary signals: B-Y, G-Y & R-Y signals (SCI)

y, yr you; your

Y/B ratio term used to describe a type of dichromatism – an observer sees only 2 colours when examining the solar spectrum, blue & yellow, separated by a white patch The relative extent of the 2 colours is the Y/B ratio (SCI)

YA young adults (publishing genre)

YAAC Youth Action Against Crime (*Soweto*)

YAP young aspiring professional

y-axis the lateral or pitch axis of an aircraft (SCI)

YC Youth Custody (*now YOI*) (PRP)

YC Young Conservative (POL)

YCDBSOYA You Can't Do Business Sitting On Your Arse (*inscription on tie-clip worn by George Heas (1910–96) when Canadian Trade Minister*) (COM)

Y-chromosome one of a pair of heterochromosomes, in the heterogametic sex, associated with sex determination (SCI)

Y-class insulation A class of insulating material to which is assigned a temperature of 90°C (SCI)

Y-connection an alternative name for star connection (SCI)

Y-cut special cut of a quartz crystal normal to the mechanical (Y) axis (SCI)

Yeo yeomanry

YFC Young Farmers' Club

YHA Youth Hostel Association

YIG yttrium iron garnet (*a material which has a lower acoustic attenuation loss than quartz & which has been considered for use in delay lines*) (SCI)

Y-level Wye level – a type of level whose essential characteristic is the support of the telescope which is similar to that of the Wye theodolite

YMCA Young Men's Christian Association

YMCA yesterday's meal cooked again

Yn US air fare: night/off-peak coach

Y-network 3-branch star network (SCI)

YO young offender (PRP)

YOI Young Offenders' Institution (PRP)

YOP yopper

YP young prisoner (PRP)

Y-parameter the short-circuit admittance parameter of a transistor (SCI)

Y-plates pair of electrodes to which voltage producing vertical deflection of spot is applied in accordance with Cartesian coordinate system (SCI)

yr younger

Yr(s) your(s)

YS-L Yves (Matieu-) Saint-Laurent (*French couturier 1936–*) (COM)

yst youngest

YUMP young upwardly-mobile manual person

yuppie young urban/upwardly-mobile professional person

Y-voltage voltage between any line & neutral of a 3- or 6-phase system – also called voltage to neutral (SCI)

YWCA Young Women's Christian Association

Z

Z FW Woolworth Company (COM)

Z Ackiova Spolecnost Ceskoslovenska Zborojovka (*Czechoslovakia 1927–36*)

Z zenith (point of celestial sphere exactly overhead) (NAV)

z symbol for figure of merit (SCI)

z zero

z zone

z f zero frequency (SCI)

Z marker beacon a form of marker beacon radiating a narrow conical beam along the vertical axis of the cone of silence of a radio range (NAV)

Z, Zn azimuth angle (*angle a star makes to the northern or southern points of a meridian*) (NAV)

Z1, Z2, Z3 primitive computers home-made by Konrad Zuse 1936, 1939, 1941 (SCI)

za pizza (*USA*)

ZANU Zimbabwe African National Union (POL)

ZAPU Zimbabwe African People's Union (POL)

zB zum Beispiel (*German: for example*)

ZETA zero-energy thermonuclear apparatus (SCI)

ZEV zero emission vehicle (runs on compressed air)

ZIP, zip (code) zone Improvement plan (USPO)

ZKES zero kinetic energy spectroscopy (*investigating – among other things – why Guinness bubbles sink*) (SCI)

Z-line in striated or voluntary muscle of vertebrates, the line found at either end of a sarcomere. It carries a system of submicroscopic transverse tubules which are in contact with the sarcoplasmic reticulum & are thought to transmit action potentials from the outer sarcolemma of the muscle fibres to the inner fibres. (SCI)

z-modulation variations in intensity in the electron beam of a CRT which form the display or picture on a sweep or raster (SCI)

zod zodiac

ZOE zinc oxide and eugenol (*dental cement*)

ZONDA part of Aerolineas Argentinas

ZPG zero population growth

Zssg zusammensetzung(en) (*German: compound word(s)*)

zw zwischen (*German: between; among*)

zZ(t) zur Zeit (*German: at the time; at present; for the time being*)

2   National Insurance leaflets & forms

BEL Benefit enquiry line

BR19 Form – How to get a Retirement Pension Forecast

CA01 Leaflet – National Insurance Contributions for Employees

CA02 Leaflet – National Insurance Contributions for Self-Employed People with Small Earnings

CA03 Leaflet – National Insurance Contributions for Self-Employed People: Class 2 & Class 4

CA04 Leaflet – National Insurance Contributions: Class 2 & Class 3 – Direct Debit – The easier way to pay

CA07 Leaflet – National Insurance – Unpaid & Late Paid Contributions

CA08 Leaflet – National Insurance – Voluntary Contributions

CA09 Leaflet – National Insurance for Widows

CA10 Leaflet – National Insurance for Divorced Women

CA12 Leaflet – Training for Further Employment & Your National Insurance Record

CA13 Leaflet – National Insurance Choices for Married Women

CA5445 Form – Class 2 Self-Employed National Insurance Contributions – Certificate of Exception

CA5603 Form – Application to pay Class 3 NI Contributions

CA62 Leaflet – Unhappy with our Service?

CF11 Form – Notification of Self-Employment

CF11A Form – Application to Pay Class 3 National Insurance Contributions

CF351N Form – Direct Debit Mandate

CF411 Form – How To Protect your State Retirement Pension if you are looking after someone at home

CF88 Form – Application for a National Insurance Number Card

CH1 Leaflet – Child Benefit

CH11 Leaflet – One Parent Benefit

CTB1 Leaflet – Council Tax Benefit

CWP1 Leaflet – Social Fund – Cold Weather Payment

DS700 Claim pack – Invalid Care Allowance

DS702 Leaflet – Attendance Allowance

DS704 Leaflet – Disability Living Allowance

DWA1 Claim pack – Disability Working Allowance

FB8 Leaflet – Maternity Allowance

FB8 Leaflet – Statutory Maternity Pay

FC1 Claim pack – Family Credit

HC11 Leaflet – Health Costs

HRP Home Responsibilities Protection

IB201 Leaflet – Incapacity Benefit

IB202 Leaflet – Incapacity Benefit – Information for New Customers

ICA Invalid Care Allowance

IS20 Leaflet – Income Support

LEL Lower Earnings Limit

LPL Lower Profits Limit

NI12 Leaflet – Unemployment Benefit

NI14 Leaflet – Guardian's Allowance

NI17A Leaflet – Statutory Maternity Pay

NI196 Leaflet – Social Security benefit rates

NI244 Leaflet – Statutory Sick Pay

NI252 Leaflet – Severe Disablement Allowance

NI38 Leaflet – Social Security abroad

NI6 Leaflet – Industrial Injuries Disablement Benefit

NI9 Leaflet – Hospital rates

NIL196 Leaflet – Social Security Benefit Rates, Northern Ireland

NP45 Leaflet – A Guide to Widows' Benefits

NP45 Leaflet – Widows' Benefits

NP46 Leaflet – A Guide to Retirement Pension

NP46 Leaflet – Retirement Pension

PN1 Leaflet – Pneumoconiosis, Byssinosis & Miscellaneous Diseases Benefit Scheme

RPFA Unit Retirement Pension Forecast

RR1 Leaflet – Housing Benefit

SB16 Leaflet – Social Fund

SDA Severe Disability Allowance

SDA Severe Disablement Allowance

SERPS State Earnings-Related Pension Scheme

SMP Statutory Maternity Pay

UEL Upper Earnings Limit

UPL Upper Profits Limit

WPA1 War Pensions

WPA9 Leaflet – War Pensions

WSı Leaflet – Workmen's Compensation Supplementation

3 Music – instruments, voices & instructions

A starting note of the Aeolian (*minor*) scale

A at; by; for; with; in; to; in the manner of

AB, ab a stop no longer required in organ music (*German: off*)

Acc accompaniment; accompanied by

Acht (*German: eight; care*)

Adel (*German: nobility*)

AEUIA (AEVIA) 'word' incorporating the vowels of Alleluia – *see* EUOUAE

Affekt (*German: full of fervour*)

Agevole (*Italian: comfortable; easily*)

Agit agitato

Alle indication after a solo passage that all are to enter (*German: all*)

Allo allegro (*Italian: bright; cheerful; lively; quick*)

Alt alt (*Italian: high*)

Âme anima (*French, Italian: soul – soundpost of a stringed instrument*)

Amp amplified; amplifier

An an (*German: on; by; to; at – to draw an organ stop*)

Anh Anhang (*German: appendix*)

Anim animato (*Italian: to be performed in a lively manner*)

Anon anonymous(ly)

Appx appendix

Arr arrangement; arranged by/for

As al segno (*Italian: to the sign – either forwards or back*)

Attrib attribution; attributed to

Aut autumn

B starting note of the Locrian (*Hypoæolian*) scale

Barit baritone

Be Be (*German: flat sign*)

Bg/Bog Bogen (*German – bow*)

BMV Beatae Mariae Virginis – *see* BVM (*Latin: Blessed Mary the Virgin*)

BWV Bach Werke Verzeichnis (*catalogue of works of JS Bach published 1950; compiled by Wolfgang Schmieder b 1901*)

C starting note of the Ionian (*major*) scale

C used as a time signature for 4/4 (*not an abbreviation for 'common' time but a relic of broken circle of early mensural notation*)

Ca coll'arco (*Italian: with the bow*)

Cant canticle

Cap capacity

Carn carnival

Cb col basso (*Italian: with the bass*)

Cd, cd colla destra (*Italian: with the right (hand)*)

Chin Chinese

Clt clarinet

Collab in collaboration with

Con with

Conc concerto

Cond conductor; conducted by

Cont continuo

Cps cycles per second (*now Hertz*)

Cresc crescendo (*Italian: getting louder*)

Cs, cs colla sinistra (*Italian: with the left (hand)*)

D starting note of the Dorian scale

D Deutsch catalogue (*of the works of Schubert*)

D Dounias catalogue (*of the works of Tartini*)

DC, Dc, dc da capo (*Italian: 'from the head' – go back to beginning*)

Decresc decrescendo (*Italian: getting softer*)

Ded dedication; dedicated to

Dir director; directed by

Div divisi (*Italian*); divisés (*French: divided – in orchestral score where same section plays different music*)

Dms drums

Doh one of the notes in solmisation scale – *see* ut

DS, Ds, ds dal segno (*Italian: from the sign*)

Dur dur (*German: major*)

E starting note of the Phrygian scale

Ed editor; edited by

Edn edition

Elec electric; electronic

Ens ensemble

Esp especially

EUOUAE (EVOVAE) 'word' consisting of the vowels of seculorum Amen – last words of the Gloria Patri doxology (*see* AEUIA)

Ex, exx example(s)

F starting note of the Lydian scale

F Fanna thematic list (*of the works of Vivaldi*)

f forte (*Italian: loud*)

f, ff folio(s)

f, ff following page(s)

fa 4th note in solmisation scale

FAE sonata frei aber einsam (*German: free, but alone*) by Brahms, Dietrich & Schumann

Fag fagotto (*Italian: bassoon*)

ff fortissimo (*Italian: very loud*)

fff as loud as possible

fia fia (*German: sharp*)

fz forzato (*Italian: forced*)

G starting note of the Mixolydian scale

G Gérard's thematic catalogue (*of the works of Boccherini*)

G identifies a work by Beethoven in a list published in the 2nd edition of Grove's Dictionary (1904–10) which supplements existing opus numbers by assigning new ones (beyond 138) to works that lack them

GP general pause (*all players in orchestra silent at that moment*)

Gr Fl grosse Flöte (*German: concert flute*)

Gr Tr grosse Trommel (*German: bass drum*)

grad gradual

gui, gtr guitar

H Hoboken catalogue (*of the works of Joseph Haydn*)

H *German* B (*note*)

Hb Hoboe (*German: oboe*)

Hn horn

Hpd harpsichord

Hrf Harfe (*German: harp*)

Inst(s) instrument(s)

Int introit

K serial number of a Mozart work in the 1862 catalogue compiled by Ludwig von Köchel (1800–77)

K, Kirk serial number of Scarlatti sonata in the catalogue compiled by the American musicologist Ralph Kirkpatrick (b 1911–84)

Kb Kontrabass (*German: double bass*)

Kbd(s) keyboard(s)

Kl Klarinette (*German: clarinet*)

Kl Fl kleine Flöte (*German: piccolo*)

KV + number Köchel-Verzeichnis (*same as* K)

L links (*German: left hand*)

L serial number of a Scarlatti sonata in the catalogue prepared by Alessandro Longo (Naples 1906–8)

La 6th note in solmisation scale

Leg legato

LH left hand

Lib libretto

Lo loco (*Italian: place- used after a sign indicating performance an octave higher or lower than written, cancelling original sign*)

Man mano (*Italian: hand*)

Man manual (*German: manual – in organ music*)

Mand mandolin

Mar marimba

MD main droite (*French: with the right hand*); mano destra (*Italian: with the right hand*)

Mez mezzo-soprano (*Italian: half-soprano ie voice half-way between soprano and contralto*)

Mf mezzo forte (*Italian: half loud*)

MG main gauche (*French: with the left hand; see* MS)

Mi 3rd note in solmisation scale

MM Maelzel's metronome

Moll moll (*German: minor*)

Mov, move movement

Mp mezzo piano (*Italian: half soft; not too soft*)

MS mano sinistra (*Italian: with the left hand; see* MG)

MS(S) manuscript(s)

Nd no date of publication

No number

Np no place of publication

O in music for violin (*open string or harmonic*)

O in English keyboard music (*use the thumb*)

Ob oboe

Obbl obbligato

OIOUEAE 'world without end, Amen'

Op, Opp opus; opera

Oph ophicleide

Opt optional

Orch orchestra(l)

Org organ

P piano (*Italian: softly*)

P, p pedal (*in keyboard music*)

P, p pédalier (*French: pedal board*); positif (*French: choir organ*) [*in French organ music*]

P, Pest catalogue of Scarlatti's works prepared by Giorgio Pestelli (*Turin 1967*)

PB&D piano, bass & drums

Ped pedale (*Italian: use the pedal*)

Perc percussion

Pf, pfte, pno pianoforte

Pic piccolo

Piu piu forte (*Italian: more loud*)

Piva (*Italian: pipe or bagpipe*)

Pizz pizzicato (*Italian: plucking*)

Pk Pauken (*German: kettledrums*)

Pk pedalkoppel (*German: (in organ music) pedal coupler*)

Pno piano

Posthv posthumous(ly)

Pp pianissimo (*Italian: very softly*)

Pp, ppp (*Italian: very, very softly; as softly as possible*)

Prol prologue

Ps Posaune (*German: trombone*)

Ps Psalm

Pt part

Pubd published

Pubn publication

Qnt quintet

Qt quartet

R Ryom catalogue (*of the works of Vivaldi - see* RV)

R abbreviation for works by Liszt according to the catalogue by Peter Raabe (1931, 2/1968)

R photographic reprint

r recto – right hand page of score

R&B rhythm & blues

rall rallentando (*Italian: slackening the pace*)

re 2nd note in solmisation scale

rec recorder

recit recitative

red reduction; reduced for

rf, rinf rinforzando (*Italian: enforcing*)

RH right hand

RISM International Inventory of Musical Scores

rit ritenuto (*Italian: held back; slower*)

ritard ritardando (*Italian: holding back*)

RV Ryom Verzeichnis (*German: Ryom catalogue – standard thematic catalogue of the works of Vivaldi drawn up by Peter Ryom (Leipzig 1974, supplement Poitiers 1979*)

S soprano (*Italian*)

S al segno (*Italian: sign*)

S subito (*Italian: suddenly*)

S sinistra (*Italian: left*)

S Schmieder (*see* BWV)

S soprano (*instrument*)

SATB (*vocal music for*) soprano, alto, tenor & bass

Sax saxophone

SCTB (*vocal music for*) soprano, contralto, tenor & bass

Ser series

Sf sforzando (*Italian: forcing*)

Sff sforzatissimo (*Italian: very forced*)

Sfp sforato-piano (*Italian: strongly accented note followed by a quiet one*)

Sin sino (*Italian: until – eg sin al segno: go on 'until the sign'*)

So 5th note in solmisation scale

Str string(s)

Su (*Italian: on; near – on a certain string*)

Su (*Italian: up – up-bowed*)

Suppl supplement(ary)

Sym symphony; symphonic

Synth synthesizer

T tenor (*voice*)

T, ten tenor (*instrument*)

Te 7th note in solmisation scale

Ten tenuto (*Italian: held; sustained*)

Timp timpani

Tmb trombone

Ton Tonart (*German: key*)

Tpt trumpet

Tr treble (*voice*); trumpet; trill

Trans translation; translated by

Transcr transcription; transcribed by

Trbn trombone

Trge triangle

Ts tasto solo (*Italian: only bass notes to be played rather than filled in harmonies*)

Uc una corda (*Italian: depress soft pedal*)

Unacc unaccompanied

Unattrib unattributed

Unperf unperformed

Unpubd unpublished

Ut 1st note in solmisation scale system using syllables in association with pitches – used in oral teaching of melodies

V voci (*Italian: voices*)

V verso (*reverse of recto*)

V, Vo violin

V, vv voice(s)

V, vv verse(s)

Va (*Italian: go on; goes on; continue*)

Va, vla viola

Vc cello; violoncello

Vib vibraphone

Vif, vive vivement (*French: lively; briskly*)

Viz videlicet (*Latin: namely*)

Vl, vn violin

Vle violone

Vol volume

Vs volta subito (*Italian: turn over quickly*)

WoO Werk ohne Opuszahl (*German: work without opus number – often used for Beethoven's works published after his death*)

WQ Wotquenne catalogue (*of the works of C P E Bach*)

Ww woodwind

Xyl xylophone

Z Zimmerman catalogue (*of the works of Purcell*)

OT OLD TESTAMENT

Gen Genesis

Exod Exodus

Lev Leviticus

Num Numbers

Deut Deuteronomy

Josh The Book of Joshua

Judg The Book of Judges

Ruth The Book of Ruth

I Sam; 1 Sam The First Book of Samuel

II Sam; 2 Sam The Second Book of Samuel

I Kgs; 1 Kgs The First Book of Kings

II Kgs; 2 Kgs The Second Book of Kings

I Chr; 1 Chr The First Book of the Chronicles

II Chr; 2 Chr The Second Book of the Chronicles

Ez, Ezra Ezra

Neh The Book of Nehemiah

Est, Esther The Book of Esther

Job The Book of Job

Ps The Book of Psalms

Prov The Proverbs

Eccles Ecclesiastes; or, the Preacher

SS, S of Sol The Song of Solomon

Isa The Book of the Prophet Isaiah

Jer The Book of the Prophet Jeremiah

Lam The Lamentations of Jeremiah

Ezek The Book of the Prophet Ezekiel

Dan The Book of Daniel

Hos Hosea

Joel Joel

Am, Amos Amos

Obad Obadiah

Jonah Jonah

Mic Micah

Nah, Nahum Nahum

Hab Habakkuk

Zeph Zephaniah

Hag Haggai

Zech Zechariah

Mal Malachi

Apoc APOCRYPHA

I Esd; 1 Esd I Esdras

II Esd; 2 Esd II Esdras

Tob, Tobit Tobit

Jud, Judith Judith

Rest of Est Rest of Esther

Wis of Sol Wisdom of Solomon

Ecclus Ecclesiasticus

Bar Baruch

Pr of Az Prayer of Azariah

S of Three The Song of the Three Children

Sus Daniel & Susanna

B&D, Bel & Sn Bel & the Dragon; Daniel, Bel & the Snake

Pr of Man Prayer of Manasseh

I Macc; 1 Macc I Maccabees

II Macc; 2 Macc II Maccabees

NT NEW TESTAMENT

Matt The Gospel According to Saint Matthew

Mark The Gospel According to Saint Mark

Luke The Gospel According to Saint Luke

John The Gospel According to Saint John

Acts The Acts of the Apostles

Rom The Epistle of Paul the Apostle to the Romans

I Cor; 1 Cor The First Epistle of Paul the Apostle to the Corinthians

II Cor; 2 Cor The Second Epistle of Paul the Apostle to the Corinthians

Gal The Epistle of Paul the Apostle to the Galatians

Eph The Epistle of Paul the Apostle to the Ephesians

Phil The Epistle of Paul the Apostle to the Philippians

Col The Epistle of Paul the Apostle to the Colossians

I Thess; 1 Thess The First Epistle of Paul the Apostle to the Thessalonians

II Thess; 2 Thess The Second Epistle of Paul the Apostle to the Thessalonians

I Tim; 1 Tim The First Epistle of Paul the Apostle to Timothy

II Tim; 2 Tim The Second Epistle of Paul the Apostle to Timothy

Titus The Epistle of Paul to Titus

Phil, Philem The Epistle of Paul to Philemon

Heb The First Epistle of Paul the Apostle to the Hebrews

Jas The General Epistle of James

I Pet; 1 Pet The First Epistle General of Peter

II Pet; 2 Pet The Second Epistle General of Peter

I John; 1 John The First Epistle General of John

II John; 2 John The Second Epistle of John

III John; 3 John The Third Epistle of John

Jude The General Epistle of Jude

Rev The Revelation of St John the Divine (*not 'Revelations'*)

5   Communications

5.1   Amateur radio (ham) shorthand

?AA please repeat all after . . .

?AB please repeat all before . . .

?BN please repeat all between . . .

73s best regards

88s love & kisses (*the meeting of two pairs of lips*)

ABT about

ADR address

AGN again

ANI any

ANT antenna

BA buffer amplifier

BC broadcast

BCI broadcast interference

BCL broadcast listener

BCNU be seeing you

BD bed

BFO beat frequency oscillator

BK to interrupt a transmission in progress

BK break in

BLV believe

BUG semi-automatic CW key

C yes (*si*)

CANS headphones

CC crystal controlled

CFM confirm
CK check
CL closing down
CLD called
CNT cannot
CO crystal oscillator
CONDX conditions
CPSE counterpoise
CQ calling all stations
CRD card
CUAGN see you again
CUD could
CUL see you later
CW continuous wave (*ie Morse transmission*)
DE separates call signs of caller and callee
DF direction finding/finder
DR dear
DX long distance
DXCC DX Century Club
ECO electron-coupled oscillator
ELBUG electronic key
ENUF enough
ER here
ES and
FB fine business
FCC Federal Communications Commission
FD frequency doubler
FER for
FM frequency modulator/modulated
FOC First Class Operators' Club
FONE telephone
FREQ frequency
GA go ahead, good afternoon
GB goodbye
GBA give better address
GD good day
GE good evening

GG going
GLD glad
GM good morning
GN good night
GND ground (*earth*)
GUD good
HAM amateur transmitter
HI laughter (*H-I-H-I*)
HPE hope
HR here, hear
HRD heard
HV have
HVY heavy
HW how
IARU International Amateur Radio Union
II repetition
INPT input
K please transmit
LID poor operator
LSN listen
MNI many
MO master oscillator
MOD modulation/modulator
MSG message
MTR metre(s)
NBFM narrow-band frequency modulation
ND nothing doing
NIL nothing to send
NR number
NW now
OB old boy
OC old chap
OG old girl
OK agreed, correct
OM old man
OP operator
OT old timer
PA power amplifier
PP push-pull

PSE please

PWR power

All the Q-codes may be used either as a call or its response

QAV I am calling . . .

QCF . . . (*callsign*) is using . . . frequency

QCM There seems to be a defect in your transmission

QRA The name of my station is . . .

QRB The distance between our stations is . . .

QRG *Caller:* Please tell me my exact frequency *Responder:* Your exact frequency is

QRH Does my frequency vary? Yes

QRI What is the tone of my transmission? Your tone is T1 (*rough & hissing*) — T9 (purest DC)

QRJ Your signals are very weak

QRK What is the readability of my signals? Your readability is R1 (*unreadable*) — R5 (*perfectly readable*)

QRL Are you busy? I am busy, please don't interfere

QRM Are you being interfered with? Yes

QRN Are you troubled by static? Yes

QRO Shall I increase power? Yes

QRP Shall I decrease power? Yes

QRQ Shall I send faster? Yes

QRS Shall I send more slowly? Yes

QRT Shall I stop sending? Yes

QRU Have you anything for me? No

QRV Are you ready? Yes

QRW Please tell . . . I am calling

QRX When will you call me again? At . . . hrs

QRZ Who is calling? . . . on . . . kHz

QSA What is my signal strength? S1 (*faint*) — S9 (*extremely strong*)

QSB Are my signals fading? Yes

QSD Is my keying defective? Yes

QSK I can hear between my signals

QSL Please acknowledge receipt I hereby acknowledge receipt

QSM Repeat the last message

QSO Can you communicate with . . . ? I can communicate with . . . direct (*or by relay through . . .*)

QSP Will you relay to . . . ? Yes

QSV Shall I send a series of Vs? Yes

QSW I will transmit on . . . kHz

QSY Shall I change to another frequency? Yes (*on . . . kHz*)

QSZ Shall I send each word more than once? Send each word twice

QTH What is your location? My location is . . .

QTR What is the time? The time is . . .

R received

RAC raw AC

RAOTA Radio Amateur Old Timers' Association

RCC Rag Chewers' Club

RCD received

RCVR receiver

RPRT report

RPT repeat, I repeat

RST readability, signal strength & tone

RX receive/receiver

SA say

SED said

SIG signal

SINPO code signal strength, interference, noise, fading, overall rating; each quantity is measured 1 bad to 5 good

SKED schedule

SN soon
SRI sorry
SSB single sideband
SSB single side band
STN station
SUM some
SW short wave
SWL short-wave listener
TFC traffic
TKS thanks
TMW tomorrow
TNX thanks
TRX transceiver
TV television
TVI television interference
TX transmit/transmitter/
transmission
TX transmitter
U you
UR your
VFO variable-frequency oscillator
VY very
W word(s)
W watts
WA word after
WAC worked all continents
WB word before
WID with

WKD worked
WKG working
WL will, well
WUD would
WX weather
XMTR transmitter
XTAL crystal
XYL ex-young lady (= *wife*)
YF wife
YL young lady
ZAN I am receiving nothing
ZAP please acknowledge
ZCK check your keying
ZCL transmit your call letters
intelligibly
ZDF your frequency is drifting
ZDM your dots are missing
ZFO your signals have faded
ZGS your signals are getting
stronger
ZGW your signals are getting
weaker
ZOK I am receiving OK
ZRN you have a rough note
ZSU your signals are unreadable
ZWO send words once
ZWT send words twice

5.2 Telephone dials

DIGIT	GPO	BT 1996	FRANCE	SCANDINAVIA 1960s	AUSTRALIA
1	—	—	—	C	QZ
2	ABC	ABC	ABC	ABD	ABC
3	DEF	DEF	DEF	EFG	DEF
4	GHI	GHI	GHI	HIK	GHI
5	JKL	JKL	JKL	LMN	JKL
6	MN	MNO	MN	OPR	MNO
7	PRS	PQRS	PRS	STU	PRS
8	TUV	TUV	TUV	VXY	TUV
9	WXY	WXYZ	WXY	Æ Ø	WXY
0	OQ	—	OQZ	—	—

5.3 Old telephone exchanges

BIRMINGHAM

Acocks Green 021-706
Ashfield 021-351
Aston Cross 021-359
Bearwood 021-429
Birchfield 021-356
Blackheath 021-559
Broadwell 021-552
Calthorpe 021-440
Castle Bromwich 021-747
Central 021-236
East 021-327
Edgbaston 021-454
Erdington 021-373
Four Oaks 021-308
GPO 021-262
Great Barr 021-357
Halesowen 021-550
Harborne 021-427
Highbury 021-444

Hillside 021-445
James Bridge 021-526
King's Norton 021-458
Marston Green 021-779
Maypole 021-474
Midland 021-643
Northern 021-554
Priory 021-475
Rubery 021-453
Selly Oak 021-472
Sheldon 021-743
Shirley 021-744
Smethwick 021-558
Solihull 021-705
South 021-449
Springfield 021-777
Setchford 021-783
Stone Cross 021-558
Streetly 021-353
Sutton Coldfield 021-354

Tipton 021-557
Victoria 021-772
Wednesbury 021-556
West Bromwich 021-553
Woodgate 021-422

EDINBURGH

Abbeyhill 031-661
Caledonian 031-225
Colinton 031-441
Corstorphine 031-334
Craiglockhart 031-443
Davidson's Mains 031-336
Deans 031-332
Donaldson 031-337
Fairmilehead 031-445
Fountainbridge 031-229
GPO 031-550
Granton 031-552
Leith 031-554
Liberton 031-664
Morningside 031-447
Musselburgh 031-667
Newington 031-667
Pentland 031-449
Portobello 031-669
Waverley 031-556

GLASGOW

Baillieston 041-771
Barrhead 041-881
Battlefield 041-649
Bearsden 041-942
Bell 041-552
Bishopsbriggs 041-772
Bridgeton 041-554
Busby 041-644
Cambuslang 041-641
Central 041-221
City 041-248
Clydebank 041-952

Cranhill 041-774
Croftfoot 041-634
Douglas 041-332
Drumchapel 041-944
Giffnock 041-638
Govan 041-445
GPO 041-220
Halfway 041-882
Ibrox 041-427
Jordanhill 041-954
Kelvin 041-334
Kirkintiloch 041-776
Langside 041-632
Maryhill 041-946
Merrylee 041-637
Milngavie 041-956
Moss Heights 041-883
Newton Mearns 041-639
Paisley 041-889
Parkhead 041-556
Pollok 041-423
Possil 041-336
Provanmill 041-770
Renfrew 041-886
Rutherglen 041-647
Scotstoun 041-959
Shettleston 041-778
South 041-429
Springburn 041-558
Stepps 041-779
Tannahill 041-887
Thornly Park 041-884
Western 041-339

LIVERPOOL

Aintree 051-525
Allerton 051-724
Anfield 051-263
Argosy 051-274
Arrowebrook 051-677
Birkenhead 051-647

Bootle 051-922
Bromborough 051-334
Caldy 051-625
Central 051-236
Childwall 051-722
Claughton 051-652
Cressington Park 051-422
Eastham 051-327
Ellesmere Port 051-355
Garston 051-427
Gateacrea 051-428
GPO 051-229
Great Crosby 051-924
Hale 051-425
Hooton 051-339
Hunts Cross 051-486
Huyton 051-489
Irby 051-648
Kirkby 051-547
Lark Lane 051-727
Lydiate 051-593
Maghull 051-526
Maritime 051-227
Mountwood 051-608
New Brighton 051-639
North 051-207
Prescot 051-426
Rock Ferry 051-645
Royal 051-709
Sefton Park 051-733
Simonswood 051-546
Stanley 051-226
Stoneycroft 051-228
Wallasey 051-638
Waterloo 051-928
Windes 051-424
Willaston 051-345

MANCHESTER

Altrincham 061-928
Ardwick 061-273

Ashton-under-Lyme 061-330
Blackfriars 061-834
Bramhall 061-439
Broughton 061-792
Bury (Lancashire) 061-764
Central 061-236
Cheetham Hill 061-740
Chorlton-cum-Hardy 061-881
Collyhurst 061-205
Deansgate 061-832
Denton 061-336
Disbury 061-445
Droylsden 061-370
East 061-223
Eccles 061-789
Failsworth 061-681
Gatley 061-428
GPO 061-863
Heaton Moor 061-432
Hulme Hall 061-485
Hyde 061-368
Longford 061-865
Main (Oldham) 061-624
Medlock Head 061-633
Mercury 061-437
Middleton 061-643
Moss Side 061-226
Pendleton 061-736
Prestwich 061-773
Pyramid 061-962
Radcliffe 061-723
Ringway 061-980
Rusholme 061-224
Sale 061-973
Stalybridge 061-338
Stepping Hill 061-483
Stockport 061-480
Swinton 061-794
Trafford Park 061-872
Urmston 061-748

Walken 061-790
Whitefield 061-766
Woodley 061-430
Wythenshawe 061-998

LONDON

Abbey 01-222
Acorn 01-992
Addiscombe 01-654
Advance 01-980
Albert Dock 01-476
Alperton 01-998
Ambassador 01-262
Amherst 01-985
Archway 01-272
Arnold 01-904
Atlas 01-568
Avenue 01-283
Balham 01-672
Barnet 01-449
Battersea 01-228
Bayswater 01-229
Beckenham 01-650
Belgravia 01-235
Bermondsey 01-237
Bexleyheath 01-303
Bishopsgate 01-247
Bluebell 01-656
Bowes Park 01-888
Brixton 01-274
Brunswick 01-278
Buckhurst 01-504
Bushey Heath 01-950
Byron 01-422
Bywood 01-668
Canonbury 01-226
Central 01-236
Chancery 01-242
Cherrywood 01-540
Chiswick 01-994
City 01-248

Clerkenwell 01-253
Clissold 01-254
Clocktower 01-552
Colindale 01-205
Concord 01-864
Coombe End 01-949
Coppermill 01-520
Covent Garden 01-240
Crescent 01-550
Croyden 01-688
Crystal Palace 01-659
Cunnigham 01-286
Danson Park 01-304
Derwent 01-337
Dickens 01-359
Diligence 01-903
Dollis Hill 01-450
Dominion 01-592
Drummond 01-908
Dryden 01-204
Duncan 01-690
Ealing 01-567
East 01-987
Edgware 01-952
Edmonton 01-807
Elgar 01-965
Elstree 01-953
Eltham 01-850
Empress 01-603
Enfield 01-363
Enterprise 01-368
Euston 01-387
Ewell 01-393
Fairlands 01-644
Feltham 01-890
Field End 01-868
Finchley 01-346
Fitzroy 01-348
Flaxman 01-352
Fleet Street 01-353

Molesey 01-979
Monarch 01-606
Moorgate 01-600
Mountview 01-340
Mulberry 01-889
Municipal 01-686
Museum 01-636
National 01-628
New Cross 01-639
Noble 01-602
North 01-607
Nuffield 01-848
Paddington 01-723
Palmers Green 01-886
Park 01-727
Peckham Rye 01-732
Perivale 01-997
Pinner 01-866
Plumstead 01-855
Pollards 01-764
Popesgrove 01-892
Primrose 01-722
Prospect 01-876
Putney 01-788
Raglan 01-556
Ravensbourne 01-460
Redpost 01-733
Regent 01-734
Reliance 01-735
Renown 01-736
Richmond (Surrey) 01-940
Rippleway 01-594
Riverside 01-748
Rodney 01-703
Royal 01-709
Scott 01-720
Seven Kings 01-590
Shepherds Bush 01-743
Shoreditch 01-739
Silverthorn 01-529

Skyport 01-759
Sloane 01-730
Snaresbrook 01-530
Southall 01-574
Spartan 01-249
Speedwell 01-455
Springpark 01-777
Stamford Hill 01-800
Stepney Green 01-790
Stonegrove 01-958
Streatham 01-769
Sullivan 01-799
Sunnyhill 01-203
Swiss Cottage 01-794
Sydenham 01-778
Tabard 01-822
Tate Gallery 01-828
TCY 01-829
Teddington Lock 01-977
Temple Bar 01-836
Terminus 01-837
Thornton Heath 01-684
Tideway 01-692
Tottenham 01-808
Townley 01-693
Trafalgar 01-839
Trevelyan 01-553
Trojan 01-870
TSW 01-879
Tudor 01-883
Tulse Hill 01-674
Turnham Green 01-995
Twickenham Green 01-894
Underhill 01-863
Uplands 01-660
Upper Clapton 01-806
Valentine 01-554
Vandyke 01-874
Victoria 01-834
Vigilant 01-642

Viking 01-845

Virginia 01-349

Wanstead 01-989

Waring Park 01-302

Waterloo 01-928

Waxlow 01-578

Welbeck 01-935

Wembley 01-902

Western 01-937

Whitehall 01-930

Widmore 01-464

Willesdan 01-459

Wimbledon 01-946

Woolwich 01-854

Wordsworth 01-907

6   Paper & printing

6.1   Named sizes of printing paper

Name   in x in

Foolscap 17 x 13.5

Double Foolscap 27 x 17

Crown 20 x 15

Double Crown 30 x 20

Post 19.25 x 15.5

Double Post 31.5 x 19.5

Double Large Post 33 x 21

Sheet & 1/2 Post 23.5 x 19.5

Demy 22.5 x 17.5

Double Demy 35 x 22.5

Music Demy 20 x 15.5

Medium 23 x 18 **Royal** 24 x 20

Super Royal 27.5 x 20.5

Elephant 28 x 23

Imperial 30 x 22

6.2   Named sizes of writing & drawing papers

Name   in x in

Pott 15 x 12.5

Brief 16.5 x 13.25

Double Demy 31 x 20

Double Large Post 33 x 21

Double Post 30.5 x 19

Double Foolscap 26.5 x 16.5

Sheet & 1/2 Foolscap 24.5 x 13.5

Sheet & 1/3 Foolscap 22 x 13.5

Foolscap 17 x 13.5

Pinched Post 18.5 x 14.75

Post 19 x 15.25

Demy 20 x 15.5

Copy or Draft 20 x 16

Large Post 21 x 16.5

Medium 22 x 17.5

Royal 24 x 19

Super Royal 27 x 19

Cartridge 26 x 21

Elephant 28 x 23

Imperial 30 x 22

Colombier 34.5 x 23.5

Atlas 34 x 26

Grand Eagle 42 x 28.75

Double Elephant 40 x 26.75

Antiquarian 53 x 31

Emperor 72 x 48

6.3   Named sizes of brown paper

Name   *in x in*
Kent Cap 21 x 18
Bag Cap 24 x 19.5
Haven Cap 26 x 21
Imperial Cap 29 x 22

Double Four Pound 31 x 21
Elephant 34 x 24
Double Imperial 45 x 29
Casing 46 x 36 6.4

6.4   Bound books

Size   *in x in*
Demy 16mo 5.625 x 4.375
Demy 18mo 5.75 x 3.75
Foolscap Octavo (8vo) 6.75 x 4.25
Crown 8vo 7.5 x 5
Large Crown 8vo 8 x 5.25
Demy 8vo 8.375 x 5.625
Medium 8vo 9.5 x 6
Royal 8vo 10 x 6.25
Super Royal 8vo 10.25 x 6.875
Imperial 8vo 11 x 7.5

Foolscap Quarto (4to) 8.5 x 6.75
Crown 4to 10 x 7.5
Demy 4to 11.25 x 8.75
Royal 4to 12.5 x 10
Imperial 4to 15 x 11
Crown Folio 15 x 10
Demy Folio 15.5 x 11.25
Royal Folio 20 x 12.5
Music 14 x 10.25 6.5

6.5   ISO paper sizes

*The sides of a sheet of an ISO size are in the ratio 1: 2, so if a sheet is cut in
half on the long side, the ratio remains the same. Moreover, an A0 sheet is
1m² in area.*

Size   *mm x mm*
4A   3364 x 4756
3A   2378 x 3364
2A   1682 x 2378
1A   1189 x 1682
A0   841 x 1189
A1   594 x 841
A2   420 x 594
A3   297 x 420

A4   210 x 297
A5   148 x 210
A6   105 x 148
A7   74 x 105
A8   52 x 74
A9   37 x 52
A10   26 x 37

The B range is for use when there is no suitable size in the A range.

Size	mm x mm		B5	176 x 250
B0	1000 x 1414		B6	125 x 176
B1	707 x 1000		B7	88 x 125
B2	500 x 707		B8	62 x 88
B3	353 x 500		B9	44 x 62
B4	250 x 353		B10	31 x 44

6.6   Archaic type sizes

Of these, only pica (to rhyme with biker) remains as a line measure of 12-point ems.

Name	Point size		Bourgeois	9
Diamond	4 ½		Long Primer	10
Pearl	5		Small Pica	11
Ruby	5 ½		Pica	12
Nonpareil	6		English	14
Minion	7		Great Primer	18
Brevier	8		Double Pica	24

7 Medicine

7.1 Medical science

fracture

++ much; many

° nil; nothing; no (*as in* °J = *no jaundice*)

µg microgram

Δ diagnosis

ΔΔ differential diagnosis

°JACCO no jaundice, anaemia, cyanosis, clubbing or oedema (*often seen at start of note of clinical examination*)

1/24 one hour

2/7 two days

3/52 three weeks

4/12 four months

5FU cutotoxic chemotherapy drug used in bowel cancer

373 37 weeks and 3 days

A&E Accident and Emergency

A&W alive & well

A/V i) anteverted; ii) arterio-venous; iii) atrio-ventricular

A1 in the best of health

Aa ana (*Greek: of each*)

AABB American Association of Blood Banks

AAL anterior axillary line

AAPTSD American Association for the Promotion of Teaching Speech to the Deaf (*founded by Alexander Graham Bell*)

ABG arterial blood gases

ABPI Association of the British Pharmaceutical Industry

Ac ante cibum (*Latin: before food*)

ACE inhibitor angiotensis-converting enzyme

ACG apex cardiogram

ACh acetylcholine

ACP acid calcium phosphate

ACTH adrenocorticotropic hormone (*corticotropin; a protein hormone of the anterior pituitary gland controlling many secretory processes of the adrenal cortex. Used medically for the same conditions as cortisone & corticosterone*)

ACTH-RH ACTH releasing hormone

ADA adenosine deaminase

ADEPT antibody-directed enzyme pro-drug therapy

ADH anti-diuretic hormone

ADHD attention deficit hyper-activity disorder (*treat with Ritalin*)

ADI acceptable daily intake

ADP adenosine diphosphate

AE air entry

AEG air encephalogram

Aet aetas (*age*)

AF atrial fibrillation

AFB acid-fast bacillus

AFP alpha-fetoprotein

AGL acute granulocytic leukaemia

AGN acute glomerulonephritis

AH Alice Heim (*Cambridge psychologist and compiler of AH series of psychometric tests*)

AHS alien hand syndrome

AI i) aortic incompetence; ii) artificial insemination

AID artificial insemination donor

AIDS acquired immune deficiency syndrome

AJ ankle jerk (*reflex: see also* BJ, KJ, SJ, TJ)

AK above knee (*as in AKA = above knee amputation*)

ALa alanine

ALD adrenoleukodystrophy

ALG antilymphocyte globulin

Alk.phos alkaline phosphatase

ALL acute lymphoblastic leukaemia

ALS anti-lymphocyte/lymphocytic serum

Alt die alternis diebus (*Latin: alternate days*)

AMA American Medical Association

AMI acute myocardial infarction

AML acute myelogenous leukaemia

AMP adenosine monophosphate

An anaemia

ANDI abnormal development & involution

ANF antinuclear factor

ANK appointment not kept

Anti-D this gamma globulin must be given by injection to Rhesus negative mother who delivers/aborts Rhesus positive child/foetus to prevent mother developing antibodies which could damage a subsequent Rhesus positive baby

Ao aorta

AP i) anteroposterior ii) artificial pneumothorax

Ap ante prandium (*Latin: before a meal (in prescriptions)*)

APC aspirin, phenacitin & caffeine

Apgar Apgar score: means of recording baby's condition at and shortly after birth by observing and "scoring" (0, 1 or 2) 5 variables. (*Apgar 10 = perfect condition. Apgar 0 = stillbirth*)

APH antepartum haemorrhage

APKD adult polycystic kidney disease

APR abdominal-perinal resection

APUD amine precursor uptake & decarboxylation

ARD acute respiratory disease

ARDS adult respiratory distress syndrome

ARI acute respiratory infection/insufficiency

ARM artificial rupture of membranes (*labour*)

AS i) aortic stenosis; ii) ankylosing spondylitis

As arsenic

ASB anencephaly and spina bifida

ASCUS atypical squamous cells of uncertain significance

ASD atrial septal defect

ASO antistreptolysin

ASPEN American Society for Parenteral & Enteral Nutrition

AST aspartate aminotransferase

ATN acute tubular necrosis

ATP adenosine triphosphate (*an important coenzyme in various biological reactions, involving the transfer of phosphate bond energy*)

ATPase an enzyme that converts ATP to ADP

Au gold

AUA American Urological Association

AVB antioventricular block

AVPU alert, visual, pain, unresponsive

AVT arginine vasotoxin (*produced in the brain of the blue-head wrasse; induces gender-specific behaviour*)

AW above the waist

AXR abdominal X-ray

AZT azidothymidine

B i d bis in die (*Latin: twice a day*)

B-eucaine benzamine, formerly used as a local anaesthetic

Ba barium

Bact bacteria

Bacteriol bacteriological; bacteriology

BaE barium enema

BAL bronchoalveolar lavage

BAL British anti-lewisite (*dimercaprol; antidote to gas & metal poisoning*)

BaM barium meal

BASIC British Association for Immediate Care

BBA born before arrival

BBB i) blood-brain barrier; ii) bundle branch block

BCC basal-cell carcinoma

BCG bacille Calmette-Guérin (*anti TB vaccine*)

BD to be given/taken twice a day

Bd bis in die (*Latin: twice a day*)

BDA British Dyslexia Association

BDA British Dental Association

BDA British Diabetic Association

BDL below detectable limits

BFMS British False Memory Society (*protection from psychotherapeutic seek-and-ye-shall-find*)

BHA butylated hydroxyanisole

BHHI British Home & Hospital for Incurables

BHT butylated hydroxytoluene

BIBA brought in by ambulance

BID brought in dead

Bid bis in die (*Latin: twice a day*)

BIPP 1 part bismuth subnitrate (*1 part*), 2 parts iodoform (*2 parts*), & paraffin (*wound dressing paste*)

BIRT Brain Injury and Rehabilitation Trust

BJ biceps jerk (*reflex: see* AJ)

BK below knee

BKPA British Kidney Patient Association

BM bowel movement

BMA British Medical Association

BMI body mass index

BMJ British Medical Journal

BMR basal metabolic rate

BNF (plus date) British National Formulary (*prescriber's bible supplied free to all NHS doctors*) *New edition each year*

BNO bowels not open

BO body odour

BO bowels open

BOD biological/biochemical oxygen demand

BP British Pharmacopoeia

BP i) blood pressure; ii) boiling point

BPA Bereaved Parents' Association

BPC British Pharmaceutical Codex

BPM beats per minute

BPRO Blind Persons' Resettlement Officer

BRC Biotechnology Research Council

BS Bachelor of Surgery

BS i) breath sounds; ii) bowel sounds; ii) blood sugar

BSA body surface area

BSE bovine spongiform encephalopathy

BSI British Society for Immunology

BSL British Sign Language

BSR i) blood sedimentation rate; ii) British Society of Rheumatology

BSSAA British Snoring & Sleep Apnoea Association

BST bovine somatotropin (*natural growth hormone to increase milk yield in cows*)

BT bleeding time

BUMS Bristol University Medical School

BV bacterial vaginosis

BV biological value (*measure of protein quality*)

BV i) blood vessel; ii) blood volume

BW i) below the waist; ii) body water; iii) body weight

C carbon

C cum (*Latin: with*)

C&P cystoscopy and pyelography

C&R convalescence and rehabilitation

C1, C2 etc cervical vertebrae

C3 inferior or in poor health

CA chronological age

CA cardiac arrest

Ca cases

Ca i) carcinoma; cancer; ii) calcium

CABG coronary artery bypass graft(ing) (*pronounced 'cabbage'*)

CAEs contingent after effects

CAH congenital adrenal hyperplasia (*faulty enzyme causing subject to grow up too fast*)

CAPD continuous ambulatory peritoneal dialysis

Caps capsules

CAR child abuse register

CARE communicated authenticity, regard, empathy (*qualities a therapist needs*)

CAST computer-assisted sonic tomography

CAT computerised axial tomography

Cat cataplasma (*Latin: a poultice*)

CBD common bile duct

CBF cerebral blood flow

CBR complete bed rest

Cc i) carcinoma (*cancer*); ii) cubic centimetre

CCCR closed chest cardiac resuscitation

CCDC Consultant for Commercial Disease Control

CCF congestive cardiac failure

CCU Coronary Care Unit

CD cluster of differentiation (*a numerical system for classifying antigens expressed on the surface of leucocytes*)

CD controlled drug

Cd cadmium

CDH i) congenital disease of the heart; ii) congenital dislocated hip(s)

CF cystic fibrosis

CF citrovorum factor

CFC central flood cell

CFS chronic fatigue syndrome (*was PVD; became ME; alternatives: CSD, MMD, FBF*)

CFU colony-forming unit

CGL chronic granulocytic leukaemia

CHA chronic haemolytic anaemia

CHB complete heart block

CHC Child Health Clinic

CHC Community Health Council

CHD coronary heart disease

ChE cholinesterase

ChM Master of Surgery

CHO carbohydrate

CI contraindications

CI i) clubbing (*of fingers or toe nails*) ii) chlorine

CIN cervical intraepithelial neoplasia (*grading cervical smears*)

CJD Creutzfeldt-Jakob disease

CLL chronic lymphoid leukaemia

CMC carboxymethylcellulose

CMF cyclophosphamide, methotrexate & fluorouracil

CML chronic myeloid leukaemia

CMR cerebral metabolic rate

CMV cytomegalovirus

CN I-XII cranial nerves 1-12

CNS central nervous system

CO complaining of

Co I coenzyme I (*nicotinamide adenine dinucleotide – NAD*)

Co II coenzyme II (*nicotinamide adenine dinucleotide phosphate – NADP*)

CO2 carbon dioxide

CoA coenzyme A

COAD chronic obstructive airways disease

COC cottaging or cruising

COD chemical oxygen demand

COETT cuffed oral endotracheal tube (*see* COT *and* ETT)

COLD chronic obstructive lung disease

COMA Committee on Medical Aspects of Food Policy (*UK*)

Cong congius (*Latin: gallon*)

CONI care of the next infant (*after a cot death*)

COPD chronic obstructive pulmonary disease

CoQ ubiquinone (*a coenzyme*)

CORD chronic obstructive respiratory disease

COSHH control of substances hazardous to health

COT cuffed oral tube (*endotracheal tube used for ventilating a patient who cannot breath unaided*)

CPA Community Practitioners' Association

CPAG Community Pharmacy Action Group

CPAG Child Poverty Action Group

CPAP continuous positive airway pressure

CPB cardiopulmonary bypass

CPD cephalopelvic disproportion (*baby too big to pass through pelvis*)

CPE chronic pulmonary emphysema

CPM counts per minute

CPP cerebral perfusion pressure

CPPB constant positive pressure breathing

CPPV continuous positive pressure ventilation

CPR cardiopulmonary resuscitation

Cr chromium

CRC Cancer Research Campaign

Crit critical

CRMF Cancer Relief Macmillan Fund

CRS Congenital Rubella Syndrome

CRT Cognitive Research Trust

CS caesarean section

Cs caesium

CSAG Clinical Standards Advisory Group

CSB chemical stimulation of the brain

CSD chronic syndrome disorder (*see* CFS)

CSF cerebrospinal fluid

CSF colony stimulation factor

CSM Committee for Safety of Medicines

CSOM chronic suppurative otitis media

CST i) convulsive shock therapy; ii) cavernous sinus thrombosis

CT computerised tomography

CT cerebral (or coronary) thrombosis

CTG cardiotacograph (*trace during labour of baby's heart and mother's contractions*)

CTR cardiothoracic ratio

CTS carpal tunnel syndrome

Cu copper

CV i) cardiovascular; ii) cerebrovascular

CVA cerebrovascular accident (*rupture or blockage of blood vessel in the brain – a cerebral haemorrhage, or stroke*)

CVP central venous pressure

CVP cardiovascular pressure

CVS chorionic villus/villi sampling

CVS clean voided specimen

CX powder to clean & disinfect skin

Cx cervix

CXR chest X-ray

Cy cyanosis

D value decimal reduction time

D&C dilation and curettage

D&V diarrhoea and vomiting

D- & l- dextrorotatory & laevorotatory optical activity (*obsolete, replaced by (+) & (-)*)

D/S dextrose saline

D/W i) discussed with; ii) dextrose in water

DA developmental age

DAH disordered action of the heart

DBP diastolic blood pressure

DD i) dangerous drug; ii) differential diagnosis

DDAVP trade name for desmopressin

DE dextrose equivalent value

DFib defibrillator

DHA District Health Authority

DHEA dehydroepiandrosterone (*a hormone whose gradual depletion is thought to contribute to ageing; hence it is dubbed 'the fountain of youth'*)

DI donor insemination (*see* AID)

DI diabetes insipidus

DIC disseminated intravascular coagulation

DICI direct intracytoplasmic injection

DIT diet-induced thermogenesis

DLE discoid lupus erythematosus

DLRM Doctors & Lawyers for Responsible Medicine

DM diabetes mellitus

DMD Duchenne muscular dystrophy

DNA i) did not attend; ii) deoxyribonucleic acid

DNO District Nursing Officer

DNR do not resuscitate

DOA dead on arrival

DOB date of birth

DOC 11-deoxycorticosterone

Dol urg dolore urgente (*Latin: when the pain is severe*)

DPN diphosphopyridine nucleotide (*obsolete name for NAD*)

DPT i) dental pantomogram; ii) diphtheria-pertussis-tetanus (*vaccines*)

Dr Doctor; debtor

Dr drachm

DS i) disseminated (multiple) sclerosis; ii) Down's syndrome

DT delirium tremens

DTA differential thermal analysis

DTP i) distal tingling on percussion; ii) diphtheria, tetanus, pertussis

DU duodenal ulcer

DVM Doctor of Veterinary Medicine

DVT deep-vein thrombosis

Dx diagnosis

DXR deep x-ray

EAHF eczema, asthma, hay fever

EBF erythroblastosis fetalis

ECB exploration of common bile duct

ECF extracellular fluid

ECG electrocardiogram

ECM external cardiac massage

ECT electroconvulsive therapy

ECV extracellular volume

ED emotionally disturbed

EDC expected date of confinement

EDD expected date of delivery

EDTA ethylene diamine tetra-acetic acid

EEA index essential aminoacid index

EEG electroencephalogram/graph (*brain recording*)

EFA essential fatty acids

EGDF embryonic growth and development factor

EGRAC test enzyme activation tests

EH equilibrium humidity

EHL electrostatic lithotripsy

EIA enzyme immunoassay

EJ elbow jerk (*see* AJ)

EKG electro-cardiogram/ cardiograph

ELISA enzyme-linked immunosorbent assay

EMEA European Medicines Evaluation Agency

EMF i) electromotive force; ii) endomyocardial fibrosis

EMS Emergency Medical Service

EMT Emergency Medical Technician

ENO effervescent antacid – sodium bicarbonate, tartaric acid & citric acid

ENP Emergency Nurse Practitioner

ENT ear, nose & throat (*otolaryngology*)

EOA examination, opinion and advice

EOL end of life

EPA eicosapentaenoic acid (*in fish oils*)

EPIC European Prospective Investigation into Cancer (*diet research*)

EPO erythropoietin (*hormone that boosts red blood cell production*)

EQ emotion(al) quotient

ER endoplasmic reticulum

ER emergency room

ERCP endoscopic retrograde cholangiopancreatography

ESN educationally subnormal

ESP i) end-systolic pressure; ii) extrasensory perception

ESPEN European Society for Parenteral & Enteral Nutrition

ESR erythrocyte sedimentation rate

ESWL extracorporeal shock wave lithotripsy

ETC i) estimated time of conception; ii) examined through clothes

EtOH ethyl alcohol (*paperwork code for a drunk*)

ETT endotracheal tube (*see* COT *above*)

EUA examination under anaesthesia

Ex aq ex aqua (*Latin: from water*)

Ext extractum (*Latin: extract*)

F value sterilising measurement = 1 minute at 121.1°C

f fiat (*Latin: let it be made*)

FACT Focus on Alternative & Complementary Therapies

FAD flavin adenine dinucleotide (*a coenzyme formed from vitamin B_2 (riboflavin); essential for using oxygen*)

FAO Food & Agriculture Organisation (*of the UN*)

FAS foetal alcohol syndrome

FB i) finger's breadth; ii) foreign body

FBC full blood count

FBS foetal blood sampling (*carried out during labour to check baby's condition*)

FDA Food & Drug Administration (*US*)

FDIU foetal death *in utero*

Fe iron

FEUO for external use only

FFA free fatty acids

FFI fit and free from infection

FH i) family history; ii) familial hypercholesterolaemia

FHHR foetal heart heard regular

FHNH foetal heart not heard

FHR foetal heart rate

FHSA Family Health Services Authority

FIGLU formiminoglutamic acid

FIGLU test a test for folic acid nutritional status based on FIGLU excretion

FIUO for internal use only

FLK funny-looking kid

FMF foetal movements felt

FMN flavin mononucleotide (*riboflavin phosphate from vitamin B*)

FNAC fine needle aspiration cytology

FOB faecal occult blood

FOOH fell on outstretched hand

FOREST Freedom of Right to Enjoy Smoking Tobacco

FP freezing point

FPA Family Planning Association

FPC Family Practitioner Committee

FRJM full range of joint movement

FROM full range of movement

FSE foetal scalp electrode

FSH follicle-stimulating hormone

FSH family and social history

FTA fluorescent treponemal antibody

FTBD full term, born dead

FTND full term, normal delivery

FTT failure to thrive

FTVD full term vaginal delivery

FU follow up

FVC forced vital capacity (*a respiratory function test*)

Fx fracture

G6P glucose 6 phosphate

G6PD glucose 6 phosphate dehydrogenase

GA general anaesthetic

GA gestational age

GA, Gam-Anon Gamblers Anonymous

GABA gamma-aminobutyric acid

GALT gut-associated lymphoid tissue

GASP Group Against Smokers' Pollution; Group Against Steroid Prescription

GB gall bladder

GC gonococcus

GCS Glasgow coma scale ($3-15$)

GF growth factor

GFR glomerular filtration rate

GH General Hospital

GH growth hormone

GI gastro-intestinal

GI tract gastro-intestinal tract

GIFT gamete intrafallopian transfer

GIG Genetic Interest Group

GIP gastric inhibitory peptide

GITT glucose insulin tolerance test

GM genetically modified

GM general medicine

GMC General Medical Council

GMS glyceryl monostearate

GNC General Nursing Council

GnRH gonadotrophin releasing hormone

GOMER get out of my emergency room

GORD gastro-oesophageal reflux disease

GOSH Great Ormond Street Hospital

GOT glutamic oxaloacetic transaminase

GP general practitioner

GPI general paralysis of the insane

GRID gay-related immune disease

GSR galvanic skin response

gt, gtt, gutt gutta; guttae (*Latin: drop, drops*)

GTT glucose tolerance test

GU genito-urinary

GU gastric ulcer

GUT genito-urinary tract

GVHD graft-versus-host disease

H hydrogen

H&SE Health & Safety Executive

HAA hospital activity analysis

HACSG Hyperactive Children's Support Group

Haust haustus (*Latin: draught*)

Hb haemoglobin

HBD has been drinking

HbF foetal haemoglobin

HbH haemoglobin H

HbS sickle cell haemoglobin

HCM hypertrophic cardiomyopathy

Hct haemocyte

HDL high-density lipoprotein

HDU high-dependency unit

HEA Health Education Authority

HeLa cell Henrietta Lacks (*who died of cancer in 1951, but whose cultured cells live on in laboratories the world over – name originally disguised as Helen Lane or Lancaster*)

HELLP syndrome haemolysis, elevated liver enzymes & low platelet count

HFEA Human Fertilisation & Embryology Authority

HFPPV high frequency positive pressure ventilation

Hg mercury

HGAC Human Genetics Advisory Committee

HIB meningitis

HISS Hospital Information Support System

HIV human immunodeficiency virus

HLA system human leucocyte antigen

HLG human chorionic gonadotrophin

HMD hyaline membrane disease

HMG CoA hydroxymethylglutaryl CoA

HMO Health Maintenance Organisation

Hn hac nocte (*Latin: this night*)

HOCM hypertrophic obstructive cardiomyopathy

Hor decub hora decubitus (*Latin: at bedtime*)

HPC history of presenting complaint

HPI history of present(ing) illness

HpRL prolactin

HPV human papillomavirus

HR heart rate

HRT hormone replacement therapy

HS heart sounds

Hs hora somni (*Latin: at bedtime*)

HSE i) Health and Safety Executive; ii) herpes simplex encephalitis

HSPS Henoch-Schönlein purpura syndrome

HTLV human T-cell leucocyte/ lympho(cyto)tropic virus

HV Health Visitor

HV hallux valgus

HV, hv high voltage

HVS high vaginal swab

Hx history

I incisor

I&D incision and drainage

I&O intake and output

IA intra-arterial

IADHS inappropriate antidiuretic hormone syndrome

IBS irritable bowel syndrome

IC immunochemical

IC(U) intensive care (unit)

ICD International Classification Of Disease

ICF intracellular fluid

ICIDH International Classification of Impairments, Disabilities & Handicaps

ICP intracranial pressure

ICRC International Committee of the Red Cross

ICS intercostal space (*usually as xICS, where x = a number from 1-11*)

ICSH Interstitial-Cell-Stimulating Hormone

ID, id intradermal

IDD insulin dependent diabetes

IDDM insulin-dependent diabetes mellitus

IEM inborn error or metabolism

IFB inflammatory bowel disease

IFFT International Federation of Forensic Toxicologists

IFS information fatigue syndrome

Ig immunoglobulin

IgA immunoglobulin A

IGBM International Group on Breastfeeding Monitoring

IgD immunoglobulin D

IgE immunoglobulin E

IgG immunoglobulin G

IgM immunoglobulin M

IHD ischaemic heart disease

IHEEM Institute of Healthcare Engineering & Estate Management (*estd 1943*)

IJ internal jugular (*vein*)

IM i) intramuscular; ii) infectious mononucleosis

IMP integrating motor pneumotachograph

IMP inosine monophosphate

IMR infant mortality rate

IMS Indian Medical Service

IMV intermittent mandatory ventilation

INR international normalised ratio

IOFB intra-ocular foreign body

IOP intra-ocular pressure

IPCRESS Induction of Psychoneuroses by Conditioned Reflex with Stress (*as in* The IPCRESS File, *a film*)

IPEMB Institution of Physics & Engineering in Medicine & Biology (*BES + IPMS merged 1995*)

IPMS Institute of Physical Scientists in Medicine (*see* IPEMB)

IPPA inspection, palpation, percussion, auscultation

IPPR intermittent positive pressure respiration

IPPV intermittent positive pressure ventilation

IQ intelligence quotient (*the norm is 100; to be shocked that half the population has an IQ of less than 100 shows a lack of understanding of the principle*)

Ir iridium

IRM innate releasing mechanism

ISC intermittent self-catheterisation

ISM Institute of Sports Medicine

ISMO nitrate treatment for angina

ISQ in status quo (*unchanged*)

IT intrathecal

IT(U) intensive therapy (*unit*)

ITCH information technology for children in hospital

ITP idiopathic thrombocytopenic purpura

ITT insulin tolerance test

IU immunising unit

IU international unit

IU(C)D intra-uterine (contraceptive) device

IUD intrauterine device

IUGR intra-uterine growth retardation

IUP intrauterine pressure

IUT intensive therapy unit

IV intravenous

IVC inferior vena cava

IVD intravertebral disc

IVF in vitro fertilisation

IVGGT intravenous glucose tolerance test

IVH intraventricular haemorrhage

IVI intravenous infusion (*drip*)

IVP intravenous pyelography

IVT intravenous transfusion

IVU intravenous urography

Ix investigations

I-PSS international prostate symptoms score (*for qualifying patients' ease of urinating – medical humour manifested*)

J jaundice

JABS justice, awareness & basic support (*parental campaign to promote awareness of possible side effects of inoculations*)

JJ jaw jerk

Jnd just noticeable difference

JRC Junior Red Cross

JV jugular vein

JVP jugular vein pressure

K potassium

K group factor of spacial ability

KJ knee jerk (*reflex: see* AJ)

KKIH King Khalid International Hospital (*Kingdom of Saudi Arabia*)

KKLS kidneys, liver, spleen

KPa kilopascal (*approximately 7.5mmHg*)

KPTT kaolin partial thromboplastin time

KS Kaposi's sarcoma

L i) litre ii) left

L&A light and accommodation

L&W living and well

L-dopa levodopa

L1, L2 etc lumbar vertebrae

LA local anaesthetic

Laetrile laevo-mandelonitrile-beta-glucoronic acid

Las label as such (*note on drug prescription*)

LBB left bundle branch

LBBB left bundle branch block

LBF liver blood flow

LBH length, breadth, height

LBP lower back pain

LBW low birth weight

LCF Leonard Cheshire Foundation

LD50 lethal dose 50% (*an index of toxicity – the dose of a toxic compound that causes death in 50% of test animals*)

LDC London Diagnostic Centre

LDL low-density lipoproteins

LE lupus erythematosus

LEPRA Leprosy Relief Association

LFTs liver function tests; lung function tests

LGSIL low grade squamous intraepithelial lesions

LH little house (*water closet; originally outside earth closet*)

LH luteinising hormone (*causes growth of the corpus luteum of the ovary & stimulates activity in the interstitial cells of the testis*)

LIB lump in breast

LIF left iliac foss

LIH left inguinal hernia

LKS liver, kidney, spleen

LMN lower motor neurone

LMP last menstrual period

LN lymph node

LOA left occiput anterior (*position of baby's head at delivery: see also* LOP, ROA, ROP, LOL, ROL, OA, OP)

LOC loss of consciousness

LOL left occipitolateral (*see* LAO)

LOM limitation of movement

LOP left occiput posterior

LOPS length of patient stay

LP Lecturer Practitioner

LP lumbar puncture

LPN Licensed Practical Nurse

LRCP Licentiate of the Royal College of Physicians

LRT lower respiratory tract

LRTI lower respiratory tract infection

LS letter sent

LSCS lower segment caesarean section (*the 'normal' type of caesarean section*)

LSHTM London School of Hygiene & Tropical Medicine

LSKK liver, spleen, kidneys

LTM long-term memory

LUQ left upper quadrant

LUSCS lower uterine segment caesarean section

LVF left ventricular failure

LVH left ventricular hypertrophy

M molar

M menarche (*started periods*)

M misce (*Latin: mix*)

M medicine

M et sign misce et signa (*Latin: mix and label*)

M ft mist misce fiat mistura (*Latin: mix and let a mixture be made*)

M/F male/female

MA mental age

MACS Micro Anophthalmic Children's Society

MAGPI operation meatal advancement & glanuloplasty operation

MAI myobacterium avium intercellare

MAL mid axillary line

Mane in the morning

MAO monoamine oxidase

MAOI monoamine oxidase inhibitor

MAP mean arterial pressure

MASH Mobile Army Surgical Hospital

MB Bachelor of Medicine

MBD minimal brain dysfunction

MC&S microscopy culture & sensitivity

MCA Medicines Control Agency

Mcg microgram

MCL mid clavicular line

MCV mean cell volume

Md more dicto (*Latin: as directed*)

MDR TB multiple-drug-resistant TB

Mdu more dicto utendus (*Latin: to be used as directed*)

ME myalgic encephalopathy (*was CFS*)

Med medical; medicine

MELAS mitochondrial encephalomyopathy, lactic acidosis and stroke

MESMAC Men who Enjoy Sex with Men Action in the Community

MF myelofibrosis

Mg magnesium

Mg milligram

MGM/F maternal grandmother/father

MI mitral insufficiency

MI i) myocardial infarction; ii) medical inspection

MIC minimum inhibitory concentration

MIND National Association for Mental Health

Mist mistura (*Latin: mixture*)

Mist mixture

Mit mitte (*Latin: send*)

Mitte 1/12 supply/give/send/provide (eg *instruction to pharmacist to provide patient with eg, 1 month's supply of drugs*)

Ml millilitres

MLC mixed lymphocyte culture

MLD mean/median/minimum lethal dose

MLR mixed lymphocyte reaction

MM malignant melanoma

MM i) multiple myeloma; ii) mucous membrane

MMD magical mystery disease (*see* CFS)

MmHg millimetres of mercury (*pressure*)

MMol millimol

MMPI Minnesota Multi-Phasic Personality Inventory

MMR measles, mumps & rubella (*inoculation for children*)

MN Master of Nursing

MNB Medical Negligence Board

MND motor-neurone disease

MNDA motor-neurone disease association

MO Medical Officer

Mo morphine

MOEH Medical Officer for Environmental Health

MOF multiple organ failure

MOH Medical Officer of Health

MOPP ch mechlorethamine, vincristine, procarbazine & prednisone

MPC maximum permissible concentration

MPC Medical Practices' Committee

MPD maximum possible dose

MPH Master of Public Health

MPS mucopolysaccharide (*19 MPS diseases affecting the body's enzymes, and leading to degeneration*)

MR medium release

MRCS Master of the Royal College of Surgeons

MRI magnetic resonance imaging (= *NMRI*)

MRSA methicillin-resistant *staphylococcus aureus* (*dubbed 'the silent epidemic' by the Royal College of Nursing*)

MS multiple sclerosis

MS mitral stenosis

MSBP Münchausen's syndrome by proxy

MSDS manufacturer's safety data sheet

MSF Médecin sans Frontières

MSH melanocyte-stimulating hormone

MSM Men Who Have Sex With Men (*in a PSE*)

MSN Master of Science in Nursing

MST morphine sulphate

MSU mid-stream specimen of urine

MT Medical Technologist

MUAC mid-upper-arm-circumference (*for assessing nutritional status*)

MUGA scan multiple-gated arteriography

MWO Mental Welfare Officer

N nitrogen

N balance nitrogen balance

N conversion factor nitrogen conversion factor

N&V nausea and vomiting

N-oil substances used to replace fat in a recipe food

N/S normal size; not significant

Na sodium

NAA no apparent abnormalities

Naafa National Association for the Advancement of Fat Acceptance (*US*)

NAC National Abortion Campaign

NACNE National Advisory Committee on Nutrition Education (*UK*)

NAD no abnormality detected

NAD, NADP nicotinamide adenine dinucleotide/phosphate (*co-enzymes – see* Co I & Co II)

NAFARE National Association for Families & Addiction Research & Education (*US*)

NAHAT National Association of Health Authorities and Trusts

NaHCO₃ sodium bicarbonate (*alkaline substance: inter alia given to counteract metabolic acidosis following oxygen deprivation*)

NAI non-accidental injury

NBM nil by mouth

NBPA National Back-Pain Association

NBTS National Blood Transfusion Service (*obsolete*)

NCHS standards National Center for Health Statistics (*US*)

standards (*tables of weight and age used for assessing growth and nutritional status of children*)

NCT National Childbirth Trust

ND Notifiable Disease

NDCS National Deaf Children's Society

NDpCal net dietary protein energy ratio

NDRA National Deafblind & Rubella Association

NDV Newcastle disease virus

NEC necrotising enterocolitis

NEFA non-esterified fatty acids

NEL no effect level

NEO-DHC neohesperidin dihydrochalcone

NET naso-endotracheal tube

NF necrotising fasciitis (*self-destructive disease*)

NFE nitrogen-free extract

NFR, NFn not for resuscitation; not for crash (*n is the number of the crash team – let the patient die in peace*)

NFTD normal full term delivery

NG i) naso-gastric; ii) carcinoma/cancer (*neoplastic growth = new growth*)

Ng nanogram

NICU neonatal death

NIDDM non insulin dependant diabetes mellitus

NIH National Institute of Health (*US*)

NK cell natural killer

NKDA no known drug allergies

NLM (*used by paediatricians*) nice looking mother

NMCS no malignant cells seen

NMR nuclear magnetic resonance

NMRI nuclear magnetic resonance imaging

NMSC non-melanoma skin cancer(s)

NND neonatal death

No 606 salvarsan

No 914 neo-salvarsan

Noct/nocte at night

NOF neck of femur

NP neuropsychiatry; neuropsychiatric

NPCO negative patient-care outcome (= *death*)

NPPI negative pressure patient isolator

NPR net protein ratio

NPU net protein utilisation

NS normal saline

NSAID non-steroidal anti-inflammatory drugs

NSD i) normal spontaneous delivery; ii) nominal standard dose

NSF National Schizophrenia Fellowship

NSI non-specific illness

NSP non-starch polysaccharides

NSR normal sinus rhythm

NSS National Surveillance Scheme

NSU non specific urethritis

NTBR not to be resuscitated (*see* NFR)

NTD neural tube defect

NTP normal temperature and pressure

NTR no treatment required

NWB non weight bearing

NZMA New Zealand Medical Association

O octarius (*Latin: pint*)

O&C onset and course

O2 (or O) oxygen

OA i) occipito-anterior (*see* LOA); ii) osteo arthritis

OAD obstructive airways disease

OAP over anxious parent

OCP oral contraceptive pill

Od overdose (*of drugs*)

OE on examination

OGD oesophagogastroduodenoscopy

OHS Occupational Health Service

Om omni mane (*Latin: every morning*)

On omni nocte (*Latin: every evening*)

ONTRA orders not to resuscitate

OP occipito-posterior (*see* LOA)

Op(s) operation(s)

ORIF open reduction & internal fixation

ORT oral rehydration therapy

Orthop orthopnoea (*breathlessness on lying flat*)

OT Occupational Therapy/Therapist

OT Operating Theatre

OTC over the counter

P pharmacy only

P pulse

P or period

P oc pro oculis (*Latin: for the eyes*)

P/S polyunsaturated/saturated ratio

P/S ratio ratio between poly-unsaturated and saturated fatty acids

P4000 a class of synthetic sweeteners

Paa parti effecti applicandus (*Latin: to be applied to the affected part*)

PABA para-amino benzoic acid

PAFO pissed and fell over

PAH polycyclic aromatic hydrocarbon (*possibly carcinogenic*)

PAIN parents against injustice (ie, *wrongfully accused of child abuse*)

PAL physical activity level

PALS paediatric advanced life support

PAN polyarteritis nodosa

PAR physical activity ratio

PARNUTS an EU term for foods prepared for particular nutritional purposes

PAS 4-aminosalicylic acid – a form of sodium salt used in the treatment of TB

PASG pneumatic anti-shock garment

PAT paroxysmal atrial tachycardia

PBI protein-bound iodine

PC post cibum

PCB polychlorinated biphenyl (*unpleasant chemical*)

PCM protein-calorie malnutrition

PCO2 partial pressure of carbon dioxide

PCP pneumocystis carinii pneumonia

PCS Prostate Cancer Society

PCV packed cell volume

PCWP pulmonary capillary wedge pressure

PD peritoneal dialysis

PD, pd per diem (*Latin: per day*)

PDA patent ductus arteriosus

PDGF platelet-derived growth factor

PDT photodynamic therapy

PE i) pulmonary embolism; ii) pre-eclampsia

PEFR peak expiratory flow rate

PEG percutaneous endoscopic gastronomy

PEM protein-energy malnutrition

PER protein efficiency ratio

PERL pupils equal & reactive to light

PERLA pupils are equal and react to light and accommodation

PET polyethylene terephthalate (*a clear plastic used in bottles & packaging*)

PET positron emission tomography

PET pre-eclamptic toxaemia

PFI Private Finance Initiative (*NH*)

PFT pulmonary function test

Pg picogram

PGA pteroylglutamic acid

PGH pituitary growth hormone

PGM/F paternal grandmother/ father

PGR psychogalvanic response

PH past/previous history

PH potential hydrogen

PH negative log of hydrogen ion activity: 'acidity and alkalinity' scale: low is acidic: high is alkaline: pH7.4 is normal body level

PHA phyto haemagglutinin

Phar, phar, Pharm, pharm pharmaceutical, pharmacy, pharmacopoeia

Pharmacol pharmacology

PHB ester *methyl, ethyl & propyl esters of* p-hydroxybenzoic *acid* (*parabens*) *used with their sodium salts as antimicrobial*

PHLS Public Health Laboratory Service

PICU paediatric intensive care unit

PID pelvic inflammatory disease

PID prolapsed intervertebral disc

PIP proximal interphalangeal

PK psychokinesis

PKD polycystic kidney disease

PKU phenylketonuria (*heel-prick test for newborns*)

PL product licence

PL prolactin

PLWA person living with AIDS

PM post mortem (*Latin: after death – an autopsy*)

PMF progressive massive fibrosis

PMH past medical history

PMH previous menstrual history

PMO post-menopausal osteoporosis

PMT pre-menstrual tension

PN percussion note

PN (R) percussion note (resonant)

Pn plutonium

PND post-natal depression

PND paroxysmal nocturnal dyspnœa

PNH paroxysmal nocturnal haemoglomeria

PNO Principal Nursing Officer

Po per os (*Latin: by mouth*)

PO₂ partial pressure of oxygen

POH past/previous obstetric history

POM prescription-only medicine

POP plaster of Paris

POS polycystic ovary syndrome

POSSUM from POSM – patient-operated selector mechanism

PP plumbum pendulans (*swinging the lead*)

PP i) placenta privia; ii) private patient

PP factor/vitamin pellagra preventive (*niacin, a vitamin of the B complex*)

Pp post prandium (*Latin: after a meal*)

PPB positive pressure breathing

PPH postpartum haemorrhage

PPLO pleuropneumonia-like organisms

Ppm parts per million

PPP Private Patients' Plan

PR per rectum

PR pulse rate

PRE protein retention efficiency

PRI population reference intake (*of nutrients*)

Prn pro re nata (*Latin: when needed*)

PROM premature rupture of membranes

PRV polycythaemia rubra vera

PS pulmonary stenosis

PSA promoting stress & anxiety

PSA prostatic-specific antigen

PSE public sex environment (*PC term for a public lavatory in a homosexual sense*)

PSW Psychiatric Social Worker

Psych, psychol psychology; psychological

PT prothrombin time

PT physical therapy

PT physical training

PTA prior to admission

PTC percutaneous transhepatic cholangiopancreatography

PTD permanent total disability

PTH parathyroid hormone

PTSD post-traumatic stress disorder

PTT prothrombin time

PU pass urine

PU per urethra

PUFAs polyunsaturated fats/fatty acids

PULHEEMS physical capacity, upper and lower limbs, hearing, hearing, eyesight, emotional capacity, mental stability (*used in military medical assessments – sometimes known as 'having your pulheems done'*)

Pulv pulvis (*Latin: powder*)

PUO pyrexia of unknown origin

PV peritoneo-venous

Pv i) per vaginum (*Latin: by the vagina*) ii) polyoma virus

PVD persistent virus disease (*was yuppie flu; became CFS*)

PVN patient very nervous

PVS persistent vegetative state

PVS postviral syndrome

PWA person with AIDS

PWS Prader-Willi Syndrome (*congenital disorder – short stature, mental retardation, hypotonia, abnormally small hands and feet, hypogonadism and uncontrolled appetite, leading to extreme obesity described by Professor Andrea Prader of Zurich and Heinrich Willi in 1956*)

P-generation parental generation

Q-sign tongue lolling from open mouth, indicative of the patient's condition

Q-sort a sorting psychology test

QALY quality adjusted light years

Qd quater in die (*Latin: 4 times a day*)

QDS to be given/taken 4 times a day

Qh quatis horis (*Latin: four hourly*)

Qid quater in die (*Latin: 4 times a day*)

Qq quaque (*Latin: every*)

Qqh quater quaque hora (*Latin: every fourth hour*)

Qs quantum sufficit (*Latin: as much as is sufficient*)

R right

R treatment

r recipe (*Latin: take thou*)

R&S ritonavir & saquinavir (*supposed HIV suppressant cocktail*)

RA reading age

RA rheumatoid arthritis

RADAR Royal Association for Disability & Rehabilitation

RAGE receptor for advanced glycation end products (*possible target in brain for retarding Alzheimer's disease*)

RAP right atrial pressure

RAST radioallergosorbent tests (*for food allergy*)

RBB right bundle branch

RBBB right bundle branch block

RBC red blood cell (*erythrocyte*)

rbe relative biological effectiveness (*dose*)

RCP Royal College of Pathologists

RCT randomized clinical trial

RD reaction of degeneration (*term used in physiotherapy for abnormal responses to the electrical reactions of muscles*)

RDA recommended daily (or dietary) allowance (or amount) (*of nutrients*)

RDS respiratory distress syndrome

REBA rapid entire body assessment

Rh rhesus (*blood type: can cause problems if mother is rhesus negative and father is rhesus positive*)

REM (sleep) rapid eye movement (sleep) (*part of the sleep cycle which coincides with dreaming*)

REM, rem Roentgen equivalent man (*former unit of radioactivity*)

rep repetatur (*Latin: let it be repeated*)

rep dos repetatur dosis (*Latin: let the dose be repeated*)

RERF Radiation Effects Research Foundation

RES reticuloendothelial system

Rescare National Society for Mentally-handicapped people in Residential Care

RET rational-emotive therapy

rF VIII recombinant factor VIII (*synthetic alternative clotting agent for people with haemophilia*)

RGN Registered General Nurse

Rh rhesus factor

RHD i) rheumatic heart disease; ii) rhesus haemolytic disease

RIA research into aging

RIC raised intracranial pressure

RICE rest, ice, compress & elevate

RIDDOR Reporting of Diseased & Dangerous Occurrences Regulations 1995

RIF right iliac fossa

RIH right inguinal hernia

RLF retrolental fibroplasia

RM Registered Midwife

RNA ribonucleic acid

RNI reference nutrient intake

RNIB Royal National Institute for the Blind

RNID Royal National Institute for the Deaf

RNO Regional Nursing Officer

ROA right occiput anterior (*see* LOA)

ROC Research into Ovarian Cancer

ROL right occipito-lateral (*see* LOA)

ROM range of movement

ROP right occiput posterior (*see* LOA)

RP retinitis pigmentosa

RPF retroperitoneal fibrosis

RPMS Royal Postgraduate Medical School

RPV relative protein value

RQ respiratory quotient

RS respiratory system

RSI repetitive strain injury

RSM Royal Society of Medicine

RT reaction time

RTC Regional Transfusion Centre (*within NBTS; obsolete*)

RTI respiratory tract infection

RU486 abortion pill ™

RULA rapid upper limb assessment

RUQ right upper quadrant

Rx recipe (*Latin: take thou*)

S speculum (*Journal of the Mediaeval Academy of America*)

S without (*Latin: sine*)

S/B seen by

S/D systolic/diastolic (*heart and circulation*)

S/m sadomasochism

S/N signal to noise ratio

S1, 2 etc sacral vertebrae

SA node sinoatrial node

SAGB Schizophrenia Association of Great Britain

SAMI socially acceptable monitoring instrument

SAMS South African Medical Services

SANE, Sane Schizophrenia – A National Emergency

SB i) serum bilirubin; ii) stillbirth

Sb antimony

SBE sub-acute bacterial endocarditis

SBP systolic blood pressure

SBR strict bed rest

SC subcutaneous

SCA sickle cell anaemia

SCAN suspected child abuse and neglect

SCBU Special Care Baby Unit

SCI spinal chord injury

SCID severe combined immunodeficiency disease

SCIEH Scottish Centre for Infection & Environmental Health

SCU special care unit

SDA specific dynamic action

SDHD sudden death heart disease

SDS Safety Data Sheet

SE starch equivalent

SE side effects

SFU suitable for upgrade

SGOT serum glutamic oxaloacetic transaminase

SGPT serum glutamic pyruvic transaminase

SH social history

Si dol urg si dolor urgeat (*Latin: if the pain is severe*)

SIDS sudden infant death syndrome

SIG stroppy ignorant git

SIMV synchronised intermittent mandatory ventilation

Sig signetur (*Latin: let it be labelled*)

Sig signa (*Latin: label*)

SJ supinator jerk (*reflex: see* AJ)

SJA St John Ambulance (*Brigade or Association – NOT St John's*)

SL sub lingual (*under the tongue*)

SLD severe learning difficulties

SLE systemic lupus erythematosus

SLR straight leg raising

SM systolic murmur

SMS sucrose monostearate

Sn tin

SNF solids-not-fat

SO2 sulphur dioxide (*a preservative*)

SOA swelling of ankles

SOB (OE) short of breath (on exertion)

SOL space-occupying lesion

SOS, sos i) si opus sit (*Latin: if necessary*); ii) see other sheet

SOSAS severe obstructive sleep apnoea syndrome

SPE sucrose polyesters

SPECT single photon emission computed tomography

SPUC Society for the Protection of the Unborn Child

SRCN State Registered Children's Nurse

SRD State Registered Dietician (*UK*)

SRH Sue Ryder Home

SRN State Registered Nurse

SROM spontaneous rupture of membranes (*labour*)

SRSV small round structured virus

SSN severely subnormal

SSP Specialist Skills Practitioner

SSPE sub-acute sclerosing panencephalitis

SSRI serotonin-specific re-uptake inhibitor

Stat immediately

STD sexually transmitted disease(s)

STM short-term memory

STOP suction termination of pregnancy

Stp standard temperature and pressure

SUDEP sudden unexpected death in epilepsy

Supp suppositories

SVC superior vena cava

SVD spontaneous vaginal delivery

SVT supraventricular tachycardia

SWD short wave diathermy

SXR skull x-ray

Sym symptom

Syr syrupus (*Latin: syrup*)

T&A tonsils and adenoids

T&E tired & emotional (*slightly inebriated*)

T+4 term (*ie date baby due*) plus four days

T-2/52 term less 2 weeks

T1, T2 etc thoracic vertebrae

T3 tri-iodothyronine (*a thyroid hormone*)

T38.6 temperature 38.6 degrees (*nowadays mostly centigrade*)

T4 thyroxine (*a thyroid hormone*)

TAB (vaccine) (*a mixed preparation of killed bacteria for immunisation against*) typhoid and paratyphoid A & B

Tab tablet

TAH total abdominal hysterectomy

Tal qual talis qualis (*Latin: just as they come*)

TATT syndrome tired all the time

TCI2/52 to come in, in two weeks time

TCA tricyclic antidepressant

TCRE transcervical resection of the endometrium

Td ter in die (*Latin: three times a day*)

Tda ter die summendum (*Latin: three times a day*)

TDS three times a day

TEE tried everything else (*now it's homeopathy*)

TEETH tried everything else try homoeopathy

TEF thermatic effect of food

TENS transcutaneous electrical nerve stimulation (*therapeutic relief of labour pains, arthritis* etc)

Tert qq hora tertia quaque hora (*Latin: every third hour*)

TGH to go home

TGS trichlorogalactosucrose

Therap, therapeut therapeutic(s)

THR total hip replacement

THT Terrence Higgins Trust

TIA transient ischaemic attack

TICTAC The Index CD of Tablets & Capsules

Tid ter in die (*Latin: three times a day*)

TIL tumour infiltration factor

TJ triceps jerk (*see* AJ)

TKac transketolase activation coefficient

TLC i) thin layer chromatography; ii) total lung capacity; iii) tender loving care (ie *nursing, no more doctoring*)

TLV i) total lung volume; ii) tuberculin test

TM Transcendental Meditation

TNF tumour necrosis factor

TNM Classification of the spread of cancer by the American Joint Committee on Cancer; T = size of tumour, N = presence & extent of lymph-node involvement, M = presence of distant spread.

TOBEC total body electrical conductivity

TOF total organ failure tox, toxicol toxicology

TPA an emergency medication for heart attack

TPA, TPA tissue plasminogen activator

TPN total parental nutrition

TPR temperature, pulse & respiration

TRT testosterone replacement therapy (*may help osteoporosis*)

TSH thyroid stimulating hormone

TTA to take away

TTH to take home

TTP thrombotic thrombocytopenic purpura (*breaks up red blood cells, which can damage vital organs*)

TUBE totally unnecessary breast examination

TURP trans-urethral resection of the prostate

TVF tactile vocal fremitus

U&E urea and electrolytes (*biochemical tests*)

UC ulcerative colitis

UCR unconditioned reflex

UCS unconditioned stimulus

UFA unesterified fatty acids

UKHCA UK Home Care Association

UKTS UK Transplant Service

UMDS United Medical & Dental Schools (*Guy's + St Thomas's Medical School*)

UMN upper motor neurone

Ung unguentum (*Latin: ointment*)

UO urinary output

UQ useless quack (*CS Lewis's doctor – 'strong on Thomas Aquinas, poor on urinary infections'*)

URI upper respiratory infection

URT upper respiratory tract

URTI upper respiratory tract infection

USS ultra sound scan

Ut dict ut dictum(*Latin: as directed*)

UTI urinary tract infection

UTP uridine triphosphate

UV, uv ultraviolet

UVA ultraviolet-A (*accelerates skin ageing; contributes to cancer*)

UVB ultraviolet-B (*causes skin burning and cancer*)

UVC ultraviolet-C (*filtered out by the earth's atmosphere*)

V ventral

V- symbol for verbal ability

V-Z varicella-zoster

V-ZV varicella-zoster virus

V/V vulva and vagina

VA visual acuity

VC vital capacity (*respiratory function test*)

VD venereal disease (*now STD*)

VE vaginal examination

VER visual evoked response

VES Voluntary Euthanasia Society

VF ventricular fibrillation

VGH very good health

VHDL very high-density lipoprotein

VIP vasoactive intestinal peptide

VIPER visually impaired personal electronic reader (*for barcodes in shops, and by extension, other information*)

Vitamin PP pellagra preventive (*niacin*)

VLDL very low-density lipoproteins

VSD ventricular septal defect

VSIL 'very sick indeed' list (*or 'very seriously ill' list*)

VT ventricular tachycardia

VV varicose veins

Vx vertex

W/O wash out

W/o i) water in oil; ii) without

WAIS Wechsler Adult Intelligence Scale

WBC white blood corpuscle/white blood cell count

WCC white cell count

WCEDM World Congress on Emergency & Disaster Medicine

Wd ward

WISC Wechsler Intelligence Scale for Children

WR Wasserman reaction

X-zone transitory region of the inner zones of the adrenal cortex

XR X-ray

XRT X-ray therapy

XS cross section

XX sex chromosomes (*normal female*)

XY sex chromosomes (*normal male*)

ZIFT zygote intra-fallopian transfer

7.2 Animals & veterinary science

ACA American Cat Association

ACE mixture alcohol (*1 part*), chloroform (*2 parts*), ether (*3 parts*) (*inhaled anaesthetic*)

ACFA American Cat Fanciers' Association

ACTA Animal Consultants' & Trainers' Association

ACTH adrenocorticotrophin

Ad lib feeding animals help themselves

ADH antidiuretic hormone

ALAC American Lhasa Apso Club

ANTU alphanaphthylthiourea (*rodent poison*)

ARC Agricultural Research Council (*control functions of some UK Veterinary Research Institutes*)

ARC Animal Rescue Centre

B coli bacillus coli (*now known as E coli – qv*)

B virus fatal herpes-type disease of man transmitted from monkeys

BBA British Beekeepers' Association

BCG vaccine bacillus Calmette-Guérin vaccine (*for cats & dogs where owner has TB*)

BGS British Goat Society

BHB British Horseracing Board

BHC benzene hexachloride (*parasiticide*)

BHPS British Hedgehog Preservation Society (*Knowbury House SY8 3LQ*)

BHS beta-haemolytic streptococcus

BHS British Horse Society

BIPP bismuth nitrate, iodoform & medicinal soft paraffin (*antiseptic & soothing wound treatment*)

BTO British Trust for Ornithology

BVA British Veterinary Association

BWD bacillary white diarrhoea/disease (*of young chickens caused by salmonella pullorum*)

CC contemporary comparison (*progeny testing in cattle – see RBV*)

CCA Canadian Cat Association

CCK contagious conjunctivo-keratitis

CDV canine distemper virus

CFA Cat Fanciers' Association

CFAGB Circus Friends' Society of Great Britain

CFF Cat Fanciers' Federation

Ch champion

ChCh champion of champions

CITES Convention on International Trade in Endangered Species

CIWF Compassion In World Farming

CPL Cats' Protection League

CRD chronic respiratory disease

CVH canine virus hepatitis

CVL Central Veterinary Laboratory

DDT dichloro-diphenyl-trichlor-ethane (*a potent parasiticide*)

DLH domestic long-hair (*veterinary description of cat*)

DNA desoxyribonucleic acid (*a constituent of bacteria, viruses & plasmids; the basis of genetic engineering*)

DNOC dinitro-ortho-cresol (*weedkiller acting as cumulative poison in animals*)

DNP very similar to DNOC

DOCA desoxycorticosterone acetate (*post-operative treatment for Cushing's disease in cats & dogs*)

Dow ET-57 oral systemic insecticide to control cattle warbles

DRUAV Diagnostic & Research Units in Avian Virology

DSH domestic short hair (*veterinary description of cat*)

E coli *escherichia coli* – formerly known as *B coli* (*gives rise to various bowel disorders in different animals*)

ELISA test for brucellosis & salmonellosis

FCV feline calcivirus

Fel V feline leukaemia virus

FIA feline infectious anaemia

FIE feline infectious enteritis

FIFe Fédération Internationale Féline (*Europe's main cat fancy, encompassing associations in several other continents – formerly FIFE Fédération Internationale Féline d'Europe*)

FIP feline infectious peritonitis

FLF four-legged friend

FPL feline panleukaemia

FUS feline urological syndrome (*urolithiasis, sometimes caused by eating dry food*)

FVR feline viral rhinotracheitis

FZS Fellow of the Zoological Society

GCCF Governing Council of the Cat Fancy

GSD German Shepherd dog (*once the Alsatian*)

HETP an organo-phosphorus insecticide used in both agriculture & horticulture – *see* TEPP

Hh hands high (*of a horse, measured at the withers; 1 hand = 4"*)

HI test haemagglutination-inhibition test (*for Newcastle disease of poultry*)

IBK infectious bovine keratitis

IBR infectious bovine rhinotracheitis

ICC improved contemporary comparison (*began to supersede CC & RBV in 1974*)

IFAW International Fund for Animal Welfare

ILT infectious laryngotracheitis

INH isonicotylhydrazile (*a TB treatment*)

Invert invertebrate

IWC International Whaling Commission

Jizz general impression & size (*birdwatchers' jargon if they can't identify a bird*)

KC Kennel Club (*canine regulator*)

Lab Labrador retriever

LD50 value a statistical estimate of the amount of poison per body-weight needed to kill 50% of a large population of test animals

Lug lugworm

M&B 693 Sulphapyridine – a sulphonamide drug

MCH malignant head catarrh

MLC Meat & Livestock Commission

Mong mongrel (*Australia*)

N neuter; neutered cat

NAWT National Animal Welfare Trust

NCDL National Canine Defence League

NDV Newcastle disease virus

NFW New Zealand flatworm

NZCF New Zealand Cat Fancy

PAM pyridine-2-aldoxime methiodide (*antidote to parathion poisoning used with atropine*)

PAS para-aminosalicylic acid (*TB treatment for zoo animals*)

PAT Pets as Therapy

PETA People for the Ethical Treatment of Animals

PFMA Pet Foods Manufacturers Association

PMS pregnant mare's serum

PPD purified protein derivative (*used in TB testing*)

PPLO pleuro-pneumonia-like organisms

PSE pale soft exudative muscle (*a condition of pig carcases which may occur when pH falls below 6*)

Q fever a disease of cattle, sheep & goats which is communicable to man, usually by drinking untreated affected milk and resembles food-poisoning or influenza

Qu queen (*adult female cat*)

RAVC Royal Army Veterinary Corps

RBST Rare Breeds Survival Trust

RBV relative breeding value (*of cattle – see* CC & ICC)

RCVS Royal College of Veterinary Surgeons

RIA radio immunoassay

SAAUK Society for the Acclimatisation of Animals in the UK (*founded by Frank Buckland*)

Shub shubunkin

SNF solids-not-fat (*milk containing less than the statutory percentage; may be unacceptable for human consumption*)

SOS Save Our Sheep (*live animal export protest group*)

Sp qu spayed queen

SPF specific pathogen-free (*pigs removed from uterus & reared in sterile conditions*)

SWHP Society for the Welfare of Horses & Ponies

T tom cat

TCE trichlorethylene (*trilene – a less-toxic anaesthetic for small animals than chloroform*)

TEPP *see* HETP

TICA The Independent Cat Association (*USA*)

TWAD Tail-Waggers Against Docking

UCF United Cat Federation (*USA*)

UDN ulcerative dermatic necrosis (*a disease of salmon*)

VHD viral haemorrhagic disease (*of rabbits*)

VLA Veterinary Laboratories Agency

VO Veterinary Officer

VPP virus pneumonia of pigs

WAG Awards Willing & Giving Awards (*for heroic animals*)

WDCS Whale & Dolphin Conservation Society

WGAS Wood Green Animal Shelter

WWF Worldwide Fund for Nature (*formerly World Wildlife Fund*)

ZSL Zoological Society of London

8 Geography & the forces of nature

8.1 Ordnance survey & mapping

(C) close (*boulders*) (*OFD*)

(m) medium (*boulder density*) (*OFD*)

(o) open (*boulder density*) (*OFD*)

(Scat) scattered (*density*) (*OFD*)

(um) unmade

A alley; approach; arcade; area; avenue

A/D asphalt disc

AAT Analytical Aerial Triangulation

ABUT abutment

Acad Academy

Ad Co, Admin Co Administrative County

Adj adjacent

AG Art gallery

AGL above ground level

AL alley

ALB air light beacon

Allot Gdns allotment gardens

Alt altitude

Alts alterations

Amb Sta Ambulance Station

AND Administrative Names Diagram

ANG angle

AOD above Ordnance datum

AP air point

AP Amsterdamsch Peil (*Amsterdam level – the mean level used as a datum for levels in Holland, Belgium and Northern Germany*)

AP, APP approach

APPROX approximately

AR, ARC arcade

AUX auxiliary

Av, Ave avenue

B baulk; bank; base; basin; bay; boiler; boulevard; bridge; broad; broadway; brow

B break in house numbers (*OFD*)

B Md boundary mound

B Mk boundary mark

B Rod brass rod

B-P, BY-PS by-pass

Bapt Baptist

BATT battlement

BB base of bank; buried block

BC Borough Constituency, Burgh Constituency

BD boulevard

BDY broadway

Bdy boundary

Bdy M boundary mark; boundary mound

BG burial ground

BH bier house

BK bank (*building*)

BK H bake house

Bk bank

Bks Barracks

BLDG(S), Bldg(s), Blg building(s)

BM Bench Mark

BN barn

Bn broken (*hedge or bank*) (*OFD*)

BO H boiler house

Bo boulder

Bol bollard

Boro Borough

Boro Const Borough Constituency

BP boundary post; boundary plate

BR brass rivet

BR bridle road; bridge; brow

BR H brew house
Br bridge
Br P braced post
Brac/RG bracken & rough grassland (*OFD*)
BS boundary stone
Bty battery
Burgh Const Burgh Constituency
Burial Gd burial ground
Bus omnibus
BUTT buttress
BVD boulevard
BY broadway
C Cam; canal; carriage; causeway; centre of; channel; chase; circle; circus; cliff; close; cock; community (*Wales*); conduit; coniferous (*OFD*); cop; corner; course of; Court; covered; crane; creek; crescent; croft; cross; culvert; cut
C in W Church in Wales
C of E Church of England
C of S Church of Scotland
Calv Calvinist
Car Pk car park (*OFD*)
CAS, Cas castle
CATH, Cath, Cathl cathedral
CB centre of bank; centre of basin; centre of baulk; centre of broad; coal bin; County Borough
CC centre of canal; chisel cut (*mark*); coal cover; County Constituency; County Council
CCLW centre of channel at low water
CCS centre of covered stream
CD centre drain; centre of drain
CDK centre drain at kerb
CDS cul de sac
Cemy cemetery
Cen centre (*OFD*)
CF, CFT croft
CG cattle grid (*OFD*)

CG Lookout coastguard lookout
CG Sta Coastguard Station
CH chase; church; club house, coach house; coal house
Ch Yd church yard
CHA chase
Chap Chapel
Chr Sc Ch Christian Science Church
Chy chimney
Cin cinema
CIR, CIRC circle; circus
Cis, CN cistern
CL close; close (*density*) (*OFD*)
CL B coal bin
CL H coal house
Cl close (*place*)
CLUB HO club house
CM chalk/crayon mark
Cn capstan
Cnl Council
CNR corner
Cnr corner (*OFD*)
Co Cnl County Council
Co Const County Constituency
Co of City County of City
Co-ed co-educational
Co-ord(s) co-ordinate(s)
COCS centre of old course of stream
CoH cow house
Col collects (*OFD*)
Coll college
Colly colliery
Comm Centre community centre
Comps computations
Conc concrete
Congl Congregational
Conv Home Convalescent Home
Cop coppice (*OFD*)
Corpn Corporation

Corpn Yd Corporation Yard

Cott cottage

CP centre punched (*mark*); cess pool/pit; Civil Parish

CPA comparator point (*air*)

CPG comparator point (*ground*)

CR centre of railway; centre of river; centre of road; continuous revision; crescent

Cr centre (*of stone marking triangulation point*)

Cr crosses (*OFD*)

Crem Crematorium

CRES, Cres crescent

CS centre of stream; cess pool/pit; cross

Cse course

CSWY causeway

CT cart track

CT H cart house

CT S cart shed

CT, Ct Court

CU classification unchanged (*OFD*); cut

Cul culvert (*OFD*)

Cvt Convent

CW causeway; centre of wall

D dale; dam; ditch; dock; double; down; drain; drive; drove

D Slip double slip (railway) (*OFD*)

D Well, DW draw well

DB dust bin

DD double ditch; double drain

Def defaced

Dept Department

Det detached

Det Ring detector ring

DF double fence; drain frame

DF, D Fn drinking fountain

DG double gate (level crossing) (*OFD*); drying ground

Dial sun dial

DIS, Dis disused

Dismtd Rly dismantled railway

Dist District

Div division

Dk dock

DL dale

DOR Date of Revision (*OFD*)

DOS Date of Survey (*OFD*)

DP dung pit

DR, Dr drive

DRO, DV drove

DS double stream (*OFD*)

DW draw well; double wall (*OFD*)

E east; edge of; embankment; end (*OFD*); esplanade; eyot

ED Electoral Division; European Datum

EDM electromagnetic distance measurement

EK edge of kerb

El electric; electricity

El Gen Sta electricity generating station

El P electricity pillar; electricity pole

El Sub Sta electricity sub station

El Tfmr electricity transformer

El Tmfr Sta electricity transformer station

El Wks electricity works

ELB electric light bracket

ELS electric light standard

EM embankment; end of motorway (*OFD*)

EMB embankment

Emp employment

Emp Ex Employment Exchange

Eng Wks Engineering Works

ENT entrance

ES end of straight (railway) (*OFD*)

ESP, ESPL esplanade

ETL electricity transmission line

Euro Const European Assembly
   Constituency

Ex exchange

F face of; fence; fleet; flyover; folly;
   foot; freeboard; furrow

F Sta Fire Station

FA fire alarm

Fall waterfall

FAP fire alarm pillar

FB filter bed; foot bridge

FB, F Br foot bridge

FBM Fundamental Bench Mark

FC Forestry Commission

FC, F Ch Free Church

FD foundations (*OFD*)

FE Sta Fire Engine Station

FF face of fence

FH fire hydrant

FL face left

FL BR flush bracket

Fl Sk flare stack

FL-O, F flyover

Fm farm

FN felt nail

Fn fountain

FN/W felt nail & washer

Fo,

F folly

FP face of paling; fire plug; foot
   path

FR face right; flat rock (*OFD*)

FS flagstaff

Ft feet

FW face of wall

G gap; gardens; gate; grass; green;
   grove

G Yd graveyard

G, GD, Gdns gardens

Gas Gov gas governor

GC gas column

GD ground

Gen Sta generating station

Geo geodetic

GH green house

Gl glass (*OFD*)

GN, Gn green

Govt Government

GP gas plug; guide post (signpost)

GPO General Post Office

GR, Gr grove

GS Gantry Support (*OFD*)

GSL ground surface level (*OFD*)

GT gate

GT P, Gt P gate post; pillar (*OFD*)

GV gas valve

GVC gas valve compound

H harbour; hedge; heights; high;
   hill; hole; hollow; house;
   hydrant; hydraulic

H, HT, HTS heights

Ha hectares

Hd head

HL hill

HNT house number trace

Ho house

HOL hollow

Hos, Hospl Hospital

HP highest point

HPO Head Post Office

HQ headquarters

HR hedge row

HW hollow; hollow way

HWM high water mark

HWMMT high water mark of
   medium tides

HWMOST high water mark of
   ordinary spring tides

HWMOT high water mark of
   ordinary tides

HWMS high water mark (springs)

I island; isle

IDT instrumental detail trace

IH inspection hole or hatch

Indpt, Indt independent
Infmy Infirmary
Inft infant
Ins inches
Inst institute
Instn institution
Int intersection; intersected
IP iron pipe
IR iron rod
IRB Sta Inshore Rescue Boat Station
Isoln Hospl Isolation Hospital
Iss issues (*OFD*)
J, JN, Junc junction
JMI junior mixed & infants
K kerb
Km P kilometre post
Km kilometres
KN kiln
KS kitchen sink
L lade; lake; lamp; lane; lawn; lea; lead; leat; loch; lochan; lock; lockspit; lynchet
L Ho lighthouse
L Tan left tangent
L Twr lifting tower
L, La lane
Lat latitude
Lav lavatory
LB letter box; London Borough
LB Ho Lifeboat House
LB Sta Lifeboat Station
LC level crossing
LCC London County Council
LDP long distance path
LE lea
LG loading gauge
LH lamp house
Liby library
LK, LKN lime kiln
LN lawn

Loco Shed locomotive shed
Long longitude
LP lamp post
Lr lower
LRO local reference object
LT London Transport
LWL low water level
LWM low water mark
LWM(S) low water mark (springs)
LWMMT low water mark of medium tides
LWMOST low water mark of ordinary spring tides
LWMOT low water mark of ordinary tides
LWN lawn
LWR last walk round
M mark; marsh; masonry; mead; mere; metre(s); mews; mile(s); moat; mooring; mound; mount
M metres
Mag Var magnetic variation
MB Municipal Borough
MC minor control
MCPA minor control point album
MCTS minor control traverse station
MD mound
Me mead
Meml memorial
Met Metropolitan
Met Sta meteorological station
Met metalled (*OFD*)
Meth Methodist
Mg P mooring post
MH malt house; man hole
MH & MLW mean high & mean low water
MH & MLWS mean high & mean low water springs
MHW mean high water
MHWS mean high water springs

Min Tech Ministry of Technology

Misn Mission

Misn Ch Mission Church

Mkt market

Mkt Ho Market House

MLW mean low water

MLWS mean low water springs

MO matter of opinion (*OFD*)

Mon monument

Mort mortuary

MP mile post; mooring post

MPU mail pick-up

MR mooring ring

Mr manor

MS mews; mile stone

MSD Master Survey Drawing

MSL mean sea level

MT mount

Mt mountain

MT(s) medium tide(s)

Mtl Hospl Mental Hospital

Multi Car Park multistorey car park

Munl municipal

Mus museum

N north; no name or number (*OFD*)

N Bd Notice Board (*OFD*)

NBM New Bench Mark

NC non-coniferous (*OFD*)

NCB National Coal Board

ND no division (*OFD*)

No number

Noncon Nonconformist

NS, N Sq not square (*OFD*)

NT National Trust

NTL normal tide limit

NTS National Trust for Scotland

O office; old; orchard

Obsy observatory

Oct octagonal (*OFD*)

OE original error (*OFD*)

OFD on field document (*mentioned on original survey, but not appearing on map made therefrom*)

ON oven

OPP opposite

OR orchard; outcropping rock (*OFD*)

Orch orchard (*OFD*)

OS out stipple (*OFD*)

OSBM Ordnance Survey Bench Mark

OST(s) ordinary spring tide(s)

OT(s) ordinary tide(s)

P paling; parade; pass; passage; path; pavement; pillar; place; plate; plug; pole; pond; pool; post; precinct; promenade; pump; pylon

PA path

PAB published abstract bolt

Paint M paint mark

Pal palace

PAR parade

PARA parapet

Parly Parliamentary

PASS passage

Pav pavilion

PC public convenience

PCB Police call box

PD detail point (point of detail)

Pd Pond (*OFD*)

Per Cur perpetual curacy

PG passage

PH Public House

Ph Parish

Pillar (OS) triangulation pillar

Pks pecks (*OFD*)

Pkt picket

PL pipe line (*OFD*)

Pl place

Plantn plantation

PLB pillar letter box

PN pipe nail
PN/W pipe nail & washer
PO Post Office
POD detail point (point of detail)
Pol Ho Police House
Pol Sta Police Station
PP primary point
Pp pump
Pp Ho pump house
Ppg Sta pumping station
PR periodic revision; promenade
PRE precinct
Presb Presbyterian
Presby Presbytery
Prim Meth Primitive Methodist
PRODN production
PROM promenade
PS pass
PSH Parish
PT precinct
Pt point
Pte private (*OFD*)
PTP Police telephone pillar or post
PTS permanent traverse station
    Pub public (*OFD*)
PW place of worship PY piggery
Py privy
Q, QY quay
R race; railway; ride; ridge; river;
    road; rocks; root of; row
R Tan right tangent
RAC RAC call box
Range rifle range
RB Royal Borough
RC Roman Catholic
RD Rural District
Rd road
RDG ridge
Rec rectory
Recn recreation
Recn Gd recreation ground

Rems of remains of
Resr reservoir
RG ridge; bracken/rough grassland
    (*OFD*)
RH road house; root of hedge
RL roof line (*OFD*)
Rly Sta Railway Station
Rly, Ry railway
RO reference object; referring
    object; retain original (*OFD*)
rp revision point
RS rain spout
RW row
S scar; sewer; side; side of; sink;
    sink stones; slope; sluice; south;
    spur; square; stairs; steps; stone;
    strand; stream; street
S Br signal bridge
S Gantry signal gantry
S Sta signal station
SA Salvation Army
San sanatorium
SAND Sub-Areas Name Diagram
SB signal box
SC stop cock
Sc scrub (*OFD*)
Sch school
SD side; single drain; single ditch
    (*OFD*)
SD strand; sun dial
Sd sound
Sec secondary
SF side fence; side furrow
SG sewer grate
SH summer house
Sh Fd sheep fold (*OFD*)
Sk sketched (*OFD*)
Sks sinks (*OFD*)
SL signal lamp; signal light
Sl sluice
SM sloping masonry (*OFD*)
Smy smithy

SN Scientific Network

SP sewer pipe; signal post; spur

Sp spire; spreads (*OFD*)

Spr spring

SQ, Sq square

SR side of river

SRS stairs

SS saints; single stream (*OFD*)

SSlip single slip (*OFD*)

ST spring tides

ST stable

St saint; stone; street

Sta, Stn station

Std standard

STPS, STS steps

STRS stairs

Sts steps (*OFD*)

Sun Sch Sunday School

Sur surface

Sur B surface block

SV sewer vent; spirit vaults

SW sloping wall (*OFD*)

Sw switch

T tank; tap; terrace; tides; top of; track; trough

TA Territorial Army; Territorial & Army Volunteer Reserve

Tachy tacheometer; tacheometry

TAD Trig Availability Diagram

TB top of bank

TC travelling crane

TCB telephone call box

TCP telephone call post or pillar; temporary control point

TE, Ter, Terr terrace

Tech Coll Technical College

Tel Ex Telephone Exchange

Tel Line telephone line

Tel P telephone pole

Ter terminus

Tert tertiary

TG toll gate

TH tool house; Town Hall

Tk tank; track

Tk F track of fence

Tk H track of hedge

Tk S track of stream

TLH tool house

TM threshing mill

Toll toll bridge or gate

TP telegraph pole; turnpike

TR, Tr trough

Trav traverse

Trav C travelling crane

Trig Sta Trigonometrical Station

Ts traverse station

TV Sta television station

TWL top water level (*OFD*)

Twr tower

U Ref Ch United Reformed Church

UD Urban District

UF United Free

ULC upper level of through communication

Und undefined

Undenom undenominational

Under Constn under construction

Unitn Unitarian

Univ University

UP United Presbyterian

Upr upper

UTM universal transverse mercator

V vale; valve; ventilator; view; villas

V Ho valve house

VA vale; vertical angle; voluntary assisted

VC valve cover; voluntary controlled

VI vertical interval; villas

Vic vicarage

VIL villas

Vr ventilator

VW view

W walk; wall; water; watershed; way; weir; well; west; wharf; wood

W Meth Wesleyan Methodist

W Post wooden post

War Meml war memorial

WB weighbridge

WC water closet; water column

Wd El Gen wind electricity generator

Wd Pp wind pump

Wes Wesleyan

Wes Meth Wesleyan Methodist

WF wharf

WH wash house; water house

WK, WLK walk

Wks works

WM water main; weighing machine; witness mark

WMP warning & monitoring post (*Royal Observer Corps*)

WN wire nail

WP water plug; wooden peg

Wr Bd Water Board

Wr Pt water point

Wr T, WT water tap

Wr Twr water tower

Wr Wks water works

WS work shop

WT Sta wireless telegraphy station

WV water valve

WWL winter water level

WY way

XC cross cut

Y yard; Youth Hostel

Yd yard

YH Youth Hostel (*OFD*)

YMCA Young Men's Christian Association

YWCA Young Women's Christian Association

8.2 Points of the compass

N	north	**S**	south
N by E	north by east	**S by W**	south by west
NNE	north north east	**SSW**	south south west
NE by N	north east by north	**SW by S**	south west by south
NE	north east	**SW**	south west
NE by E	north east by east	**SW by W**	south west by west
ENE	east north east	**WSW**	west south west
E by N	east by north	**W by S**	west by south
E	east	**W**	west
E by S	east by south	**W by N**	west by north
ESE	east south east	**WNW**	west north west
SE by E	south east by east	**NW by W**	north west by west
SE	south east	**NW**	north west
SE by S	south east by south	**NW by N**	north west by north
SSE	south south east	**NNW**	north north west
S by E	south by east	**N by W**	north by west

8.3 Meteorology

A Arctic air mass

AA Antarctic air mass

AFOS automation of field operations & services

AP, ap atmospheric pressure

ASL above sea level

AWS Automatic Weather Station

CET Central England temperature

CFM chlorofluoromethane

CL condensation level

DALR dry adiabatic lapse rate

DP dew-point temperature

E Equatorial air mass

EDIS Environmental Data Information Service

ELR environmental lapse rate

ESA European Space Agency

ESSA Environmental Survey Satellite

FC funnel cloud

FGGE First GARP Global Experiment

GARP Global Atmospheric Research Program

GATE GARP Atlantic Tropical Experiment

GCM general circulation model

GN grid north

GOES Geostationary Operational Environmental Satellite

HWM higher water mark

IPCC Intergovernmental Panel on Climate Change

Lat latitude

LCL lifting condensation level

LFC level of free convection

Long longitude

LWM low(er) water mark

MALR moist adiabatic lapse rate

METEOSAT a meteorological satellite controlled by ESA

MHW mean high water

MLW mean low water

MN magnetic north

MSG METEOSAT second generation

NASA National Aeronautics & Space Administration

NESS National Environmental Satellite Service

NMC National Meteorological Center

NOAA National Oceanic & Atmospheric Administration

NWP numerical weather prediction

P Polar air mass

RAMOS Remote Automatic Meteorological Observing Station

RMS Royal Meteorological Society

SALR saturated adiabatic lapse rate

SAWS Synoptic Automatic Weather Station

SID sudden ionospheric disturbance

SMS Synchronous Meteorological Satellite

SRRG self-recording raingauge

T tropical air mass

TIROS television infra-red observation satellite

TN true north

WMO World Meteorological Organisation

WWW World Weather Watch

8.4   Köppen's world-wide climate classification

A	tropical rain climates	**S", w"**	summer or winter dry season climate with rainy season split in two
B	arid climates		
C	temperate rain climates		
D	boreal forest & snow	**f**	moist climates with no marked dry season
E	cold snow climates (*treeless*)		
		M	monsoon climates
AC&D	tree climates	**D**	coldest month
BS	Steppe grassland	**g**	Ganges type climate (*warmest before summer solstice then rainy*)
BW	warm deserts		
W	desert waste		
E	Tundra & Polar	**H**	hot
ET	Tundra with dwarf trees & mosses	**I**	isothermal
		K	cold winter climate
EF or F	Polar desert with no vegetation	**L**	lukewarm
		N	foggy
W	winter dry season	**N'**	moist, not foggy
S', w'	summer or winter dry season climates with rains in late summer or autumn	**T'**	Cape Verde Islands type climate (*warmest in autumn*)
X	early summer wet, late summer dry	**T"**	Sudan type (*coolest after summer solstice*)

8.5   Synoptic weathercode

A	steadiness of barometer	**Nh**	low cloud cover
Ch	name of highest cloud	**Pp**	change of pressure
Cl	name of lowest cloud	**PPP**	sea level atmospheric pressure
Cm	name of middle cloud		
Dd	true direction of wind	**TdTd**	dew point temperature
ff	wind speed in knots	**TT**	air temperature
H	height of lowest cloud	**VV**	horizontal visibility
IIiii	location of weather block and its situation	**W**	past weather
		Ww	present weather situation
N	cloud cover		

8.6 Weather in the British Isles

AC	anticyclonic type		NW	north westerly type
C	cyclonic type		S	southerly type
E	Easterly type		W	westerly type
N	northerly type			

8.7 Meridional weather

ACG	anticyclogenetic(esis)		MAM	March, April, May (*spring in Europe*)
CG	cyclogenetic(esis)			
T	temperature		JJA	June, July, August (*summer in Europe*)
S	sunshine			
R	rainfall		SON	September, October, November (*autumn in Europe*)
P	pressure			
F	force		ITCZ, ITZ	Inter-Tropical Convergence Zone (*doldrums*)
W	wet			
N	normal		SI	solar index
D	dry		SE	solar energy
L	liquid		TWZ	trade wind zone
V	vapour		DVI	dust veil index (*volcanic eruptions*)
DJF	December, January, February (*winter in Europe*)			

8.8 Cloud classification

Ac	altocumulus		Cu	cumulus
Acc	altocumulus castellatus		Fc	fractocumulus
As	altostratus		Fn	fractonimbus
Cb	cumulonimbus		Fs	fractostratus
Cc	cirrocumulus		Nb	nimbus
Ci	cirrus		Ns	nimbostratus
Cm	cumulonimbus mammatus		Sc	stratocumulus
Cs	cirrostratus		St	stratus

8.9 Beaufort scale (wind strength)

0	calm (*mph 0*)	7	very strong wind (*mph 35*)
1	light airs (*mph 2*)	8	gale (*mph 43*)
2	light breeze (*mph 5*)	9	severe gale (*mph 50*)
3	gentle breeze (*mph 10*)	10	storm (*mph 59*)
4	moderate wind (*mph 15*)	11	severe storm (*mph 69*)
5	fresh wind (*mph 21*)	12	hurricane (*mph 74+*)
6	strong wind (*mph 28*)		

8.10 US torro force (tornado strength)

FC	funnel cloud	6	moderately devastating
0	light	7	strongly devastating
1	mild	8	severely devastating
2	moderate	9	severely devastating
3	strong	10	intensely devastating
4	severe	11	intensely devastating
5	intense	12	super tornado

8.11 Richter scale

There are two scales used to measure earthquakes, the Richter Scale and the Mercalli Scale

RICHTER SCALE	MERCALLI SCALE	
1	<3	felt only by seismographs
2	3 – 3.4	feeble (*just noticeable by some people*)
3	3.5 – 4	slight (*similar to passing of heavy lorries*)
4	4 – 4.4	moderate (*rocking of loose objects*)
5	4.5 – 4.8	quite strong (*felt by most people even when sleeping*)
6	4.9 – 5.4	strong (*trees rock and some structural damage caused*)
7	5.5 – 6	very strong (*walls crack*)
8	6.1 – 6.5	destructive (*weak buildings collapse*)
9	6.6 – 7	ruinous (*houses collapse and ground pipes crack*)
10	7.1 – 7.3	disastrous (*landslides, ground cracks and buildings collapse*)
11	7.4 – 8.1	very disastrous (*few buildings remain*)
12	8.1>	catastrophic (*ground rises and falls in waves*)

8.12 Schove's suggested scale of sunspot strengths

SSS	extremely strong	MW	moderate to weak
SS	very strong	W	weak
S	strong	WW	very weak
MS	moderate to strong	WWW	extremely weak
M	moderate	X	unknown

8.13 The constellations

And	Andromeda (*Princess Enchained*)	**CrA**	Corona Australis (*Southern Crown*)
Ant	Antlia (*Bilge Pump*)	**CrB**	Corona Borealis (*Northern Crown*)
Aps	Apus (*Bird of Paradise*)		
Aql	Aquila (*Eagle*)	**Crt**	Crater (*Cup*)
Aqr	Aquarius (*Water Carrier*)	**Cru**	Crux (*Southern Cross*)
Ara	Altar	**CRV**	Corvus (*Crow*)
Arg	Argo Navis (*Ship of the Argonauts*)	**CVn**	Canes Venatici (*Hunting Dogs*)
Ari	Aries (*Ram*)	**Cyg**	Cygnus (*Swan*)
Aur	Auriga (*Charioteer*)	**Del**	Delphinus (*Dolphin*)
Boö	Boötes (*Herdsman*)	**Dor**	Dorado (*Swordfish*)
Cae	Caelum (*Chisel*)	**Dra**	Draco (*Dragon*)
Cam	Camelopardalis (*Giraffe*)	**Equ**	Equuleus (*Colt*)
Cap	Capricornus (*Horned Goat*)	**Eri**	Eridanus (*Great River*)
Car	Carina (*Keel*)	**For**	Fornax (*Furnace*)
Cas	Cassiopeia (*Queen Enthroned*)	**Gem**	Gemini (*The Twins*)
		Gru	Grus (*Crane*)
Cen	Centaurus (*Centaur*)	**Her**	Hercules
Cep	Cepheus (*Monarch*)	**Hor**	Horologium (*Clock*)
Cet	Cetus (*Whale*)	**Hya**	Hydra (*Marine Monster*)
Cha	Chamaeleon (*Chameleon*)	**Hyd**	Hydrus (*Water Snake*)
Cir	Circinus (*Compasses*)	**Ind**	Indus (*Indian*)
CMa	Canis Major (*Great Dog*)	**Kif Aus**	Kiffa Australis (*Southern Breadbasket*)
CMi	Canis Minor (*Little Dog*)		
Cnc	Cancer (*Crab*)	**Kif Bor**	Kiffa Borealis (*Northern Breadbasket*)
Col	Columba (*Dove*)		
Com	Coma Berenices (*Berenice's Hair*)	**Lac**	Lacerta (*Lizard*)
		Leo	Lion

Lep	Lepus (*Hare*)	**Pup**	Puppis (*Stern*)
Lib	Libra (*Scales*)	**Pyx**	Pyxis (*Binnacle*)
LMi	Leo Minor (*Little Lion*)	**Ret**	Reticulum (*Net*)
Lup	Lupus (*Wolf*)	**Scl**	Sculptor (*Sculptor's Workshop*)
Lyn	Lynx		
Lyr	Lyra (*Lyre*)	**Sco**	Scorpio (*Scorpion*)
Mal	Malus (*Mast*)	**Sct**	Scutum (*Shield*)
Men	Mensa (*Table*)	**Ser**	Serpens (*Serpent*)
Mic	Microscopium (*Microscope*)	**Sex**	Sextant
Mon	Monoceros (*Unicorn*)	**Sge**	Sagitta (*Arrow*)
Mus	Musca (*Fly*)	**Sgr**	Sagittarius (*Archer*)
Nor	Norma (*Rule*)	**Tau**	Taurus (*Bull*)
Oct	Octans (*Octant*)	**Tel**	Telescopium (*Telescope*)
Oph	Ophiuchus (*Serpent Bearer*)	**TrA**	Triangulum Australe (*Southern Triangle*)
Ori	Orion (*Hunter*)		
Pav	Pavo (*Peacock*)	**Tuc**	Tucana (*Toucan*)
Peg	Pegasus (*Winged Horse*)	**UMa**	Ursa Major (*Great Bear*)
Phe	Phoenix	**UMi**	Ursa Minor (*Little Bear*)
Pic	Pictor (*Painter's Easel*)	**Vel**	Vela (*Sails*)
PsA	Piscis Australis (*Southern Fish*)	**Vir**	Virgo (*Virgin*)
		Vol	Volans (*Flying Fish*)
Psc	Pisces (*Fishes*)	**Vul**	Vulpecula (*Little Fox*)

9.1 Genealogy

Admin Letters of Administration
AgLab agricultural labourer
AGRA Association of Genealogists & Record Agents
B Burial Register
B born
B, bd buried
Betw between
Bp, bpt baptised
C Christening Register
C, ca circa (*Latin: about*)
Cal calendar
Chan Proc Chancery Proceedings
Cit citizen
CLRO Corporation of London Record Office
CMB all three types of Parish Register
Co County
CRO County Record Office
D died
D bn de bonis non administratis
Dau daughter
DNB Dictionary of National Biography
Dsp decessit sine prole (*Latin: died without (legitimate) issue*)
Dvm decessit vita matris (*Latin: died within mother's lifetime*)
Dvp decessit vita patris (*Latin: died within father's lifetime*)
Exch . . . Exchequer, Court of . . .
F of
F Feet of Fines
FEI Funeral Entry, Ireland
FHG Fellow of the Institute of Heraldic & Genealogical Studies
FHS Family History Society
fo folio

fp foreign parts
FR Hist Fellow of the Royal Historical Society
FS female servant
FSA Fellow of the Society of Antiquaries
FSG Fellow of the Society of Genealogists
fun ent funeral entry
FWK framework knitter
gent gentleman
GLRO Greater London Record Office
GRD Genealogical Research Directory
GRO General Register Office
HEIC Honourable East India Company
Hist MSS Comm Royal Commission on Historical Manuscripts
IGI International Genealogical Index
Ind of independent means
IOLR India Office Library & Records
IPM Inquisition Post Mortem
J journeyman
K killed
M Marriage Register
M, md married
Mem membrane
MI Monumental Inscription
ML Marriage Licence records
MS male servant
MS manuscript
NLW National Library of Wales
NRA National Register of Archives
Ob obiit (*Latin: he died*)

Otp of this Parish
PCC Prerogative Court of Canterbury
PCY Prerogative Court of York
PeC Peculiar Court
Ped pedigree
Pr proved/proven
PRO Public Record Office
RD Registration District
reg registered
RO Record Office

S&h son & heir
SP State Papers
Sp sine prole (*Latin: without issue*)
TS typescript
Unm unmarried
VCH Victoria History of the Counties of England
Visit visitation of a county by a herald
WO War Office

9.2 Heraldry

Ar	argent – silver or white (*metal*)	**Ped**	pedigree
Az	azure – blue (*colour*)	**Ppr**	proper
Chev	chevron	**Purp**	purpure – purple (*colour*)
Engr	engrailed	**Ramp**	rampant
Gu	gules – red (*colour*)	**Sa**	sable – black (*colour*)
Or	gold – yellow (*metal*)	**Sang**	sangine – (*blood coloured*)
Pass	passant	**Vert**	vert – green (*colour*)

9.3 Knitting

Alt	alternate	**foll**	following
B	back of stitch	**g st**	garter stitch
Beg	beginning	**In**	inch(es)
C	contrast shade of yarn	**Inc**	increase; increasing
CB	slip next stitch on cable needle to back of work, k1, now p1 from cable needle	**K up**	pick up & knit
		K, k	knit
		K-wise	knitwise
CF	slip next stitch on cable needle to front of work, p1, now k1 from cable needle	**M**	main shade of yarn
		M1	make a stitch
Cm	centimetre(s)	**M2**	make 2 stitches
Dec	decrease; decreasing	**M3**	make 3 stitches
DK	double knitting wool	**Mm**	millimetre(s)
F	front of stitch	**P up**	pick up & purl

P, p	purl	Tbl	through back of loop
Patt	pattern	Tog	together
Psso	pass slipped stitch over	Tw2	slip next stitch, k1, Psso st just knitted and k into back of it
rem	remaining		
rep	repeat		
Rs	right side	Ws	wrong side
Sl	slip	Ybk	yarn back between needles
Sl st	slip stitch		
St st	stocking stitch	Yfwd	yarn forward
St, sts	stitch; stitches	Yon	yarn over needle
		Yrn	yarn round needle

9.4   Crochet

Alt	alternate(ly)	ISR	International size range (of hooks)
Approx	approximately		
Beg	begin; beginning	No	number
Ch	chain(s)	Patt	pattern
Cl	cluster(s)	rem	remain; remaining
Cm	centimetre(s)	rep	repeat
Cont	continue; continuing	RS	right side of work
Dc	double crochet	Sl st	slip stitch (seaming)
Dec	decrease	Sp	space
Dtr	double treble	Ss	slip stitch (crochet)
foll	follow; following	St, sts	stitch; stitches
gr	group(s)	Tog	together
grm	gram(s)	Tr	treble
Htr	half treble	Tr tr	triple treble
In	inch(es)	WS	wrong side of work
Inc	increase	Yrh	yarn round hook

9.5 Chess

B	black	**KP**	King's pawn
BCF	British Chess Federation	**KR**	King's rook
Cas	castle (*verb – exchanging King with King's rook, or 'castling long' with Queen's rook*)	**KRP**	King's rook's pawn
		Kt, N	Knight
		N, Kt	Knight
Ch	check	**P**	pawn
Chm	checkmate	**Q, qu**	Queen
Ep	en passant (*pawn takes while passing*)	**QB**	Queen's Bishop
		QBP	Queen's Bishop's pawn
GM	Grandmaster	**QKt, QN**	Queen's Knight
IGM	International Grandmaster	**QKtP, QNP**	Queen's Knight's pawn
IM	International Master		
K	King	**QP**	Queen's pawn
KB	King's Bishop	**QR**	Queen's rook
KBP	King's Bishop's pawn	**QRP**	Queen's rook's pawn
KKt, KN	King's Knight	**R**	rook
KKtP, KNP	King's Knight's pawn	**W**	white

9.6 Horse racing

AJ	amateur jockey	**H**	head (*winning distance*)
B	brought down	**J**	jockey
B	bay	**M**	mile
BF	beaten favourite	**M**	mare
BHB	British Horseracing Board	**N**	neck (*winning distance*)
Bl	black	**No**	nose (*winning distance*)
Br	brown	**O**	owner
C	won over course	**P**	pulled up
C	colt	**R**	refused
Ch	chestnut	**R**	roan
D	won over same distance	**S**	stallion
D	disqualified	**SH**	short head (*winning distance*)
DH	dead heat		
F	fell	**SP**	starting price
F	furlong	**T**	trainer
F	filly	**U**	unseated rider
G	gelding	**W**	white
Gr	grey	**Y**	yearling

9.7   Holiday accommodation

A	approved	Ln	linen
B/W	black & white television	M	microwave
C	commended	Me	meter point
CHB	central heating boiler	MW	mid week booking
DL	de-luxe	S	shower
EL	early & late season	SC	self catering
F	fridge/freezer	SD	spin dryer
H	highly commended	TV	colour television
H&C, h&c	hot & cold	WM	washing machine
IHS	immersion heater switch		

9.8.1   Cricket

B	bowled	M	maiden over
B&s	bowled & stumped	MCC	Marylebone Cricket Club
C	caught	No	not out
C&b	caught & bowled	Nb	no ball
CC	Cricket Club	NCA	National Cricket Association
ECF	European Cricket Federation	SCG	Sydney Cricket Ground
HW, hw	hit wicket	St	stumped
ICC	International Cricket Council	TCCB	Test & County Cricket Board
Lb	leg bye	W	wide
LBW, lbw	leg before wicket	W, wkt	wicket

9.8.2   Baseball

1st B	1st baseman	LF	left fielder
2nd B	2nd baseman	P	pitcher
3rd B	3rd baseman	RF	right fielder
C	catcher	S	shortstop
CF	center fielder		

9.8.3   Rounders

1st P	1st post	**B**	bowler
2nd P	2nd post	**BS**	back stop
3rd P	3rd post	**D**	deep (*x3*)
4th P	4th post		

9.8.4   Softball

FP	fast pitch	
SP	slow pitch	

9.8.5   Soccer

CF	centre forward	**LHB**	left half-back
CHB	centre half-back	**OL**	outside left
G	goalkeeper	**OR**	outside right
IL	inside left	**RB**	right back
IR	inside right	**RHB**	right half-back
LB	left back		

9.8.6   Football (American rules)

Offense team		*Defense team*	
C	centre	**DT**	defense tackle (*x2*)
G	guard (*x2*)	**DE**	defense end (*x2*)
T	tackle (*x2*)	**LB**	line backer (*x3*)
E	end (*x2*)	**DB**	defense back (*x4*)
QB	quarter back		
B	back (*x3*)		

9.8.7   Football (Canadian rules)

Offense team		*Defense team*	
C	centre	DT	defense tackle (*x2*)
G	guard (*x2*)	DE	defense end (*x2*)
T	tackle (*x2*)	LB	line backer (*x2*)
TE	tight end	CB	corner back (*x2*)
SE	split end	DB	defense back (*x2*)
QB	quarter back	S	safety
RB	running back (*x3*)	MLB	middle line backer
F	flanker		

9.8.8   Football (Australian rules)

BP	back pocket	FF	full forward
C	centre	FP	forward pocket
CHB	centre half back	HB	half back flank
CHF	centre half forward	HF	half forward flank
F	follower	R	rover (*ruck*)
FB	full back		

9.8.9   Rugby Union

C 3/4	centre three-quarter (*x4*)	SH	scrum half-back (2)
F	forward	SOH	stand-off half-back (*x2*)
FB	full back (*x2*)	W 3/4	wing three-quarter (*x4*)

9.8.10   Rugby League

2H	second-row half (*x2*)	PF	prop forward (*x2*)
C 3/4	centre three-quarter (*x2*)	SH	scrum half-back
FB	full back	SOH	stand-off half-back
H	hooker	W 3/4	wing three-quarter (*x2*)
LF	loose forward		

9.8.11   Speedball (men)

C	centre	**LH**	left half back
FB	full back	**RE**	right end
GG	goal guard	**RF**	right forward
LE	left end	**RG**	right guard
LF	left forward	**RH**	right half back
LG	left guard		

9.8.12   Speedball (women)

C	centre	**LW**	left wing
CH	centre half back	**RF**	right full back
G	goalkeeper	**RH**	right half back
LF	left full back	**RI**	right inner
LH	left half back	**RW**	right wing
LI	left inner		

9.8.13   Field Hockey

CF	centre forward	**LW**	left wing
CH	centre half	**RB**	right back
G	goalkeeper	**RH**	right half
LB	left back	**RI**	right inner
LH	left half	**RW**	right wing
LI	left inner		

9.8.14   Ice Hockey

C	centre	**LW**	left wing
G	goalkeeper	**RD**	right defence
LD	left defence	**RW**	right wing

9.8.15   Netball

C	centre		GS	goal shooter
G	goalkeeper		WA	wing attack
GA	goal attack		WD	wing defence
GD	goal defence			

9.8.16   Athletics

CR	Commonwealth record		OR	Olympic record
ER	European record		PB	personal best
GR	Games record		WR	World record
NR	National record			

10   Number

10.1   Multipliers & submultipliers

PREFIX	FACTOR X	SYMBOL	BRITISH TERMINOLOGY†
atto	10^{-18}	a	trillionth
femto	10^{-15}	f	thousand billionth
pico	10^{-12}	p	billionth
nano	10^{-9}	n	thousand millionth
micro	10^{-6}	µ	millionth
milli	10^{-3}	m	thousandth
centi	10^{-2}	c	hundredth
deci	10^{-1}	d	tenth
deca	10	Da	tenfold
hecto	10^{2}	H	hundredfold
kilo*	10^{3}	k	thousandfold
mega	10^{6}	M	millionfold
giga	10^{9}	G	thousand millionfold
tera	10^{12}	T	billionfold
peta	10^{15}	P	thousand billionfold
exa	10^{18}	E	million billionfold

* note that the computer K (kilo) = 1,024

† note that the true British billion is 10^{12}, while others
  may take the billion as 10^{9}

10.2 Roman numerals

I, i (final) j 1

V, v 5

X, x 10

L, l 50

C, c 100

D, d 500

M, m 1,000

— a vinculum placed over a number multiplies it by 1,000

10.3 Arithmetic & maths

A 10 in hexadecimal notation

Adj adjoint

Alg algebra; algebraic

Antilog antilogarithm

ATN arc tangent

B 11 in hexadecimal notation

BCD binary-coded decimal

Bit binary unit

C 12 in hexadecimal notation

Cdf cumulative distribution function

Cir, circ circular; circulation; circumference

Circum circumference

Const constant

Cos cosine

Cosec cosecant

Cosh hyperbolic cosine

Cot, cotan cotangent

COV covariance

Csc cosecant

Ctn cotangent

Ctr centre

D 13 in hexadecimal notation

Dn elliptic function

DSM diagnostic & statistical manual

E 14 in hexadecimal notation

EX-OR, X-OR exclusive OR (*a logical operation*)

F 15 in hexadecimal notation

FFT fast Fourier transform

FP forward perpendicular

GCF,

Gcf greatest common factor

GCM,

Gcm greatest common measure

grad gradient

GWN good with numbers

HCF highest common factor (*the highest number which will divide all the numbers in a set*)

Hyp hypotenuse

I symbol used to represent the imaginary number whose square = -1

IFF, iff if, and only if

J unit vector on y-axis

J imaginary number $\sqrt{-1}$

K unit vector on z-axis

LCD, lcd lowest common denominator

LCF lowest common factor

LCM lowest common multiple (*the smallest number exactly divisible by all the numbers in a set*)

Log logarithm

Loglog logarithm of logarithm

LQR linear quadratic regulator

Math mathematics (*USA & Canada*)

Maths mathematics (*UK*)

N an unknown number

N, Np neper

N, num, nos number(s)

NAND not and (*a logical operator*)

NOR not or (*a logical operator*)

Obl oblong; oblique

Op opposite

OR or (*a logical operation*)

Par parallel

Pe probable error

QED quid erat demonstrandum (*Latin: which was to be proved*)

r ruled; radius

R,

R,

Rad radius

rad radian

rad radix

rms root mean square (*the square root of the average of the squares of a set of numbers or quantities*)

rot rotation

S(s) section(s)

SD standard deviation

Sec secant

Sin sine

Sinh hyperbolic sine (pronounced 'shine')

SOH, CAH, TOA sine = opposite/ hypotenuse, cosine = adjacent/ hypotenuse, tangent = opposite/ adjacent (*trigonometric mnemonic propounded by Perse School maths master Victor Sederman RIP*)

Sq square

Sr steradian

Tan tangent

Tanh hyperbolic tangent (pronounced 'tan-h')

TF transfer function

Trig trigonometry; trigonometrical

U union

Vert vertical

X an unknown quantity

X-axis the horizontal axis of a graph

Y-axis the axis perpendicular to & in the horizontal plane through the x-axis of a graph

Z-axis the axis at right-angles to both the x- and y-axes

Σ**(S)** sum of

π the ratio of the circumference of a circle to its diameter approximately 22/7 or 3.141 592 653 6 to 10 places

10.4 Quantities & units

SI UNITS

Base Units

m metre (*si base unit of length*)

kg kilogram (*si base unit of mass*)

s second (*si base unit of time*)

A ampère (*si base unit of electric current*)

K kelvin (*si base unit of thermodynamic temperature*)

Cd candela (*si base unit of luminous intensity*)

Mol mole (*si base unit of amount of substance*)

Supplementary Units

rad radian (*SI supplementary unit of plane angle*)

sr steradian (*SI supplementary unit of solid angle*)

Derived Units

m² square metre (*si derived unit of area*)

m³ cubic metre (*si derived unit of volume*)

ms⁻¹ metre per second (*si derived unit of velocity*)

rad s⁻¹ radian per second (*si derived unit of angular velocity*)

ms⁻² metre per second squared (*si derived unit of acceleration*)

rad s⁻² radian per second squared (*si derived unit of angular acceleration*)

Hz hertz (*si derived unit of frequency*)

kgm⁻³ kilogram per cubic metre (*si derived unit of density*)

kgms⁻¹ kilogram metre per second (*si derived unit of momentum*)

kgm²s⁻¹ kilogram metre squared per second (*si derived unit of angular momentum*)

kgm² kilogram metre squared (*si derived unit of moment of inertia*)

N newton (*si derived unit of force*)

Pa pascal (*si derived unit of pressure or stress*)

J joule (*si derived unit of work, energy or quantity of heat*)

W watt (*si derived unit of power*)

Nm⁻¹ newton per metre (*si derived unit of surface tension*)

Nsm⁻² newton second per metre squared (*si derived unit of dynamic viscosity*)

m²s⁻¹ metre squared per second (*si derived unit of kinematic viscosity*)

°C degree celsius (*si derived unit of temperature*)

Wm⁻¹°C⁻¹ watt per metre degree celsius (*si derived unit of thermal conductivity*)

JK⁻¹ joule per kelvin (*si derived unit of heat capacity*)

Jkg⁻¹K⁻¹ joule per kilogram kelvin (*si derived unit of specific heat capacity*)

Jkg⁻¹ joule per kilogram (*si derived unit of specific latent heat*)

C coulomb (*si derived unit of electric charge*)

V volt (*si derived unit of potential difference or emf*)

ohm (*si derived unit of electric resistance*)

S siemens (*si derived unit of electric conductance*)

F farad (*si derived unit of electric capacitance*)

H henry (*si derived unit of inductance*)

Wb weber (*si derived unit of magnetic flux*)

T tesla (*si derived unit of magnetic flux density*)

A ampère (*si derived unit of magnetomotive force*)

Lm lumen (*si derived unit of luminous flux*)

Lx lux (*si derived unit of illumination*)

Bq becquerel (*si derived unit of radiation activity*)

Gy gray (*si derived unit of radiation absorbed dose*)

°C⁻¹ thermal coefficient of linear expansion per degree celsius

K⁻¹ thermal coefficient of linear expansion per kelvin

GENERAL UNITS
(*including the SI Units*)

A ampère (*si base unit of electric current*)

A ampère (*si derived unit of magnetomotive force*)

A are(s) (*metric measure of land*)

API scale American Petroleum Institute scale (*of relative density, similar to Baumé Scale*)

ASA American Standards Association film speed rating.

At ampere-turn

Atm standard atmosphere, a practical unit of pressure defined as 101.325 kn/m2 or 1.01325 bar.

AU astronomical unit

Avoir avoirdupois

B, 1B, 2B etc black (*degree of softness of pencil lead* (UK))

B, b breadth

B, b, Bn, bn billion

B- ratio of velocity to velocity of light

B/S, b/s bags

B/S, b/s bales

BA British Association screw thread

BA ohm a unit of resistance adopted by the British Association in 1865 and now superseded

Bar, bbl, bl barrel

BB double black (*soft lead pencil*)

Bd, bdl bundle

Bé Baumé

BeV US variant of gev, giga-electron-volt, unit of particle energy, 10^9 electron volts, 1.606×10^{-10} j.

BHN Brinell hardness number

BHP, bhp brake horse power

Bl bale

Bm board measure

BOT ohm Board of Trade ohm (*the international ohm*)

Bot, btl bottle

BOTU Board of trade unit (*the commercial unit of electrical energy equal to 1 kilowatt-hour*)

Bq becquerel (*si derived unit of radiation activity*)

Brl barrel(s)

BSB British Standard brass (*a Whitworth-profile screw thread used for thin-walled tubing, with 26 tpi irrespective of diameter*)

BSB British Standard brass thread

BSF British Standard fine (*a Whitworth-profile screw thread, but with finer pitch for a given diameter*)

BSP British Standard pipe thread (*or British Standard gas thread, a screw thread of Whitworth profile but designated by the bore of the tube*)

BSS British Standards specification

BSW British Standard Whitworth thread (*the pre-metric British screw thread having a profile angle of 55° and a radius at root and crest of 0.1373 x pitch*)

BTU Board of Trade unit

BTU, BThU, Btu, btu British Thermal Unit

Bu bushel

BWG Birmingham wire gauge

Bx box

C coulomb (*si derived unit of electric charge*)

C/s *see* cps

Cal Calorie (*big 'c': nutritional kilogram-calorie*)

Cal calibre

Cal calorie

Cc cubic centimetre

C$_d$ drag factor

Cd candela (*si base unit of luminous intensity*)

Cent centum (100); centime

cg centigram

CGS unit centimetre-gram-second unit (*partially superseded by mksa and si units to avoid inconsistencies in the definition of the thermal calorie and electrical quantities*)

Cgs unit centimetre-gram-second

Ch chain

CHU or Chu centigrade heat unit = pound-calorie

Cl class, classification

Clo unit of thermal insulation of clothing

clt/s centilitre/s

cm^3 cubic centimetre

Cp candlepower

Cps cycle(s) per second (*now hertz*)

Ct carat

Cwt hundredweight (*112lb avoirdupois*)

dB decibel

Deg degree(s)

dN decineper

Doz dozen (*12; baker's dozen = 13*)

Dpi dots per inch

Dsp/s dessertspoon/s

Dwt pennyweight

E symbol for potential difference, especially electromotive force of voltaic cells

E eddy diffusivity

E electric field strength

E electromotive force

E energy

E molar extinction coefficient

E emissivity; linear strain; permitivity

EMF electromotive force

Esu electrostatic unit

EV electron-volt

F faraday

F free energy

F farad (*si derived unit of electric capacitance*)

fir firkin

fl dr fluid dram

fl oz fluid ounce

Fm, Fthm fathom(s)

FPS foot-pound-second (*system of units*)

freq frequency

ft foot; feet

ft^2 square foot

ft^3 cubic foot

Fur furlong

fur furlong (*0.125 mile*)

g gauss (*unit of magnetic induction*)

g gravity

g acceleration due to gravity

g gram

g, Gal, Gall gallon

g, Gi gill (*4 fl oz*)

Gall, gal gallon

GeV giga-electron-volt (*unit of particle energy*)

GHz gigahertz (10^9 Hz)

gi gill

GPM gallons per minute.

gr grain

gr wt gross weight

Gro, gr gross (*twelve dozen* – 144. *Teacher: what is 'gross darkness? Tommy: please, sir, 144 times darker than dark!*)

GSM grams per square metre (*'grammage' – a measure of the substance of paper*)

gv gravimetric volume

Gy gray (*si derived unit of radiation absorbed dose*)

H henry

H magnetic field strength

H enthalpy

H henry (*si derived unit of inductance*)

H Planck's constant

H specific enthalpy

H, h height

Ha hectare

Hh hands high (*of a horse, measured at the withers; 1 hand = 4"*)

Hhd hogshead

HP, hp horse power

Hz hertz (*si derived unit of frequency*)

Hz (cps) cycles per second

I ionic strength

I electric current

I luminous intensity

I Van't Hoff's factor

IA international ångstrom

Ïf activity coefficient for molar concentration; partition function

IHP indicated horse power

Imp, imp imperial; imperial

Imp gal, gall imperial gallon

ISA international standard atmosphere

IU international unit

J electric current density; magnetic polarisation

J polar moment of inertia

J joule (*si derived unit of work, energy or quantity of heat*)

J j (*used by electrical engineers as mathematician's i*)

JK⁻¹ joule per kelvin (*si derived unit of heat capacity*)

Jkg⁻¹ joule per kilogram (*si derived unit of specific latent heat*)

Jkg⁻¹K⁻¹ joule per kilogram kelvin (*si derived unit of specific heat capacity*)

K kelvin (*si base unit of thermodynamic temperature*)

K⁻¹ thermal coefficient of linear expansion per kelvin

kb kilobar

kc kilocycle

kc/s kilocycles per second (*now kilohertz*)

kcal kilocalorie

kCi kilocurie (*radioactivity* = 1000 *curies*)

KCPS kilocycles per second

KE kinetic energy

keV kilo-electron-volt

kg kilogram (*si base unit of weight*)

kgm⁻³ kilogram per cubic metre (*si derived unit of density*)

kgms⁻¹ kilogram metre per second (*si derived unit of momentum*)

kgm² kilogram metre squared (*si derived unit of moment of inertia*)

kgm²s⁻¹ kilogram metre squared per second (*si derived unit of angular momentum*)

kHz kilohertz (*see* cps)

kVA kilovolt-ampere

kVAr kilovar

kVp kilovolts, peak

KWh kilowatt-hour

L self-inductance

L litre ($1 dm^3$)

L linear coefficient of thermal expansion

L thermal conductivity

L wavelength

Lb pound (*Latin: librum*)

Lm lumen (*si derived unit of luminous flux*)

Lx lux (*si derived unit of illumination*)

M million

M medium size

M mutual inductance

M luminous emittance

m milli ($x\ 10^{-3}$)

M mile

M mass of electron

M electromagnetic moment

m metre (*si base unit of length*)

Ms⁻¹ metre per second (*si derived unit of velocity*)

ms⁻² metre per second squared (*si derived unit of acceleration*)

M² square metre (*si derived unit of area*)

M²s⁻¹ metre squared per second (*si derived unit of kinematic viscosity*)

M³ cubic metre (*si derived unit of volume*)

Mag magnitude

Mc/s megacycles per second (*replaced in si units by Mhz*)

Meas measure

Med medium

MeV mega electron volts

MHz megahertz

MKSA metre-kilogram-second-ampère system of units (*adopted by international electrotechnical commission in place of all other systems of units*)

ml millilitre

mm millimetre

Mmf magnetomotive force

Mol mole (*si base unit of amount of substance*)

Mol wt molecular weight

MPH, mph miles per hour

N newton

N modulus of rigidity

N number of molecules

N number of turns

N neutron number

N newton (*si derived unit of force*)

N index of refraction

N, N A Avogadro number

Nm⁻¹ newton per metre (*si derived unit of surface tension*)

Nsm⁻² newton second per metre squared (*si derived unit of dynamic viscosity*)

Nt nit (*unit of luminance = 1 candela m²*)

P electric polarisation

P power

P pressure

P poise

P electric dipole moment

P impulse

P momentum

P pressure

Pa pascal (*si derived unit of pressure or stress*)

Pc per cent

Pct per cent (*US*)

PE potential energy

pF picofarad

Pt(s) pint(s)

Q throughput

Q quantity of water discharged

Q charge

Q symbol of merit for an energy-storing device, resonant system or tuned circuit

Q the quantity of heat which enters a system

Q(q), q(q), qto quarto(s)

Q(s), qr(s), quart(s) quarter(s)

Q, ql quintal

Q, qr(s) quire(s) (*formerly 24 sheets, now 25 sheets*)

Q, qt quart

Qq quartos

Qty quantity

R the gas constant

R the Rydberg constant

R Rankine scale (*absolute scale of temperature based on fahrenheit scale*)

R rontgen unit of X-ray dosage

°R Réaumur scale of temperature

r with subscript, a symbol for specific refraction

r, Rd rod

rad radian (*si supplementary unit of plane angle*)

rad s-1 radian per second (*si derived unit of angular velocity*)

rad s-2 radian per second squared (*si derived unit of angular acceleration*)

rd rutherford (*unit of radioactive decay rate*)

Rhm rontgen-hour-metre

rm ream (*20 quires; 500 sheets*)

rmm relative molecular mass

rms power root-mean-square power (*the effective mean power level of an alternating electric supply*)

rms value root mean square value (*the measure of any alternating waveform*)

RPM, rpm revolutions per minute

S area

S entropy

S Poynting vector

S small

S siemens (*si derived unit of electric conductance*)

S distance along a path

S solubility

S specific entropy

S diameter of a molecule

S conductivity

S normal stress

S Stefan-Boltzmann constant

S surface charge density

S surface tension

S wave number

s second (*si base unit of time*)

Sc, scr scruple

Sk sack

Sq in square inch(es)

Sq m square metre(s)

Sq yd square yard(s)

Sr steradian (*si supplementary unit of solid angle*)

St stone = 14 lbs

St short ton

SU strontium unit

T tablespoon

T tesla (*si derived unit of magnetic flux density*)

T tonne (*metric ton*)

T a time interval, especially half-life or mean life

T troy weight

T ton(s); tonne(s)

T teaspoon

Tehp total equivalent brake horse-power

TGT turbine gas temperature.

Tn with subscript, a symbol for transport number

Tsp/s teaspoon/s

U litre per second = the ratio of throughput of a gas or vapour to the partial pressure difference across a system in a steady state

U internal energy

U potential difference; tension

U magnetic permeability

U specific internal energy

U_n = symbol for velocity of ions

V potential; potential difference; electromotive force

V volume V volt (*si derived unit of potential difference or emf*)

V velocity

V the specific volume of a gas

ν **(n)** Poisson's ratio

V (n) kinematic viscosity

V (n) frequency

V, v volume

V1 critical speed

VAr volt-ampères reactive; a unit of reactive power

V_{no} maximum permissible indicated air speed, a safety limitation imposed because of strength or handling limitations

V_{no} normal operating speed, usually of an airliner or other civil aircraft

Vol volume

V_r rotation speed

W total load

W electrical energy

W weight

W work

W radiant energy

W watt (*si derived unit of power*)

W work

W range

W weight

Wm⁻¹°C⁻¹ watt per metre degree celsius (*si derived unit of thermal conductivity*)

Wb weber (*si derived unit of magnetic flux*)

Wt weight

X mole fraction

X-unit unit for expressing the wavelength of x-rays or gamma-rays equivalent approximately to 10^{-13}m 1xu = 1 002 02 +- 0 000 03 x 10^{-13}m

Y electric flux

Y magnetic field strength

Y admittance

Yd, yd yard(s)

Z gram-equivalent weight

Z number of molecular collisions per second

Z atomic number

Z impedance

Z section modulus

Z valency of an ion

ζ electrokinetic potential

[R] with subscript, a symbol for molecular refraction

°C degree celsius (*si derived unit of temperature*)

°C⁻¹ thermal coefficient of linear expansion per degree celsius

°F degree fahrenheit

μ micron (*obsolete*)

μμ micromicro (*obsolete – see* pico (10^{-12}))

μμF micromicrofarad

ω ohm (*si derived unit of electric resistance*)

11.1 Units of currency

Some currencies have local abbreviations. Occasionally currencies change and it takes time for the rest of the world to catch up.

number

$ dollar(s)

$, US $ US dollar (*United States of America, Guam, American Samoa, Turks & Caicos Islands, British Virgin Islands, US Virgin Islands, Puerto Rico*)

A$ Australian dollar (*Australia, Kiribati, Nauru, Norfolk Island, Tuvalu*)

AD Algerian dinar

Af Afghanistan afghani

AFI Aruban florin

Arg$ Argentine peso

B Venezuelan bolivar

Ba Panamanian balboa

Ba$ Bahamian dollar

BD Bahrain dinar

Bda$ Bermuda dollar

Bds$ Barbados dollar

BFr Belgian franc

BN banknote

Bol Bolivian boliviano

BOP Bolivian peso (*ISO currency*)

Br Ethiopian birr

Br$ Brunei dollar

Bt Thailand baht

BuFr Burundi franc

Bz$ Belize dollar

C$ Canadian dollar

C$ Nicaraguan cordoba

C$ Ghana cedi

CFAFr African Financial Community franc (*Benin, Burkina Faso (formerly Upper Volta), Cameroon, Central African Republic, Chad, Congo, Equatorial Guinea, Gabon, Ivory Coast, Mali, Niger, Senegal, Togo*)

CFPFr French Pacific Community franc (*French Polynesia, New Caledonia, Wallis & Futuna Islands*)

Ch$ Chilean peso

CI$ Cayman Islands dollar

CI$ Cook Islands dollar

Col$ Colombian peso

Cr Brazilian cruzeiro

¢Rc Costa Rican colon

Ct(s) cent(s)

Cub$ Cuban peso

Cur currency

CVEsc Cape Verde Islands escudo

C£ Cyprus pound

D Vietnamese dong

D denarius (*Latin: penny*) *UK before decimalisation*

Db São Tomé & Principe dobra

Den Macedonian denar

Dh dirham (*Morocco, UAE, Western Sahara*)

Di Gambia dalasi

DjFr Djibouti franc

DKr Danish krone (*Denmark, Faroe Islands, Greenland*)

Dm Armenian dram

DM, D-Mark, M German mark, Deutschmark

Dol dollar(s)

Dr Greek drachma

DR$ Dominican Republic peso

€ Euro

EC$ East Caribbean dollar (*Anguilla, Antigua & Barbuda, Dominica, Grenada, Montserrat, St Kitts & Nevis, Saint Lucia, Saint Vincent & the Grenadines*)

ECU European Currency Unit

ÉRM exchange-rate mechanism

ESc El Salvador colon

Esc escudo (*Portugal, Azores, Madeira*)

E£ Egyptian pound

E£ Egyptian pound

F Hungarian forint

F$ Fiji dollar

F, Fr French franc (*France, Andorra, Comoros, Guinea, Reunion, Saint Pierre & Michelon*)

FI£ Falkland Islands pound

FI Netherlands florin

FI florin (*2/-, two bob or, in modern parlance, 10p*)

FMk Finland markka

Fr Local franc (*French Guiana, Guadeloupe, Martinique*)

G Paraguayan guarani

G$ Guyanese dollar

G(s), G(s), Gn(s) guinea(s) (*£1.1s or, in modern parlance, £1.05*)

GBP Guinea-Bissau peso

GBP GB pound (*sterling – ISO currency*)

Gde Haiti gourde

Gib£ Gibraltar pound

Gld Netherlands guilder

G£ Guernsey pound

HK$ Hong Kong dollar

Hr Ukrainian hryuna

ID Iraqi dinar

IKr, ISK Icelandic new krona

IoM£ Isle of Man pound

IR Indian rupee

I£, IR£ Irish punt (*pound*)

J$ Jamaican dollar

JD Jordan dinar

JPY Japanese yen (*ISO currency*)

J£ Jersey pound

K Zambian kwacha

Ka Papua New Guinea kina

Kc Czech Republic koruna

Kcs Koruna (*former Czechoslovakia*)

KD Kuwaiti dinar

Kn Croatian kuna

Kp Laos kip

KRL Kampuchean riel

Kro Estonian kroon

KSh Kenya shilling

Kt Burmese kyat

Kw Angolan kwanza

L lira (*Italy, San Marino*)

L Romanian leu (*plural: lei*)

L$ Liberian dollar

L, La Honduras lempira

La Latvian lats

LD Libyan dinar

Le Sierra Leone leone

LFr Luxembourg franc

Li or Ei Swaziland lilangeni (*plural: emalangeni*)

Lit Lithuanian litas

Lk Albanian lek

LM Maltese lira

Lo Lesotho loti

LSD librae, solidi, denarii (*Latin: pounds, shillings & pence in Britain until 15 February 1971*)

Lv Bulgarian lev

L£ Lebanese pound

Ma Azerbaijan manat

Ma Lesotho maluti

Ma$ Malaysian dollar or ringgit

MAD Moroccan dirham (*ISO currency*)

Mex$ Mexican peso

MgFr Madagascar franc

MK Malawi kwacha

MnFr Monégasque franc

MOP Macau pataka (*ISO currency*)

MR Mauritius rupee

Mt Mozambique metical

MvR Maldivian rufiya

N̦ Bhutan ngultrum

N Nigerian naira

NAFI Netherlands Antilles florin
NAGld Netherlands Antilles guilder
NKr Norwegian krone
NKW North Korean won
NR Nepalese rupee
NT$ New Taiwan dollar
NZ$ New Zealand dollar (*Niue, Pitcairn*)
OR Omani rial
P Botswana pula
P, p penny, pence
Pa peseta (*Spain, Andorra, Balearic Islands, Canary Islands*)
Pat Macau pataca
Pf German pfennig
PP Philippine peso
PR Pakistan rupee
Q Guatemala quetzal
QR Qatar riyal
R rand (*South Africa, Namibia*)
R rupee(s)
Rb Belarus rouble
RI Iranian rial
RI Brazilian real
Rp Indonesian rupiah
Rub former Soviet Union rouble
RwFr Rwanda franc
S Peruvian new sol
S shilling
S$ Singapore dollar
SAR Saudi Arabian riyal
Sch Austrian schilling
SFI Surinam florin
SFr Swiss franc or franken (*Switzerland, Liechtenstein*)
SGld Surinam guilder
SI$ Solomon Islands dollar
Sk Israeli shekel
Sk Slovak koruna
SKr Swedish krona
SKW South Korean won
SLR Sri Lanka rupee

SOS Somali shilling (*ISO currency*)
SoSh Somali shilling
SR Seychelles rupee
Stg sterling
Su Ecuador sucre
Sy£ Syrian pound
S£ Sudanese pound
T Slovenian tolar
T$ Tongan pa'anga
Ta Western Samoan tala
TD Tunisian dinar
Te Kazakhstan tenge
Tk Bangladeshi taka
TL Turkish lira
TOP Tongan pa'anga (*ISO currency*)
TSh Tanzanian shilling
TT$ Trinidad & Tobago dollar
Tug Mongolian tughrik or tögrög
U Mauritanian ouguiya
UrugN$, NUr$ Uruguayan new peso
USD US dollar (*ISO currency*)
USh Ugandan shilling
VL Vatican City lira
VT Vanuatu vatu
WS$ Western Samoan tala
Y Chinese yuan
YD South Yemeni dinar
YR Yemen rial (*Yemen Arab Republic*)
YuD Yugoslavian dinar
Z Zaire zaire
Z$ Zimbabwe dollar
Zl Polish zloty
£ United Kingdom pound (*sterling*) (*UK, St Helena, Gibraltar, Guernsey, Jersey, Isle of Man, Pitcairn Island*)
£A Australian pound (*now obsolete currency*)
£E Egyptian pound (*currency*)
£T Turkish pound (*currency*)
¥ Japanese yen

11.2 Standard banking currency codes – by code

AED	Abu Dhabi; Dubai; Sharjah; UAE
AFA	Afghanistan
ALL	Albania
AMD	Armenia
ANG	Netherlands; Antilles
AOK	Angola
ARA	Argentina
ATA	Austria
AUD	Australia; Kiribati; Nauru; Tuvalu
AWG	Aruba
AZM	Azerbaijan
BAD	Bosnia
BBD	Barbados
BDT	Bangladesh
BEF	Belgium
BGL	Bulgaria
BHD	Bahrain
BIF	Burundi
BMD	Bermuda
BOB	Bolivia
BRE	Brazil
BSD	Bahamas
BTN	Bhutan
BWP	Botswana
BYB	Belarus
BZD	Belize
CAD	Canada
CHF	Switzerland; Liechtenstein
CLP	Chile
CNY	China
COP	Colombia
CRC	Costa Rica
CUP	Cuba
CVE	Cape Verde Islands
CYP	Cyprus (South)
CZK	Czech Republic
DEM	Germany
DJF	Djibouti
DKK	Denmark
DOP	Dominican Republic
DZD	Algeria
ECS	Ecuador
EEK	Estonia
EGP	Egypt
ESP	Spain; Andorra
ETB	Ethiopia
FID	Fiji
FIK	Faroe Islands
FIM	Finland
FKP	Falkland Islands
FRF	France; Andorra; French Guyana; French Overseas Territories; Guadeloupe; Martinique; Monaco; Reunion; Saint Pierre & Miquelon
GEL	Georgia
GHC	Ghana
GIP	Gibraltar
GMD	Gambia
GNF	Guinea
GRD	Greece
GTQ	Guatemala
GWP	Guinea-Bissau
GYD	Guyana
HKD	Hong Kong
HNL	Honduras
HRK	Croatia
HTG	Haiti
HUF	Hungary
IDR	Indonesia
IEP	Ireland
ILS	Israel
INR	India
IQD	Iraq

IRR	Iran	NIC	Nicaragua
ISK	Iceland	NLG	Netherlands
ITL	Italy; San Marino	NOK	Norway
JMD	Jamaica	NPR	Nepal
JOD	Jordan	NZD	New Zealand; Cook Islands
JPY	Japan	OMR	Oman
KES	Kenya	PEN	Peru
KGS	Kyrgyzstan	PGK	Papua New Guinea
KHR	Cambodia	PHP	Philippines
KMF	Comoro Islands	PKR	Pakistan
KPW	Korea (North)	PLZ	Poland
KRW	Korea (South)	PTE	Portugal
KWD	Kuwait	PYG	Paraguay
KYD	Cayman Islands	QAR	Qatar
KZT	Kazakhstan	ROL	Romania
LAK	Laos	RUR	Russia; Tajikistan
LBP	Lebanon	RWF	Rwanda
LKR	Sri Lanka	SAR	Saudi Arabia
LRD	Liberia	SBD	Solomon Islands
LSL	Lesotho	SCR	Seychelles
LTL	Lithuania	SDP	Sudan
LUF	Luxembourg	SEK	Sweden
LVL	Latvia	SGD	Singapore
LYD	Libya	SHP	Saint Helena
MAD	Morocco	SIT	Slovenia
MDL	Moldavia	SKK	Slovakia
MGF	Malagasy Republic	SLL	Sierra Leone
MKD	Macedonia	SOS	Somalia
MMK	Burma; Myanmar	SRG	Surinam
MNT	Mongolia	STD	Sao Tomé & Principe
MOP	Macau	SVC	El Salvador
MRO	Mauritania	SYP	Syria
MTL	Malta	SZL	Swaziland
MUR	Mauritius	THB	Thailand
MVR	Maldives	TMM	Turkmenistan
MWK	Malawi	TND	Tunisia
MXN	Mexico	TOP	Tonga
MYR	Malaysia	TRL	Cyprus (North)
MZM	Mozambique	TRL	Turkey
NAD	Namibia	TTD	Trinidad & Tobago
NGN	Nigeria	TWD	Taiwan

TZS	Tanzania	XCD	Anguilla; Antigua; Barbuda; Dominica; Grenada; Montserrat; Saint Kitts & Nevis; Saint Lucia; St Vincent & the Grenadines; Eastern Caribbean Countries
UGX	Uganda		
USD	United States of America; Guam; Panama; Puerto Rico; Turks & Caicos Islands; Virgin Islands (*US & British*)		
		XOF	Benin; Burkina Faso; Ivory Coast; Mali; Niger; Senegal; Togo; West African States
UYP	Uruguay		
UZS	Uzbekistan		
VEB	Venezuela	XPF	French Polynesia; New Caledonia; Tahiti
VND	Vietnam		
VUV	Vanuatu	YER	Yemen
WST	Western Samoa	YUD	Yugoslavia
XAF	Cameroun; Central African Republic; Central African States; Chad; Congo; Equatorial Guinea; Gabon	ZAR	South Africa
		ZMK	Zambia
		ZRZ	Zaire
		ZWD	Zimbabwe

11.3 Standard banking currency codes – by country

AED	Abu Dhabi	XCD	Barbuda
AFA	Afghanistan	BYB	Belarus
ALL	Albania	BEF	Belgium
DZD	Algeria	BZD	Belize
FRF	Andorra	XOF	Benin
ESP	Andorrs	BMD	Bermuda
AOK	Angola	BTN	Bhutan
XCD	Anguilla	BOB	Bolivia
XCD	Antigua	BAD	Bosnia
ARA	Argentina	BWP	Botswana
AMD	Armenia	BRE	Brazil
AWG	Aruba	BGL	Bulgaria
AUD	Australia	XOF	Burkina Faso
ATA	Austria	MMK	Burma; Myanmar
AZM	Azerbaijan	BIF	Burundi
BSD	Bahamas	KHR	Cambodia
BHD	Bahrain	XAF	Cameroun
BDT	Bangladesh	CAD	Canada
BBD	Barbados	CVE	Cape Verde Islands

KYD	Cayman Islands	DEM	Germany
XAF	Central African Republic	GHC	Ghana
XAF	Central African States	GIP	Gibraltar
XAF	Chad	GRD	Greece
CLP	Chile	XCD	Grenada
CNY	China	FRF	Guadeloupe
COP	Colombia	USD	Guam
KMF	Comoro Islands	GTQ	Guatemala
XAF	Congo	GNF	Guinea
NZD	Cook Islands	GWP	Guinea-Bissau
CRC	Costa Rica	GYD	Guyana
HRK	Croatia	HTG	Haiti
CUP	Cuba	HNL	Honduras
TRL	Cyprus (North)	HKD	Hong Kong
CYP	Cyprus (South)	HUF	Hungary
CZK	Czech Republic	ISK	Iceland
DKK	Denmark	INR	India
DJF	Djibouti	IDR	Indonesia
XCD	Dominica	IRR	Iran
DOP	Dominican Republic	IQD	Iraq
AED	Dubai	IEP	Ireland
XCD	Eastern Caribbean Countries	ILS	Israel
ECS	Ecuador	ITL	Italy
EGP	Egypt	XOF	Ivory Coast
SVC	El Salvador	JMD	Jamaica
XAF	Equatorial Guinea	JPY	Japan
EEK	Estonia	JOD	Jordan
ETB	Ethiopia	KZT	Kazakhstan
FKP	Falkland Islands	KES	Kenya
FIK	Faroe Islands	AUD	Kiribati
FID	Fiji	KPW	Korea (North)
FIM	Finland	KRW	Korea (South)
FRF	France	KWD	Kuwait
FRF	French Guyana	KGS	Kyrgyzstan
FRF	French Overseas Territories	LAK	Laos
XPF	French Polynesia	LVL	Latvia
XAF	Gabon	LBP	Lebanon
GMD	Gambia	LSL	Lesotho
GEL	Georgia	LRD	Liberia
		LYD	Libya
		CHF	Liechtenstein

LTL	Lithuania	**QAR**	Qatar
LUF	Luxembourg	**FRF**	Reunion
MOP	Macau	**ROL**	Romania
MKD	Macedonia	**RUR**	Russia
MGF	Malagasy Republic	**RWF**	Rwanda
MWK	Malawi	**SHP**	Saint Helena
MYR	Malaysia	**XCD**	Saint Kitts & Nevis
MVR	Maldives	**XCD**	Saint Lucia
XOF	Mali	**FRF**	Saint Pierre & Miquelon
MTL	Malta	**ITL**	San Marino
FRF	Martinique	**STD**	Sao Tomé & Principe
MRO	Mauritania	**SAR**	Saudi Arabia
MUR	Mauritius	**XOF**	Senegal
MXN	Mexico	**SCR**	Seychelles
MDL	Moldavia	**AED**	Sharjah
FRF	Monaco	**SLL**	Sierra Leone
MNT	Mongolia	**SGD**	Singapore
XCD	Montserrat	**SKK**	Slovakia
MAD	Morocco	**SIT**	Slovenia
MZM	Mozambique	**SBD**	Solomon Islands
NAD	Namibia	**SOS**	Somalia
AUD	Nauru	**ZAR**	South Africa
NPR	Nepal	**ESP**	Spain
NLG	Netherlands	**LKR**	Sri Lanka
ANG	Netherlands Antilles	**XCD**	St Vincent & the Grenadines
XPF	New Caledonia		
NZD	New Zealand	**SDP**	Sudan
NIC	Nicaragua	**SRG**	Surinam
XOF	Niger	**SZL**	Swaziland
NGN	Nigeria	**SEK**	Sweden
NOK	Norway	**CHF**	Switzerland
OMR	Oman	**SYP**	Syria
PKR	Pakistan	**XPF**	Tahiti
USD	Panama	**TWD**	Taiwan
PGK	Papua New Guinea	**RUR**	Tajikistan
PYG	Paraguay	**TZS**	Tanzania
PEN	Peru	**THB**	Thailand
PHP	Philippines	**XOF**	Togo
PLZ	Poland	**TOP**	Tonga
PTE	Portugal	**TTD**	Trinidad & Tobago
USD	Puerto Rico	**TND**	Tunisia

TRL	Turkey	**VEB**	Venezuela
TMM	Turkmenistan	**VND**	Vietnam
USD	Turks & Caicos Islands	**USD**	Virgin Islands (US & British)
AUD	Tuvalu		
AED	UAE	**XOF**	West African States
UGX	Uganda	**WST**	Western Samoa
USD	United States of America	**YER**	Yemen
UYP	Uruguay	**YUD**	Yugoslavia
UZS	Uzbekistan	**ZRZ**	Zaire
VUV	Vanuatu	**ZMK**	Zambia
		ZWD	Zimbabwe

11.4 Forms of money

M0 Narrow money - notes & coins in public circulation together with cash in banks' tills and their operational balances with the bank of England. Term in current use.

M1 Notes & coins in circulation & deposited in current bank accounts. Term no longer used in UK.

M2 M1 plus private sector holdings of building societies & national savings; ordinary accounts & bank deposit accounts. Term no longer used in UK.

M3 M2 plus interest-bearing, non-sterling deposit accounts held by UK residents & other certificates of deposit. Term no longer used in UK.

M4 M0 plus all deposits in UK banks and building societies. Designed to measure spending power. Term in current use.

11.5 Bullion &c

AGR Australian Gold Refineries (*gold refiner*)

BIS Bank for International Settlement

BLCo Britannia Refined Metals Limited (*UK silver refiner*)

CMB Casa da Moeda do Brasil (*gold refiner*)

CP Peru Empress Minera del Centro del Peru (*silver refiner*)

CREST new equity settlement system which replaced the Stock Exchange system in 1996 – it does not stand for anything

E Engelhard Corporation (*US silver refiner*)

GEMMs Gilt-Edged Market Makers

IMM Industrial Minera Mexico SA (*gold refiner*)

JM Johnson Matthey (*gold refiner*)

JMI Johnson Matthey Incorporated (*gold refiner*)

KAR K A Rasmussen Hamar A/S (*silver refiner*)

KUE Kennecott Copper Corporation, USA

LBMA The London Bullion Market Association

MTFS Medium Term Financial Strategy

NFL National Loans Fund

NMR N M Rothschild (*gold refiner*)

RPIX Retail Prices Index excluding mortgage interest

RR Ltd Rand Refinery Ltd (*South African silver refiner*)

SEMPSA Sociedad Española de Metales Preciosis SA (*silver refiner*)

SIB Securities & Investments Board

UGDO Usine Genevoise de Degrossissage d'Or (*gold refiner*)

ZTM Zaklady Metalurgiczne Trzebinia (*Polish silver refiner*)

11.6   In the City

€ new unit of currency of EMU, came into effect on 1 January 1999: initial signatories Austria, Finland, Ireland, France, Germany, Italy, Portugal, Spain, Belgium, the Netherlands and Luxembourg

A Actuaries

AEFA American Express Financial Advisers

AEX Amsterdam Stock Exchange

AIF Authorised Investment Fund

AIM Alternative Investment Market

Amex The American Stock Exchange

APACS Association for Payment Clearing Services

AUTIF Association of Unit Trusts and Investment Funds

BBA British Bankers Association

BTP Buoni del Tesoro Poliennali (*Italian Bond*)

BVCA British Venture Capital Association

C Call Option (*buy, as opposed to put option = sell; see* LIFFE)

Con, Consols Consolidated Annuities (*Government Stock*)

CAC Compagnie des Agents de Change (*French Stockbrokers' Association*)

CAR Compounded Annual Rate

CBOT, CBT Chicago Board of Trade (*US futures exchange*)

CFR Code of Federal Regulations

CGO Central Gilts Office

CHAPS Clearing House Automated Payment System

CIF Cost, Insurance and Freight

CME Chicago Mercantile Exchange

CMO Central Moneymarkets Office

COMEX Commodity Exchange (*New York*)

CPT Cost per thousand

CSCE Conference on Security and Co-operation in Europe

CSDs Central Securities Depositories

DAX Deutsche Aktien-Index (*German Share Price Index*)

DTB Deutsche Terminbörse (*Frankfurt Futures Exchange*)

EASDAQ Independent Pan-European Stock Market

EASI The EASDAQ All Share Index

EBA ECU Banking Association

ECU, Ecu European Currency Unit

EIB European Investment Bank

EMS European Monetary System

EMF European Monetary Fund

EMU, Emu Economic and Monetary Union

ERM Exchange Rate Mechanism

ESCB European System of Central Banks

Eurex European Exchange

EURO.NM a pan-European grouping of regulated stocks markets dedicated to innovative companies with big growth potential

EURO.NM Belgium Brussels Stock Exchange

Extel Exchange Telegraph (*News Agency*)

FBSA Foreign Banks and Securities Houses Association

FCA Federation of Commodity Associations

GRR Fédération des Experts-Comptable Européene

FI Free in (*Commerce*)

FIA Fellow of the Institute of Actuaries

FIA Futures Industry Association

FIA Federal Insurance Administration

FIB Fellow of the Institute of Bankers

FLA Finance and Leasing Association

FLP Financial Law Panel

FOA Futures and Options Association

FOB Free on board (*commerce*)

FRGs Floating Rate Gilts

FSA Financial Services Act 1986

FT Financial Times

FTI Financial Times Information

FTSE,

FT-SE,

Footsie Financial Times Stock Exchange 100 index

FX Foreign Exchange

GAD Government Actuary's Department

G7 Group of Seven (*leading Industrial Nations*)

GEMMA Gilt-Edged Market Makers' Association

GEMMs Gilt-Edged Market Makers

HCPI Harmonised Consumer Price Index

HSBC Hong Kong and Shanghai Banking Corporation

IBB Invest in Britain Bureau

ICSDs International Central Securities Depositories

ICO International Coffee Organisation

IDBs Inter-Dealer Brokers

IFC International Finance Corporation

IFC International Finance Corporation (*UN affiliate*)

IFMA Institutional Fund Managers' Association

IGs Index-Linked Gilts

ILU Institute of London Underwriters

IMMTA International Money Markets Trading Association

INSECTS INdices on SECTorS

IPE International Petroleum Exchange

IPMA International Primary Markets Association

ISDA International Swaps and Derivatives Association

ISE International Stock Exchange

ISMA International Securities Markets Association

JSE Johannesburg Stock Exchange

KSE Karachi Stock Exchange

LCH London Clearing House

Le Nouveau Marché Paris Stock Exchange

LIBA London Investment Banking Association

LIBID London Inter-bank Bid rate

LIBOR London Inter-bank Offer Rate

LIFFE, Liffe London International Financial Futures & Options Exchange (*pronounced 'life'; traders hand signalling known as 'open outcry'*)

LIRMA London International Insurance and Reinsurance Market Association

LME London Metal Exchange

MATIF Marché à terme des instruments Financiers (*French: Financial Futures Market*)

MFI Monetary Financial Institution

MMC The Monopolies and Mergers Commission

MOS Mail Order Sales

MOPS Mail Order Protection Scheme

MSCI Index Morgan Stanley Capital International World Index

NAPF National Association of Pension Funds

NASDAQ National Association of Security Dealers Automated Quotations (*System*)

NCB National Central Bank

Neuer Markt Deutsche Börse (*German: German Stock Exchange*)

Nikkei The Japanese Stock Exchange

NMAX Amsterdam Exchange

NSSR National Savings Stock Register

NYCSCE New York Coffee, Sugar & Cocoa Exchange

NYMEX New York Mercantile Exchange

NYSE New York Stock Exchange

OEIC Open-Ended Investment Company

ONS Office for National Statistics

OSE Osaka Stock Exchange

OSE index OSE index

P/E price-earnings ratio

PSA Public Securities Association (*New York*)

RIE Registered Investment Exchange

RPA Retail Prices Index

RTGS Real-Time Gross Settlement

S&P Standard & Poor

SEAQ Stock Exchange Automated Quotations

SE Stock Exchange

SES Singapore Stock Exchange

SETT settlement

SFA Securities and Futures Authority

SIB Securities and Investments Board

SOFFEX Swiss Options & Financial Futures Exchange

SWIFT Society for Worldwide Interbank Funds Transfer

TARGET Trans-European Automated Real-time Gross settlement Express Transfer system

The Hex General Index Helsinki Stock Exchange General Index

The KSE-100 Karachi Stock Exchange – 100 index

TOPIC Teletext Output Price Information Computer (Stock Exchange)

12   Times & seasons

AR anno regni (*Latin: in the year of the reign*)

A, Apr April

A, Aug August

Ab Ab (*Jewish calendar month 11/12*)

AC ante Christum

AD anno domini (*Latin: in the year of our Lord; see* CE)

Ad1 Adar I; First Adar (*Jewish calendar month 6*)

Ad2 Adar II; Second Adar (*Jewish intercalated month 7*)

AH anno hegirae (*Latin: in the year of the Hegira - Mohammed's migration to Medina = 622CE*)

AM anno mundi (*Latin: in the year of the world*)

Am ante meridien (*Latin: before noon*)

Ann annual

ARR anno regni/regis/reginae (*Latin: in the year of the reign of our king/queen*)

AST Atlantic Standard Time

AUC ab urbis conditae *or* ab urbe condita (*Latin: in the year from the foundation of the city (Rome), reckoned as 753BCE*)

Aut autumn

BC before Christ (ie *counting backwards from the supposed year of Jesus's birth, as determined by the Council of Nicea in 325; see* BCE)

BCE before the common era

BH bank holiday(s)

BP before present (*present = 1950*)

Bru, Brum Brumaire (*French Revolutionary calendar month 2*)

BST British summer time

CDT central daylight time (*USA & Canada*)

CE common era

CET central European time

Chron, chronol chronological, chronology

Contemp contemporary

CST central standard time (*USA & Australia*)

CT central time

D, Dec December

D, dy day(s)

Dhu1 Dhu Al-Qa'da (*Muslim month 11*)

Dhu2 Dhu Al-Hijja (*Muslim month 12*)

DST double summer time

EDT eastern daylight time

El Elul (*Jewish calendar month 12/13*)

EST eastern standard time (*USA & Australia*)

ETA estimated time of arrival

ETD estimated time of departure

Etr Easter

F Friday

F, Feb February

Flo, Flor Floréal (*French Revolutionary Calendar month 8*)

Fri,

Frim Frimaire (*French Revolutionary Calendar month 3*)

Fru, Fruc Fructidor (*French Revolutionary Calendar month 12*)

FY fiscal year

Ger, Germ Germinal (*French Revolutionary Calendar month 7*)

GF Good Friday

GMAT Greenwich mean astronomical time

GMN Greenwich mean noon

GMT Greenwich mean time (on the Meridian; England is half-an-hour wide)

GT Greenwich time

H, hr hour(s)

IGY international geophysical year

Int interim

Iy Iyyar (*Jewish calendar month 8/9*)

J, Jan January

J, Jan January

J, Jul July

J, Jun June

Jum1 Jumada Al-Aula (*Muslim month 5*)

Jum2 Jumada Al-Ukhra (*Muslim month 6*)

Kis Kislev (*Jewish calendar month 3*)

LC lunar cycle

Lt local time

M Monday

M May

M month

M, Mar March

M, min minute(s)

Mar Marcheshvan (Heshvan) (*Jewish calendar month 2*)

Med medi(a)eval

Mes, Mess Messidor (*French Revolutionary Calendar month 10*)

MEZ Mitteleuropäische Zeit (*German: Central European Time*)

Mg milligram

Mich Michaelmas

Min. minute(s)

Mo month

MST mountain standard time (*USA*)

MTBF mean time between failures (*a measure of reliability*)

Muh Muharram (*Muslim month 1*)

N noon

N, Nov November

Nis Nisan (*Jewish calendar month 7/8*)

Niv Nivôse (*French Revolutionary Calendar month 4*)

NS new style (*dates in the Gregorian calendar - in England on and after 12 September 1752*)

NS new style

O, Oct October

OS old style

P past

Per period

Plu, Pluv Pluviôse (*French Revolutionary Calendar month 5*)

PM post meridian (*Latin: after noon*)

Pra Prairial (*French Revolutionary Calendar month 9*)

Pres present

Prox proximo

PST pacific standard time (*USA & Canada*)

Rab1 Rabi' Al-Awal (*Muslim month 3*)

Rab2 Rabi' Al-Akhir (*Muslim month 4*)

Raj Rajab (*Muslim month 7*)

Ram Ramadan (*Muslim month 9*)

s second/s (*Note – sec is incorrect*)

S a semiannual

S, Sab Sabbath

S, Sat Saturday

S, Sep, Sept September

S, Sun, $ Sunday

Saf Safar (*Muslim month 2*)

SAT south australian time

SC solar cycle

SHA sidereal hour angle

Sha Shawwal (*Muslim month 10*)

Sha'b Shaban (*Muslim month 8*)

Sheb Shebat (*Jewish calendar month 5*)

Siv Sivan (*Jewish calendar month 9/10*)

Spr spring

ST sidereal time

Sum summer

TAI temps atomique international (*French: international atomic time*)

Tam Tammuz (*Jewish calendar month 10/11*)

Teb Tebet (*Jewish calendar month 4*)

Th, Thur Thursday

The, Therm Thermidor (*French Revolutionary Calendar month 11*)

Tish Tishri (*Jewish calendar month 1*)

Tu, Tues Tuesday

UT universal time

UTC universal time co-ordinated

Ven, Vend Vendémiaire (*French Revolutionary Calendar month 1*)

Ven, Vent Ventôse (*French Revolutionary Calendar month 6*)

W, Wed Wednesday

Wint winter

Wk week

WST western standard time (*Australia*)

Y, yr year(s)

Yo year old

YTD, ytd year to date

13   de Bono's thinkwords

ADI agreement, disagreement and irrelevance

AGO aims, goals and objectives

APC alternatives, possibilities and choices

CAF consider all factors

C&S consequence and sequel

CoRT Cognitive Research Trust

EBS examine both sides

FI-FO inFormation In - inFormation Out (*not to be confused with 'first in, first out'*)

FQ fishing question (*searching for possible answers*)

HV&LV high values and low values

L-game a game for two with only one L-shaped piece each plus a couple of neutral pieces

OPV other people's views

PISCO purpose, input, solution, choice, operation

PMI plus, minus, interesting

Po a provocative word describing the forward use of an idea which comes from hy**po**thesis, sup**po**se, **po**ssible, **po**etry

SQ shooting question (*requiring yes or no answer*)

TEC target and task, expand and explore, contract and conclude

4M me, mates, moral, mankind (*a set of values*)

14 Transport
14.1 Land – road

14.1.1 Motor vehicle manufacturers

AAG Allgemeine Automobil-Gesellschaft (*German car marque 1900–02*)

AC Auto-Carrier (*English car marque 1908–*)

AJS Albert John Stevens (*1 of 4 brothers*) 1909

ALDA Ah – la délicieuse automobile (*French marque 1912–22*)

Amilcar Lamy & Akar (*French marque 1921–1939*)

ATS Automobili Turismo Sport (*Italian marque 1962–64*)

BAT Berlinetta Aerodinamica Tecnica (*Italian car marque*)

BMW Bayerische Motoren Werke (*German: Bavarian Motor Factory*)

BNC Bollack, Netter et Cie (*French marque 1923–31*)

BSA Birmingham Small Arms (*English marque 1907–40*)

CEMSA Costruzioni Elettromeccaniche SA (*Italian marque 1946–50*)

CGV Charron, Giradot et Voigt (*French marque 1901–30*)

DAF Van Doorne's Automobielfabrieken

DAT Den, Aoyama & Takeuchi (*Japanese 1912–26; see* Datsun)

Datsun DAT gave up car manufacture in 1926, and started again in 1931 as Datson (Son of Dat), changed to Datsun because 'son' = 'loss' in Japanese.

DB Deutsch and Bonnet (*German marque 1938-61*)

DKW (*originally Dampfkraftwagen, popularly Des Knaben Wunsch, then* Deutsche Kraftfahrtzeug Werke, *popularly* Das Kleine Wunder (*German marque 1928–66*)

DMW Dawson Motor Works (*1945–*)

EHP Les Établissements Henri Précloux (*French marque 1921–29*)

Elva Elle va! (*'she goes!' English car marque 1955–68*)

ERF E R Foden (*British lorry marque*)

FAST Fabbrica Automobili Sport Torino (*Italian car marque 1919–25*)

FIAT Fabbrica Italiana di Automobili Torino In 1906 F.I.A.T. became FIAT: 'let it be made'

FN Frazer Nash (*English car marque 1924–60*)

GM General Motors (*Corporation*)

GMC General Motors Corporation (*brand name for trucks*)

GN Godfrey & Frazer-Nash (*British car marque 1910–25*)

GWK Grice, Wood & Keiller (*British car marque 1911–31*; the Keiller of marmalade fame)

HE Herbert Engineering (*British car marque 1920–31*)

HRG Halford, Robins & Godfrey (*see* GN; *British car marque 1936–56*)

JZR Jezerbel (*a kit car*)

K Chrysler Corporation FWD cars

Leaf Lea-Francis (*English Marque 1904–06, 1920–35, 1937–53, 1960*)

MATRA Mécanique-Aviation-Traction (*French car marque 1965–79*)

MV Agusta Meccanica Verghera (*Italian 1945–1978*)

NAG Neue Automobil-Gesellschaft (*German car marque 1902–34*)

OK-Supreme Humphries & Dawes Ltd (*1899*)

OM Officine Meccaniche (*Italian car marque 1918–34*)

OSCA Officine Specializzate Construzione Automobili Fratelli Maserati (*Italian car marque 1947–67*)

REO Ransom Eli Olds (*ex-Oldsmobile;* car marque USA *1904–36*)

S&M Smith & Mabley (*USA marque 1904–14*)

Saab Svenska Aeroplan Aktiebolaget (*Swedish marque 1949–*)

SARA Société des Applications (Automobiles) du Refroidissement par Air (*French marque 1923–30*)

SAVA Société Anversoise pour Fabrication des Voitures Automobiles (*Belgian marque 1910–23*)

SCAT Società Ceirno Automobili Torino (*Italian marque 1906–32*)

SEAT Sociedad Española de Automobiles de Tourismo

SIATA Società Italiana Applicazioni Transformazioni Automobilistiche (*Italian marque 1926–70*)

SIGMA Société Industrielle Genevoise de Mécanique et d'Automobiles (*Swiss 1909–14*)

SIMA Société Industrielle de Matériel Automobile (*French marque 1924–29*)

SIMCA Société Industrielle de Mécanique et Carrosserie Automobile (*French marque 1934–78*)

STAR Società Torinese Automobili Rapid (*Italian marque 1904–21*)

TVR Trevor Wilkinson & Bernard Williams (*British marque 1956–*)

Volvo Latin: I roll

VW Volkswagen (*people's car*)

ZIL Zavod Imieni Likhachev (*Russian marque 1956–*)

14.1.2a Vehicle registration & licensing – index marks & their areas

We give some indication of the antiquity of the marks for the benefit of Vintage & Veteran car buffs. A star* after the letter(s) indicates that they were introduced at the very start of vehicle registration under the Motor Car Act of 1903, which became effective on 1 January 1904. The dates of later introductions are shown either in the second (present-day area) column or, if the area has changed, after the original area in the third column. So, for example, AG presently represents Hull, but originally represented Ayrshire from 1925.

	PRESENT AREA	ORIGINAL AREA IF DIFFERENT
A*		London
AA*	Bournemouth	Southampton
AB*	Worcester	Worcestershire
AC*	Coventry	Warwickshire
AD*	Gloucester	Gloucestershire
AE*	Bristol	
AF*	Truro	
AG	Hull	Ayr 1925
AH*	Norwich	Norfolk
AI*		Meath County
AJ*	Middlesbrough	Yorkshire: North Riding
AK*	Sheffield	Bradford
AL*	Nottingham	Nottinghamshire
AM*	Swindon	Wiltshire
AN*	Reading	West Ham
AO*	Carlisle	Cumberland
AP*	Brighton	East Sussex
AR*	Chelmsford	Hertfordshire
AS*	Inverness	Nairn
AT*	Hull	
AU*	Nottingham	
AV	Peterborough	Aberdeen 1926
AW*	Shrewsbury	Shropshire
AX*	Cardiff	Monmouthshire
AY*	Leicester	Leicestershire
AZ		Belfast 1928
B*		Lancashire
BA*	Manchester	Salford

BB*	Newcastle upon Tyne	
BC*	Leicester	
BD*	Northampton	Northamptonshire
BE*	Lincoln	Lincolnshire: Parts of Lindsey
BF	Stoke-on-Trent	
BG*	Liverpool	Birkenhead 1931
BH*	Luton	Buckinghamshire
BI		Monaghan
BJ*	Ipswich	East Suffolk
BK*	Portsmouth	
BL*	Reading	Berkshire
BM*	Luton	Bedfordshire
BN*	Manchester	Bolton
BO*	Cardiff	
BP*	Portsmouth	West Sussex
BR*	Newcastle upon Tyne	Sunderland
BS*	Aberdeen	Orkney
BT*	Leeds	Yorkshire: East Riding
BU*	Manchester	Oldham
BV	Preston	Blackburn 1930
BW	Oxford	Oxfordshire
BX*	Haverfordwest	Carmarthenshire
BY	London NW	Croydon
BZ		Down 1930
C*		Yorkshire: West Riding
CA*	Chester	Denbighshire
CB*	Manchester	Blackburn
CC*	Bangor	Caernarvonshire
CD	Brighton 1920	
CE*	Peterborough	Cambridgeshire
CF	Reading	West Suffolk 1908
CG	Bournemouth	Southampton County 1931
CH*	Nottingham	Derby
CI*		Queen's County
CJ*	Gloucester	Hertfordshire
CK*	Preston	
CL*	Norwich	
CM*	Liverpool	Birkenhead
CN	Newcastle upon Tyne	Gateshead 1920
CO*	Exeter	Plymouth

CP*	Huddersfield	Halifax
CR*	Portsmouth	Southampton
CS*	Glasgow	Ayr 1934
CT*	Lincoln	Lincolnshire: Parts of Kesteven
CU*	Newcastle upon Tyne	South Shields
CV	Truro	Cornwall 1929
CW*	Preston	Burnley
CX*	Huddersfield	
CY*	Swansea	
CZ		Belfast 1932
D*		Kent
DA*	Birmingham	Wolverhampton
DB*	Manchester	Stockport
DC*	Middlesbrough	
DD	Gloucester	Gloucestershire 1921
DE*	Haverfordwest	Pembrokeshire
DF 1926, DG 1930	Gloucester	
DH*	Dudley	Walsall
DI*		Roscommon
DJ*	Liverpool	St Helens
DK*	Manchester	Rochdale
DL*	Portsmouth	Isle of Wight
DM*	Chester	Flintshire
DN*	Leeds	York
DO*	Lincoln	Lincolnshire: Parts of Holland
DP*	Reading	
DR	Exeter	Plymouth 1926
DS*	Glasgow	Peebles
DT	Sheffield	Doncaster 1927
DU*	Coventry	
DV	Exeter	Devon 1929
DW*	Cardiff	Newport (Mon)
DX*	Ipswich	
DY*	Brighton	Hastings
DZ		Antrim County 1932
E*		Staffordshire
EA*	Dudley	West Bromwich
EB*	Peterborough	Isle of Ely
EC*	Preston	Westmorland

ED*	Liverpool	Warrington
EE*	Lincoln	Grimsby
EF*	Middlesbrough	West Hartlepool
EG*	Peterborough	Soke of Peterborough
EH*	Stoke -on-Trent	
EI*		County Sligo
EJ*	Haverfordwest	Cardiganshire
EK*	Liverpool	Wigan
EL*	Bournemouth	
EM*	Liverpool	Bootle
EN*	Manchester	Bury
EO*	Preston	Barrow-in-Furness
EP*	Swansea	Montgomeryshire
ER	Peterborough	Cambridgeshire 1922
ES*	Dundee	Perth
ET*	Sheffield	Rotherham
EU*	Bristol	Brecknockshire
EV	Chelmsford	Essex 1931
EW*	Peterborough	Huntingdonshire
EX*	Norwich	Great Yarmouth
EY*	Bangor	Anglesey
EZ		Belfast 1935
F*		Essex
FA*	Stoke-on-Trent	Burton-on-Trent
FB*	Bristol	Bath
FC	Oxford	
FD*	Dudley	
FE*	Lincoln	
FF*	Bangor	Merioneth
FG	Brighton	Fife 1925
FH*	Gloucester	
FI*		Tipperary: North Riding
FJ*	Exeter	
FK*	Dudley	Worcester
FL*	Peterborough	Soke of Peterborough
FM*	Chester	
FN*	Maidstone	Canterbury
FO*	Gloucester	Radnorshire
FP*	Leicester	Rutland
FR*	Preston	Blackpool

FS	Edinburgh 1931	
FT*	Newcastle upon Tyne	Tynemouth
FU	Lincoln	Lincolnshire: Parts of Lindsey 1922
FV	Preston	Blackpool 1929
FW	Lincoln	Lincolnshire: Parts of Lindsey 1929
FX*	Bournemouth	Dorset
FY*	Liverpool	Southport
FZ		Belfast 1938
G*		Glasgow 1921
GA, GB	Glasgow 1921	
GC	London SW	London 1929
GD	Glasgow 1925	
GE	Glasgow 1928	
GF	London SW	London 1930
GG	Glasgow 1930	
GH, GJ, GK	London SW	London 1930
GL	Truro	Bath 1932
GM	Reading	Motherwell & Wishaw 1921
GN, GO, GP	London SW	London 1931
GR	Newcastle upon Tyne	Sunderland 1933
GS	Luton	Perth 1928
GT	London SW	London 1931
GU	London SE	London 1929
GV	Ipswich	West Suffolk 1930
GW	London SE	London 1931
GX, GY	London SE	London 1932
GZ		Belfast 1942
H*		Middlesex
HA	Dudley	Smethwick 1907
HB	Cardiff	Merthyr Tydfil 1908
HC	Brighton	Eastbourne 1911
HD	Huddersfield	Dewsbury 1913
HE	Sheffield	Barnsley 1913
HF	Liverpool	Wallasey 1913
HG	Preston	Burnley 1930
HH	Carlisle 1914	
HI*		Tipperary: South Riding
HJ	Chelmsford	Southend-on-Sea 1914
HK	Chelmsford	Essex 1915
HL	Sheffield	Wakefield 1915

HM	London C	East Ham 1915
HN	Middlesbrough	Darlington 1921
HO	Bournemouth	Southampton (County) 1917
HP	Coventry 1919	
HR	Swindon	Wiltshire 1919
HS*	Glasgow	Renfrewshire
HT	Bristol 1920	
HU	Bristol 1924	
HV	London C	East Ham 1929
HW	Bristol 1927	
HX	London C	Middlesex 1930
HY	Bristol 1930	
HZ		Tyrone 1944
IA*		County Antrim
IB*		Armagh
IC*		County Carlow
ID*		County Cavan
IE*		County Clare
IF*		County Cork
IH*		County Donegal
IJ*		County Down
IK		County Dublin
IL*		Fermanagh
IM*		County Galway
IN*		County Kerry
IO*		County Kildare
IP*		County Kilkenny
IR*		King's County
IT*		Leitrim
IU		County Limerick
IW*		County Londonderry
IX*		County Longford
IZ		County Mayo 1920
J*		County Durham
JA	Manchester	Stockport 1929
JB	Reading	Berkshire 1932
JC	Bangor	Caernarvonshire 1931
JD	London C	West Ham 1929
JE	Peterborough	Isle of Ely 1933
JF	Leicester 1930	

JG	Maidstone	Canterbury 1929
JH	Reading	Hertfordshire 1931
JI*		Tyrone
JJ	Maidstone	London 1932
JK	Brighton	Eastbourne 1928
JL	Lincoln	Lincolnshire: Parts of Holland 1932
JM	Reading	Westmorland 1931
JN	Chelmsford	Southend-on-Sea 1930
JO	Oxford 1930	
JP	Liverpool	Wigan 1934
JR	Newcastle upon Tyne	Northumberland 1932
JS*	Inverness	Ross & Cromarty
JT	Bournemouth	Dorset 1933
JU	Leicester	Leicestershire 1932
JV	Lincoln	Grimsby 1930
JW	Birmingham	Wolverhampton 1931
JX	Huddersfield	Halifax 1932
JY	Exeter	Plymouth 1932
K*		Liverpool
KA	Liverpool 1925	
KB	Liverpool 1914	
KC	Liverpool 1920	
KD	Liverpool 1927	
KE	Maidstone	Kent 1920
KF	Liverpool 1930	
KG	Cardiff 1931	
KH	Hull 1925	
KJ	Maidstone	Kent 1931
KK	Maidstone	Kent 1922
KL	Maidstone	Kent 1924
KM	Maidstone	Kent 1925
KN	Maidstone	Kent 1917
KO	Maidstone	Kent 1927
KP	Maidstone	Kent 1928
KR	Maidstone	Kent 1929
KS*	Edinburgh	Roxburgh
KT	Maidstone	Kent 1913
KU	Sheffield	Bradford 1922
KV	Coventry 1931	
KW	Sheffield	Bradford 1926

KX	Luton	Buckinghamshire 1928
KY	Sheffield	Bradford 1931
L*		Glamorganshire
LA	London NW	London 1910
LB	London NW	London 1908
LC*	London NW	London
LD	London NW	London 1909
LE	London NW	London 1911
LF	London NW	London 1912
LG	Chester	Cheshire 1928
LH	London NW	London 1913
LI*		County Westmeath
LJ	Bournemouth 1929	
LK	London NW	London 1913
LL	London NW	London 1914
LM	London NW	London 1914
LN	London NW	London 1906
LO	London NW	London 1915
LP	London NW	London 1915
LR	London NW	London 1916
LS	Edinburgh	Selkirk 1923
LT	London NW	London 1918
LU	London NW	London 1919
LV	Liverpool 1932	
LW, LX, LY	London NW	London 1919
M		Cheshire
MA, MB	Chester	Cheshire
MC	London NE	Middlesex 1917
MD	London NE	Middlesex 1920
ME	London NE	Middlesex 1921
MF	London NE	Middlesex 1923
MG	London NE	Middlesex 1924
MH*	London NE	Middlesex
MI		County Wexford 1930
MJ	Luton	Bedfordshire 1932
MK	London NE	Middlesex 1925
ML, MM	London NE	Middlesex 1926
MN	not used	
MO	Reading	Berkshire 1922
MP	London NE	Middlesex 1927

MR	Swindon	Wiltshire 1924
MS*	Edinburgh	Stirling
MT, MU	London NE	Middlesex 1928–29
MV	London SE	Middlesex 1931
MW	Swindon	Wiltshire 1927
MX	London SE	Middlesex 1912
MY	London SE	Middlesex 1929
N*		Manchester
NA	Manchester 1913	
NB	Manchester 1919	
NC	Manchester 1920	
ND	Manchester 1923	
NE	Manchester 1925	
NF	Manchester 1926	
NG	Norwich	Norfolk 1930
NH*	Northampton	
NI*		County Wicklow
NJ	Brighton	East Sussex 1932
NK	Luton	Hertfordshire 1919
NL	Newcastle upon Tyne	Northumberland 1921
NM	Luton	Bedfordshire 1921
NN	Nottingham	Nottinghamshire 1921
NO	Chelmsford	Essex 1921
NP	Worcester	Worcestershire 1921
NR*	Leicester	Leicestershire 1921
NS	Glasgow	Sutherland
NT	Shrewsbury	Shropshire 1921
NU	Nottingham	Derbyshire 1923
NV	Northampton	Northamptonshire 1931
NW	Leeds 1921	
NX	Dudley	Warwickshire 1921
NY	Cardiff	Glamorganshire 1921
O*		Birmingham
OA	Birmingham 1913	
OB	Birmingham 1915	
OC	Birmingham 1933	
OD	Exeter	Devon 1931
OE	Birmingham 1919	
OF	Birmingham 1929	
OG	Birmingham 1930	

OH	Birmingham 1920	
OI*		Belfast
OJ	Birmingham 1932	
OK	Birmingham 1922	
OL	Birmingham 1923	
OM	Birmingham 1924	
ON	Birmingham 1925	
OO	Chelmsford	
OP	Birmingham 1926	
OR	Portsmouth	Southampton (County) 1922
OS	Glasgow	Wigtown 1921
OT	Portsmouth	Southampton (County) 1926
OU	Bristol	Southampton (County) 1928
OV	Birmingham 1931	
OW	Portsmouth	Southampton 1931
OX	Birmingham 1927	
OY	London NW	Croydon 1931
P*		Surrey
PA	Guildford	Surrey 1913
PB	Guildford	Surrey 1919
PC	Guildford	Surrey 1921
PD	Guildford	Surrey 1923
PE	Guildford	Surrey 1925
PF	Guildford	Surrey 1926
PG	Guildford	Surrey 1929
PH	Guildford	Surrey 1927
PI*		Cork
PJ	Guildford	Surrey 1931
PK	Guildford	Surrey 1928
PL	Guildford	Surrey 1930
PM	Guildford	East Sussex 1922
PN	Brighton	East Sussex 1927
PO	Portsmouth	West Sussex 1929
PP	Luton	Buckinghamshire 1923
PR	Bournemouth	Dorset 1923
PS*	Aberdeen	Zetland (Shetland)
PT	Newcastle upon Tyne	County Durham 1922
PU	Chelmsford	Essex 1923
PV	Ipswich 1932	
PW	Norwich	Norfolk 1923

PX	Portsmouth	West Sussex 1923
PY	Middlesbrough	Yorkshire: North Riding 1923
R*		Derbyshire
RA	Nottingham	Derbyshire 1926
RB	Nottingham	Derbyshire 1929
RC	Nottingham	Derby 1931
RD	Reading 1928	
RE	Stoke-on-Trent	Staffordshire 1921
RF	Stoke-on-Trent	Staffordshire 1924
RG	Newcastle upon Tyne	Aberdeen (City) 1928
RH	Hull 1930	
RI*		Dublin
RJ	Manchester	Salford 1931
RK	London NW	Croydon
RL	Truro	Cornwall 1924
RM	Carlisle	Cumberland 1924
RN	Preston 1928	
RO	Luton	Hertfordshire 1925
RP	Northampton	Northamptonshire 1924
RR	Nottingham	Nottinghamshire 1925
RS*	Aberdeen	Aberdeen (City)
RT	Ipswich	East Suffolk 1925
RU	Bournemouth 1924	
RV	Portsmouth	Portsmouth 1930
RW	Coventry 1924	
RX	Reading	Berkshire 1927
RY	Leicester 1925	
S*		Edinburgh
SA*	Aberdeen	
SB*	Glasgow	Argyll
SC	Edinburgh 1927	
SCY		Scilly Isles (Truro)
SD	Glasgow	Ayr
SE*	Aberdeen	Banff
SF	Edinburgh 1924	
SG	Edinburgh 1918	
SH*	Edinburgh	Berwick
SJ*	Glasgow	Bute
SK*	Inverness	Caithness
SL*	Dundee	Clackmannan

SM*	Carlisle	Dumfries
SN*	Dundee	Dunbarton
SO*	Aberdeen	Moray
SP	Dundee	Fife
SR*	Dundee	Angus
SS*	Aberdeen	East Lothian
ST*	Inverness	
SU*	Glasgow	Kincardine
SV*	spare	Kinross
SW*	Carlisle	Kirkudbright
SX*	Edinburgh	West Lothian
SY*	spare	Midlothian
T		Devon
TA	Exeter	Devon
TB	Liverpool	Lancashire
TC	Bristol	Lancashire
TD, TE	Manchester	Lancashire
TE	Manchester	Lancashire 1927
TF	Reading	Lancashire 1929
TG	Cardiff	Glamorganshire 1930
TH	Swansea	Carmarthenshire 1929
TI*		Limerick
TJ	Liverpool	Lancashire 1932
TK	Exeter	Dorset 1927
TL	Lincoln	Lincolnshire: Parts of Kesteven 1928
TM	Luton	Bedfordshire 1927
TN	Newcastle upon Tyne 1925	
TO	Nottingham 1924	
TP	Portsmouth 1924	
TR	Portsmouth	Southampton 1925
TS*	Dundee	
TT	Exeter	Devon
TU	Chester	Cheshire 1925
TV	Nottingham 1929	
TW	Chelmsford	Essex 1925
TX	Cardiff	Glamorganshire 1926
TY	Newcastle upon Tyne	Northumberland 1925
U*		Leeds
UA	Leeds 1927	
UB	Leeds 1929	

UC	London C	London 1928
UD	Oxford	Oxfordshire 1926
UE	Dudley	Warwickshire 1925
UF	Brighton 1925	
UG	Leeds 1923	
UH	Cardiff 1925	
UI*		Londonderry
UJ	Shrewsbury	Shropshire 1932
UK	Birmingham	Wolverhampton 1925
UL	London C	London 1929
UM	Leeds 1925	
UN	Exeter	Denbighshire 1927
UO	Exeter	Devon 1926
UP	Newcastle upon Tyne	County Durham 1927
UR	Luton	Hertfordshire 1928
US	Glasgow 1933	
UT	Leicester 1927	
UU, UV,		
UW	London C	London 1929
UX	Shrewsbury	Shropshire 1927
UY	Worcester	Worcestershire 1927
V*		Lanark
VA	Peterborough	Lanark 1923
VB	Maidstone	Croydon 1927
VC	Coventry 1929	
VD	series withdrawn	Lanark 1933
VE	Peterborough	Cambridgeshire 1928
VF	Norwich	Norfolk 1927
VG	Norwich 1927	
VH	Huddersfield 1927	
VJ	Gloucester	Herefordshire 1927
VK	Newcastle upon Tyne 1929	
VL	Lincoln 1928	
VM	Manchester 1928	
VN	Middlesbrough	Yorkshire: North Riding 1929
VO	Nottingham	Nottinghamshire 1928
VP	Birmingham 1928	
VR	Manchester 1929	
VS*	Luton	Greenock
VT	Stoke-on-Trent 1927	

VU	Manchester 1930	
VV	Northampton 1930	
VW	Chelmsford	Essex 1927
VX	Chelmsford	Essex 1929
VY	Leeds	York 1928
W*		Sheffield
WA	Sheffield 1919	
WB	Sheffield 1924	
WC	Chelmsford	
WD	Dudley	Warwickshire 1930
WE	Sheffield 1927	
WF	Sheffield	Yorkshire: East Riding 1926
WG	Sheffield	Stirling 1930
WH	Manchester	Bolton 1927
WJ	Sheffield 1930	
WK	Coventry 1926	
WL	Oxford 1925	
WM	Liverpool	Southport 1927
WN	Swansea 1927	
WO	Cardiff	Monmouthshire 1927
WP	Worcester	Worcestershire 1931
WR	Leeds	Yorkshire: West Riding 1915
WS*	Bristol	
WS1– WS500	Leith	
WS 501–	Edinburgh 1934	
WT	Leeds	Yorkshire: West Riding 1923
WU	Leeds	Yorkshire: West Riding 1925
WV	Brighton	Wiltshire 1931
WW	Leeds	Yorkshire: West Riding 1927
WX	Leeds	Yorkshire: West Riding 1929
WY	Leeds	Yorkshire: West Riding 1921
X*		Northumberland
XA, XB, XC, XD, XE	spare	London 1920
XF	spare	London 1921
XG	spare	Middlesbrough 1930
XH	spare	London 1921
XI		Belfast 1921
XJ	spare	Manchester 1932
XK, XL,		

XM	spare	London 1922
XN, XO, XP	spare	London 1923
XR	spare	London 1924
XS*	spare	Paisley
XT, XU	spare	London 1924
XV	spare	London 1928
XW	spare	London 1924
XX, XY	spare	London 1925
Y*		Somerset
YA, YB, YC, YD	Taunton	Somerset 1921
YB	Taunton	Somerset 1924
YC	Taunton	Somerset 1927
YD	Taunton	Somerset 1930
YE, YF	London C	London 1927
YG	Leeds	Yorkshire: West Riding 1932
YH	London C	London 1927
YI		Dublin 1921
YJ	Brighton	Dundee 1932
YK, YL, YM	London C	London 1925
YN, YO, YP, YR	London C	London 1926
YS	Glasgow 1935	
YT, YU	London C	London 1927
YV, YW, YX	London C	London 1928
YY	London C	London 1932
Z		Dublin County 1927
ZA		Dublin 1933
ZB		Cork 1935
ZC		Dublin 1937
ZD		Dublin 1940
ZI		Dublin 1927
ZZ		Dublin & the Council of any County which adjoins Northern Ireland

14.1.2b Vehicle registration & licensing – by location

INDEX MARKS	CENTRE
BS, PS, RS, SA, SE, SO, SS	Aberdeen
CC, EY, FF, JC	Bangor
DA, JW, OA, OB, OC, OE, OF, OG, OH, OJ, OK, OL, OM, ON, OP, OV, OX, UK, VP	Birmingham
AA, CG, EL, FX, HO. JT, LJ, PR, RU	Bournemouth
AP, CD, DY, FG, HC, JK, NJ, PN, UF, WV, YJ	Brighton
AE, EU, FB, HT, HU, HW, HY, OU, TC, WS	Bristol
AX, BO, DW, HB, KG, NY, TG, TX, UH, WO	Cardiff
AO, HH, RM, SM, SW	Carlisle
AR, EV, HJ, HK, JN, NO, OO, PU, TW, VW, VX, WC	Chelmsford
CA, DM, FM, LG, MA, MB, TU	Chester
AC, DU, HP, KV, RW, VC, WK	Coventry
DH, EA, FD, FK, HA, NX, UE, WD	Dudley
ES, SL, SN, SP, SR, TS	Dundee
FS, KS, LS, MS, SC, SF, SG, SH, SX	Edinburgh
CO, DR, DV, FJ, JY, OD, TA, TK, TT, UN, UO	Exeter
CS, DS, GA, GB, GD, GE, GG, HS, NS, OS, SB, SD, SJ, SU, US, YS	Glasgow
AD, CJ, DD, DF, DG. FH, FO, VJ	Gloucester
PA, PB, PC, PD, PE, PF, PG, PH, PJ, PK, PL, PM	Guildford
BX, DE, EJ	Haverfordwest
CP, CX, HD, JX, VH	Huddersfield
AG, AT, KH, RH	Hull
AS, JS, SK, ST	Inverness
BJ, DX, GV, PV, RT	Ipswich
BT, DN, NW, UA, UB, UG, UM, VY, WR, WT, WU, WW, WX, WY, YG	Leeds
AY, BC, FP, JF, JU, NR, RY, UT	Leicester
BE, CT, DO, EE, FE, FU, FW, JL, JV, TL, VL	Lincoln
BG, CM, DJ, ED, EK, EM, FY, HF, JP, KA, KB, KC, KD, KF, LV, TB, TJ, WM	Liverpool
HM, HV, HX, JD, UC, UL, UU, UV, UW, YE, YF, YH, YK, YL, YM, YN, YO, YP, YR, YT, YU, YV, YW, YX, YY	London C
MC, MD, ME, MF, MG, MH, MK, ML, MM, MP, MT, MU	London NE

BY, LA, LB, LC, LD, LE, LF, LH, LK, LL, LM, LN, LO, LP, LR, LT, LU, LW, LX, LY, OY, RK	London NW
GU, GW, GX, GY, MV, MX, MY, GC, GF, GH, GJ, GK, GN, GO, GP, GT	London SE
BH, BM, GS, KX, NK, NM, PP, RO, TM, UR, VS	Luton
FN, JG, JJ, KE, KJ, KK, KL, KM, KN, KO, KP, KR, KT, VB	Maidstone
BA, BN, BU, CB, DB, DK, EN, JA, NA, NB, NC, ND, NE, NF, RJ, TD, TE, VM, VR, VU, WH	Manchester
AJ, DC, EF, HN, PY, VN	Middlesbrough
BB, BR, CN, CU, FT, GR, JR, NL, PT, RG, TN, TY, UP, VK	Newcastle upon Tyne
BD, NH, NV, RP, VV	Northampton
AH, CL, EX, NG, PW, VF, VG	Norwich
AL, AU, CH, NN, NU, RA, RB, RC, RR, TO, TV, VO	Nottingham
BW, FC, JO, UD, WL	Oxford
AV, CE, EB, EG, ER, EW, FL, JE, VA, VE	Peterborough
BK, BP, CR. DL, OR, OT, OW, PO, PX, RV, TP, TR	Portsmouth
BV, CK, CW, EC, EO, FR, FV, HG, RN	Preston
AN, BL, CF, DP, GM, JB, JH, JM, MO, RD, RX, TF	Reading
AK, DT, ET, HE, HL, KU, KW, KY, WA, WB, WE, WF, WG, WJ	Sheffield
AW, NT, UJ, UX	Shrewsbury
BF, EH, FA, RE, RF, VT	Stoke-on-Trent
CY, EP, TH, WN	Swansea
AM, HR, MR, MW	Swindon
YA, YB, YC, YD	Taunton
AF, CV, GL, RL	Truro
AB, NP, UY, WP	Worcester

14.1.3   International vehicle identification

By country

AFG	Afghanistan	A	Austria
AL	Albania	BS	Bahamas
GBA	Alderney	BRN	Bahrain
DZ	Algeria	BD	Bangladesh
AND	Andorra	BDS	Barbados
RA	Argentina	B	Belgium
AUS	Australia	BH	Belize
		DY	Benin

RB	Botswana		**HK**	Hong Kong
BR	Brazil		**H**	Hungary
BRU	Brunei		**IS**	Iceland
BG	Bulgaria		**IND**	India
RU	Burundi		**RI**	Indonesia
BUR	Burma		**IR**	Iran
K	Cambodia		**IRQ**	Iraq
CDN	Canada		**IRL**	Ireland
RCA	Central African Republic		**GBM**	Isle of Man
RCH	Chile		**IL**	Israel
CO	Colombia		**I**	Italy
RCB	Congo		**JA**	Jamaica
CR	Costa Rica		**J**	Japan
CI	Côte d'Ivoire		**GBJ**	Jersey
C	Cuba		**HKJ**	Jordan (*Hashemite Kingdom of*)
CY	Cyprus		**EAK**	Kenya
CS	Czech Republic		**ROK**	Korea (*Republic of*)
DK	Denmark		**KWT**	Kuwait
WD	Dominica		**LAO**	Laos
DOM	Dominican Republic		**LV**	Latvia
EC	Ecuador		**RL**	Lebanon
ET	Egypt		**LS**	Lesotho
ES	El Salvador		**LB**	Liberia
EW	Estonia		**LAR**	Libya
ETH	Ethiopia		**FL**	Liechtenstein
FR	Faroe Islands		**LT**	Lithuania
FJI	Fiji		**L**	Luxembourg
FIN	Finland		**RM**	Madagascar (*Republic of Malagasy*)
F	France			
WAG	Gambia		**MW**	Malawi
D	Germany		**MAL**	Malaysia
GH	Ghana		**RMM**	Mali
GBZ	Gibraltar		**M**	Malta
GB	Great Britain		**RIM**	Mauritania
GR	Greece		**MS**	Mauritius
WG	Grenada		**MEX**	Mexico
GCA	Guatemala		**MC**	Monaco
GBG	Guernsey		**MA**	Morocco
GUY	Guyana		**SWA**	Namibia (*South-West Africa*)
RH	Haiti		**NL**	Netherlands

NA	Netherlands Antilles	**TR**	Turkey
NZ	New Zealand	**EAU**	Uganda
NIC	Nicaragua	**USA**	United States of America
RN	Niger	**ROU**	Uruguay
WAN	Nigeria	**V**	Vatican City
N	Norway	**YV**	Venezuela
PK	Pakistan	**VN**	Vietnam
PA	Panama	**WS**	Western Samoa
PNG	Papua New Guinea	**ADN**	Yemen
PY	Paraguay	**YU**	Yugoslavia
PE	Peru	**ZRE**	Zaire
RP	Philippines	**Z**	Zambia
PL	Poland	**ZW**	Zimbabwe
P	Portugal		
RO	Romania		
RUS	Russia		*By code*
RWA	Rwanda	**A**	Austria
RSM	San Marino	**ADN**	Yemen
SN	Senegal	**AFG**	Afghanistan
SY	Seychelles	**AL**	Albania
WAL	Sierra Leone	**AND**	Andorra
SGP	Singapore	**AUS**	Australia
ZA	South Africa	**B**	Belgium
E	Spain	**BD**	Bangladesh
CL	Sri Lanka	**BDS**	Barbados
WL	St Lucia	**BG**	Bulgaria
WV	St Vincent & the Grenadines	**BH**	Belize
SME	Suriname	**BR**	Brazil
SD	Swaziland	**BRN**	Bahrain
S	Sweden	**BRU**	Brunei
CH	Switzerland	**BS**	Bahamas
CS	Slovakia	**BUR**	Burma
SYR	Syria	**C**	Cuba
RC	Taiwan	**CDN**	Canada
EAT	Tanzania	**CH**	Switzerland
EAZ	Tanzania (*Zanzibar*)	**CI**	Côte d'Ivoire
T	Thailand	**CL**	Sri Lanka
TG	Togo	**CO**	Colombia
TT	Trinidad & Tobago	**CR**	Costa Rica
TN	Tunisia	**CS**	Czech Republic
		CS	Slovakia

CY	Cyprus	IS	Iceland
D	Germany	J	Japan
DK	Denmark	JA	Jamaica
DOM	Dominican Republic	K	Cambodia
DY	Benin	KWT	Kuwait
DZ	Algeria	L	Luxembourg
E	Spain	LAO	Laos
EAK	Kenya	LAR	Libya
EAT	Tanzania	LB	Liberia
EAZ	Tanzania (*Zanzibar*)	LS	Lesotho
EAU	Uganda	LT	Lithuania
EC	Ecuador	LV	Latvia
ES	El Salvador	M	Malta
ET	Egypt	MA	Morocco
ETH	Ethiopia	MAL	Malaysia
EW	Estonia	MC	Monaco
F	France	MEX	Mexico
FIN	Finland	MS	Mauritius
FJI	Fiji	MW	Malawi
FL	Liechtenstein	N	Norway
FR	Faroe Islands	NA	Netherlands Antilles
GB	Great Britain	NIC	Nicaragua
GBA	Alderney	NL	Netherlands
GBG	Guernsey	NZ	New Zealand
GBJ	Jersey	P	Portugal
GBM	Isle of Man	PA	Panama
GBZ	Gibraltar	PE	Peru
GCA	Guatemala	PK	Pakistan
GH	Ghana	PL	Poland
GR	Greece	PNG	Papua New Guinea
GUY	Guyana	PY	Paraguay
H	Hungary	RA	Argentina
HK	Hong Kong	RB	Botswana
HKJ	Jordan (*Hashemite Kingdom of*)	RC	Taiwan
I	Italy	RCA	Central African Republic
IL	Israel	RCB	Congo
IND	India	RCH	Chile
IR	Iran	RH	Haiti
IRL	Ireland	RI	Indonesia
IRQ	Iraq	RIM	Mauritania

RL	Lebanon	TG	Togo
RM	Madagascar (*Republic of Malagasy*)	TN	Tunisia
		TR	Turkey
RMM	Mali	TT	Trinidad & Tobago
RN	Niger	USA	United States of America
RO	Romania	V	Vatican City
ROK	Korea (*Republic of*)	VN	Vietnam
ROU	Uruguay	WAG	Gambia
RP	Philippines	WAL	Sierra Leone
RSM	San Marino	WAN	Nigeria
RU	Burundi	WD	Dominica
RUS	Russia	WG	Grenada
RWA	Rwanda	WL	St Lucia
S	Sweden	WS	Western Samoa
SD	Swaziland	WV	St Vincent & the Grenadines
SGP	Singapore	YU	Yugoslavia
SME	Suriname	YV	Venezuela
SN	Senegal	Z	Zambia
SWA	Namibia (*South-West Africa*)	ZA	South Africa
SY	Seychelles	ZRE	Zaire
SYR	Syria	ZW	Zimbabwe
T	Thailand		

14.1.4   Car franchise codes

Alf	Alfa Romeo	Lan	Lancia
Ast	Aston Martin	Lot	Lotus
Bit	Bitter	LR	Land Rover
Bri	Bristol	Maz	Mazda
Cit	Citroen	Mer	Mercedes-Benz
Dai	Daihatsu	Mit	Mitsubishi
DJ	Daimler; Jaguar	Mor	Morgan
Fer	Ferrari	Nis	Nissan
Fia	Fiat	Ope	Opel
For	Ford	Peu	Peugeot
Hon	Honda	Por	Porsche
Hyu	Hyundai	Pro	Proton
Isu	Isuzu	Ran	Range Rover
Lad	Lada	Rel	Reliant

Ren	Renault		Suz	Suzuki
Rov	Rover Group		Tal	Talbot
RR	Rolls Royce; Bentley		Toy	Toyota
SAA	Saab		Vau	Vauxhall
Sea	SEAT		Vol	Volvo
Sko	Skoda		VW	Volkswagen
Sub	Subaru		Yug	Yugo

14.1.5　　Motorcycle franchise codes

Ben	Benelli		Lam	Lambretta
Bet	Beta		Mor	Morini
Bim	Bimota		Mot	Moto Guzzi
Cag	Cagiva		Nev	Neval
Duc	Ducati		Puc	Puch
Enf	Enfield		Sco	Scott
Har	Harley Davidson		Suz	Suzuki
Hon	Honda		Tri	Triumph
Jaw	Jawa		Ves	Vespa
Kaw	Kawasaki		Yam	Yamaha

14.2.1　　Older British railway companies

A & NJR Ashby & Nuneaton Joint Railway (*LNW & Midland*)

ADR, ANSWDRC Alexandra (*Newport & South Wales*) Docks & Railway Company

AJR Axholme Joint Railway

B & LJR Bourne & Lynn Joint Railway

BACLR Bere Alston & Calstock Light Railway

BCR Bishop's Castle Railway

BDR Barry Dock & Railways

BER Bristol & Exeter Railway

BGR Birmingham & Gloucester Railway

BJ GWR & LNWR (*later GWR & LMSR Joint*)

BJS Bristol Joint Station (*GWR + LMS*)

BLR Brackenhill Light Railway

BM & LNWJ Brecon & Merthyr & LNW Joint

BMR Brecon & Merthyr Railway

BPR, BP &

GVR Burry Port Gwendraeth Valley Railway

BR British Rail(ways)

BRB British Railways Board

BRYR Barry Railway

BTC British Transport Commission

BWHA Bideford, Westward Ho! & Appledore Railway

BWR Bodmin & Wadebridge Railway

C & OJ Croydon & Oxted Joint Railway (*LBSCR + SECR*)

Cal R Caledonian Railway

Cam R Cambrian Railways

Car R Cardiff Railway

CCR Chester & Crewe Railway

CCSJC Carlisle Citadel Station Joint Committee

CER Clifton Extension Railway (*GW + Midland*)

CER Central Electric Railway

CFDR Central Forest of Dean Railway

CGUR City of Glasgow Union Railway

CK & PR Cockermouth Keswick & Penrith Railway

CLC Cheshire Lines Committee (*GC + GN + Midland*)

CMDPLR Cleobury Mortimer & Ditton Priors Light Railway

CMLR Campbeltown & Macrihanish Light Railway

Corris R Corris Railway

CVR Colne Valley Railway

CWJR Cleator & Workington Junction Railway

D & AJR Dundee & Arbroath Joint Railway (*NBR + Cal*)

Dist Metropolitan District Railway

DJC (Carlisle) Dentonholme Joint Committee (*G&SW + Midland + NB*)

DVLR Derwent Valley Light Railway

DVR Dearne Valley Railway

E Lincs R East Lincolnshire Railway

Eas Easingwold Railway

ECHR Easton & Church Hope Railway

ECJS East Coast Joint Stock

EGR Edinburgh & Glasgow Railway

EKR East Kent Railway

EKR East Kent Railway

ELR East London Railway (*GE + LB&SC + Met + Met Dist + SE&C*)

ELR East London Railway

EMR Eastern & Midlands Railway

EWJR East & West Junction Railway

EWYUR East & West Yorkshire Union Railway

F & MJR Furness & Midland Joint Railway

FBR Forth Bridge Railway

FDR Forest of Dean Railway

Fest, FR Festiniog Railway

FP & WRJR Fleetwood Preston & West Riding Junction Railway

FR Furness Railway(s)

FRRH Fishguard & Rosslare Railways & Harbours

FYNR Freshwater, Yarmouth & Newport Railway

G&PJR Glasgow & Paisley Joint Railway (*Cal + G&SW*)

GB & KJR Glasgow, Barrhead & Kilmarnock Joint Railway (*GSWR + Cal*)

GC & LNWJ Great Central & London & North Western Joint Railway

GC & MJ Great Central & Midland Joint Line

GCR Great Central Railway

GER Great Eastern Railway

GER & Mid Great Eastern & Midland Railway

GFE Grunty Fen Express (*GER*)

GJR Grand Junction Railway

GKER Garstang & Knott End Railway

GLR Garston & Liverpool Railway

GN & GC Great Northern & Great Central Joint Railway

GN & LNWR Great Northern & London & North Western Joint Lines

GN & LYJ Great Northern & Lancashire & Yorkshire Joint Railways

GNR Great Northern Railway

GNSR Great North of Scotland Railway

GSWR Glasgow & South Western Railway

GTC (Carlisle) Goods Traffic Committee (*Cal + G&SW + L&NW + Midland*)

GVR Gwendraeth Valley Railway

GVT Glyn Valley Tramway

GW & LNE J Great Western & London & North Eastern Joint Railway

GW & LSWR Great Western & London & South Western Joint Railway

GW & Met Great Western & Metropolitan Joint Committee

GW & RR Great Western & Rhymney Joint Railway

GWR Great Western Railway

GWR & GCR Great Western & Great Central Joint Committee

GWR & LMS Great Western Railway & London Midland & Scottish Railway (*several lines operated jointly*)

GWR & Mid J Great Western & Midland Railways

H&C Hammersmith & City (*GW + Met*)

H&O Halifax & Ovenden Joint (*GN + LYR*)

HB&GCJ Hull & Barnsley & Great Central Joint Committee

HBGC & MJC Hull & Barnsley, Great Central & Midland Joint Committee

HBR Hoylake & Birkenhead Railway

HBR Hull & Barnsley Railway

HCR Hammersmith & City Railway (*Met + GWR*)

HHL Halifax High Level (*GN + LYR*)

HJR Halesowen Joint Railway

HR Highland Railway

IMR Isle of Man Railway

IWCR Isle of Wight Central Railway

IWR Isle of Wight Railway

K&BJR Kilsyth & Bonnybridge Joint Railway (*Cal + HBR*)

KER Knott End Railway

KER Kington & Eardisley Railway

KESR Kent & East Sussex Railway

KWR Kendal & Windermere Railway

LBR Lynton & Barnstaple Railway

LBR Leicester & Birmingham Railway

LBR London & Birmingham Railway

LBSCR London Brighton & South Coast Railway

LC&DR London, Chatham & Dover Railway (*when Lucy Caine (Hall Caine's sister) accompanied Dante Gabriel Rossetti to the South Coast by train, he teased her that their initials were interwoven on the carpet*)

LCR Lancaster & Carlisle Railway

LCR Liskeard & Caradon Railway

LDECR Lancashire Derbyshire & East Coast Railway

LEGR Lewes & East Grinstead Railway

LER London Electric Railway

LHL Leeds High Level

LKR Leominster & Kington Railway

LLR Liskeard & Looe Railway

LMR Llanelli & Mynydd Mawr Railway

LMS & LNER London Midland & Scottish and London & North Eastern Joint Railway

LMS (or LMSR) London Midland & Scottish Railway

LMSR (NCC) London Midland & Scottish Northern Counties Committee

LNER London & North Eastern Railway

LNWR London & North Western Railway

LNWR & Cal London & North Western & Caledonian Joint

LNWR & FR London & North Western and Furness Railway Joint Lines

LNWR & GWR London & North Western & Great Western Joint Railway

LNWR & LYR London & North Western and Lancashire & Yorkshire Joint Lines

LNWR & NER London & North Western and North Eastern Railway Joint Lines

LOR Liverpool Overhead Railway (*The Dockers' Umbrella*)

LSWR London & South Western Railway

LTSR London Tilbury & Southend Railway

LUR Lancashire Union Railway (*LNWR + LYR*)

LYR Lancashire & Yorkshire Railway

LYR & GNR Lancashire & Yorkshire and Great Northern Railway Cos

M & GNJR Midland & Great Northern Joint Railway

M & SWJR Midland & South Western Junction Railway

Macc Comm Macclesfield Committee (*renamed from Macclesfield Bollington & Marple Railway*)

Mawd Mawddwy Light (*Cambrian*)

MCR Maryport & Carlisle Railway

MCR Midland Counties Railway

MDHB Mersey Docks & Harbour Board

MER Manx Electric Railway

Met Metropolitan Railway

Met & GCJC Metropolitan & Great Central Joint Committee

Met & LNE Metropolitan and London & North Eastern Joint

Met R Metropolitan Railway

MGNJR Midland & Great Northern Joint Railway

MGWR Midland Great Western Railway (*Ireland*)

Mid & LNWR Midland and London & North Western Railway Joint Lines

Mid & NER Midland & North Eastern Railway Co

Mid R Midland Railway

MJC Methley Joint Committee (*LYR + NER + GNR*)

MMR Manchester & Milford Railway

Monk R Monkland Railways

MR Mersey Railway

MRC Co Monmouth Railway & Canal Co

MSCR Manchester Ship Canal Railways

MSJAR Manchester South Junction & Altrincham Railway (*GC + LNWR*)

MSLR Manchester, Sheffield & Lincolnshire Railway

MSLR Mid-Suffolk Light Railway

Mum Swansea & Mumbles Railway

MWR Mid-Wales Railway

N & BR Neath & Brecon Railway

NBJR Northampton & Banbury Junction Railway

NBR North British Railway

NCR Newcastle & Carlisle Railway

NCR Northern Counties Railway

NDCJLR North Devon & Cornwall Junction Light Railway

NER North Eastern Railway

NLLR North Lindsey Light Railway

NLR North London Railway

NNSTR Newcastle North Shields & Tynemouth Railway

NPF North Pembroke & Fishguard Railway

NSJC Norfolk & Suffolk Joint Committee (*GER + M&GNR*)

NSLR North Sunderland Light Railway

NSR North Staffordshire Railway

NUJ North Union Joint Railway (*LNWR + LYR*)

NV Nidd Valley Railway

NWNGR North Wales Narrow Gauge Railway

NYMR North Yorkshire Moors Railway

O&IJR Otley & Ilkley Joint Railway

OAGBR Oldham, Ashton & Guide Bridge Railway (*GC + LNWJ*)

OAT Oxford & Aylesbury Tramroad (*Met + GCJ*)

OWWR Oxford Worcester & Wolverhampton Railway

P & LJR Preston & Longbridge Joint Railway (*LNWR + LYR*)

P & WJR Portpatrick & Wigtown Joint Railway (*Cal + GCWR + Mid + LNWR*)

PBHR Paisley Barrhead & Hurlet Railway

PCBR Portmadoc, Croesor & Beddgelert Railway

PCNR Pontypridd Caerphilly & Newport Railway

PDJR Princes Dock Joint Railway (*Cal + G&SW + NB*)

PDSWJR Plymouth Devonport & South Western Junction Railway

PJ Penrith Joint Station

PLA Port of London Authority

PR Peebles Railway

PTRD Co Port Talbot Railway & Docks Co

PWR Preston & Wyre Railway (*LNWR + LYR*)

QYMJR Quaker's Yard & Merthyr Joint Railway (*GW + Rhymney*)

R & LNW Rhymney & LNW Joint

RCT Rye & Camber Tramway

RHDR Romney, Hythe & Dymchurch Railway

RKFR Rowrah & Kelton Fell Railway

RR Rhymney Railway

RSBR Rhondda & Swansea Bay Railway

S & WJR Severn & Wye Joint Railway (*GWR + LMS*)

SDJC Somerset & Dorset Joint Line Committee

SDR Snailbeach District Railways

SDR South Devon Railway

SDR Stockton & Darlington Railway

SDR Sheffield District Railway (*GC + Midland*)

SECR South Eastern & Chatham Management Committee

SER South Eastern Railway

SHDR Seacombe Hoylake & Deeside Railway

SHR Shrewsbury & Hereford Railway

SJS Stalybridge Joint Station

SKR Swinton & Knottingley Railway (*Midland + NE*)

SMJC Sheffield & Midland Joint Committee

SMJR Stratford-upon-Avon and Midland Junction Railway

SMR Snowdon Mountain Railway

SMR Shropshire & Montgomery Railway

SR Southern Railway

SR & LMS Southern Railway and London Midland & Scottish Joint Railway

SSR Sittingbourne & Sheerness Railway

SSR South Staffordshire Railway

ST Selsey Tramways

St HCR Co St Helens Canal & Railway Co

SUR Stafford & Uttoxeter Railway

SURCC Shropshire Union Railways & Canal Co

SWJR Severn & Wye Joint Railway (*GW + Midland*)

SWJR Shrewsbury & Welshpool Joint Railway (*GW + L&NW*)

SWMR South Wales Minerals Railway

SWR Southwold Railway

SYJL South Yorkshire Joint Line Committee (*GCR, GNR, LYR, Mid & NER*)

TalR Talyllyn Railway

TBJ Taff Bargoed Joint Railway (*GWR + RR*)

TFGR Tottenham & Forest Gate Railway (*LTS + Midland*)

THJR Tottenham & Hampstead Junction Railway (*GER + Mid*)

TRE The Railway Executive

TVLR Tanat Valley Light Railway (*Cambrian*)

TVR Taff Vale Railway

TWT Thetford & Watton Tramway

VLR Van Light Railway (*Cambrian*)

VOTR Vale of Towy Railway (*LNWR + GWR Joint*)

VRR Vale of Rheidol Railway

W & PJ Weymouth & Portland Joint Railway (*GW + LSWR*)

W&LLR Welshpool & Llanfair Light Railway (*Cambrian*)

W&MJR Wrexham & Minera Joint Railway (*GW + L&NW*)

WBJR Whitechapel & Bow Joint Railway (*LTS + Met Dist*)

WCEJR Whitehaven, Cleator & Egremont Joint Railway (*Furness + L&NW*)

WCJC Wath Curve Joint Committee (*GC = Midland + NE*)

WCJS West Coast Joint Stock

WCP Weston, Clevedon & Portishead Railway

WCR West Cornwall Railway

WJC Watford Joint Committee

WJPS Wakefield Joint Passenger Station

WLEJR West London Extension Joint Railway (*GW + L&NW + LB&SC + L&SW*)

WLJ West London Joint (*LNWR + GWR*)

WLR West Lancashire Railway

WMCQR Wrexham Mold & Connah's Quay Railway

WMR West Midland Railway

WR Wirral Railway

WRGJC West Riding & Grimsby Joint Committee (*GN + GC*)

WSCR Woodside & South Croydon Railway (*LB&SC + SE&C*)

WSMR West Somerset Minerals Railway

WT Wantage Tramway

WUT Wisbech & Upwell Tramway

WVR Wye Valley Railway

YNR York & Newcastle Railway

14.2.2   Train Operating Companies

AR Anglia Railways Train Services Ltd

CRC Cardiff Railway Company Ltd

CSC Connex South Central Ltd

CSE Connex South Eastern Ltd

CT Central Trains Ltd

CT The Chiltern Railway Co Ltd

CTR2 Channel Tunnel Route 2 (*via Sevenoaks*)

CTR3 Channel Tunnel Route 3 (*via Redhill*)

Eurostar Eurostar (UK) Ltd

EWS, EW&S English, Welsh & Scottish Railway Ltd

Freightliner Freightliner Ltd

GE Gatwick Express Ltd

GER Great Eastern Railway Ltd

GNER Great North Eastern Railway Ltd

GNRTS Greater Nottingham Rapid Transit System

GWT Great Western Trains Co Ltd

LTS Rail LTS Rail Ltd

LUL London Underground Ltd

ME Merseyrail Electrics Ltd

MML Midland Main Line Ltd

NLL North London Line

NLR North London Railways Ltd

NWRR North West Regional Railways Ltd

RfD Railfreight Distribution Ltd

RRNE Regional Railways North East Ltd

RRNE Regional Railways North East

ScotRail ScotRail Railways Ltd

SHRT South Hampshire Rapid Transit

SW&W South West & West Railways Ltd

SWIFT South Wales Integrated Fast Transit

SWT South West Trains Ltd

TLR Thameslink Rail Ltd

VCC Virgin Cross Country Trains Ltd

WAGN West Anglia Great Northern Railway Ltd

WCL InterCity West Coast Ltd

AHB Automatic Half Barrier

AMP Asset Maintenance Plan

APT Advanced Passenger Train

ATP Automatic Train Protection

AWG Adhesion Working Group

BAA British Airports Authority

BR British Rail

BRB British Railways Board

BRR British Rail Research

BRV Brake Release Valve

CCTV Closed Circuit Television

Cge Carriage

CPR Canadian Pacific Railway

CRA Critical Resource Agency

CRID Current Rail Indicator Device (*Safety on the Track – 'juice-box'*)

CSR Cab Secure Radio

CWR Continuous Welded Rail

DART Dublin Area Rapid Transport

DART Digital Advanced Radio for Trains

DIRFT Daventry International Rail Freight Terminal

DIRT Daventry International Rail Terminal

DMU Diesel Multiple Unit

DOO Driver-Only Operation

EC European Community

ECC Engineering Control Centre

ECML East Coast Main Line (*King's Cross-Inverness*)

ECS Empty Coaching/Carriage Stock

EI Elevated Railway

EMU Electrical Multiple Unit

EPS Eurostar Passenger Services

ERTMS European Rail Traffic Management System

ESR Emergency Speed Restrictions

Eurailpass European Railway Passenger Ticket

EWC Engineering Works Controller

FFG Freight Facilities Grant

FOC Freight Operating Company

FTA Freight Transport Association

GB Great Britain

GE Great Eastern

GWML Great Western Main Line

H&C Hammersmith & City

HEL Heathrow Express Link

HMRI Her Majesty's Railway Inspectorate

HST high-speed train

ICC integrated control centre

ICECR InterCity East Coast Railway

IECC integrated electronic control centre

IMC Infrastructure Maintenance Company

INLORS Inner London Orbital Route Strategy

KX King's Cross (*London railway terminus*)

L&CR London & Continental Railways

LMD Light Maintenance Depot

LRT Light Rail Transport

LTA London Transport Authority

M million

MCC Management Control Centre

NMC Network Management Centre

NMS Network Management Statement

NMS Network Management System

NRN National Radio Network

NSE Network South-East

OLE overhead line equipment

ORR Office of the Rail Regulator

OUSE outer, up, southbound, eastbound (*see* WIND)

PSB panel signal box

PSR permanent speed restriction

PTA Passenger Transport Authority

PTE Passenger Transport Executive

PTE Passenger Transport Executive

PUG passenger upgrade

R, R, Rly, Rwy, Ry railway

RA route availability

RAC Royal Automobile Club

RASB Rolling Stock Acceptance Board

RHA Road Haulage Association

RPL Rail Property Ltd

RTA Rapid Transit Authority

RTS rapid transit system

RUC Railway Users' Committee

RUCC Rail Users' Consumer Council

S car stop at end of line

S&T Signalling & Tele-communications (*Railway Department*)

SB signal box

SCD short-circuit device (*for switching off railway traction current in an emergency*)

SELLA Salisbury to Exeter Line Local Authorities

SICA Signalling Infrastructure Condition Assessment

SO Saturdays only

SOR Save Our Railways

SPAD signal passed at danger

SPIC site person in charge

SPT Strathclyde Passenger Transport

SRP Station Regeneration Program

SWISS South West Infrastructure and Signalling Strategy

SX Saturdays excepted

TBS transmission-based signalling (*now replaced by TCS*)

TCS train control system

TENs Trans-European Networks

TOC Train Operating Company

TPWS train protection warning system

TRP track replacement project

Ts terminus

TSR temporary speed restriction

TVG French HST

UIC Union Internationale Chemins de Fer (*French: International Union of Railways*)

UK United Kingdom

VDC volts direct current

VS-OE Venice Simplon Orient Express

WA West Anglia

WARM West Anglia Route Modernisation

WCML West Coast Main Line (*Euston–Glasgow*)

WDM wrong directional movement

WIND Westbound Inner Northbound Down (*Railway Line Designation – see* OUSE)

WYPTE West Yorkshire Passenger Transport Executive

14.3.1 International civil aircraft markings

AN	Nicaragua	N	USA
AP	Pakistan	OB	Peru
B	China or Taiwan	OD	Lebanon
CB	Bolivia	OE	Austria
CC	Chile	OH	Finland
CCCP	Soviet Union	OK	Czechoslovakia
CF	Canada	OO	Belgium
CR, CS	Portugal & Colonies	OY	Denmark
CU	Cuba	PH	Netherlands
CX	Uruguay	PI	Philippines
CZ	Principality of Monaco	PJ	Curaçao
D	Western Germany	PK	Indonesia
EC	Spain	PP, PT	Brazil
EI, EJ	Ireland	PZ	Surinam
EL	Liberia	RX	Panama
EP	Iran	SE	Sweden
ET	Ethiopia	SN	Sudan
F	France & French Union	SP	Poland
		SU	Egypt
G	United Kingdom	SX	Greece
HA	Hungary	TC	Turkey
HB	Switzerland	TF	Iceland
HC	Ecuador	TG	Guatemala
HH	Haiti	TI	Costa Rica
HI	Dominican Republic	VH	Australia
HK	Colombia	VP, VQ, VR	British Colonies & Protectorates
HL	Korea		
HS	Thailand	VT	India
HZ	Saudi Arabia	XA, XB, XC	Mexico
I	Italy	XH	Honduras
JA	Japan	XT	China
JY	Jordan	XY, XZ	Burma
LN	Norway	YA	Afghanistan
LV	Argentina	YE	Yemen
LX	Luxembourg	YI	Iraq
LZ	Bulgaria	YK	Syria
MC	Monte Carlo	YR	Romania

YS	El Salvador	ZP	Paraguay
YU	Yugoslavia	ZS, ZT, ZU	South Africa
YV	Venezuela	4R	Ceylon
ZA	Albania	4X	Israel
ZK, ZL, ZM	New Zealand	5A	Libya
		9G	Ghana

14.3.2   Airlines of the world

An airline code with no interpretation is not presently in use

AA	American Airlines	**American** AA	
AB	Air Cortéz	**AN**	Ansett Airlines of Australia
AC	Air Canada (*Canadian International airline*)	**AO**	Aloha Airlines
		AP	Aspen Airways
AD	Antilles Airboats	**AQ**	Air Anglia
AE	Air Ceylon	**AR**	Aerolineas Argentinas
AF	Air France ('*the world's largest airline*')	**AS**	Alaska Airlines
		AT	Royal Air Maroc
AG	Aeronaves del Centro	**AU**	Austral Lineas Aéreas
AH	Air Algerie	**AV**	Avianca
AI	Air India (*international Indian airline service*)	**Avensa** VE	
		Avianca Aeroovias Nacionales de Colombia (*Spanish: National Airlines of Colombia*)	
Air Canada AC			
Air France AF			
Air India AI		**AW**	
Air NZ NZ, TE		**AX**	Air Togo
Air UK United Kingdom airlines (*Air Anglia and BIA*)		**AY**	Finnair
		AZ	Alitalia
Air West ZX ('*serving 100 cities in the Western United States, Canada and Mexico*')		**BA**	British Airways
		BB	Air Great Lakes
AJ	All Island Air	**BC**	Brymon Airways
AK	Altair Airlines	**BD**	British Midland Airways
AL	Allegheny Airlines (*now USAir*)	**BE**	
		BF	Iowa Airlines and Horizon Airways
Alaska Alaska Airlines			
Alitalia AZ (*international Italian airline*)		**BG**	Bangladesh Biman
		BH	Air US
AM	Aeroméxico	**BI**	Royal Brunei Airlines

BJ	Bakhtar Afghan Airlines	CN	James Air
BK	Chalk's International Airline	CO	Continental Airlines (*Air Micronesia*)
BL	Air BVI	**Continental**	CO
BM	Aero Transporti Italiani	CP	CP Air
BN	Braniff International Airways	**CP Air**	Canadian Pacific Airlines
BO	Bouraq Indonesia Airlines	CQ	Aero-Chaco
BOAC	British Overseas Airways Corporation	CR	
BP	Air Botswana	CS	Colorado Airlines
BQ	Business Jets	CT	Command Airways
BR	British Caledonian Airways	CU	Cubana Airlines
Braniff	BN	CV	
British European	British European Airways	CW	St Andrews Airways
BS	Auxaire-Brétagne	CX	Cathay Pacific Airways
BT	Air Martinque (*Satair*)	CY	Cyprus Airways
BU	Braathens SAFE Airtransport	CZ	Cascade Airways
BV	Northwest Skyways	DA	Dan-Air Services
BW	BWIA International	DB	Brittany Air International
BX		DC	Trans Catalina Airlines
BY	Burlington	DD	Command Airways
BZ	Davey Air Services	DE	Downeast Airlines
CA	CAAC (*Civil Aviation Administration of China*)	**Delta**	DL
CB	Commuter Airlines	DF	Air Nebraska
CC	Crown Aviation	DG	Darien Airlines
CD	Trans-Provincial Airlines	DH	Tonga Air Service
CE	Air Virginia	DI	Delta Air (*Germany*)
CF	Faucett	DJ	Air Djibouti
CG	Clubair	DK	Decatur
CH	Express Airways	DL	Delta Air Lines
CI	China Airlines	DM	
CJ	Colgan Airways	DN	Skystream Airlines
CK	Connair	DO	Dominicana de Aviación
CL	Capitol International Airways	DP	Cochise Airlines
CM	COPA (*Compañia Panameña de Avición*)	DQ	
		DR	Advance Airlines
		DS	Air Senegal
		DT	TAAG-Angola Airlines
		DU	Roland Air
		DV	Ede-Aire

DW	DLT Deutsche Regional	FG	Ariana Afghan Airlines
DX	Danair	FH	Mall Airways
DY		FI	Flugfelag-Icelandair
DZ	Douglas Airways	**Finnair**	Finnish Airlines
EA	Eastern Airlines	FJ	Air Pacific
Eastern	EA	FK	Geelong Air Travel
EB	Eagle Airlines	FL	Frontier Airlines
EC	Air Ecosse	FM	
ED	Sunbird	FN	Air Carolina
EE	Eagle Commuter Airlines	FO	Southern Nevada
EF	Far Eastern Air Transport	FP	Simmons
EG	Japan Asia Airways	FQ	Compagnie Aérienne du Languedoc
EH	Roederer Aviation		
EI	Air Lingus (*Irish*)	FR	Susquehanna
EJ	New England Airlines	FS	Key Airlines
EK	Masling Commuter Services	FT	
		FU	Air Littoral
EL	Nihon Kinkyori Airways	FV	Frisia Luftverkehr
EI AI	LY	FW	Wright Airlines
EM	Hammond's Air Service	FX	Mountain West Airlines
EN	Aire Caravane	FY	Metroflight Airlines and Great Plains Airline
EO	Aeroamérica		
EP	Tropic Air Services	FZ	Air Chico
EQ	TAME	GA	Garuda Indonesian Airways
ER		GB	Air Inter Gabon
ES	Airways of New Mexico	GC	Lina-Congo
ET	Ethiopian Airlines	GD	Air North
EU	Empresa Ecuatoriana de Aviación	GE	Maui Commuter
		GF	Gulf Air
EV	Atlantic Southeast	GG	Gem State Airlines
EW	East-West Airlines	GH	Ghana Airways
EX	Eagle Aviation	GI	
EY	Europe Aero Service	GJ	Ansett Airlines of South Australia
EZ			
FA	Finnaviation	GK	Laker Airways
FB		GL	
FC	Chaparral Airlines	GM	Scheduled Skyways System
FD	Wiscair	GN	Air Gabon
FE	Florida Airlines and Air South	GO	
		GP	Gadag Air Seebaederflug
FF	Air Link	GQ	Big Sky Airlines

GR	Aurigny Air Services	IC	Indian Airlines
GS		ID	Apollo Airways
GT	Gibraltar Airways	IE	Soloman Islands Airways
GU	Aviateca	IF	Interflug
GV	Talair	IG	Alisarda
GW	Golden West Airlines	IH	Itavia
GX	Great Lakes Airlines	II	Imperial Airlines
GY	Guyana Airways	IJ	Touraine Air Tranport
GZ	Indiana Airways	IK	Eureka Aero Industries
HA	Hawaiian Air Lines	IL	Island Air
HB	Air Melanesiae	IM	Jamaire
HC	Haiti Air International	Imperial	II
HD	Air Mont	IN	East Hampton Air
HE	Green Bay Aviation	IO	Air Paris
HF	First Air	IP	Executive Airlines
HG	Harbor Airlines	IQ	Caribbean Airways
HH	Somali Airlines	IR	Iran National Airlines
HI	Hensley Flying Service	Irish	EI
HJ		IS	Eagle Air
HK	South Pacific Island Airways	IT	Air Inter
		IU	Midstate Airlines
HL		IV	Chaparral Aviation
HM	Air-Mahe	IW	International Air Bahama
HN	NLM-Dutch Airlines	IX	Trans Air Express
HO	Charterair	IY	Yemen Airways
HP	Air Hawaii	IZ	Arkia-Israel Inland Airlines
HQ	Heussler Air Service	JA	Bankair
HR	Eastern Caribbean Airways	JAL	JL
HS	Marshall's Air	Japan	JL
HT	Air Tchad	JB	Pioneer Airways
HU	Trinidad and Tobago Air Services	JC	Rocky Mountain Airways
		JD	Toa Domestic Airlines
Hughes	Hughes Air West	JE	Yosemite Airlines
HV	Air Central	JF	LAB Flying Service
HW	Havasu Airlines	JG	Swedair
HX	Cosmopolitan Aviation	JH	Nordeste-Lineas Aéreas Regionais
HY	Metro Airlines		
HZ	Henebery Aviation	JI	Gull Air
IA	Iraqi Airways	JJ	Astec Air East
IB	Iberia Air Lines of Spain	JK	
Iberia	IB	JL	Japan Air Lines

JM	Air Jamaica	KY	Sun West
JN	Air Bama	KZ	Oriens & King
JO	Holiday Airlines	LA	LAN Chile
JP	Indo-Pacific International	LB	Lloyd Aereo Boliviano
JQ	Trans-Jamaican Airlines	LC	Loganair
JR	Delta Air	LD	LADE (*Lineas Aéreas del Estado*)
JS			
JT	Air Oregon	LE	Magnum Airlines
JU	Yugoslav Airlines	LF	Linjeflyg
JV	Bearskin Lake	LG	Luxair (*Luxembourg Airlines*)
JW	Royal American		
JX	Bougair	LH	Lufthansa (*German Airlines*)
JY	Jersey European		
JZ	Alamo Commuter Airlines	LI	LIAT (*Leeward Islands Transport*)
KA	Coastal Plains Commuter	LJ	Sierra Leone Airways
KB	Burnthills	LK	Letaba Airways
KC	Aeromech	LL	Bell-Air
KD	Kendell Airlines	LM	ALM (*Antillianaanse Luchtvaart Maatschappij – Dutch–Antillean Airline Company*)
KE	Korean Air Lines		
KF	Catskill Airways		
KG	Catalina Airlines		
KH	Cook Island Airways	LN	Libyan Arab Airlines
KI	Time Air	LO	LOT (*Polish Airlines*)
KJ	Sea Airmotive	LP	Air Alpes
KL	Royal Dutch Airlines (*KLM – Koninklijke Luchtvaart Maatschappij*)	LQ	Inland Empire Airlines
		LR	LACSA (*Lineas Aéreas Costarricenses*)
KLM	KL	LS	Marco Island Airways
KM	Air Malta	LT	Great Sierra
KN	Air Kentucky	LU	
KO	Kodiak Western Alaska Airlines	**Lufthansa** LH	
KP		LV	LAV (*Linea Aeropostal Venezolaña*)
KQ	Kenya Airways	LW	Air Nevada
KR	Kar-Air (*Finland*)	LX	Crossair
KS	Peninsula Airways	LY	El Al Israel Airlines
KT	Turtle Airways	LZ	Balkan (*Bulgarian Airlines*)
KU	Kuwait Airways	MA	MALEV (*Magyar Legikolekedesi Vallat – Hungarian Air Lines*)
KV	Transkei Airways		
KW	Dorado Wings		
KX	Cayman Airways	MB	Countrywide

MC	Rapidair	NK	NORCANAIR
MD	Air Madagascar	NL	Air Liberia
ME	Middle East Airlines/Air Liban	NM	Mt Cook Airlines
		NN	Air Trails
MF	Red Carpet Flying Service	NO	Air North
MG	Pompano Airways	**Northwest** NW	
MH	Malaysian Airline System	NP	Desert Pacific
MI	Mackey International Airlines	NQ	Cumberland Airlines
		NR	NORONTAIR
MJ	Lineas Aereas Privadas Argentinas	NS	Nuernberger
		NT	Lake State Airways
MK	Air Mauritius	NU	Southwest Airlines
ML	Aviation Services	NV	Northwest Territorial Airways
MM	Sociedad Aeronautica Medellin		
		NW	Northwest Orient Airlines
MN	COMAIR (*Commercial Airways*)	NX	New Zealand Air Charter
		NY	New York Airways
MO		NZ	Air New Zealand (*domestic*)
MP	Atlantis Airlines	OA	Olympic Airways
MQ	Magnum Airlines	OB	Opal Air
MR	Air Mauritanie	OC	Air California
MS	Egyptair	OD	Aerocondor
MT	Mac Knight Airlines	OE	Samoan
MU	Misrair	OF	Noosa Air
MV	MacRobertson-Miller Airline Service	OG	Air Guadeloupe
		OH	Comair
MW	Maya Airways	OI	TAVINA (*Trans-Colombiana de Aviación*)
MX	Mexicana de Aviación		
MY	Air Mali	OJ	Air Texana
MZ	Merpati Nusantara Airlines	OK	Czechoslovak Airlines
NA	National Airlines	OL	ÖLT (*Östfriesische Lufttransport*)
National NA			
NB	New Haven Airways	OM	Air Mongol (*MIAT*)
NC	Newair	ON	Air Nauru
ND	Nordair	OO	Sunaire Lines
NE	Air New England	OP	Air Panamá Internacional
NF	EJA/Newport	OQ	Royale Airlines
NG	Green Hill Aviation	OR	Air Comores
NH	All Nippon	OS	Austrian Airlines
NI	LANICA (*Lineas Aéreas de Nicaragua*)	OT	
		OU	Otonabee Airways
NJ	Namakwaland Lugdiens		

OV		PZ	LAP (*Lineas Aéreas Paraguayas*)
OW	Trans Mountain Airlines		
OX	Air Atlantic Airlines	QA	
OY	New Jersey Airways	Qantas	QF
OZ	Ozark Air Lines	QB	Quebecair
PA	Pan American World Airways	QC	Air Zaire
		QD	Trans-Brasil
Pan Am	PA	QE	Air Tahiti
PB	Air Burundi	QF	Quantas Airways
PC	Fiji Air	QG	Sky West Aviation
PD	Pem Air	QH	Air Florida
PE	People Express	QI	
PF	Trans Pennsylvania Airlines	QJ	Lesotho Airways
		QK	Mexico Air Service
PG	Florida Commuter	QL	
PH	Polynesian Airlines	QM	Air Malawi
Philippine	PR	QN	Bush Pilots Airways
PI	Piedmont Aviation	QO	Bar Harbor Airlines
PJ		QP	Sunbird
PK	Pakistan International	QQ	Emmet County
PL	Aero Peru	QR	
PM	Pilgrim Airlines	QS	Cal Sierra
PN	Princeton Aviation	QT	Vaengir (*Wings Air Iceland*)
PO	Aeropelican Intercity Commuter Air Services	QU	Uganda Airlines
		QV	Lao Aviation
PP	Phillips Airlines	QW	Air Turks and Caicos
PQ	PRINAIR (*Puerto Rican International Airlines*)	QX	Century Airlines
		QY	Aero Virgin Islands
PR	Phillippine Airlines	QZ	Zambia Airways
PS	PSA (*Pacific Southwest Airlines*)	RA	Royal Nepal Airlines
		RB	Syrian Arab Airlines
PT	Provincetown–Boston Airline	RC	Republic
PU	PLUNA – Primeras Lineas Uruguayos de Navegación Aérea (*Spanish: First Uruguayan Aerial Navigation Lines*)	RD	
		RE	
		RF	Rossair
		RG	VARIG (*Viação Aérea Rio Grandense*)
PV	Eastern Provincial Airways		
PW	Pacific Western Airlines	RH	Air Zimbabwe
PX	Air Niugini (*Air New Guinea*)	RI	Eastern Airlines
		RJ	Royal Jordanian Airlines (*ALIA*)
PY	Surinam Airways		

RK	Air Afrique	**SR**	Swissair
RL	Crown International Airlines	**SS**	South Coast Airlines
		ST	Belize Airways
RM	Wings West	**SU**	Aeroflot (*Russian International Airlines*)
RN	Royal Air International		
RO	TAROM (*Romanian Air Transport*)	**SV**	Saudi Arabian Airlines
		SW	Namib Air
Route of the Red Baron LH		**Swissair** SR	
RP	Precision Airlines	**SX**	Christman Air System
RQ	Maldives International Airlines	**SY**	Air Alsace
		SZ	ProAir Services
RR		**TA**	Taca International
RS	Aeropesca	**TAP**	TP
RT	Norving	**TB**	Tejas Airlines
RU	Britt Airways	**TC**	Air Tanzania
RV	Reeve Aleutian Airways	**TD**	
RW	Republic	**TE**	Air New Zealand (*international*)
RX	Capitol Air Service		
RY	Perkiomen Airways	**TF**	Veeneal
RZ	Arabia (*Arab International*)	**TG**	Thai Airways (international)
SA	South African Airways		
SABENA SN		**TH**	Thai Airways (*domestic*)
SAS	SK	**TI**	Texas International Airlines
SB			
SC	Cruzeiro do Sul	**TJ**	Oceanair
SD	Sudan Airways	**TK**	Turk Hava Yollari
SE	Southeast Skyways	**TL**	
SF	Scruse Air	**TM**	DETA – Direção de Exploração dos Transportes Aéreos (*Portuguese: Directorate of Exploration of Aerial Transport – Mozambique Airline*)
SG	Atlantis		
SH	SAHSA (*Servicio Aéreo de Honduras SA*)		
SI	Air Sierra		
SJ	Stewart Island	**TN**	Trans-Australia Airlines
SL	Rio-Sul	**TO**	
SM		**TP**	TAP – Transportes Aéros Portugueses (*Portuguese Air Transport*)
SN	SABENA (*Belgian Airlines*)		
SO	Austrian Air		
SP	SATA – Sociedade Açoriana de Transportes Aéreos (*Portuguese: Azores Air Transport Line*)	**TQ**	Las Vegas Airlines
		TR	Royal Air
		TS	
		TT	Royal West
SQ	Singapore Airlines	**TU**	Tunis Air

TV	Transamerica	**VB**	Westair Commuter Airlines
TW	Trans World Airlines		
TWA	TW	**VC**	TAC – Transportes Aéreos del Cesar
TX	Transportes Aéreos Nacionales		
		VD	
TY	Air Caledonie	**VE**	AVENSA – Aerovias Venezolanas (*Spanish: Venezuelan Airlines*)
TZ	SANSA – Servicios Aereos Nacionales		
UA	United Airlines	**VF**	Golden West
UB	Burma Airlines	**VG**	City Flug
UC	LADECO – Linea del Cobre (*Spanish: Copper Line*)	**VH**	Air Volta
		VI	Vieques Airlink
		VJ	Trans-Colorado
UD	Georgian Bay	**VK**	Air Tungaru
UE	United Air	**VL**	Mid-South Commuter Airlines
UF	Sydaero		
UG	Norfolk Island Airlines	**VM**	Ocean Airways
UH	Austin Airways	**VN**	Hang Khong Vietnam
UI	Flugfelag Nordurlands	**VO**	Tyrolean Airways
UJ		**VP**	VASP – Viação São Paulo (*Portuguese: São Paulo Airline*)
UK	British Island Airways (*Air UK*)		
UL	Air Lanka	**VQ**	
UM		**WR**	Transportes Aéreos de Cabo Verde
UN	East Coast Airlines		
United	UA	**VS**	
UO	Direct Air	**VT**	Air Polynesie
UP	Bahamas Air	**VU**	Air Ivoire
UQ	Suburban Airlines	**VV**	Semo Aviation
UR	Empire Airlines	**VW**	Ama-Flyg
USAir	*formerly Allegheny Airlines*	**VX**	Aces
UT	UTA (*Union de Transports Aeriens*)	**VY**	Coral Air
UU	Reunion Air	**VZ**	Aquatic Airways
UV	Universal Airways	**WA**	Western Airlines
UW	Perimeter Airlines	**WB**	SAN – Servicios Aéreos Nacionales (*Spanish: National Air Services*)
UX	Air Illinois		
UY	Cameroon Airlines		
UZ	Nefertiti	**WC**	Wien Air Alaska
VA	VIASA – Venezolana Internacional de Aviación (*Spanish: Venezuelan International Aviation*)	**WD**	
		WE	Votec
		Western	WA
		WF	Wideroes Flyveselskap

WG	ALAG – Alpine Luft Transport AG (*German: Alpine Air Transport Company*)
WH	Southeastern Commuter Airlines
WI	Swift-Aire Lines
WJ	Torontair
WK	Westkuestenflug
WL	Bursa Hava Yollari
WM	Windward Island Airways International
WN	Southwest Airlines
WO	World Airways
WP	Princeville Airways
WQ	Wings Airways
WR	Wheeler Flying Service
WS	Northern Wings (*Quebecair*)
WT	Nigeria Airways
WU	Rhine Air
WV	Midwest Aviation
WW	Trans-West
WX	Ansett Airlines of New South Wales
WY	Indiana Airways
WZ	Trans Western Airlines of Utah
XA	
XB	
XC	
XD	
XE	South Central
XF	Cobden Airways
XG	Air North
XH	
XI	
XJ	Mesaba Aviation
XK	AEROTAL – Aerolineas Territoriales de Colombia (*Spanish: Territorial Airlines of Colombia*)

XL	
XM	
XN	
XO	Rio Airways
XP	Avior
XQ	Caribbean International
XR	
XS	
XT	Executive Transportation
XU	Trans Mo Airlines
XV	Mississippi Valley Airways
XW	Walker's Cay Air Terminal
XX	Valdez Airlines
XY	Munz Northern
XZ	Air Tasmania
YA	
YB	Hyannis Aviation
YC	Alaska Aeronautical Industries
YD	Ama Air Express
YE	Pearson Aircraft
YF	
YG	
YH	Trans New York
YI	Intercity
YJ	Commodore
YK	Cyprus Turkish Airways
YL	Montauk Caribbean Airways and Ocean Reef Airways
YM	Mountain Home Air Service
YN	Nor-East Commuter Airlines
YO	Heli-Air-Monaco
YP	Pagas Airlines
YQ	Lakeland
YR	Scenic Airlines
YS	San Juan Airlines
YT	Sky West
YU	Aerolineas Dominicanas

YV	Mesa Aviation	ZM	Trans-Central
YW	Will's Air	ZN	Tennessee Airways
YX	Société Aeronautique Jurassienne	ZO	Trans-California
		ZP	Virgin Air
YY		ZQ	Lawrence Aviation
YZ	Linhas Aéreas da Guine-Bissau	ZR	Star Airways
		ZS	Grand Canyon Airlines
ZA	Alpine Aviation	ZT	SATENA – Servicio Aeronavegación a Territorios Nacionales (*Spanish: Aeronavigation Service to National Territories*)
ZB	Air Vectors		
ZC	Royal Swazi National Airways		
ZD	Ross Aviation		
ZE	Pacific National		
ZF	Berlin USA	ZU	Zia Airlines
ZG	Silver State	ZV	Air Midwest
ZH	Royal Hawaiian Airways	ZW	Air Wisconsin
ZI	Lucas Air Transport	ZX	Air West Airlines
ZJ		ZY	Air Pennsylvania
ZK	Shavano Air	ZZ	
ZL	Hazelton Air Services		

14.4.1   British Isles fishing ports registration

BFP	British Fishing Ports Registration	BM	Brixham
		BN	Boston
A	Aberdeen	BO	Bo'ness (*Borrowstounness*)
AA	Alloa	BR	Bridgwater
AB	Aberystwyth	BS	Beaumaris
AD	Ardrossan	BU	Burntisland
AH	Arbroath	BW	Barrow
AR	Ayr	C	Cork, Republic of Ireland
B	Belfast	CA	Cardigan
BA	Ballantrae	CE	Coleraine
BD	Bideford	CF	Cardiff
BE	Barnstaple	CH	Chester
BF	Banff	CK	Colchester
BH	Blyth	CL	Carlisle
BK	Berwick upon Tweed	CN	Campbeltown
BL	Bristol	CO	Caernarvon

CS	Cowes	L	Limerick, Republic of Ireland
CT	Castletown	LA	Llanelly
CY	Castlebay	LE	Lyme
D	Dublin, Republic of Ireland	LH	Leith
DA	Drogheda, Republic of Ireland	LI	Littlehampton
DE	Dundee	LK	Lerwick
DH	Dartmouth	LL	Liverpool
DK	Dundalk, Republic of Ireland	LN	King's Lynn
DL	Deal	LO	London
DO	Douglas	LR	Lancaster
DR	Dover	LT	Lowestoft
DS	Dumfries	LY	Londonderry
E	Exeter	M	Milford
F	Faversham	ME	Montrose
FD	Fleetwood	ML	Methil
FE	Folkestone	MN	Maldon
FH	Falmouth	MR	Manchester
FR	Fraserburgh	MT	Maryport
FY	Fowey	N	Newport
G	Galway, Republic of Ireland	N	Newry
GE	Goole	NE	Newcastle
GH	Grangemouth	NN	Newhaven
GK	Greenock	NS	New Ross
GN	Granton	OB	Oban
GR	Gloucester	P	Portsmouth
GU	Guernsey	PD	Peterhead
GW	Glasgow	PE	Poole
GY	Grimsby	PH	Plymouth
H	Hull	PL	Peel
HE	Hale	PN	Preston
HH	Harwich	PW	Padstow
HL	Hartlepool	PZ	Penzance
IE	Irvine	R	Ramsgate
IH	Ipswich	RN	Runcorn
J	Jersey	RO	Rothesay
K	Kirkwall	RX	Rye
KY	Kirkcaldy	RY	Ramsey
		S	Skibbereen, Republic of Ireland
		SA	Swansea

SC	Scilly	TT	Tarbert
SD	Sunderland	UL	Ullapool
SE	Salcombe	W	Waterford, Republic of Ireland
SH	Scarborough		
SM	Shoreham	WD	Wexford, Republic of Ireland
SN	North Shields		
SO	Sligo, Republic of Ireland	WH	Weymouth
SR	Stranraer	WI	Wisbech
SS	St Ives	WK	Wick
ST	Stockton	WN	Wigtown
SU	Southampton	WO	Workington
SY	Stornoway	WT	Westport, Republic of Ireland
T	Tralee, Republic of Ireland		
TH	Teignmouth	WY	Whitby
TN	Troon	Y	Youghal, Republic of Ireland
TO	Truro		

14.4.2   International Yacht Racing Union – National codes

A	Argentina	I	Italy
AR	United Arab Republic	IR	Republic of Ireland
B	Belgium	K	United Kingdom
BA	Bahamas	KA	Australia
BL	Brazil	KB	Bermuda
BU	Bulgaria	KC	Canada
CA	Cambodia	KG	Guyana
CY	Ceylon	KGB	Gibraltar
CZ	Czechoslovakia	KH	Hong Kong
D	Denmark	KI	India
E	Spain	KJ	Jamaica
EC	Ecuador	KK	Kenya
F	France	KR	Southern Rhodesia; Zambia; Malawi
G	West Germany		
GO	East Germany	KS	Singapore
GR	Greece	KT	West Indies
H	Holland	KZ	New Zealand
HA	Netherlands Antilles	L	Finland

LE	Lebanon	RI	Indonesia
LX	Luxembourg	RM	Romania
M	Hungary	S	Sweden
MA	Morocco	SA	South Africa
MO	Monaco	SE	Senegal
MX	Mexico	SR	USSR
N	Norway	T	Tunisia
NK	Korea	TH	Thailand
OE	Austria	TK	Turkey
P	Portugal	U	Uruguay
PH	Philippines	US	USA
PR	Puerto Rico	V	Venezuela
PU	Peru	X	Chile
PZ	Poland	Y	Yugoslavia
RC	Cuba	Z	Switzerland

15   Geographical areas

15.1 UK postcodes

AB	Aberdeen	CV	Coventry & Warwickshire
AL	St Albans	CW	Crewe
B	Birmingham	DA	Dartford
BA	Bath	DD	Dundee
BB	Blackburn & Burnley	DE	Derby
BD	Bradford	DG	Dumfries
BH	Bournemouth	DH	Durham
BL	Bolton	DL	Darlington
BN	Brighton	DN	Doncaster
BR	Bromley	DT	Dorchester
BS	Bristol	DY	Dudley
BT	Northern Ireland	EH	Edinburgh
CA	Carlisle	EN	Enfield
CB	Cambridge	EX	Exeter
CF	Cardiff	FK	Falkirk
CH	Chester & Deeside	FY	Fylde
CM	Chelmsford	G	Glasgow
CO	Colchester	GL	Gloucester
CR	Croydon	GU	Guildford
CT	Canterbury	HA	Harrow

HD	Huddersfield		**OX**	Oxford
HG	Harrogate		**PA**	Paisley
HP	Hemel Hempstead		**PE**	Peterborough
HR	Hereford		**PH**	Perth
HS	Hebrides		**PL**	Plymouth
HU	Hull		**PO**	Portsmouth
HX	Halifax		**PR**	Preston
IG	Ilford		**RG**	Reading
IP	Ipswich		**RH**	Redhill
IV	Inverness		**RM**	Romford
KA	Kilmarnock		**S**	Sheffield
KT	Kingston-upon-Thames		**SA**	Swansea
KW	Kirkwall		**SG**	Stevenage
KY	Kirkcaldy		**SK**	Stockport
L	Liverpool & The Wirral		**SL**	Slough
LA	Lancaster		**SM**	Sutton
LD	Llandrindod Wells		**SN**	Swindon
LE	Leicester		**SO**	Southampton
LL	Llandudno		**SP**	Salisbury
LN	Lincoln		**SR**	Sunderland
LS	Leeds		**SS**	Southend-on-Sea
			ST	Stoke-on-Trent
London			**SY**	Shrewsbury & Mid-Wales
E	East		**TA**	Taunton
EC	East Central (City)		**TD**	Borders
N	North		**TF**	Telford
NW	North West		**TN**	Tonbridge
SE	South East		**TQ**	Torquay
SW	South West		**TR**	Truro
W	West		**TS**	Cleveland
WC	West Central		**TW**	Twickenham
			UB	Uxbridge
LU	Luton		**WA**	Warrington
M	Manchester		**WD**	Watford
ME	Medway		**WF**	Wakefield
MK	Milton Keynes		**WN**	Wigan
ML	Motherwell		**WR**	Worcester
NE	Newcastle upon Tyne		**WS**	Walsall
NG	Nottingham		**WV**	Wolverhampton
NN	Northampton		**YO**	York
NP	Newport (Gwent)		**ZE**	Lerwick
NR	Norwich			
OL	Oldham			

15.2 British counties pre-1974

England
Beds Bedfordshire
Berks Berkshire
Bucks Buckinghamshire
Cambs Cambridgeshire & the Isle of Ely
Ches Cheshire
Corn Cornwall
Cumb Cumberland
Derbys Derbyshire
Devon Devonshire
Dor Dorset
Dur, Co Dur Durham
Essex Essex
Glos Gloucestershire
Hants Hampshire
Here Herefordshire
Here & Worc Hereford & Worcester
Herts Hertfordshire
Hunts Huntingdonshire
IoM, I of M Isle of Man
IoS, Is of Sc Isles of Scilly
IoW, I of W Isle of Wight
Kent Kent
Lancs Lancashire
Leics Leicestershire
Lincs Lincolnshire
Mddx Middlesex
Norf Norfolk
Northants Northamptonshire
Northd, Northumb Northumberland
Notts Nottinghamshire
Oxon Oxfordshire
Rut Rutland
Som Somerset
Ssx Sussex

Staf Staffordshire
Suff Suffolk
Sy Surrey
Warw Warwickshire
Westm Westmorland
Wilts Wiltshire
Worcs Worcestershire
Yorks Yorkshire

Wales
Angle Anglesey
Breck Brecknockshire
Caern Ca(e)rnarvonshire
Carm Carmarthenshire
Card Cardiganshire
Denb Denbigh
Fl Flint
Glam Glamorganshire
Meri Merionethshire
Monm Monmouthshire
Mont Montgomeryshire
Pembs Pembrokeshire
Rad Radnorshire

Scotland
Aber Aberdeenshire
Arg Argyllshire
Ayr Ayrshire
Banf Banffshire
Berw Berwickshire
Caith Caithness
Clack Clackmannanshire
Dumbar Dumbartonshire
Dumfrie Dumfriesshire
Edin Edinburgh
Elg Elgin
Fife Fifeshire

Forf	Forfarshire	**Peeb**	Peeblesshire
Hadd	Haddingtonshire	**Per**	Perthshire
Inver	Invernessshire	**R&C**	Ross & Cromarty
Kin	Kinrossshire	**Renf**	Renfrewshire
Kincar	Kincardineshire	**Roxb**	Roxburghshire
Kirkud	Kirkudbrightshire	**Selk**	Selkirksshire
Lan	Lanarkshire	**Stirl**	Stirlingshire
Lin	Linlithgow	**Suther**	Sutherland
Nairn	Nairn	**Wig**	Wigtonshire

15.3 UK counties & metropolitan areas post-1974

COUNTY OR AREA	ABBREVIATION	ROYAL MAIL APPROVED ABBREVIATION; OTHERS SHOULD BE WRITTEN IN FULL (ON LETTERS)
England		
Avon	Avn	
Bedfordshire	Beds	Beds
Berkshire	Berks	Berks
Buckinghamshire	Bucks	Bucks
Cambridgeshire	Cambs	Cambs
Cheshire	Ches	
Cleveland	Clev	
Cornwall	Corn	
Cumbria	Cumb	
Derbyshire	Derbys	
Devon	Devon	
Dorset	Dors	
Durham	Dur Co	Durham
East Sussex	E Ssx	E Sussex
Essex	Exx	
Gloucestershire	Glos	Glos
Greater London	GL	
Greater Manchester	GM	
Hampshire	Hants	Hants
Hereford & Worcester	H&W	
Hertfordshire	Herts	Herts
Humberside	Humb	
Isle of Wight	IOW	

Kent	Kent	
Lancashire	Lancs	Lancs
Leicestershire	Leics	Leics
Lincolnshire	Lincs	Lincs
Merseyside	Mers	
Middlesex	Mx	Middx
Norfolk	Nflk	
North Humberside	N Huml	N Humberside
North Yorkshire	N Yorks	N Yorkshire
Northamptonshire	Northan	Northants
Northumberland	Northd	Northd
Nottinghamshire	Notts	Notts
Oxfordshire	Oxon	Oxon
Shropshire	Salop	Salop
Somerset	Som	
South Humberside	S Humb	S Humberside
South Yorkshire	S Yorks	S Yorkshire
Staffordshire	Staffs	Staffs
Suffolk	Sflk	
Surrey	Sry	
Tyne & Wear	T&W	Tyne & Wear
Warwickshire	Warks	Warks
West Midlands	W Mids	W Midlands
West Sussex	W Ssx	W Sussex
West Yorkshire	W Yorks	W Yorkshire
Wiltshire	Wilts	Wilts
Worcestershire	Worcs	Worcs

Scotland

Borders	Bdrs	
Central	Cent	
Dumfries & Galloway	D & G	
Fife	Fife	
Grampian	Gramp	
Highland	Hghld	
Lothian	Loth	
Orkney	Ork	
Shetland	Shetd	
Strathclyde	Strath	
Tayside	Tays	
Western Isles	W Is	

Wales

Clwyd	Clwyd	
Dyfed	Dyfed	
Mid Glamorgan	M Glam	M Glam
South Glamorgan	S Glam	S Glam
West Glamorgan	W Glam	W Glam
Gwent	Gwent	
Gwynedd	Gynd	
Powys	Pwys	

Northern Ireland

Antrim	Ant	
Armagh	Arm	
Down	Down	
Fermanagh	Ferm	
Londonderry	Londy	Co Derry
Tyrone	Tyr	

15.4 Counties of Ireland

Ireland was originally a kingdom divided into four provinces: Ulster, Leinster, Munster & Connacht (Connaught). Six of the nine counties in Ulster now comprise Northern Ireland while three remain in the Republic of Ireland.

Ulster: Northern Ireland

Ant	Antrim
Arm	Armagh
Down	Down
Ferm	Fermanagh
Londy	Londonderry
Tyr	Tyrone

Ulster: Republic of Ireland

Cav	Cavan
Dngl	Donegal
Mongh	Monaghan

Leinster

Carl	Carlow
Dub	Dublin
Kild	Kildare
Kilk	Kilkenny
Laois	Laois
Long	Longford
Louth	Louth
Meath	Meath
Ofly	Offaly
Wex	Wexford
Wklw	Wicklow
Wmth	Westmeath

Munster

Clare	Clare
Cork	Cork
Kerry	Kerry
Lim	Limerick
Tipp	Tipperary
Wat	Waterford

Connacht		**Mayo**	Mayo
Gal	Galway	**Rosc**	Roscommon
Leit	Leitrim	**Sligo**	Sligo

15.5 British motorways

M1	London – Leeds	**M56**	North Cheshire Motorway
M2	Rochester – Faversham	**M61**	Greater Manchester –
M3	Sunbury – Southampton		Preston
M4	London – Pont Abraham	**M62**	Liverpool – Humberside
M5	Birmingham – Exeter	**M63**	Manchester Ring Road
M6	Rugby – Carlisle	**M65**	Calder Valley Motorway
M8	Edinburgh – Bishopton	**M66**	Greater Manchester
M9	Edinburgh – Dunblane	**M67**	Hyde Bypass
M10	St Albans – M1 link	**M69**	Coventry – Leicester
M11	London – Cambridge	**M73**	East of Glasgow
M18	Rotherham – Humberside	**M74, A74(M)**	
M20	Swanley – Folkestone		Glasgow – Gretna
M23	Hooley – Crawley	**M80**	Glasgow – Stirling
M25	London Orbital Motorway	**M876**	Bonnybridge – Kincardine
M27	Cadnam – Portsmouth		Bridge
M40	London – Birmingham	**M90**	Forth Road Bridge – Perth
M42	Bromsgrove – Measham	**A1(M)**	Doncaster Bypass
M53	Mersey Tunnel – Chester	**A1(M)**	South Mimms – Baldock
M54	Telford Motorway	**A1(M)**	Scotch Corner – Tyneside

15.6.1 The United States of America

Ala	Alabama	**Mont**	Montana
Alas	Alaska	**Nebr**	Nebraska
Ariz	Arizona	**Nev**	Nevada
Ark	Arkansas	**NH**	New Hampshire
Cal, Calif	California	**NJ**	New Jersey
Colo	Colorado	**N Mex, NM**	New Mexico
Conn	Connecticut	**NY**	New York
DC	District of Columbia	**NC**	North Carolina
Del	Delaware	**N Dak, ND**	North Dakota
Fla	Florida	**OH**	Ohio
Ga	Georgia	**Okla**	Oklahoma
Hi	Hawaii	**Oreg**	Oregon
Id, Ida	Idaho	**Pa, Penn, Penna**	
Ill	Illinois		Pennsylvania
Ind	Indiana	**RI**	Rhode Island
Ia	Iowa	**SC**	South Carolina
Kan, Kans	Kansas	**S Dak**	South Dakota
Ken, Ky	Kentucky	**Tenn**	Tennessee
La	Louisiana	**Tex**	Texas
Me	Maine	**Ut**	Utah
Md	Maryland	**Vt**	Vermont
Mass	Massachusetts	**Va**	Virginia
Mich	Michigan	**Wash**	Washington
Minn	Minnesota	**W Va**	West Virginia
Miss	Mississippi	**Wis**	Wisconsin
Mo	Missouri	**Wy, Wyo**	Wyoming

15.6.2 US State codes

AK	Alaska	MT	Montana
AL	Alabama	NC	North Carolina
AR	Arkansas	ND	North Dakota
AZ	Arizona	NE	Nebraska
CA	California	NH	New Hampshire
CO	Colorado	NJ	New Jersey
CT	Connecticut	NM	New Mexico
DC	District of Columbia	NV	Nevada
DE	Delaware	NY	New York
FL	Florida	OH	Ohio
GA	Georgia	OK	Oklahoma
HI	Hawaii	OR	Oregon
IA	Iowa	PA	Pennsylvania
ID	Idaho	RI	Rhode Island
IL	Illinois	SC	South Carolina
IN	Indiana	SD	South Dakota
KS	Kansas	TN	Tennessee
KY	Kentucky	TX	Texas
LA	Louisiana	UT	Utah
MA	Massachusetts	VA	Virginia
MD	Maryland	VT	Vermont
ME	Maine	WA	Washington
MI	Michigan	WI	Wisconsin
MN	Minnesota	WV	West Virginia
MO	Missouri	WY	Wyoming
MS	Mississippi		

15.6.3 Canadian provinces

Alb	Alberta	NWT	North West Territories
BC	British Columbia	Ont	Ontario
Man	Manitoba	PEI	Prince Edward Island
NB	New Brunswick	Qué	Québec
Nfld	Newfoundland	Sask	Saskatchewan
NS	Nova Scotia	Yuk	Yukon Territory

15.6.4 States of Mexico

Ags	Aguascalientes	**Mor**	Morelos
BC	Baja California	**Nay**	Nayarit
BC Front	Baja California Fronteriza	**NL**	Nuevo León
		Oax	Oaxaca
Cam	Campeche	**Pue**	Puebla
Chih	Chihuahua	**Qro**	Querétaro
Chis	Chiapas	**Q Roo**	Quintana Roo
Coah	Coahuila	**Sin**	Sinaloa
Col	Colima	**SLP**	San Luis Potosi
DF	Distrito Federal	**Son**	Sonora
Dgo	Durango	**Tab**	Tabasco
Gro	Guerrero	**Tam**	Tamaulipas
Gto	Guanajuato	**Tlax**	Tlaxcala
Hgo	Hidalgo	**Ver**	Veracruz
Jal	Jalisco	**Yuc**	Yucatán
Méx	México	**Zac**	Zacatecas
Mich	Michoacán		

15.6.5 States of Australia

ACT	Australian Capital Territory	**SA**	Southern Australia
		T	Tasmania
NSW	New South Wales	**V**	Victoria
NT	Northern Territory	**WA**	Western Australia
Q	Queensland		

AIM Association Européenne des Industries de Produits de Marque

BCNET Business Co-operation NETwork

BEUC Bureau of European Consumer Organisations

BIC Business Information Centre

BRITE Basic Research in Industrial Technologies for Europe

BSI British Standards Institute

CADDIA Co-operation in Automation of Data & Documentation for Exports, Imports & Agriculture

CAP Common Agricultural Policy

CCT Common Customs Tariff

CDI Centre for the Development of Industry

CECG Consumers in the European Community Group

CEDEFOP European Centre for the Development of Vocational Training

CELELEC European Committee for Electrotechnical Standardisation

CEN European Committee for Standardisation

CFMU Central Flow Management Unit (*air traffic*)

COMECON Council for Mutual Economic Assistance

COREPER COmmittee of PERmanent REpresentatives

CRAFT Co-operation Research Action For Technology

CSCE Conference on Security Co-operation in Europe

CSF Community Support Framework

CTMO Community Trade-Marks Office

CU Customs Union

DES Department of Education & Science

DG Directorates General (*has 23 departments*)

DG I External relations

DGII Economic & Financial Affairs

DGIII International Market & Industrial Affairs

DGIV Competition (Cartels) & State Aids

DGIX Personnel, Administration & Translations

DGV Employment, Social Affairs & Education

DGVI Agriculture

DGVII Transport

DGVIII Aid To Developing Countries

DGX Information, Communication & Culture

DGXI Environment, Consumer Protection & Nuclear Safety

DGXII Science And Research & Development (*including The Joint Research Centre*)

DGXIII Telecommunications, Information Industries & Innovation

DGXIX EC Budgets

DGXV Financial Institutions, Company Law & Tax

DGXVI Regional Development & Policy

DGXVII Energy

DGXVIII EC Credit & Investments (*borrowing & lending*)

DGXX Budgets (*Internal Financial Control*)

DGXXI Customs Union & Indirect Taxation

DGXXII Co-Ordination of Structural Investments

DGXXIII Enterprise Policy, Commerce, Tourism & Social Economics

DOMs French Overseas Departments (*POSEDOM Programme*)

DSE Display Screen Equipment

EAGGF European AGricultural Guarantee Fund

EBRD European Bank for Reconstruction & Development

EBU European Broadcasting Union

EC European Community

ECAS Euro Citizen Advice Service

ECAS European Citizen Action Service

ECOSOC ECOnomic & SOCial Committee

ECSC European Coal & Steel Community

ECU European Currency Unit

EEA European Economic Area

EEC European Economic Community

EEIG European Economic Interest Group

EFTA European Free Trade Area

EFTA European Free Trade Association

EHLASS European Home & Leisure Accident Surveillance System

EIB European Investment Bank

EMCF European Monetary Corporation Fund

EMF European Monetary Fund

EMS European Monetary System

EMU European & Monetary Union

EOTC European Organisation for Testing & Certification

EPC European Patent Convention

EPC European Political Co-operation

EPC European Political Co-operation

EPO European Patent Office

ERDF European Regional Development Fund

ERM Exchange Rate Mechanism

ESA European Space Agency

ESC UN Economic & Social Council

ESCB European System of Central Banks

ESCO UN Educational, Scientific & Cultural Organisation

ESF European Social Fund

ESPRIT European Strategic Programme of Research & Development in Information Technology

ETP Executive Training Programme

ETSI Executive Telecommunications Standards Institute

ETUC European Trade Union Confederation

EUA Executive Unit of Account

EUREKA EUropean REsearch Co-operation Agency Eurochambers Association of European Chambers of Commerce & Industry 'Euronet Diane' Direct Information Access for Europe

EUROSTAT STATistical Office of the EUROpean Communities (*sometimes SOEC*)

EUROTAM EUROpean ATOMic Energy Community

EUW European Union of Women

FEOGA French initials of EAGGF

FOREST Forestry Sectional Research (*Technology*)

GCC Gulf Co-operation Council

GPA Government Procurement Agreement

HS/HT Harmonised System/ Harmonised Tariff

IEC International Standards

IGC Inter Governmental Conference

ILO International Labour Organisation

INSIS Community Inter- Institutional Information System

IRFO International Road Freight Office

ITMA Institute of Trade Marks Agents

LIFE European Environment Fund

MCA Monetary Compensation Amount

MCA Monetary Compensation Amounts

MEP Member of the European Parliament

MOS Mail Order Sales

NIC New Community Instrument for Borrowing & Lending

NOW New Opportunities for Women

OECD Organisation for Economic Co-operation & Development

OEO Office of Equal Opportunities

PHARE Poland & Hungary Assistance Reconstruction Economic Programme

Plc Public Limited Company

PTD Package Travel Directive

SAD Single Administrative Document (*customs harmonised system*)

SAE Single European Act

SME's Small & Medium-sized Enterprise/s

SOEC Statistical Office of the European Communities (*sometimes EUROSTAT*)

TARIC Tariff Intègre Communautaire (*French: Integrated Community Tariff*

TED Tenders Electronic Dialling System

TEN Trans European Network TIR convention Geneva Convention on International Road Transport

UCC Universal Copyright Convention (*Geneva 1955*)

UNCTAD UN Conference on Trade & Development

UNEP UN Environmental Programme

UNESCO UN Educational, Scientific & Cultural Organisation

UNICEF UN International Children's Emergency Fund

UNIDO UN Industrial Development Organisation

WEU Western European Union

WHO World Health Organisation

WIPO World Intellectual Property Organisation

WIS Women's Information Service

XIV Fisheries

17   Chemical elements

(by atomic number)

1	H	hydrogen
2	He	helium
3	Li	lithium
4	Be	beryllium (*was glucinium*)
4	Gl	glucinum (*an old name for beryllium*)
5	B	boron
6	C	carbon
7	N	nitrogen
8	O	oxygen
9	F	fluorine
10	Ne	neon
11	Na	sodium (*Latin: natrium*)
12	Mg	magnesium
13	Al	aluminium; aluminum
14	Si	silicon
15	P	phosphorus
16	S	sulphur
17	Cl	chlorine
18	Ar	argon
19	K	potassium (*Latin: kalium*)
20	Ca	calcium
21	Sc	scandium
22	Ti	titanium
23	V	vanadium
24	Cr	chromium
25	Mn	manganese
26	Fe	iron (*Latin: ferrum*)
27	Co	cobalt
28	Ni	nickel
29	Cu	copper (*Latin: cuprum*)
30	Zn	zinc
31	Ga	gallium
32	Ge	germanium
33	As	arsenic
34	Se	selenium
35	Br	bromine
36	Kr	krypton
37	Rb	rubidium
38	Sr	strontium
39	Y	yttrium
40	Zr	zirconium
41	Cb	columbium (*now niobium*)
41	Nb	niobium (*was columbium*)
42	Mo	molybdenum
43	Tc	technetium
44	Ru	ruthenium
45	Rh	rhodium
46	Pd	palladium
47	Ag	silver
48	Cd	cadmium
49	In	indium
50	Sn	tin (*Latin: stannum*)
51	Sb	antimony (*Latin: stibium*)
52	Te	tellurium
53	I	iodine
54	Xe	xenon
55	Cs	caesium
56	Ba	barium
57	La	lanthanum
58	Ce	cerium
59	Pr	praseodymium
60	Nd	neodymium
61	Pm	promethium
62	Sm	samarium
63	Eu	europium
64	Gd	gadolinium
65	Tb	terbium
66	Ds	dysprosium (*alternative symbol to Dy*)

66	Dy	dysprosium (*see* Ds)
67	Ho	holmium
68	Er	erbium
69	Tm	thulium
70	Yb	ytterbium
71	Lu	lutetium; lutecium
72	Hf	hafnium
73	Ta	tantalum
74	W	tungsten (*alias wolfram*)
75	Re	rhenium
76	Os	osmium
77	Ir	iridium
78	Pt	platinum
79	Au	gold (*Latin: aurum*)
80	Hg	mercury (*Greek: hydrargyrum – silver water*)
81	Tl	thallium
82	Pb	lead (*Latin: plumbum*)
83	Bi	bismuth
84	Po	polonium
85	At	astatine
86	Rn	radon
87	Fr	francium
88	Ra	radium
89	Ac	actinium
90	Th	thorium
91	Pa	protactinium
92	U	uranium
93	Np	neptunium
94	Pu	plutonium
95	Am	americium
96	Cm	curium
97	Bk	berkelium
98	Cf	californium
99	Es	einsteinium
100	Fm	fermium
101	Md	mendelevium
102	No	nobelium
103	Lr	lawrencium (*formerly Lw*)

103	Lw	lawrencium (*now Lr*)
104	Rf	rutherfordium
105	Db	dubnium
106	Sg	seaborgium
107	Bh	bohrium
108	Hs	hassium
108	Mt	meitnerium

The chemical elements (by symbol)

Ac	89	actinium
Ag	47	silver
Al	13	aluminium; aluminum
Am	95	americium
Ar	18	argon
As	33	arsenic
At	85	astatine
Au	79	gold (*Latin: aurum*)
B	5	boron
Ba	56	barium
Be	4	beryllium (*was glucinium*)
Bi	83	bismuth
Bk	97	berkelium
Br	35	bromine
C	6	carbon
Ca	20	calcium
Cb	41	columbium (*now niobium*)
Cd	48	cadmium
Ce	58	cerium
Cf	98	californium
Cl	17	chlorine
Cm	96	curium
Co	27	cobalt
Cr	24	chromium
Cs	55	caesium
Cu	29	copper (*Latin: cuprum*)
Ds	66	dysprosium (*alternative symbol to Dy*)
Dy	66	dysprosium (*see* Ds)
Er	68	erbium

Es	99	einsteinium
Eu	63	europium
F	9	fluorine
Fe	26	iron (*Latin: ferrum*)
Fm	100	fermium
Fr	87	francium
Ga	31	gallium
Gd	64	gadolinium
Ge	32	germanium
Gl	4	glucinum (*an old name for beryllium*)
H	1	hydrogen
Ha	105	hahnium (*or nielsbohrium*)
He	2	helium
Hf	72	hafnium
Hg	80	mercury (*Greek: hydrargyrum - silver water*)
Ho	67	holmium
I	53	iodine
In	49	indium
Ir	77	iridium
K	19	potassium (*Latin: kalium*)
Kr	36	krypton
Ku	104	kurchatovium (*or rutherfordium*)
La	57	lanthanum
Li	3	lithium
Lr	103	lawrencium (*formerly Lw*)
Lu	71	lutetium; lutecium
Lw	103	lawrencium (*now Lr*)
Md	101	mendelevium
Mg	12	magnesium
Mn	25	manganese
Mo	42	molybdenum
N	7	nitrogen
Na	11	sodium (*Latin: natrium*)
Nb	41	niobium (*was columbium*)
Nd	60	neodymium
Ne	10	neon
Ni	28	nickel
No	102	nobelium
Np	93	neptunium
Ns	105	nielsbohrium (*or hahnium*)
O	8	oxygen
Os	76	osmium
P	15	phosphorus
Pa	91	protactinium
Pb	82	lead (*Latin: plumbum*)
Pd	46	palladium
Pm	61	promethium
Po	84	polonium
Pr	59	praseodymium
Pt	78	platinum
Pu	94	plutonium
Ra	88	radium
Rb	37	rubidium
Re	75	rhenium
Rf	104	rutherfordium (*or kurchatovium*)
Rh	45	rhodium
Rn	86	radon
Ru	44	ruthenium
S	16	sulphur
Sb	51	antimony (*Latin: stibium*)
Sc	21	scandium
Se	34	selenium
Si	14	silicon
Sm	62	samarium
Sn	50	tin (*Latin: stannum*)
Sr	38	strontium
Ta	73	tantalum
Tb	65	terbium
Tc	43	technetium
Te	52	tellurium
Th	90	thorium
Ti	22	titanium

Tl	81	thallium	Xe	54	xenon
Tm	69	thulium	Y	39	yttrium
U	92	uranium	Yb	70	ytterbium
V	23	vanadium	Zn	30	zinc
W	74	tungsten (*alias wolfram*)	Zr	40	zirconium

18 Alphabets – phonetic & comic

	Old	*New*	*Comic*
A	Able	Alfa	for orses
B	Baker	Bravo	for mutton
C	Charlie	Charlie	for thighlanders
D	Dog	Delta	for mation
E	Easy	Echo	for lution
F	Fox	Foxtrot	for vescence
G	George	Golf	for fstaff
H	How	Hotel	for voting (18)
I	tem	India	for lootin
J	Jig J	uliet	for oranges
K	King	Kilo	for restaurant
L	Love	Lima	for leather
M	Mike	Mike	for sis
N	Nan	November	for mation
O	Oboe	Oscar	for the open road
P	Peter	Papa	for comfort
Q	Queen	Quebec	for fish
R	Roger	Romeo	for mo
S	Sugar	Sierra	for you
T	Tare	Tango	for two
U	Uncle	Uniform	for mism
V	Victor	Victor	for la France
W	William	Whiskey	for quits
X	X-ray	X-ray	for breakfast
Y	Yoke	Yankee	for runts
Z	ebra	Zulu	for yourself

° deg lat zero degrees latitude (*the Equator*)

O2 both eyes

007 James Bond (*Ian Fleming's international agent*)

1/4 d farthing (*fourth of an old English penny*)

1/4 h quarter-hard

1/4 ly quarterly

1/4 ph quarter-phase

1/4

Rd quarter-round

1/2 can narcotics equal to a half can of pipe tobacco

1/2 d halfpenny (*half of an old English penny*); ha'penny

1/2

Gr half-gross (72)

1/2 h half hard

1/2

R half-round

1/2 t halftitle (*bibliography*)

1 year 1; in the beginning

1/- an old English shilling (*bob*)

1d an old English penny

1/e first edition

1er(e) first (*French*)

1 Esd The First (Apocryphal) Book of Esdras

1G one grand (£1k)

1 Hen IV King Henry IV, Part 1

1 Hen VI King Henry VI, Part 1

1/M First Mate

1mo primo (*Italian: first*)

1Ne First Book of Nephi

1° primero (*Spanish: first*)

1/O First Officer

1-p single pole

1Q first quarter (eg: *1Q99 – first quarter 1999*)

1st first

1s & 2s mixed first and second quality timber

1-wd one-wheel drive

2nd second

2do secondo (*Italian: second*)

2/e second edition

11e deuxième, seconde, second (*French: second*)

2/F two-seater fighter aircraft

2-4-D dichlorophenoxy-acetic acid (*weed killer*)

2-4-5-T trichlorophenoxy-acetic acid (*antiplant agent and defoliant*)

CHM 2, 4, 5-TP *see* fenoprop

CHM 2, 4-DES 2-(2,4-dichlorophenoxy ethyl hydrogen sulphate (*weedkiller, also disul, SES, sesin, sesone*) (CHM)

2H, H2 deuterium (*heavy hygrogen*)

2Lt, 2Lieut Second Lieutenant

MIL 2g, 3g *etc* multiples of acceleration of gravity – 981.5cm/s^2 (32.2ft/s^2) at the earth's surface

2 Hen IV King Henry IV, Part 2

2 Hen VI King Henry VI, Part 2

2 i/ic second in command

2/M Second Mate

2n diploid number

2Ne Second Book of Nephi

2NR not received; not reported

2NZEF Second New Zealand Expeditionary force (*WWII*)

MIL 2S-acid an intermediate for dyestuffs CHM

2° segundo(a) (*Spanish: second*)

2/O Second Officer

2-p double pole

2 ph two-phase

2Q second quarter

2-st two storey

2-13 drug addict

2-wd two-wheel drive

3b third base

3Bs Bach, Beethoven, Berlioz; Bach, Beethoven, Brahms; *etc (depending on your favourite composers)*

3/c three-conductor

3C Computer Control Company

3-d, 3-D three dimensional

3/e third edition

IIIe troisième (*French: third*)

3H, H3 tritium (*very heavy hydrogen*) CHM

3 Hen VI King Henry VI, Part 3

3 K's Kinder, Küche, Kirche (*German: children, cooking, church*)

3-l's latitude, lead, lookout; lead, log, lookout (dead-reckoning essentials)

3M Third Mate; Minnesota Mining & Manufacturing

3 Ne Third Book of Nephi

3° tercero(a) (*Spanish: third*)

3/O Third Officer

3-p triple pole

3Ps Pick up, Put down, Piss off (*market trader*)

3 ph three-phase

3Q third quarter

3rd third

3-Rs reading, writing, arithmetic (colloquially: readin', 'ritin', 'rithmetic)

3-st three-storey

4 level 4 (*death-dealing dose or injection of drug used by executioners*)

4/c four-conductor

4Cs before downshifting: Comfort, Compensate, Conform, Compete, *and after:* Control, Challenge, Compatibility, Cretivity

4/e fourth edition

4-F US draft classification: not eligible MIL

4H Head, Heart, Hands & Health (*US youth organisation*)

4-Ls latitude, lead, longitude, lookout

4MTA methylthio amphetamine (*flatliner constituent*)

4 Ne Fourth Book of Nephi

4° quarto, cuarto(a) (*Spanish: fourth*)

4/O Fourth Officer

4-p quadruple pole

4Q fourth quarter

4-st four-storey

4tet quartet

4th fourth

4-wb,4WB four-wheel brakes

4-wd, 4WD four-wheel drive

5/e fifth edition

Ve cinquième (*French: fifth*)

5'er, Fiver £5 note; $5 bill

5° quinto(a) (*Spanish: fifth*)

5 w's, 5WH *the* who, what, when, where *and* why *reporters attempt to include in summary paragraphs*

6/c six-conductor

6-dW Six-day War

6/e sixth edition

VIe sixième (*French: sixth*)

6° sesto(a); sexto(a) (*Spanish: sixth*)

6-pack *of beer,* etc

6-shooter revolver holding six cartridges

6th sixth

7 aa's 7 archangels (*Gabriel, Jerahmeel, Michael, Raguel, Raphael, Sariel, and Uriel*)

7ber September

7e septiembre (*Spanish: September*)

VIIe septième (*French: seventh*)

7° septimo(a) (*Spanish: seventh*)

7th seventh

8 numerical symbol for heroin (*H is the eighth letter of the alphabet*)

8bre octobre (*French: October*)

8/e eighth edition

8e octubre (*Spanish: October*)

VIIIe huitième (*French: eighth*)

8° octavo(a) (*Spanish: eighth*)

8th eighth

8va bass ottava bassa (*Italian: octave lower*)

9ber November

9bre novembre (*French: November*) noviembre (*Spanish: November*)

9/e 10/e, etc ninth, tenth edition, *etc*

9e noviembre (*Spanish: November*)

IXe neuvième (*French: ninth*)

9° nono(a); noveno(a) (*Spanish: ninth*)

9th ninth

9 to 5 everyday job

'10 1810 (*Bolvarian-type Spanish-American Revolutions and wars of liberation, 1810-1826*)

10⁻¹ deci; d

10⁻² centi; c

10⁻³ milli; m

10⁻⁶ micro; μ

10⁻⁹ nano; n

10⁻¹² pico; p

10⁻¹⁵ femto; f

10⁻¹⁸ atto; a

10² hecto; h

10³ kilo; k

10⁶ mega; M

10⁹ giga; G

10¹² tera: T

10 Aug Ecuadorian Independence Day

Xber December

10bre décembre (*French: December*) diciembre (*Spanish: December*)

10 Dec Human Rights Day (*Liberia*)

10e diciembre (*Spanish: December*)

Xe dixième (*French: tenth*)

10° decimo(a) (*Spanish: tenth*)

10th tenth

10-V the lowest – the opposite of A-1

11-11-11 eleventh hour, eleventh day, eleventh month of 1918 – when Armistice ended World War 1

12° twelvemo (*book size*)

12, 15, 18 video classification – suitable for people of these ages and over

13 numerical symbol for marijuana

IL13 interleukin 13 (*possible asthma trigger*)

14 numerical symbol for narcotics

16° sixteenmo (*book size*)

16s 16⅔ rpm phonograph records

17-D modified yellow-fever virus

18-19 Sept Chilean Independence Days

21 blackjack

.22 22-calibre ammunition, pistol, or rifle

22 s-e silencer-equipped 22-calibre revolver

23rd twenty third

23½ deg N lat Tropic of Cancer

23½ deg S lat Tropic of Capricorn

24 24 Capricci (Opus 1) (*Paganini's Twenty-four Captrices for cadenza-like unaccompanied violin*)

240 twenty-fourmo (*book size*)

25 numerical symbol for LSD (*because 25 is part of its name – d-lysergic acid diethylamide tartrate 25*)

30 finis symbol used by newspapermen at the end of an article or story

.30-'06 30-calibre American cartridge introduced in 1906 – used by US Armed Forces in World Wars I and II for rifles and machine guns

320 thirty-twomo (*book size*)

33's 33⅓ rpm phonograph records

.38 .38-calibre ammunition or pistol

40 40 acres

.44 .44-calibre ammunition or pistol

.45 .45-calibre ammunition or pistol

45's 45 rpm phonograph records

48er emigrant to America in 1848; participant in the German revolution of 1848

480 forty-eightmo (*book size*)

49er gold-rush settler who went to California in 1849

.50 50-calibre ammunition or machine gun

640 sixty-fourmo (*book size*)

66° 17 min N lat Artic Circle

66° 17 min S lat Antarctic Circle

75s 75mm cannon

78s 78 rpm phonograph records

90° N lat North Pole

90° S lat South Pole

'96 1796 (*Napoleonic Wars, 1796–1815*)

111 One-Eleven (British Aircraft Corporation STOL fan-jet aircraft) **2**

40 Convair two-engine transport aeroplane; trotting horse speed – 1 mile in 2 minutes 40 seconds; synonym for high speed

280 copper alloy (*Muntz metal*); yellow metal

606 arsphenamine compound sold as Salvarsan; 606th compound developed and tested by Paul Ehrlich for treatment of relapsing fevers and syphilis

707 Boeing Stratoliner jet-transport aeroplane

720 Boeing medium-range jet-transport aeroplane

727 Boeing jet-transport with three empennage-mounted engines

737 Boeing model 737-400: short-range twin-jet aeroplane

747 Boeing model 747-400: jumbo jet-liner

757 Boeing model 757-400: 136-seat medium-range jetliner

767 Boeing model 767-400: twin-engine wide-bodied jetliner

880 Convair 880 jet aeroplane

911 US police telephone number

990 Convair 990 fan-engine jet aeroplane

999 telephone number for the emergency services

1011 Lockheed 1011 jumbo jetliner

1812 1812 Overture by Tchaikovsky

1905er Old Bolshevik; participant in the Russian Revolution of 1905; veteran communist

'1915' Leon Trotsky's account of the dress-rehearsal Russian revolution of 1905; Shostakovich's 11th Symphony – Year 1905

2707 Boeing supersonic transport

338171 TE TE Lawrence's (*Lawrence of Arabia*) number in the British Army; he used this number rather than his name as a final defence against a world he found hostile and unresponsive

@ at

B- a stereo-isomer of a sugar CHM

B- substitution on a carbon atom (1) next but one to an atom common to two condensed aromatic nuclei, (2) next but one to the hetero-atom in a hetero-cyclic compound, (3) of a chain next but one to the functional group CHM

E- epi- (*containing an intra-molecular bridge*) SCI

ΦBK Phi Beta Kappa – philosophia biou kubernetes (Greek: philosophy, the guide of life – US national honorary society founded 1776; membership denotes high academic ability)

L symbol for absolute activity SCI

M chemical potential SCI

M meso- CHM

N coefficient of viscosity SCI

Y pseudo- SCI

Y phase displacement SCI

---

20   Symbols

! exclamation mark ✧ excl ✧ wow ✧ exclam ✧ bang ✧ shriek

hash ✧ hash mark ✧ mesh ✧ splat ✧ crunch ✧ pig-pen

= equals ✧ half-mesh

£ pound sign ✧ ch-ching

$ dollar

© copyright

& ampersand ✧ pussy and (and per se and, or Tironian sign)

' single quote ✧ forward quote ✧ opening quote ✧ spark

' closing quote ✧ backquote ✧ backspark

" double quote

" close double quote

(open parenthesis ✧ open bracket ✧ open ✧ wax

) close parenthesis ✧ close bracket ✧ close ✧ wane

( ) parenthese ✧ parens

* asterisk ✧ star ✧ splat ✧ gear

. full point ✧ point ✧ period ✧ dot ✧ spot

· decimal point ✧ centred dot

... ellipsis ✧ dot dot dot

/ oblique stroke ✧ oblique ✧ slat ✧ slash ✧ forward slash

**** backslash

; semicolon ✧ semi

: colon ✧ two-spot

- hyphen

– en-dash

— em-dash ✧ worm

__ underline ✧ flatworm

< less than ✧ angle ✧ left angle bracket ✧ open angle bracket ✧ left broket

<— angleworm

= equals

> greater than ✧ right angle ✧ right angle bracket ✧ close angle bracket ✧ right broket

? ques ✧ query ✧ what ✧ question mark

@ at ✧ at-sign ✧ whirlpool

**** backslat ✧ backslash

^ caret ✧ hat ✧ shark ✧ shark fin ✧ circumflex

{ } brackets ✧ curly brackets ✧ braces ✧ curly braces ✧ embrace & bracelet

|	vertical bar ✧ spike ✧ vertiline	´	acute accent ✧ eh
[ ]	square brackets ✧ U-turn & U-turn back	'	grave accent
		« »	guillemets (French brackets)
"	second ✧ inch ✧ double prime ✧ rabbit ears	* † ‡ § || ¶	precedence of footnote signs
'	prime ✧ foot	†	dagger ✧ obelus
~	tilde ✧ squiggle ✧ swung dash	‡	double dagger ✧ cross of Lorraine
,	tail ✧ comma	§	section mark
+	plus ✧ intersection	||	vertical equals ✧ vertiquals
%	per cent ✧ double-oh-seven	¶	para ✧ paragraph mark
‰	per thousand ✧ lorgnettes		